KU-648-511

Contents

CAMBRIDGE TEXTS IN THE HISTORY OF POLITICAL THOUGHT

JOHN MILTON
Political Writings

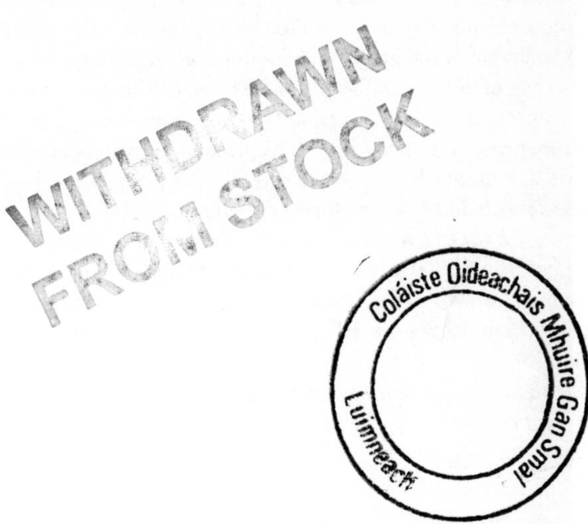

CAMBRIDGE TEXTS IN THE HISTORY OF POLITICAL THOUGHT

Series editors

RAYMOND GEUSS *Columbia University*
QUENTIN SKINNER *Christ's College, Cambridge*
RICHARD TUCK *Jesus College, Cambridge*

The series is intended to make available for students the most important texts required for an understanding of the history of political thought. The scholarship of the present generation has greatly expanded our sense of the range of authors indispensable for such an understanding, and the series will reflect those developments. It will also include a number of less well-known works, in particular those needed to establish the intellectual contexts that in turn help to make sense of the major texts. The principal aim, however, will be to produce new versions of the major texts themselves, based on the most up-to-date scholarship. The preference will always be for complete texts, and a special feature of the series will be to complement individual texts, within the compass of a single volume, with subsidiary contextual material. Each volume will contain an introduction on the historical identity and contemporary significance of the work or works concerned, as well as a chronology, notes on further reading and (where appropriate) brief biographical sketches of significant individuals mentioned in each text.

For a list of titles published in the series, please see end of book

JOHN MILTON

Political Writings

EDITED BY
MARTIN DZELZAINIS
Lecturer in English, Royal Holloway and Bedford New College, London

TRANSLATED BY
CLAIRE GRUZELIER

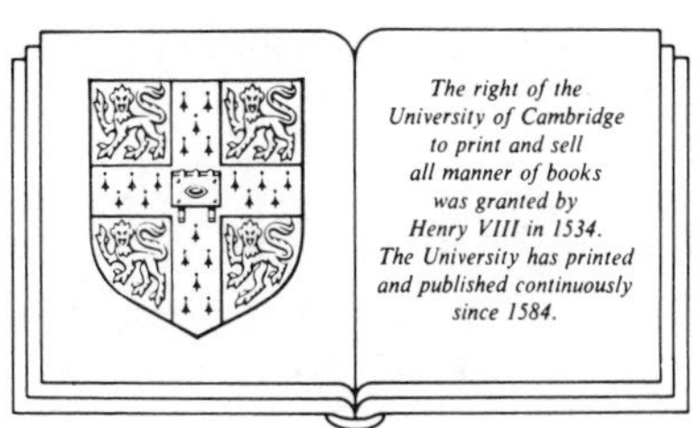

CAMBRIDGE UNIVERSITY PRESS
CAMBRIDGE
NEW YORK PORT CHESTER
MELBOURNE SYDNEY

67675

Published by the Press Syndicate of the University of Cambridge
The Pitt Building, Trumpington Street, Cambridge CB2 1RP
40 West 20th Street, New York, NY 10011, USA
10 Stamford Road, Oakleigh, Melbourne 3166, Australia

© Cambridge University Press 1991

First published 1991

Printed in Great Britain by The Bath Press, Avon

British Library cataloguing in publication data

Milton, John, *1608–1674*
Political writings. – (Cambridge texts in the history of political thought)
1. Political. Theories of Milton, John, 1608–1674
I. Title II. Dzelzainis, Martin III. Gruzelier, Claire 320.5092

Library of Congress cataloging in publication data

Milton, John, 1608–1674
[Tenure of kings and magistrates]
Political writings/John Milton; edited by Martin Dzelzainis;
translated by Claire Gruzelier.
p. cm. – (Cambridge texts in the history of political thought)
Includes bibliographical references.
Includes indexes.
Contents: The tenure of kings and magistrates – A defence of the people of England.
ISBN 0-521-34394-1. – ISBN 0-521-34866-8 (paperback)
1. Political science – Early works to 1800. 2. Divine right of kings.
I. Dzelzainis, Martin. II. Milton, John, 1608–1674. Pro populo Anglicano defensio.
English. 1991. III. Title.
IV. Series.
JC153.M55 1991
321'.6–dc20 90-1857 CIP

ISBN 0 521 34394 1 hardback
ISBN 0 521 34866 8 paperback

For Marts and Stefan

Coláiste Oideachais
Mhuire Gan Smál
Luimneach
Class No. 824.4
Acc. No. 379192

Acknowledgements

The translation of Milton's *Defence of the People of England* was made specially for this edition by Dr Claire Gruzelier. I am grateful to her for confronting all the difficulties of Milton's often tortuous Latin. For their help in preparing the rest of the edition, I am grateful to Roy Booth, John Creaser, Nicholas von Maltzahn, Ella Newton, Nigel Saul and Quentin Skinner.

M.D.

Note on the texts

The copy text for *The Tenure of Kings and Magistrates* was Bodleian Library, Rawlinson 408 4°, which may have been a presentation copy (fourth issue of the second edition) from the author. Material peculiar to the second, revised edition is enclosed in square brackets in the text; material peculiar to the first edition (denoted A), and other significant variants, can be found in the footnotes. For the dating of the second edition, see J. T. Shawcross, 'Milton's *Tenure of Kings and Magistrates*: Date of Composition, Editions, and Issues', *Papers of the Bibliographical Society of America*, 60 (1966), 1–8.

A Defence of the People of England was translated from the Latin text edited by Clinton W. Keyes in Volume VII (1932) of *The Works of John Milton*, gen. ed. Frank A. Patterson, 20 vols. (New York: Columbia University Press, 1931–40). Also consulted was Robert W. Ayers, 'Corrections to the Columbia Text of Milton's *Pro Populo Anglicano Defensio*', in *Complete Prose Works of John Milton*, ed. Don M. Wolfe *et al.*, 8 vols. (New Haven and London: Yale University Press: 1953–82), IV ii, 1146–8 (Appendix H). The *Defensio* was first published in quarto in 1651, followed by the emended 1651 folio, and the corrected and enlarged 1658 duodecimo edition. No attempt has been made to register all the variants collated by Robert W. Ayers in his 'Variants in the London Editions of Milton's *Defensio*', in *Complete Prose Works*, IV ii, 1129–39 (Appendix F). Where it was thought helpful, material peculiar to any of these editions has been enclosed in square brackets in the text and explained in the footnotes by references to 1651Q, 1651F, and 1658.

For further bibliographical information, see J. T. Shawcross, *Milton: A Bibliography for the Years 1624–1700, Medieval & Renaissance Texts and Studies*, 30 (Binghamton, New York, 1984).

Introduction

Charles I was executed on 30 January 1649. The events leading to this act, the act itself, and its consequences, dominate Milton's political writings. Within two weeks he had published a vindication of the proceedings against Charles, *The Tenure of Kings and Magistrates* (largely written while the trial was in progress), and was rewarded for his unsolicited efforts a month later by the newly constituted Council of State which appointed him as its Secretary for Foreign Tongues. Henceforth Milton was responsible not only for handling much of the Commonwealth's diplomatic correspondence but was also in effect its chief propagandist. The works he published between 1649 and 1651 – *Observations upon the Articles of Peace*, *Eikonoklastes*, and *Pro Populo Anglicano Defensio* – were all officially commissioned.

Towards the end of the decade the interregnum regime disintegrated in a succession of experiments and expedients. In 1660, with the return of Charles II imminent, Milton published two works in which he sought to stem the tide: *The Readie and Easie Way to Establish a Free Commonwealth* urged a revived commitment to republicanism, while *Brief Notes upon a Late Sermon* advocated more despairingly that, if there must be a king, it would be better to elect one rather than restore the Stuarts. Milton only narrowly escaped with his life at the Restoration and, until his death in 1674, devoted himself largely to poetry, publishing first *Paradise Lost* and then *Paradise Regained* and *Samson Agonistes*.

The foundations of these achievements were laid in a prolonged period of self-preparation. Milton was born in London in 1608, the son of a relatively well-to-do scrivener. In 1620 he entered St Paul's

School where the curriculum reflected the humanist values of its founder, John Colet. The education Milton received there led to some dissatisfaction with the scholastic emphasis of the syllabus at Christ's College, Cambridge, where he was a student from 1625 until 1632. For the next few years he studied privately, immersing himself especially in the Greek and Latin writers. This leisured existence culminated in 1638 in a fifteen-month tour of Europe during which he met Grotius and Galileo, and was enthusiastically received in several Florentine humanist academies. From the time he returned to England until summoned by the Council of State in 1649, he supported himself largely as a private tutor.

Milton's commitment to humanist values informs virtually everything he wrote, from the academic *Prolusions* (a series of bold variations on the forms of classical oratory) which he composed while at Cambridge, to his *Areopagitica* (1644), cast in the form of a speech for the liberty of unlicensed printing. *The Tenure of Kings and Magistrates* is no exception. The text of the first edition conforms to the five-part structure of the classical oration laid down by Isocrates and Cicero: exordium (pp. 3–8), narration (pp. 8–16), confirmation (pp. 16–23), refutation (pp. 23–6) and peroration (pp. 26–36). However, there is also within this structure a more simple division into positive and negative elements. On the one hand, the narration and the confirmation form a positive core of arguments devoted to an exposition of the principles of popular sovereignty while, on the other, the exordium, refutation and peroration constitute a polemic directed mainly against the Presbyterians. This in turn corresponds to the two aims which Milton sets himself on the title-page: to prove that it is lawful 'for any, who have the Power' to depose and punish a tyrant, and secondly to show 'that they, who of late so much blame Deposing, are the Men that did it themselves'. To understand why Milton saw these as his main ideological tasks, and to see how they were related, we must turn to the political situation in the winter of 1648 to 1649.

The victorious Parliamentary coalition had largely been held together by the pressures of war. Once peace came, it disintegrated. Agreement on the shape a political settlement should take proved elusive and finally impossible. A majority in the two Houses, especially the Presbyterians, wanted to negotiate with Charles and to reinstate him on terms which seemed to some outside Parliament to sacrifice the aims for which the war had been fought. The Army, a far more radical body, wanted instead to bring the king to justice and expressed its opposition to a treaty in a lengthy remonstrance. To break the ensuing stalemate, the Army staged a coup on 6 December 1648 – Pride's Purge – which by excluding recalcitrant MPs left a body (the so-called Rump) more compliant with its wishes. This intervention – the more so when it became clear that Charles would be placed on trial – provoked the bitterest response not only from Royalists but also Presbyterians and even radical groups like the Levellers.

At this critical juncture, Milton threw his weight behind the Army. One way to vindicate its actions was by the simple ploy of discrediting its opponents. The Presbyterians, despite having initially urged the most vigorous prosecution of the war against Charles, had now retreated behind the third article of the Solemn League and Covenant (1643) which pledged them to protect the king's authority and person, and this accordingly became the focus of his attack. Much of *The Tenure* is taken up with exposing this inconsistency.

Milton's animus against the Presbyterians is best encapsulated by his repeated allusions to a speech in Shakespeare's *Macbeth*:

> And be these juggling fiends no more believ'd,
> That palter with us in a double sense;
> That keep the word of promise to our ears,
> And break it to our hope.
>
> (V. 9. 19–22)

The Presbyterians had likewise 'juggl'd and palter'd with the world', and had spoken 'with a double contradictory sense' (pp. 4, 6). So, like the 'weird sisters' with whom Macbeth expressed his disillusionment, they were no more to be believed. Nor could they hope to relieve themselves of the burden of guilt any more than Lady Macbeth had been able to in her sleep; they 'were the men themselves that deposd the King, and cannot with all thir shifting and relapsing, wash off the guiltiness from thir own hands' (p. 26).

But the main way in which Milton drives home this message is to announce on no fewer than three occasions that he will rely as far as possible on specifically Presbyterian and Scottish sources (pp. 8, 10, 23). The point of this is to remind the Presbyterians that the theory of resistance which they had espoused at the start of the Civil War owed much for its development to their own distinguished sixteenth-century predecessors, John Knox and George Buchanan. Throughout *The Tenure* (most notably, and appropriately, in the refutation), Milton therefore draws on the works of Knox and Buchanan – two figures whose authority was such that they could not be disowned by, yet whose radicalism was now likely to embarrass, their seventeenth-century descendants.

What complicates this picture is that the Presbyterians, far from disowning their radical heritage, had successfully turned one of the fundamental tenets of the constitutional theory of resistance *against* the Army and its adherents. This was the distinction – orthodox in Lutheran and Calvinist tracts on resistance – between inferior magistrates and private persons: while resistance to tyrannical rule by inferior magistrates was lawful, it was never lawful for private persons to take any political initiative whatsoever. From the Presbyterian point of view, its immediate relevance was unmistakable. They argued that since the Army had been raised by Parliament, and was thus merely the agent of the inferior magistrate, it was lacking in any independent magisterial authority and ought therefore to be considered as no more than a collection of private persons. It followed from this that the Army's intervention in purging Parliament had been completely unlawful.

Milton could not ignore this line of argument if he was to succeed in exhibiting the Army's actions as legitimate. He therefore devotes the confirmation to challenging and reversing the key assumption on which the Presbyterians' case rested: that it was always unlawful for private persons to seize the political initiative from the inferior magistrate. Milton does not however mount a frontal attack on the constitutional theory but chooses instead to undermine it at a more vulnerable point.

Many of the sixteenth-century writers on resistance, while upholding the distinction between inferior magistrates and private persons, had nevertheless reluctantly treated the problem of tyrannicide in a way which did allow the individual citizen to act in certain circumstances. They usually opened their analysis with the traditional distinction between two kinds of tyrant: the tyrant by practice and the tyrant by usurpation (or tyrant without title). The former case involved them in no new departures; an otherwise legitimate ruler who degenerates into tyranny, they continue to maintain, can only be resisted by the inferior magistrate. But in the latter case a degree of flexibility enters their discussions. An example would be a foreign invader who, since he lacked any title, could be resisted by the private citizen acting in defence of his native institutions. They invariably go on to insist however that such individual resistance must cease once the invader has acquired the legitimacy he previously lacked – a teaching they illustrate by reference to the moment during Rome's transition from republic to empire at which lawful resistance turned into conspiracy and sedition.

So far, leading exponents of the constitutional theory like Peter Martyr, Beza, and the author of *Vindiciae contra tyrannos* were in complete agreement. But the Bible contained numerous instances of individual resistance to the oppressors of Israel. Whereas this posed no problem for Beza, who saw these oppressors as tyrants without title, it did for the author of the *Vindiciae*, who categorized them as tyrants by practice. For this carried with it the extremely awkward implication that there now appeared to be scriptural precedents for the very conclusion these theorists had sought to avoid: that individuals could resist even tyrants by practice. His solution – which became the standard one – was to argue that while, for example, Moses, Ehud and Jehu appear to be private persons, the fact of their having received an extraordinary calling from God meant that they should be seen as possessing an authority surpassing even that of the ordinary magistrate.

Thus when Milton chooses the story of the slaying of King Eglon by Ehud (Judges 3. 12–26) it is precisely because of the pivotal place it occupied in the controversy over who may lawfully resist a tyrant. He begins by rehearsing the arguments conventionally used to offset its alarming potential: that Eglon 'was a forren Prince, an enemie, and *Ehud* besides had special warrant from God' (p. 17). He then proceeds to dismantle them one by one.

Milton's first step is to refuse to concede that the distinction between the two types of tyrant is itself valid. He can see no material difference between a foreign usurper and a domestic tyrant: 'For look how much right the King of *Spaine* hath to govern us at all, so much right hath the King of *England* to govern us tyrannically' (p. 17). This becomes clearer still from the supra-national perspective afforded by the stoic notion of the brotherhood of man as repeatedly invoked by Cicero (e.g., *De officiis*, I, 16–17). In Cicero's view, tyrants were merely savage monsters who had renounced these common bonds and ought to be exterminated as the enemies of mankind (III, 6, 32). Milton then spells out his argument in these Ciceronian terms. It cannot be denied 'that there is a mutual bond of amity and brotherhood between man and man over all the World', and the only way in which men can be excluded – or, rather, exclude themselves – from these peaceful relations is by manifesting a hostile disposition. As Milton puts it epigrammatically, it is not 'distance of place that makes enmitie, but enmity that makes distance'. Thus any attempt 'to distinguish' between tyrants by the criteria of 'outlandish, or domestic' must be 'a weak evasion' (p. 18). A tyrant was simply someone who had segregated himself from human society and was in consequence to be treated as a 'savage Beast', a 'common enemie' and 'pest', and the 'destroyer of mankinde' (pp. 13, 17).

The result of adopting this stoic doctrine was to subvert the conventional analysis of the problem of tyrannicide. Conflating the two types of tyrant under one description meant it was no longer possible to specify circumstances in which resistance was to be undertaken exclusively by the inferior magistrate. A tyrant by practice was no less liable than a foreign usurper to be punished by a private individual.

Milton next turns to consider the remaining objections. By the logic of his own argument, he must concede that Eglon was an 'enemie', since 'what Tyrant is not?' But this was not because he had no right to govern. The Israelites had undoubtedly 'acknowlegd' him as 'thir Sovran' and made themselves 'his proper Subjects' by taking 'Oaths of Fealty and Allegeance' (p. 18). This was in effect to classify Eglon as a tyrant by practice and, as we have seen, it was usual at this point to argue that Ehud must have had, in Milton's words, a 'special warrant' from God to slay him. Milton however blocks off this avenue of escape, using two quite distinct arguments.

He points out first that, while Ehud was undeniably 'a man whom God had raysd to deliver Israel', it was nowhere specifically 'expressd' that he had received any positive command from God. Ehud had acted solely 'on just principles, such as were then and ever held allowable' (pp. 17, 19).

His second and more important argument is that it would make no difference even if we did have incontrovertible evidence of God's direct intervention. Although Jehu had received a 'special command to slay *Jehoram*', this did not make his action any the 'less imitable'. The explanation Milton gives is that where an action like Jehu's is 'grounded so much on natural reason' all that the 'addition of a command from God' can do is to 'establish the lawfulness of such an act' (p. 19). That is, a divine command establishes that a given action is lawful but is not itself what constitutes the grounds of its lawfulness; for that we must look to natural reason. To say that Ehud and Jehu were not private persons because they had been directed by God in what they did was to miss the point that the rightness of such actions was capable of being intuited in the ordinary way by any rational individual.

All this amounted to a decisive break with the Protestant tradition of voluntarism which held that whatsoever God commands is just simply because it is the will of God. For Milton the lawfulness of an action followed not from the expressed will of God, but from the fact that it was an intrinsically just and reasonable thing to do. What this implied was the possibility of forming correct ethical and moral judgements quite independently of any knowledge of revelation or scripture. So when at the start of the confirmation Milton poses the vital question of 'what the people lawfully may doe' against a tyrant, his answer is simply to say that 'no man of cleare judgement need goe furder to be guided then by the very principles of nature in him' (p. 17).

It also left the constitutional theory of resistance (and hence the Presbyterians' case) in disarray, clearing the way for Milton to secure his ideological objectives. He could now affirm the lawfulness of individual political action and so furnish a defence of the Army's conduct. Or, as he puts it on the title-page, since Parliament, the 'ordinary MAGISTRATE', had 'neglected, or deny'd' to bring the king to justice it was 'Lawfull' for 'any, who have the Power' to do so.

The individualistic, even anarchic, nature of this claim should not be underestimated – nor should its secularism. While Milton's sympathy with the 'saints' is evident, as is his tendency to invoke God's judgements in an authentically providentialist fashion, he is also at pains to distance himself and the Army from the allegations of religious enthusiasm and zealotry levelled by the Presbyterians. His scepticism about divine commands, his dissent from voluntarism, and his emphasis on reason all stem from the need to fashion a less vulnerable, because more secular, kind of argument.

The same outlook informs Milton's account of the formation of political society, and especially his discussion of the sword of justice.

For if his claim that individuals and not only magistrates could punish offenders was to carry any weight, then he had to address the question of the origins of this power. It is true that Milton closes the exordium on an uncontroversial note by saying that 'all humane power to execute' the 'wrath of God' is 'of God' (p. 8). He does not, however, seek to ground this upon divine positive law by citing any of the standard scriptural texts on the power of life and death. Instead he goes on in the narration to provide a wholly secular account of the sword of justice.

Although men 'naturally were borne free', they eventually formed 'Citties, Townes and Common-wealths' to escape the 'violence' and 'wrong' which stemmed from the Fall when they 'agreed by common league to bind each other from mutual injury, and joyntly to defend themselves against any that gave disturbance or opposition to such agreement'. The result of this agreement was however still pre-political in that it was a purely voluntary association which, while capable of defending itself from external threats, lacked any power to discipline internal deviants. Precisely 'because no faith in all was found sufficiently binding' it became 'needfull to ordaine som authoritie, that might restrain by force and punishment what was violated against peace and common right'. They accordingly took the further step which alone could create a genuinely political society: for their own 'ease' and 'order' they 'communicated' the 'autoritie and power of self-defence and preservation' which was 'originally and naturally in every one of them' either to one person or many (kings and magistrates respectively). But the status which these rulers enjoyed as the result of this transaction could be no greater than that of 'Deputies and Commissioners' who had merely been 'intrusted' with the execution of 'that justice which else every man by the bond of nature and of Cov'nant must have executed for himself, and for one another' (pp. 8–9).

Milton here committed himself to the view – without precedent in any vernacular work of political theory – that, in a state of nature, each and every individual can punish offenders against the law of nature, and that, in executing justice, the civil magistrate was exercising no new right but one which had initially been possessed by all pre-political individuals. He thus joined Grotius in flouting the orthodox view that the sword of justice belonged exclusively to the sovereign body; only came into being with it; and then only as a direct grant from God. And he went beyond what Grotius had been willing to countenance in adding that this right had not been alienated but merely entrusted to the magistrate by the people, 'with liberty . . . and right remaining in them to reassume it to themselves' (p. 16).

In short, Milton was proposing not a theory of resistance as much as a theory of revolution (analogous to the way in which a power to punish, which can be exercised on behalf of 'another', is distinct from, and less limited than, a 'power of self-defence'). The full scope of this becomes clear if we consider two further points which Milton is anxious to underline.

The first to note is that when discussing the right of deposing the king, or of altering the government in any way, Milton refers almost invariably to the 'people' rather than to parliament. To understand why, we need only look again at his outline of the procedure when the sword of justice was committed to those who were thereby constituted rulers. The sole parties to this transaction were the people, who chose, and those who were chosen, kings or magistrates. Like Buchanan, Milton makes no mention of any preliminary choice of representatives who then elect rulers on the people's behalf. Indeed, he specifically insists that all the other institutions of government – laws, oaths, and parliaments – were developed subsequently to ensure that the conditions of the original choice were observed. The bodies traditionally identified with the inferior magistrate in accounts of the ancient constitution had thus only emerged at a relatively late stage, and could not have constituted a source of political authority to the exclusion of the people. And it followed in turn that the right of deposing and punishing their kings must rest with the people themselves.

The second is that Milton's preferred way of expressing the relationship between people and ruler is to call it a 'trust'. While he does refer to a 'bond or Covnant' and (citing Buchanan) even allows that 'regal power' is 'nothing else but a mutual Covnant or stipulation between King and people' (pp. 9, 25), the word 'contract' itself never appears. Nor is the structure of his argument at all contractarian. The key difference between a trust and a contract is that a ruler who is entrusted with authority by the people unilaterally incurs an obligation to use it 'for their good in the first place, and not his own' (p. 13), whereas a ruler who enters into a contractual relation with the people derives rights as well as obligations from the contract. What this implies (a point dwelt on with much emphasis in the narration) is that a trustee can be dismissed at will without his having done anything wrong and without – since he has no special rights – suffering any wrong thereby. The people, Milton maintains, can, 'as oft as they shall judge', depose a ruler, 'though no Tyrant, meerly by the liberty and right of free born Men to be govern'd' as they wish. And while the people may of course 'reassume' power if 'it be abus'd', they can also simply 'dispose of it by any alteration, as they shall judge most conducing to the public good' (pp. 13, 16). The same claim is reiterated in yet more emphatic, almost Rousseauvian, terms in the peroration. A 'Nation' which lacks 'the power to remove, or to abolish any governour supreme, or subordinat, with the goverment it self upon urgent causes' cannot be considered 'free' but must be 'under tyranny and servitude'. Without this power they are the 'slaves and vassals' of a lord whose 'goverment, though not illegal, or intolerable' is not 'free' and is on that account alone 'to be abrogated' (pp. 32–3; and see p. 88).

It might well be asked why Milton took up such an extreme position, going further than was required to justify regicide and beyond what was officially acceptable to the Rump. (On 4 January 1649, the Commons had first proclaimed the sovereignty of the people and then promptly vested supreme power in themselves.) The most plausible answer is that he did not want to foreclose on further constitutional changes – not only the formal abolition of the monarchy and the House of Lords, but also more thoroughgoing proposals for reform like the version of the Levellers' *Agreement of the people* revised by the officers, and submitted to the Commons on 20 January. This would help to explain Milton's exhortation to adhere 'to the *present* Parlament & Army' (p. 6; my emphasis).

So open-ended a commitment proved difficult to sustain. As a functionary of the Commonwealth, Milton was required to defend the regime in its present form, and this meant changes to his theory. A dramatic instance of this, amounting almost to a *volte face*, came later that year in the second edition of *The Tenure*. Reviewing a gallery of Protestant 'Witnesses' – Luther, Zwingli, Calvin, Bucer, Paraeus, Knox, Fenner, Cartwright and Goodman – added in a lengthy coda, Milton announces that it is 'generally' their 'cleere and positive determination' that 'to doe justice on a lawless King, is to a privat man unlawful, to an inferior Magistrate lawfull' (p. 47), so reinstating, under their aegis, the very distinction he had laboured to demolish.

Milton does not, however, unequivocally make the distinction his own, and thus the extent to which the second edition of *The Tenure* represents a retreat from radicalism remains unclear (an elusiveness which also characterizes the work which was to win him a European reputation, *Pro Populo Anglicano Defensio*). Even so, it raises the question of why he was prepared to publish a second edition which he knew was, in one fundamental respect at least, inconsistent with the first. One answer may be that it was worth delivering a reminder to the Presbyterians of their habitual insistence on the complete political passivity of the individual, which ought now to operate in favour of the Commonwealth, even at the cost of introducing ambiguity where previously there had been none. Alternatively, the sudden infusion of orthodox continental opinion into a text which had previously been marked by a narrowly anti-Scottish bias could be explained by Milton's having already seen a copy of Salmasius' *Defensio Regia* (see p. 33) and becoming aware as a result of the need to construct a position which was defensible in a European as well as a domestic context.

Within weeks of the regicide, royalist exiles sought to commission a work to voice their horror at the event, mobilize opinion against the new regime, and issue a call for the rightful successor to be installed on the throne. Salmasius, the foremost Protestant scholar in Europe now that Grotius was dead, quickly offered his services. Mindful of the need to appeal to a European readership without neglecting English sensibilities, the thrust of Salmasius' *Defensio Regia*, published (anonymously) by November 1649, was at least minimally compatible with Anglicanism. He deplores the bishops' exclusion from the House of Lords and their later abolition, but, while admonishing the Presbyterians, reserves his severest criticism for the Independents. His denunciations of the regicides as religious fanatics focus on John Cook, who acted as solicitor-general at Charles' trial, and especially his speech summing up the prosecution (never delivered, but published as *King Charls his Case*). Salmasius' reply centres on two absolutist propositions; that the people are not the origin of kingly power, which derives directly from God; and that the king is *legibus solutus* (i.e., above all positive laws), and therefore accountable to God alone.

Milton's chapter-by-chapter refutation of Salmasius, *A Defence of the People of England*, finally appeared in February 1651. While it resembles *The Tenure* in being devoted as much to invective as argument, these are more freely intermixed in the manner of Cicero's *Philippics* on which it is modelled. Just as Cicero had offered himself as the saviour of the republic in the face of Antony's attempts to overthrow it, so Milton steps forward to champion the beleaguered Commonwealth against Salmasius. And just as Cicero, in the *Second Philippic* especially, had tried to undermine Antony's reputation by dwelling on his susceptibility to bribes, his attempts to improve his oratory by hiring a rhetorician, and his demeaning relationships with women (II, xiv, xvii, xxxi), so Milton seeks to destroy the personal and professional integrity of his adversary. By the end of Chapter I, the charges which Milton is to deploy throughout the work are already in place.

While Salmasius now professed to uphold the bishops' cause, he had in an earlier work advocated their abolition and replacement by a system of elders. Milton seizes on this to discredit and embarrass Salmasius at every turn, and to assume the mantle of religious orthodoxy (as he had begun to do in the second edition of *The Tenure*) by invoking the support of Luther, Zwingli, Calvin and Bucer (pp. 76, 125, 177).

Next, the fact that *Defensio Regia* had been published 'at the king's expense' is used to revile Salmasius as a hireling whose defence of royal power and Antony's 'have flowed forth from the same spring' (pp. 55, 92). As in *The Tenure*, Milton also impugns his opponent's masculinity. Salmasius is introduced as a Terentian 'eunuch' (p. 55), suffers an Ovidian metamorphosis into the nymph 'Salmacis' (p. 57), and finally falls victim to the Homeric enchantress Circe; 'accustomed to the most shameful slavery' under his wife, he has 'no taste of virtue and the liberty which is born of it' (p. 238). This picture of domestic servitude undermines Salmasius' credibility as a spokesman for patriarchalism. It also contributes to a recurrent contrast between his slavish devotion to the cause of tyranny and the regicides' virtuous and – in what for Milton, as for Cicero, amounts to a tautology – manly commitment to liberty.

Milton also takes Salmasius' rhetorical incompetence for granted. Even his avowed modesty in not aspiring to any Ciceronian heights of eloquence is turned against him (p. 64). He is a mere 'grammarian' whose every solecism Milton unfailingly subjects to ridicule (p. 56).

This broadens into the claim that, for all his learning, Salmasius has failed to understand the classical writings he has read or edited (p. 76). Having displayed contempt for his opponent's abilities, Milton turns to the questions of textual interpretation which form the battleground of Chapters II–V.

In his second chapter Salmasius had marshalled the standard Old Testament texts in support of his view that kings are *legibus solutus*. Milton's response is self-consciously to adopt the methods and mannerisms of the humanist exegete, seeking to explain the meaning of these passages by reference to their scriptural and historical context, and to show that the lessons which they yield when properly understood are contrary to those suggested by Salmasius. For example, he compiles evidence to show that when God acceded to the Israelites' wish for a king (Deuteronomy 17. 14) this was done unwillingly, and so, far from indicating approval of their desire to subjugate themselves to rulers released from all laws, offers instead divine 'testimony' that the 'decision' about which 'form of commonwealth' to choose 'has always lain in the power of all peoples and nations' (p. 80).

But Milton also displays a scepticism about the value of such lessons which is seemingly at odds with the exegetical effort required to produce them. While this sometimes takes the form it had in *The Tenure* of a rationalistic distaste for the empirical, at others it is couched in theological terms. From Chapter II onwards, Milton invariably responds to the claim that kings are divinely ordained by arguing that there is a sense in which everything in general, and hence nothing in particular, is similarly ordained – the rights of the people, for example, just as much (or as little) as the rights of kings. The outcome of employing this devalued idea of divine appointment is a strict demarcation between cases like, say, that of Moses, who indubitably could refer matters directly to God, and the rest, where there is no 'visible sign from God' (pp. 92–4). It is in the end irrelevant 'what kind of king the Israelites wanted', since the English had originally exercised 'the right of nations, without God's command or prohibition' playing any part in their choice (pp. 83, 90).

Chapter III deals with the New Testament in much the same way. It is a 'divine proclamation of liberty', the meaning of which Salmasius has distorted in developing a spurious notion of 'religious obligation', and which must now be reconstructed (pp. 105–6). The political advice of the apostles, for example, should be understood as having been addressed exclusively to private persons rather than 'senators' and 'magistrates'. No obligation on the latter not to resist tyrants can be inferred from this, nor could it have been the apostles' intention to inculcate obedience to tyrants, since the emperor at the time was not Nero, as Salmasius alleged, but Claudius, an 'honest prince' (pp. 112, 115). Once again, however, Milton does not seek to derive any specific precepts from the scriptures. Except for an ironical flourish in which he turns against Salmasius his own argument that subjects should always obey the powers that be (which would require conscientious obedience to the Commonwealth), Milton confines himself to showing that the gospel yields a consistent meaning only when interpreted in the light of a principle of liberty which the interpreter brings to the text.

Milton begins Chapter IV by taking it as axiomatic that men cannot be subject by law to a ruler who is above all law, but nevertheless condescends to 'renew the fight with precedents' (p. 130). Thus in reply to the claim that nothing corresponding to the regicide can be found anywhere in Jewish history, he reproduces his discussion of Ehud and Eglon and concludes that 'If Ehud slaughtered Eglon justly, we have justly punished Charles' (pp. 130–31). But Milton is less concerned with erecting this parallel into a precedent than with disclosing the underlying principle of justice which makes the parallel a true one. And he again uses the example of Jehu to underline the point; 'killing a tyrant was not good and lawful because God ordered it, but God ordered it because it was good and lawful' (p. 136).

Chapter V opens with a variation on this theme. Salmasius cannot hope to advance his argument by resorting to the law of nature, Milton says, because 'the law of God agrees exactly with the law of nature' and to demonstrate a proposition in terms of the former is thus already to have shown 'what is most suited to the law of nature' (p. 149). (This need not imply that the relation between the two must be exactly symmetrical, for what Milton says is consistent with the idea that the law of nature is more extensive than, and includes within it, the precepts of divine positive law.) Even though the preceding chapters have, on this view, made the task redundant, Milton agrees to examine the classical sources, and the rest of Chapter V becomes a showcase for his humanist talents.

In the following two chapters, Salmasius had mounted a direct assault on the foundations of the new regime: the theory of popular sovereignty. He argued first that when setting up a ruler the people cannot merely delegate, but must alienate, their original sovereignty. By this he meant a transfer which is full, unconditional, and irrevocable such that (in the phrase picked up by Milton) 'the power of the people ceases to exist when the power of a king begins' (p. 182). Salmasius had no difficulty with the notion of individuals entering into voluntary slavery and simply extended it to communities as a whole, the *Lex Regia* by which the Roman people had granted power to the emperor being a model of this type of contract.

Faced with these absolutist commonplaces, Milton's response in Chapters VI and VII is to reiterate that political power is best defined as a trust. He had already laid it down in Chapter III that voluntary slavery is impossible for the individual because his liberty is not unconditionally his to surrender: since 'we belong to God' it would be 'sacrilege' to 'hand ourselves over in slavery to Caesar' (p. 108). Equally, he now points out, since the king does not unconditionally own any property – he 'cannot even sell off the inheritance of the crown' – it is impossible for him to function as a master enjoying total control over his slaves (p. 185). And even if these rights were not inalienable, for the people to set up a ruler 'other than upon trust would be the height of madness' (p. 183). Thus it would be 'reasonable' to construe the *Lex Regia* as a transaction involving a 'lawful and revocable power, not a tyrannical and senseless one' (p. 184). The truth is that when the 'public welfare' demands, the people can revoke a power which they 'virtually' hold themselves (pp. 184, 190).

But Salmasius had also argued that the usual typologies were beside the point, since the Commonwealth represented an altogether unprecedented kind of government: military rule. Despite its democratic pretensions, the regime essentially consisted of a Council of State dominated by officers. This in turn wielded despotic power over what was, since the abolition of the House of Lords, an undifferentiated mass which ought to be thought of not as the people but merely a rabble.

Milton was naturally anxious to rebut the allegation that the social as well as the political order of things had been overthrown. But it was difficult to see how a defence of the revolutionary acts which had brought the Commonwealth into being could be reconciled with the claim that their outcome was nevertheless socially conservative. *The*

Tenure had ended up by appearing implausibly to press the claims of both the individual *and* the magistrate. His solution in the *Defence* is to define 'the people' in a way which avoids identification with either. Thus in the Preface, Milton insists that an embattled state is justified in concerning itself with 'the healthy and sound part' to the exclusion of the disaffected, 'whether they are commoners or aristocrats', while in Chapter I he applauds the 'sounder part' who invited the Army to act (pp. 61, 72). And in Chapters VI and VII he takes a further step, and uses the terms 'better part' (*pars potior*) and 'sounder part' (*pars sanior*) to denote those whose actions are the 'act of the people', and who can indeed be said to 'represent the whole people' (pp. 181, 193).

It is sometimes argued – following the lead given in 1652 by one of Milton's earliest and shrewdest critics, Sir Robert Filmer, in his *Observations* (a critique of Hobbes, Milton and Grotius in turn) – that this was a blunder which exposed both the narrowness of the regime's support and Milton's fundamentally apolitical concern with the interests of a spiritual elite. In fact, the capacity for citizenship even of the godly is socially defined, and said to derive from the fact that they cannot be diverted from the path of 'virtue' by either 'luxury and opulence' or 'poverty and need' (p. 194). Milton's vocabulary is moreover entirely conventional. Like Marsilius of Padua, who emphasized the role of 'the weightier part' (*pars valentior*) of the people, many later advocates of popular sovereignty often spoke of 'the people' in qualitative terms. Even Buchanan, whose commitment to radical populism is beyond doubt, insists on the primacy of those displaying the civic virtues. The *Defence* is therefore unexceptional in this respect, and its usage marks little more than a shift from the rights of the people considered severally (legitimating individual action against the Long Parliament) to an emphasis on the rights of the people considered collectively (embodied in the Rump). In effect, Milton aligns himself with the Commons' votes of 4 January 1649.

Chapters VIII to XII then proceed to give historical substance to a vision of the English constitution with, *mutatis mutandis*, the Rump as its centrepiece. Abandoning the view which he had shared with Buchanan that rulers were originally chosen directly by the people, Milton now says that the people first 'delegated' their power to a popular assembly which then created kings (p. 214). Given that the bishops and lords had been later additions to, and not constituent parts of, this body, it did not matter if they had now been abolished.

And the objection that there was no mention of a 'parliament' before the Conquest is dismissed as a verbal quibble, since 'the thing always existed' (p. 205). Nor for that matter, Milton maintains, had there even been a Conquest; William had confirmed the laws of Edward the Confessor, thereby preserving the continuity of the ancient constitution (p. 212).

Milton appears to model his account on François Hotman's *Francogallia* (1573), the main contentions of which – that the monarchy was elective, that kings were bound by their coronation oaths, and that popular assemblies not only possessed the power of electing kings but also of deposing them – he had earlier endorsed (p. 147). Armed with this analysis, Milton is able to counter Salmasius' (no less tendentious) historical arguments and assert the legitimacy of all the revolutionary acts carried out since the purge.

It is true that this still represents something of a sea-change: whereas the radical heights of *The Tenure* had been arrived at through a critique of constitutionalism, *A Defence* closes in harmony with one of its classic texts. For all the harsh invective, the underlying stance is one of studied moderation, and in this lay the key to the work's success. An impeccably Ciceronian ethos, an undoctrinaire commitment to the Commonwealth as merely the best arrangement that circumstances allowed, the disclaiming of any hostility to monarchy as such, and a disavowal of resistance except in the gravest cases, all combine to form a picture of sober self-restraint far removed from any suspicion of fanaticism.

But it would be a mistake to suppose that all traces of radicalism had been expunged from the text. Certainly many of its seventeenth-century readers did not think so. 'William Allen', the author of *Killing Noe Murder* (1657), for example, put forward arguments for the assassination of Cromwell which show every sign of having been derived from *A Defence*. It is also significant that *A Defence* appears on John Locke's book-lists from 1667 onwards (he also owned a copy of the version of *The Tenure* published in 1689). For not the least of the similarities between Locke and Milton is their adoption of a stoic perspective which allows them to assert, with the minimum of qualification, the right of the people, and even of individuals, to resist their tyrannical rulers.

Principal events in Milton's life

1608 *December*: born (9th), Bread St, London.

1620 Enters St Paul's School, London.

1625 *February*: admitted (12th) to Christ's College, Cambridge.

1629 *March*: takes his BA (26th).

1632 *July*: takes his MA (3rd), then retires to Horton for private study.

1634 *September*: his masque *Comus* performed (29th) at Ludlow Castle (published three years later).

1638 *May*: sails for France and calls on Grotius in Paris.

June to September: travels south through Italy to stay in Florence for two months. Visits Galileo.

October to December: goes on to Rome (where he visits the Vatican library, and attends a reception given by Cardinal Barberini) and then Naples.

1639 *January to May*: abandons plan of visiting Sicily and Greece and travels back through Italy with stays at Florence and Venice.

June: visits the theologian John Diodati in Geneva.

July: returns to England.

1641 *May*: publishes *Of Reformation Touching Church-Discipline*, the first of five anti-episcopal tracts.

June to July: publishes *Of Prelatical Episcopacy* and *Animadversions upon the Remonstrants Defence, Against Smectymnuus*.

1642 *January or February*: publishes *The Reason of Church-Governement*.

April: publishes *An Apology Against a pamphlet*.

Around Whitsun marries Mary Powell.

1643 *August*: *The Doctrine and Discipline of Divorce*, the first of four tracts advocating divorce by consent, published (1st).

1644 *February*: the greatly enlarged second edition of *Doctrine and Discipline* appears (2nd).
June: tract *Of Education* published (5th).
August: publishes (6th) *The Judgement of Martin Bucer, Concerning Divorce*. His works on divorce are attacked in a sermon before Parliament (13th), and petitioned against by the stationers (24th to 26th).
November: *Areopagitica* published (23rd).
December: summoned by the House of Lords for examination (28th).

1645 *March*: publishes (4th) final divorce tracts, *Tetrachordon* and *Colasterion*. Apparently shuns all public controversy for the next four years.

1646 *January*: *Poems of Mr. John Milton* appears (2nd).

1649 *January*: Charles I executed (30th).
February: *The Tenure of Kings and Magistrates* published (13th).
March: Milton invited (13th) to be Secretary for Foreign Tongues by the Council of State and appointed (15th). He is ordered (26th and 28th) to 'make some observations' on John Lilburne's *Englands new chains discovered* and on papers relating to 'designers against the peace of the Common-welth' in Ireland.
May: *Observations upon the Articles of Peace* published (16th).
October: second edition of *Tenure* probably in print.
Eikonoklastes, the official response to *Eikon Basilike* (purportedly written by Charles I, but actually by John Gauden) published (6th).
November: Salmasius' *Defensio Regia* published not later than the middle of the month.

1650 *January*: ordered by the Council of State (8th) to reply to Salmasius.

1651 *February*: *Pro Populo Anglicano Defensio* published (24th).
March: acts as licenser (17th) for *Mercurius Pragmaticus* (until the following January).

1652 *February*: first of a series of personal disasters overtakes Milton when he becomes totally blind (his sight had been failing since 1644). Publication (2nd) of Sir Robert Filmer's *Observations concerning the originall of government, upon Mr. Hobs Leviathan, Mr. Milton against Salmasius. H. Grotius De jure belli.*

April: a committee reports to the Commons (2nd) about his 'examination' for approving publication of a Socinian manifesto, the Racovian catechism, which is condemned as blasphemous.

May: his wife dies (5th) three days after the birth of their third daughter, Deborah.

June: his one son, John, dies aged one.

1654 *May*: publishes (30th) *Pro Populo Anglicano Defensio Secunda*, a reply to Pierre du Moulin's *Regii sanguinis clamor* (1652) which he said he was ordered to make though there is no official record.

1655 *April*: his salary is reduced to a life pension and he is allowed a substitute in the secretaryship.

August: *Pro Se Defensio* published (8th).

1657 *November*: marries Katherine Woodcock (12th).

1658 *February*: his wife dies (3rd) as does their daughter, Katherine, the following month.

May (?): publishes *The Cabinet-Council* from a manuscript which he believes (mistakenly) to be by Sir Walter Raleigh.

September: Cromwell dies (3rd) and is succeeded as Protector by his son Richard.

October: publishes second, enlarged edition of the first *Defensio*.

1659 *February*: publishes *A Treatise of Civil Power in Ecclesiastical causes.*

August: *Considerations touching the likeliest means to remove Hirelings out of the church* published.

1660 *February*: first edition of *The Readie & Easie Way to Establish a Free Commonwealth* published towards the end of the month.

April: second, revised and enlarged edition of *The Readie & Easie Way* published in the first week, followed within days by *Brief Notes Upon a Late Sermon.*

May: Charles II is proclaimed king (8th), returns from exile (25th) and enters London (29th). Milton goes into hiding.

June: the Commons order Milton's arrest (16th) and request a royal proclamation calling in *Eikonoklastes* and the first *Defensio*. In later debates on the bill of indemnity his name is proposed, but not accepted, as the last of those to be excluded from pardon.

August: proclamation issued (13th) calling in the two works, copies of which are burned by the hangman (28th).

October (?): arrested and imprisoned.

December: the Commons order his release (15th).

1663 *February*: marries (24th) Elizabeth Minshull.

1667 *August (?)*: *Paradise Lost* published.

1669 *June*: *Accedence Commenc't Grammar* published.

1670 *November (?)*: publishes *The History of Britain*.

1671 Publishes *Paradise Regained* and *Samson Agonistes*.

1672 *May (?)*: *Artis logicæ Plenior Institutio* published.

1673 *May (?)*: *Of True Religion, Hæresie, Schism, Toleration* published.

November (?): *Poems* published.

1674 *May*: *Epistolarum Familiarum Liber Unus* and *Prolusiones* published.

July: publishes second, revised edition of *Paradise Lost*, and *A Declaration, or Letters Patents of the Election of this present King of Poland John the Third.*

November: dies (8th?) and is buried (12th) in St Giles, Cripplegate.

1676 *September to October*: state letters prepared by Milton during the interregnum published in Amsterdam.

1681 *April (?)*: the digression excised from Milton's *History of Britain* published as *The Character of the Long Parliament.*

1682 *February (?)*: *A Brief History of Moscovia* published.

1825 Two years after the manuscript was discovered, Milton's *De Doctrina Christiana* published.

Bibliographical note

Biography

The standard accounts are W. R. Parker, *Milton: A Biography*, 2 vols. (Oxford, 1968) and, more discursively, David Masson, *The Life of Milton: Narrated in Connexion with the Literary, Historical, and Political Events of his Time*, 7 vols. (London, 1859–80). Almost all the known facts are documented by J. M. French, *The Life Records of John Milton*, 5 vols. (New Brunswick, N.J., 1949–58).

Intellectual background

For the most comprehensive survey of the sixteenth-century writings on resistance to which Milton was responding see Q. Skinner, *The Foundations of Modern Political Thought*, 2 vols. (Cambridge, 1978). (On the right to punish see, however, J. H. Burns, '*Jus Gladii* and *Jurisdictio*: Jacques Almain and John Locke', *Historical Journal*, 26 (1983), pp. 369–74.) Selections from key texts are introduced in J. H. Franklin, *Constitutionalism and Resistance in the Sixteenth Century* (New York, 1969). Two studies which carry the story forward are J. H. M. Salmon, *The French Religious Wars in English Political Thought* (Oxford, 1959), and F. Oakley, 'On the Road from Constance to 1688: the Political Thought of John Major and George Buchanan', *Journal of British Studies*, 2 (1962), pp. 1–31. See also Harro Höpfl and Martyn P. Thompson, 'The History of Contract as a Motif in Political Thought', *American Historical Review*, 84 (1979), pp. 919–44. For central themes in the seventeenth century see Richard Tuck, *Natural*

Rights Theories: Their Origin and Development (Cambridge, 1979); J. G. A. Pocock, *The Ancient Constitution and the Feudal Law*, reissue (Cambridge, 1987); and David Wootton, 'Introduction' to *Divine Right and Democracy* (Harmondsworth, 1986).

Political background

David Underdown, *Pride's Purge: Politics in the Puritan Revolution* (Oxford, 1971) and Blair Worden, *The Rump Parliament, 1648–1653* (Cambridge, 1974) are indispensable. For the evolution of the interregnum regime and its collapse see especially Austin Woolrych, *Commonwealth to Protectorate* (Oxford, 1982) and his 'Historical Introduction' to Volume VII, *Complete Prose Works of John Milton* (New Haven, 1980).

General studies of Milton's political thought, 1649–51

The outstanding study is Ernest Sirluck, 'Milton's Political Thought: The First Cycle', *Modern Philology*, 61 (1964), 209–24. The treatment in Chapter IX of P. Zagorin, *A History of Political Thought in the English Revolution* (London, 1954) – as in Part III of Christopher Hill, *Milton and the English Revolution* (London, 1977) – is somewhat perfunctory. Michael Fixler usefully highlights his 'aristocratic' tendencies in Chapter IV of *Milton and the Kingdoms of God* (Northwestern UP, 1964). Z. S. Fink's related thesis in *The Classical Republicans* (Evanston, 1945) is more convincing on the later pamphlets. The most recent survey is in Chapter VI of John B. Sanderson, '*But the People's Creatures*': *the philosophical basis of the English Civil War* (Manchester, 1989). A fascinating attempt to align his tenets with those of more systematic writers is made in Otto von Gierke, *Natural Law and the Theory of Society, 1500–1800*, trans. Ernest Barker (Cambridge, 1958), pp. 35–61, and notes.

Specific aspects of *The Tenure* and *Defence*

On his rhetoric see the excellent article by Diane Parkin Speer, 'Milton's *Defensio Prima*: *Ethos* and Vituperation in a Polemic Engagement', *Quarterly Journal of Speech*, 56 (1970), pp. 277–83, and, more generally, J. A. Wittreich, ' "The Crown of Eloquence": The Figure of the Orator in Milton's Prose Works', in *Achievements of the Left Hand*, ed. Michael Lieb and J. T. Shawcross (Amherst, Mass., 1974), pp. 3–54. For Milton's handling of his sources see Merritt Y. Hughes, 'Milton's Treatment of Reformation History in *The Tenure of Kings and Magistrates*', Chapter IX of his *Ten Perspectives on Milton* (New Haven, 1965); Ruth Mohl, *John Milton and His Commonplace Book* (New York, 1969); M. Dzelzainis, 'Milton, *Macbeth*, and Buchanan', *The Seventeenth Century*, 4 (1989), pp. 55–66; and J. Greenberg, 'The Confessor's Laws and the Radical Face of the Ancient Constitution', *English Historical Review*, 104 (1989), pp. 611–37.

Abbreviations

All works by Milton, except where stated. References in the footnotes are keyed to the Yale edition of the *Complete Prose Works of John Milton* by volume number.

A	First edition of *The Tenure of Kings and Magistrates*
AR	*Areopagitica*
C	*Colasterion*
CB	*Commonplace Book*
DDD	*The Doctrine and Discipline of Divorce*
DR	*Defensio Regia* (Salmasius)
DS	*Pro Populo Anglicano Defensio Secunda*
E	*Eikonoklastes*
HB	*The History of Britain*
M.	Milton
NPN	*A Select Library of the Nicene and Post-Nicene Fathers of the Christian Church* (First series, ed. P. Schaff)
O	*Observations upon the Articles of Peace*
PSD	*Pro Se Defensio*
R	*Of Reformation*
S.	Salmasius
T	*Tetrachordon*

THE TENURE OF KINGS AND MAGISTRATES: PROVING,

That it is Lawfull, and hath been held so through all Ages, for any, who have the Power, to call to account a Tyrant, or wicked KING, and after due conviction, to depose, and put him to death; if the ordinary MAGISTRATE have neglected, or deny'd to doe it.

And that they, who of late so much blame Deposing, are the Men that did it themselves.

Published now the second time with some additions, and many Testimonies also added out of the best & learnedest among Protestant Divines asserting the position of this book.

The Author, J. M.

LONDON,

Printed by *Matthew Simmons*, nextdoore to the Gil-Lyon in Aldersgate Street, 1650.

THE TENURE OF KINGS And MAGISTRATES.

IF men within themselves would be govern'd by reason, and not generally give up thir understanding to a double tyrannie, of Custom from without, and blind affections within, they would discerne better, what it is to favour and uphold the Tyrant of a Nation. But being slaves within doors, no wonder that they strive so much to have the public State conformably govern'd to the inward vitious rule, by which they govern themselves. For indeed none can love freedom heartilie, but good men; the rest love not freedom, but licence;[1] which never hath more scope or more indulgence then under Tyrants. Hence is it that Tyrants are not oft offended, nor stand much in doubt of bad men, as being all naturally servile; but in whom vertue and true worth most is eminent, them they feare in earnest, as by right thir Maisters, against them lies all thir hatred and suspicion.[2] Consequentlie neither doe bad men hate Tyrants, but have been alwayes readiest with the falsifi'd names of *Loyalty*, and *Obedience*, to colour over thir base compliances. And although somtimes for shame, and when it comes to thir owne grievances, of purse especially, they would seeme good Patriots, and side with the better cause, yet when others for the deliverance of thir Countrie, endu'd with fortitude and Heroick vertue to feare nothing but the curse writt'n against those *That doe the*

[1] The distinction between liberty and licence was a classical commonplace: e.g., Cicero, *De doma sua*, LI, 131; Livy, *Ab urbe condita*, III, 37, 34. For M. see *Sonnet* 12, 11; *DDD*, II, 225; *HB*, V, 131.

[2] Cf. Sallust, *Bellum Catilinae*, VII, 2: 'Nam regibus boni quam mali suspectiores sunt semperque eis aliena virtus formidulosa est'. M. placed this epigram from Sallust (his favourite historian) on the title page of *E*.

worke of the Lord negligently,[3] would goe on to remove, not only the calamities and thraldoms of a People, but the roots and causes whence they spring, streight these men, and sure helpers at need, as if they hated only the miseries but not the mischiefs, after they have juggl'd and palter'd with the world, bandied and born armes against thir King, devested him, disannointed him, nay curs'd him all over in thir Pulpits and thir Pamphlets, to the ingaging of sincere and real men, beyond what is possible or honest to retreat from, not only turne revolters from those principles, which only could at first move them, but lay the staine of disloyaltie, and worse, on those proceedings, which are the necessary consequences of thir own former actions; nor dislik'd by themselves, were they manag'd to the intire advantages of thir own Faction; not considering the while that he toward whom they boasted thir new fidelitie, counted them accessory; and by those Statutes and Lawes which they so impotently brandish against others, would have doom'd them to a Traytors death, for what they have don alreadie. 'Tis true, that most men are apt anough to civill Wars and commotions as a noveltie, and for a flash hot and active; but through sloth or inconstancie, and weakness of spirit either fainting, ere thir own pretences, though never so just, be half attain'd, or through an inbred falshood and wickednes, betray oft times to destruction with themselves, men of noblest temper joyn'd with them for causes, whereof they in their rash undertakings were not capable.[4]

If God and a good cause give them Victory, the prosecution wherof for the most part, inevitably draws after it the alteration of Lawes, change of Goverment, downfal of Princes with thir families; then comes the task to those Worthies which are the soule of that enterprize, to be swett and labour'd out amidst the throng and noises of Vulgar and irrational men. Some contesting for privileges, customs, forms, and that old entanglement of Iniquity, thir gibrish Lawes, though the badge of thir ancient slavery.[5] Others who have beene fiercest against thir Prince, under the notion of a Tyrant, and no mean incendiaries of the Warr against him, when God out of his providence

[3] M.'s marginal reference to Jer. 48:19 is wrong (A correctly gives verse 10): 'Cursed be he that doeth the work of the Lord deceitfully'. The AV suggests 'negligently' as an alternative.

[4] A: 'which they in their rash undertakings were not capable of'.

[5] Echoes the anti-Norman rhetoric which had expressed the Levellers' hostility to the common law; but, since they now opposed the king's trial on legal grounds, M. (like other Independents) is deploying such phrases *against* them.

and high disposal hath deliver'd him into the hand of thir brethren, on a suddain and in a new garbe of Allegiance, which thir doings have long since cancell'd; they plead for him, pity him, extoll him, protest against those that talk of bringing him to the tryal of Justice, which is the Sword of God, superior to all mortal things, in whose hand soever by apparent signes his testified will is to put it. But certainly if we consider who and what they are, on a suddain grown so pitifull, wee may conclude, thir pitty can be no true, and Christian commiseration, but either levitie and shallowness of minde, or else a carnal admiring of that worldly pomp and greatness, from whence they see him fall'n; or rather lastly a dissembl'd and seditious pity, fain'd of industry to begett new discord.[6] As for mercy, if it be to a Tyrant, under which Name they themselves have cited him so oft in the hearing of God, of Angels, and the holy Church assembl'd, and there charg'd him with the spilling of more innocent blood by farr, then ever *Nero*[7] did, undoubtedly the mercy which they pretend, is the mercy of wicked men; and their mercies, wee read are cruelties;[8] hazarding the welfare of a whole Nation, to have sav'd one, whom so oft they have tearm'd *Agag*;[9] and vilifying the blood of many *Jonathans*, that have sav'd *Israel*;[10] insisting with much niceness on the unnecessariest clause of thir Covnant[11] [wrested], wherein the feare of change, and the absurd contradiction of a flattering hostilitie had hamperd them, but not scrupling to give away for complements, to an implacable revenge, the heads of many thousand Christians more.

Another sort there is, who comming in the cours of these affaires, to have thir share in great actions, above the form of Law or Custom, at least to give thir voice and approbation, begin to swerve, and almost shiver at the Majesty and grandeur of som noble deed, as if they were newly enter'd into a great sin; disputing presidents, forms, and circumstances, when the Common-wealth nigh perishes for want of deeds in substance, don with just and faithfull expedition. To these I

[6] A: 'commotions' for 'discord'.

[7] Roman emperor, 54–68, noted for his cruelty. For M.'s parallels between Nero and Charles I see pp. 176, 240.

[8] M., margin, refers to Prov. 12:10.

[9] Amalekite king slain by Samuel, 1 Sam. 15:33–4.

[10] See 1 Sam. 19:1–45.

[11] Article III of the Solemn League and Covenant (25 Sept. 1643) pledged the parliaments of England and Scotland 'to preserve and defend the King's Majesty's person and authority, in the preservation and defence of the true religion and liberties of the kingdoms'. For M.'s discussion of this ambivalent clause, see *O* and *E*, III, 324–5, 493–7, 593–6 and below pp. 27–30.

wish better instruction, and vertue equal to thir calling; the former of which, that is to say Instruction, I shall indeavour, as my dutie is, to bestow on them; and exhort them not to startle from the just and pious resolution of adhering with all thir [strength &] assistance to the present Parlament & Army, in the glorious way wherin Justice and Victory hath set them; the only warrants through all ages, next under immediat Revelation, to exercise supream power, in those proceedings which hitherto appeare equal to what hath been don in any age or Nation heretofore, justly or magnanimouslie. Nor let them be discourag'd or deterr'd by any new Apostate Scarcrowes, who under show of giving counsel, send out their barking monitories and *memento's*,[12] empty of ought else but the spleene of a frustrated Faction. For how can that pretended counsel bee either sound or faithfull, when they that give it, see not for madness and vexation of thir ends lost, that those Statutes and Scriptures which both falsly and scandalously, they wrest against thir Friends and Associates, would by sentence of the common adversarie, fall first and heaviest upon thir own heads. Neither let milde and tender dispositions be foolishly softn'd from thir duty and perseverance, with the unmaskuline Rhetorick of any puling Priest or Chaplain,[13] sent as a friendly Letter of advice, for fashion sake in privat, and forthwith publisht by the Sender himself,[14] that wee may know how much of friend there was in it, to cast an odious envie upon them, to whom it was pretended to be sent in charitie. Nor let any man be deluded by either the ignorance or the notorious hypocrisie and self-repugnance of our dancing Divines,[15] who have the conscience and the boldness, to come with Scripture in thir mouthes, gloss'd and fitted for thir turnes with a double contradictory sense, transforming the sacred verity of God, to an Idol with two Faces, looking at once two several ways; and with the same quotations to charge others, which in the same case they made

[12] M. alludes to William Prynne, *A briefe memento to the present unparliamentary junto* (4 Jan. 1649), and to John Gauden, *The religious & loyal protestation* (10 Jan. 1649), p. 11, where Gauden refers to himself as 'Your faithfull Monitor'.

[13] Gauden (p. 11) urged the Army to display 'Pitty, not foolish and *feminine*, which I would have below you, but *masculine*, Heroick, truly Christian and Divine'.

[14] Gauden's work was (title page) *sent to a collonell, to bee presented to the lord Fairfax, and his generall councell of officers* on 5 Jan. 1649. Henry Hammond sent his *Humble addresse* to Fairfax on 15 Jan. 1649. See *E*, III, 548–53 and below p. 76.

[15] M. refers to the most influential of the Presbyterian tracts, *A serious and faithfull representation of the judgements of ministers of the gospell within the province of London* (18 Jan. 1649). See p. 47.

serve to justifie themselves. For while the hope to bee made Classic and Provincial Lords[16] led them on, while pluralities[17] greas'd them thick and deep, to the shame and scandal of Religion, more then all the Sects and Heresies they exclaim against, then to fight against the Kings person, and no less a Party of his Lords and Commons, or to put force upon both the Houses, was good, was lawfull, was no resisting of Superior powers; they onely were powers not to be resisted, who countenanc'd the good, and punish't the evil. But now that thir censorious domineering is not suffer'd to be universal, truth and conscience to be freed, Tithes and Pluralities to be no more, though competent allowance provided, and the warme experience of large gifts, and they so good at taking them; yet now to exclude & seize upon[18] impeach't Members,[19] to bring Delinquents without exemption to a faire Tribunal by the common National Law against murder, is now to be no less then *Corah*, *Dathan*, and *Abiram*.[20] He who but erewhile in the Pulpits was a cursed Tyrant, an enemie to God and Saints, lad'n with all the innocent blood spilt in three Kingdoms, and so to be fought against, is now, though nothing penitent or alter'd from his first principles, a lawfull Magistrate, a Sovran Lord, the Lords anointed, not to be touch'd, though by themselves imprison'd. As if this onely were obedience, to preserve the meere useless bulke of his person, and that onely in prison, not in the field, and to disobey his commands, deny him his dignity and office, every where to resist his power but where they thinke it onely surviving in thir own faction.

But who in particular is a Tyrant cannot be determin'd in a general discours,[21] otherwise then by supposition; his particular charge, and the sufficient proof of it must determin that: which I leave to Magistrates, at least to the uprighter sort of them, and of the people, though in number less by many, in whom faction least hath prevaild above the Law of nature and right reason, to judge as they find cause.

[16] The Presbyterian church was organized in *classes* (groups of parishes), provincial assemblies (for each county and for London), and a national synod.

[17] I.e., multiple church livings.

[18] A: 'on'.

[19] On 15 June 1647 eleven Presbyterian MPs were impeached by the Army in 'The Heads of a Charge'. The Commons refused to suspend them on 25 June but they withdrew voluntarily. Charges were formally submitted on 6 July, and on 7 Sept. the two who had not fled were sent to the Tower.

[20] Rebels against Moses and Aaron, Num. 16:1–33.

[21] M. avoids referring to Charles I by name throughout.

But this I dare owne as part of my faith, that if such a one there be, by whose Commission, whole massachers[22] have been committed on his faithfull Subjects, his Provinces offerd to pawn or alienation,[23] as the hire of those whom he had sollicited to come in and destroy whole Citties and Countries; be he King, or Tyrant, or Emperour, the Sword of Justice is above him; in whose hand soever is found sufficient power to avenge the effusion, and so great a deluge of innocent blood. For if all human power to execute, not accidentally but intendedly, the wrath of God upon evil doers without exception, be of God; then that power, whether ordinary, or if that faile, extraordinary so executing that intent of God, is lawfull, and not to be resisted. But to unfold more at large this whole Question, though with all expedient brevity, I shall here set downe from first beginning, the original of Kings; how and wherfore exalted to that dignitie above thir Brethren; and from thence shall prove, that turning to Tyranny they may bee as lawfully depos'd and punish'd, as they were at first elected: This I shall doe by autorities and reasons, not learnt in corners among Scisms and Heresies, as our doubling Divines are ready to calumniat, but fetch't out of the midst of choicest and most authentic learning, and no prohibited Authors, nor many Heathen, but Mosaical,[24] Christian, Orthodoxal, and which must needs be more convincing to our Adversaries, Presbyterial.[25]

No man who knows ought, can be so stupid to deny that all men naturally were borne free, being the image and resemblance of God himself, and were by privilege above all the creatures, born to command and not to obey:[26] and that they liv'd so. Till from the root of *Adams* transgression, falling among themselves to doe wrong and violence, and foreseeing that such courses must needs tend to the destruction of them all, they agreed by common league to bind each other from mutual injury, and joyntly to defend themselves against any that gave disturbance or opposition to such agreement. Hence came Citties, Townes and Common-wealths. And because no faith in all was found sufficiently binding, they saw it needfull to ordaine som

[22] M.'s estimates of the number of Protestants massacred in Ulster in 1641 vary. Cf. *O* and *E*, III, 301, 470 and below p.241.

[23] I.e., the offer of five and four counties to the Irish and Scots respectively in return for military assistance. See *E*, III, 385, 475.

[24] I.e., relating to the laws of Moses.

[25] This sentence marks the transition from the exordium to the narration.

[26] See Gen. 1:26.

authoritie, that might restrain by force and punishment what was violated against peace and common right. This autoritie and power of self-defence and preservation being originally and naturally in every one of them, and unitedly in them all, for ease, for order, and least each man should be his own partial Judge, they communicated and deriv'd either to one, whom for the eminence of his wisdom and integritie they chose above the rest, or to more then one whom they thought of equal deserving: the first was call'd a King; the other Magistrates. Not to be thir Lords and Maisters (though afterward those names in som places were giv'n voluntarily to such as had been Authors of inestimable good to the people) but, to be thir Deputies and Commissioners, to execute, by vertue of thir intrusted power, that justice which else every man by the bond of nature and of Cov'nant must have executed for himself,[27] and for one another. And to him that shall consider well why among free Persons, one man by civil right should beare autority and jurisdiction over another, no other end or reason can be imaginable. These for a while govern'd well, and with much equity decided all things at thir own arbitrement: till the temptation of such a power left absolute in thir hands, perverted them at length to injustice and partialitie. Then did they who now by tryal had found the danger and inconveniences of committing arbitrary power to any, invent Laws either fram'd, or consented to by all, that should confine and limit the autority of whom they chose to govern them: that so man, of whose failing they had proof, might no more rule over them, but law and reason abstracted as much as might be from personal errors and frailties. [While as the Magistrate was set above the people, so the Law was set above the Magistrate.][28] When this would not serve, but that the Law was either not executed, or misapply'd, they were constrain'd from that time, the onely remedy left them, to put conditions and take Oaths from all Kings and Magistrates at thir first instalment to doe impartial justice by Law: who upon those termes and no other, receav'd Allegeance from the people, that is to say, bond or Covnant to obey them in execution of those Lawes which they the people had themselves made, or assented to. And this ofttimes with express warning, that if the King or Magistrate prov'd unfaithfull to his trust, the people would be dis-

[27] Cf. Grotius, *De iure belli*, I.IV.II.I.

[28] Cf. Cicero, *De legibus*, III, I: 'ut enim magistratibus leges, ita populo praesunt magistratus'. See below p. 113.

ingag'd. They added also Counselors and Parlaments, nor to be onely at his beck, but with him or without him, at set times, or at all times, when any danger threatn'd to have care of the public safety. Therefore saith *Claudius Sesell* a French Statesman, *The Parliament was set as a bridle to the King*;[29] which I instance rather, [not because our English Lawyers have not said the same long before, but] because that [French] Monarchy is granted by all to be a farr more absolute then ours. That this and the rest of what hath hitherto been spok'n is most true, might be copiously made appeare throughout all Stories Heathen and Christian; ev'n of those Nations where Kings and Emperours have sought meanes to abolish all ancient memory of the Peoples right by thir encroachments and usurpations. But I spare long insertions, appealing to the [known constitutions of both the latest Christian Empires in Europe, the Greek[30] and] German,[31] [besides the] French,[32] Italian, Arragonian,[33] English, and not least the Scottish[34] Histories: not forgetting this onely by the way, that *William* the Norman though a Conqueror, and not unsworn at his Coronation, was compell'd the second time to take oath at S. *Albanes*,[35] ere the people would be brought to yeild obedience.

It being thus manifest that the power of Kings and Magistrates is nothing else, but what is only derivative, transferr'd and committed to them in trust from the People, to the Common good of them all, in whom the power yet remaines fundamentally, and cannot be tak'n from them, without a violation of thir natural birthright, and seeing that from hence *Aristotle*[36] and the best of Political writers have

[29] M's reference (*CB*, I, 458) to Claude de Seyssel's *La grand monarchie de France* (1519) paraphrases an edition of the Latin translation by Johann Sleidan: e.g., *De republica Galliae* (Strasburg, 1548), fo. 10a–b.

[30] I.e., Byzantine. See *CB*, I, 436 where M. notes that conditions were accepted by the emperor.

[31] See *CB*, I, 436 for a similar observation from Johann Sleidan, *De statu religionis et republicae, Carolo Quinto, Caesare, commentarii* (Strasburg, 1555), fos. 15a, 16a.

[32] M. (*CB*, I, 461) notes that France was 'an elective kingdom either to choose or depose' from Bernard de Girard, seigneur du Haillan, *L'histoire de France* (Paris, 1576), pp. 19, 123, 129.

[33] M. (*CB*, I, 442) notes from Guicciardini, *Historia d'Italia* (Florence, 1636), p. 347, that the kings of Aragon did not have absolute authority.

[34] Primarily Buchanan, *Rerum Scoticarum historia* (Edinburgh, 1582).

[35] M. (*CB*, I, 427) refers to Holinshed, *Chronicles* (London, 1587), III, 10. See below pp. 201, 212.

[36] M. (*CB*, I, 443) notes the distinction between king and tyrant in Aristotle, *Nicomachean ethics*, 1160b 1–5. For M.'s familiarity with the *Ethics* see *DDD, T*, and *C*, II, 291–2, 346, 646, 745. See below p. 240.

defin'd a King, him who governs to the good and profit of his People, and not for his own ends, it follows from necessary causes, that the Titles of Sov'ran Lord, natural Lord, and the like, are either arrogancies, or flatteries, not admitted by Emperours and Kings of best note, and dislikt by the Church both of Jews, *Isai.* 26.13.[37] and ancient Christians, as appears by *Tertullian*[38] and others. Although generally the people of Asia, and with them the Jews also, especially since the time they chose a King against the advice and counsel of God,[39] are noted by wise Authors much inclinable to slavery.[40]

Secondly, that to say, as is usual, the King hath as good right to his Crown and dignitie, as any man to his inheritance,[41] is to make the Subject no better then the Kings slave, his chattell, or his possession that may be bought and sould. And doubtless if hereditary title were sufficiently inquir'd, the best foundation of it would be found either but[42] in courtesie or convenience. But suppose it to be of right hereditarie, what can be more just and legal, if a subject for certain crimes be to forfet by Law from himself, and posterity, all his inheritance to the King, then that a King for crimes proportional, should forfet all his title and inheritance to the people: unless the people must be thought created all for him, he not for them, and they all in one body inferior to him single,[43] which were a kinde of treason against the dignitie of mankind to affirm.

Thirdly it follows, that to say Kings are accountable to none but God, is the ouerturning of all Law and government. For if they may refuse to give account, then all cov'nants made with them at Coronation; all Oathes are in vaine, and meer mockeries, all Lawes which they sweare to keep, made to no purpose; for if the King feare not God, as how many of them doe not? we hold then our lives and

[37] Isa. 26:13, 'O LORD our God, other lords beside thee have had dominion over us: but by thee only will we make mention of thy name'.

[38] M. (*CB*, I, 433) notes the reluctance of the emperor Augustus to be called 'Lord' from Tertullian, *Apologeticum*, in *Opera* (Paris, 1634; 1641), p. 31. See below pp. 122.

[39] See pp. 80, 101.

[40] E.g., Aristotle, *Politics*, VII, 7 (1327b); Cicero, *De Provinciis*, V, 10. For M.'s belief in the influence of climate and geography on temperament, see *AR*, II, 490; *HB*, V, 451.

[41] M. (*CB*, I, 441) notes from Jacques-Auguste de Thou (Thuanus), *Historiarum sui temporis* (Geneva, 1620;1626), III, 186, that the king is merely the usufructuary rather than the outright owner of the property of the realm in his possession. Cf. *O*, III, 306.

[42] A: 'but either'.

[43] An allusion to the maxim that the king is *major singulis, universis minor* ('greater than each individual citizen, but inferior to the people as whole').

estates, by the tenure of his meer grace and mercy, as from a God, not a mortal Magistrate, a position that none but Court Parasites or men besotted would maintain. [*Aristotle* therefore, whom we commonly allow for one of the best interpreters of nature and morality, writes in the fourth of his politics chap. 10. that Monarchy unaccountable, is the worst sort of Tyranny; and least of all to be endur'd by free born men.][44] And [surely] no Christian Prince, not drunk with high mind, and prouder then those Pagan *Cæsars* that deifi'd themselves, would arrogate so unreasonably above human condition, or derogate so basely from a whole Nation of men his Brethren, as if for him only subsisting, and to serve his glory; valuing them in comparison of his owne brute will and pleasure, no more then so many beasts, or vermin under his Feet, not to be reasond with, but to be trod on;[45] among whom there might be found so many thousand Men for wisdom, vertue, nobleness of mind, and all other respects, but the fortune of his dignity, farr above him. Yet some would perswade us, that this absurd opinion was King *Davids*; because in the 51 *Psalm* he cries out to God, *Against thee onely have I sinn'd*;[46] as if *David* had imagin'd that to murder *Uriah* and adulterate his Wife,[47] had bin no sinn against his Neighbour, when as that Law of *Moses* was to the King expresly, *Deut.* 17. not to think so highly of himself above his Brethren.[48] *David* therfore by those words could mean no other, then either that the depth of his guiltiness was known to God onely, or to so few as had not the will or power to question him, or that the sin against God was greater beyond compare then against *Uriah*. What ever his meaning were, any wise man will see that the pathetical words of a Psalme can be no certaine decision to a poynt that hath abundantly more certain rules to goe by. How much more rationally spake the Heathen King *Demophoon* in a Tragedy of *Euripides* then these Interpreters would put upon King *David*, *I rule not my people by Tyranny, as if they were Barbarians, but am my self liable, if I doe unjustly, to suffer justly.*[49] Not unlike was the speech of *Trajan*[50] the worthy Emperor, to one whom he made General of his Prætorian Forces. Take this drawn sword, saith he, to use for me, if I reigne well, if not, to use against me. Thus *Dion* relates.[51] And not *Trajan* onely, but *Theodosius* the yonger, a

[44] Aristotle, *Politics*, 1295a, 19–21.
[45] A: 'injurd' for 'trod on'.
[46] Ps. 51:4.
[47] 2 Sam. 11:2–17.
[48] Deut. 17:20.
[49] Euripides, *Heraclidae*, 423–4. See p. 165.
[50] Roman emperor, 98–117.
[51] See (in Greek) Dio Cassius, *Roman history*, LXVIII, 16, or (in Latin) Aurelius Victor, *De*

Christian Emperor and one of the best, causd it to be enacted as a rule undenyable and fit to be acknowledg'd by all Kings and Emperors, that a Prince is bound to the Laws; that on the autority of Law the autority of a Prince depends, and to the Laws ought submitt.[52] Which Edict of his remains yet in[53] the *Code* of *Justinian l.* 1. *tit.* 24.[54] as a sacred constitution to all the succeeding Emperors. How then can any King in Europe maintain and write himself accountable to none but God, when Emperors in thir own imperial Statutes have writt'n and decreed themselves accountable to Law. And indeed where such account is not fear'd, he that bids a man reigne over him above Law, may bid as well a savage Beast.

It follows lastly, that since the King or Magistrate holds his autoritie of the people, both originaly and naturally for their good in the first place, and not his own, then may the people as oft as they shall judge it for the best, either choose him or reject him, retaine him or depose him though no Tyrant, meerly by the liberty and right of free born Men, to be govern'd as seems to them best. This, though it cannot but stand with plain reason, shall be made good also by Scripture. *Deut.* 17.14. *When thou art come into the Land which the Lord thy God giveth thee, and shalt say I will set a King over mee, like as all the Nations about mee.* These words confirme us that the right of choosing, yea of changing thir own Goverment is by the grant of God himself in the People.[55] And therfore when they desir'd a King, though then under another form of goverment, and though thir changing displeas'd him, yet he that was himself thir King, and rejected by them, would not be

caesaribus, XIII, 9. The story was often used: e.g., 'Stephanus Junius Brutus', *Vindiciae contra tyrannos* ('Edinburgh', 1579), p. 201. See pp. 188–9.

[52] Issued at Ravenna by Theodosius II and Valentinian III in June 429: 'Digna vox maiestate regnantis legibus alligatum se principem profiteri: adeo de auctoritate iuris nostra pendet auctoritas. et re vera maius imperio est submittere legibus principatum. et oraculo praesentis edicti quod nobis licere non patimur indicamus', *Codex Iustinianus* (Berlin, 1877), p. 103 (I. 14.4). ('It is a statement worthy of the majesty of a reigning prince for him to profess to be subject to the laws; for Our authority is dependent upon that of the law. And, indeed, it is the greatest attribute of imperial power for the sovereign to be subject to the laws and We forbid to others what We do not suffer Ourselves to do by the terms of the present Edict', *The Civil Law* (Cincinnati, 1932), vol. XII, p. 86.) The 'Digna vox' was frequently cited in writings on resistance: e.g., Bucer, *In sacra quatuor evangelia, enarrationes perpetuae* (Geneva, 1553), fo. 55a; *Vindiciae*, sig. A2; Buchanan, *De iure regni apud Scotos* (Edinburgh, 1579), p. 92. M.'s phrases and the pairing of Trajan and Theodosius recall Buchanan, *Historia*, fo. 243a. Cf. *E*, III, 590–91, and see below p. 169.

[53] A: 'yet unrepeald in'.

[54] An error: M. cites correctly below, p. 169.

[55] See p. 80.

a hindrance to what they intended, furder then by perswasion, but that they might doe therein as they saw good. 1 *Sam.* 8. onely he reserv'd to himself the nomination of who should reigne over them. Neither did that exempt the King, as if he were to God onely accountable, though by his especial command anointed. Therfore *David first made a Covnant with the Elders of Israel, and so was by them anointed King*, [2 *Sam.* 5.3.] 1 *Chron.* 11.[56] And *Jehoiada* the Priest making *Jehoash* King, made a Cov'nant between him and the People, 2 *Kings* 11.17.[57] Therfore when *Roboam* at his comming to the Crown, rejected those conditions which the Israelites brought him, heare what they answer him, *What portion have we in David, or Inheritance in the son of Jesse? See to thine own House David.*[58] And for the like conditions not perform'd, all Israel before that time depos'd *Samuel*; not for his own default, but for the misgoverment of his Sons. But som will say to both these examples, it was evilly don. I answer, that not the latter, because it was expressly allow'd them in the Law to set up a King if they pleas'd; and God himself joyn'd with them in the work; though in som sort it was at that time displeasing to him, in respect of old *Samuel* who had govern'd them uprightly. As *Livy* praises the Romans who took occasion from *Tarquinius* a wicked Prince to gaine thir libertie, which to have extorted, saith hee, from *Numa*, or any of the good Kings before, had not bin seasonable.[59] Nor was it in the former example don unlawfully; for when *Roboam* had prepar'd a huge Army to reduce the Israelites, he was forbidd'n by the Prophet, 1 *Kings* 12.24. *Thus saith the Lord yee shall not goe up, nor fight against your brethren, for this thing is from me.* He calls them thir Brethren, not Rebels, and forbidds to be proceeded against them, owning the thing himself, not by single providence, but by approbation, and that not onely of the act, as in the former example, but of the fit season also; he had not otherwise forbidd to molest them. And those grave and wise Counselors whom *Rehoboam* first advis'd with, spake no such thing, as our old gray headed Flatterers now are wont, stand upon your birthright, scorn to capitulate, you hold of God, not[60] of them; for they knew no such matter, unless conditionally, but gave him politic coun-

[56] 1 Chron. 11:3. The Geneva Bible (1560) consistently has 'covenant' where the AV sometimes has 'league'.

[57] 'And Jehoiada made a covenant between the LORD and the king and the people, that they should be the LORD's people; between the king also and the people.' M. reduces the double covenant to a single one.

[58] 1 Kings 12:16.

[59] Livy, *Ab urbe condita*, II, 1.

[60] A: 'and not'.

sel, as in a civil transaction.[61] Therfore Kingdom and Magistracy, whether supreme or subordinat, is [without difference,] call'd *a human ordinance*, 1 *Pet.* 2.13. &c. which we are there taught is the will of God wee should [alike] submitt to, so farr as for the punishment of evil doers, and the encouragement of them that doe well. *Submitt* saith he, *as free men.*[62] [But to any civil power unaccountable, unquestionable, and not to be resisted, no not in wickedness, and violent actions, how can we submitt as free men?] *There*[63] *is no power but of God*, saith *Paul*, *Rom.* 13.[64] as much as to say, God put it into mans heart to find out that way at first for common peace and preservation, approving the exercise therof; els it contradicts *Peter* who calls the same autority an Ordinance of man. It must be also understood of lawfull and just power, els we read of great power in the affaires and Kingdoms of the World permitted to the Devil: for saith he to Christ, *Luke* 4.6. *All this power will I give thee and the glory of them, for it is deliver'd to me, & to whomsoever I will, I give it*: neither did he ly, or Christ gainsay what he affirm'd; for in the thirteenth of the *Revelation*[65] wee read how the Dragon gave to the beast *his power, his seate, and great autority*: which beast so autoriz'd most expound to be the tyrannical powers and Kingdoms of the earth. Therfore Saint *Paul* in the forecited Chapter[66] tells us that such Magistrates he meanes, as are, not a terror to the good but to the evil; such as beare not the sword in vaine, but to punish offenders, and to encourage the good. If such onely be mentiond here as powers to be obeyd, and our submission to them onely requir'd, then doubtless those powers that doe the contrary, are no powers ordain'd of God, and by consequence no obligation laid upon us to obey or not to resist them. And it may bee well observd that both these Apostles, whenever they give this precept, express it in termes not *concrete* but *abstract*, as Logicians are wont to speake, that is, they mention the ordinance, the power, the autoritie before the persons that execute it; and what that power is, least we should be deceav'd, they describe exactly. So that if the power be not such, or the person execute not such power, neither the one nor the other is of God, but of the Devil, and by consequence to bee resisted. From this exposition *Chrysostome* also on the same place dissents not; explaining that

61 For the advice given to Rehoboam (1 Kings 12:6–11) see pp. 134–5.
62 1 Pet. 2:13,16.
63 A: 'And *there*'.
64 Rom. 13:1.
65 Rev. 13:2.
66 Rom. 13:3–4.

these words were not writt'n in behalf of a tyrant.[67] And this is verify'd by *David*, himself a King, and likeliest to bee Author of the *Psalm* 94.20. which saith *Shall the throne of iniquity have fellowship with thee?* And it were worth the knowing, since Kings [in these dayes], and that by Scripture, boast the justness of thir title, by holding it immediately of God, yet cannot show the time when God ever set on the throne them or thir forefathers, but onely when the people chose them, why by the same reason, since God ascribes as oft to himself the casting down of Princes from the throne, it should not be thought as lawful, and as much from God, when none are seen to do it but the people, and that for just causes. For if it needs must be a sin in them to depose, it may as likely be a sin to have elected. And contrary if the peoples act in election be pleaded by a King, as the act of God, and the most just title to enthrone him, why may not the peoples act of rejection, bee as well pleaded by the people as the act of God, and the most just reason to depose him?[68] So that we see the title and just right of raigning or deposing, in reference to God, is found in Scripture to be all one; visible onely in the people, and depending meerly upon justice and demerit. Thus farr hath bin considerd briefly the power of Kings and Magistrates; how it was and is originally the peoples, and by them conferr'd in trust onely to bee imployd to the common peace and benefit; with liberty therfore and right remaining in them to reassume it to themselves, if by Kings or Magistrates it be abus'd; or to dispose of it by any alteration, as they shall judge most conducing to the public good.[69]

Wee may from hence with more ease, and force of argument determin what a Tyrant is, and what the people may doe against him. A Tyrant whether by wrong or by right comming to the Crown, is he who regarding neither Law nor the common good, reigns onely for himself and his faction: Thus St. *Basil* among others defines him.[70] And because his power is great, his will boundless and exorbitant, the fulfilling whereof is for the most part accompanied with innumerable wrongs and oppressions of the people, murders massachers, rapes, adulteries, desolation, and subversion of Citties and whole Provinces, look how great a good and happiness a just King is, so great a

[67] Chrysostom, *Homilies* (23, on Romans), *NPN*, XI, 512–13.

[68] See pp. 94, 135.

[69] This sentence marks the transition from the narration to the confirmation.

[70] M. (*CB*, I, 453) notes the distinction between a king and a tyrant made by St Basil in commenting on the sayings of Solomon in *Opera omnia* (Paris, 1618), I, 456.

mischeife is a Tyrant; as hee the public father of his Countrie, so this the common enemie. Against whom what the people lawfully may doe, as against a common pest, and destroyer of mankinde, I suppose no man of cleare judgement need goe furder to be guided then by the very principles of nature in him. But because it is the vulgar folly of men to desert thir own reason, and shutting thir eyes to think they see best with other mens, I shall shew by such examples as ought to have most waight with us, what hath bin done in this case heretofore. The *Greeks* and *Romans*, as thir prime Authors witness, held it not onely lawfull, but a glorious and Heroic deed, rewarded publicly with Statues and Garlands,[71] to kill an infamous Tyrant at any time without tryal: and but reason, that he who trod down all Law, should not be voutsaf'd the benefit of Law. Insomuch that *Seneca* the Tragedian brings in *Hercules* the grand suppressor of Tyrants, thus speaking,[72]

—— —— Victima haud ulla amplior
Potest, magisque opima mactari Jovi
Quam Rex iniquus —— —— ——
—— —— There can be slaine
No sacrifice to God more acceptable
Then an unjust and wicked King —— ——

But of these I name no more, lest it bee objected they were Heathen; and come to produce another sort of men that had the knowledge of true Religion. Among the Jews this custom of tyrant-killing was not unusual. First *Ehud*, a man whom God had raysd to deliver Israel from *Eglon* King of *Moab*, who had conquerd and rul'd over them eighteene years, being sent to him as an Ambassador with a present, slew him in his own house.[73] But hee was a forren Prince, an enemie, and *Ehud* besides had special warrant from God. To the first I answer, it imports not whether forren or native: For no Prince so native but professes to hold by Law; which when he himself overturns, breaking all the Covnants and Oaths that gave him title to his dignity, and were the bond and alliance between him and his people, what differs he from an outlandish King, or from an enemie? For look how much right the King of *Spaine* hath to govern us at all, so much right hath the King of *England* to govern us tyrannically. If he, though

[71] E.g., Xenophon, *Hiero*, IV, 5; Cicero, *Pro Milone*, XXIX, 80. See pp. 162–3.
[72] Seneca, *Hercules furens*, 922–4. See p. 171.
[73] Judges 3:12–23. Cf. *An abridgment of the late remonstrance of the army, with some marginall attestations* (27 Dec., 1648), sig. B1v.

not bound to us by any League, comming from *Spaine* in person to subdue us or to destroy us, might lawfully by the people of *England* either bee slaine in fight, or put to death in captivity, what hath a native King to plead, bound by so many Covnants, benefits and honours to the welfare of his people, why he through the contempt of all Laws and Parlaments, the onely tie of our obedience to him, for his own wills sake, and a boasted prerogative unaccountable, after sev'n years warring and destroying of his best Subjects, overcom, and yeilded prisoner, should think to scape unquestionable, as a thing divine, in respect of whom so many thousand Christians destroy'd, should lie unaccounted for, polluting with their slaughterd carcasses all the Land over, and crying for vengeance against the living that should have righted them. Who knows not that there is a mutual bond of amity and brother-hood between man and man over all the World,[74] neither is it the English Sea that can sever us from that duty and relation: a straiter bond yet there is between fellow-subjects, neighbours, and friends; But when any of these doe one to another so as hostility could doe no worse, what doth the Law decree less against them, then op'n enemies and invaders? or if the Law be not present, or too weake, what doth it warrant us to less then single defence, or civil warr? and from that time forward the Law of civil defensive warr differs nothing from the Law of forren hostility. Nor is it distance of place that makes enmitie, but enmity that makes distance. He therfore that keeps peace with me, neer or remote, of whatsoever Nation, is to mee as farr as all civil and human offices an Englishman and a neighbour: but if an Englishman forgetting all Laws, human, civil and religious, offend against life and liberty, to him offended and to the Law in his behalf, though born in the same womb, he is no better then a Turk, a Sarasin, a Heathen. This is Gospel, and this was ever Law among equals; how much rather then in force against any King whatever,[75] who in respect of the people is confessd inferior and not equal: to distinguish therfore of a Tyrant by outlandish, or domestic is a weak evasion. To the second that he was an enemie, I answer, what Tyrant is not? yet *Eglon* by the Jewes had bin acknowledgd as thir Sovran; they had serv'd him eighteen yeares, as long almost as we our *William* the Conqueror, in all which time he could not be so unwise a Statesman but to have tak'n of them Oaths of Fealty and Allegeance,

[74] Cf. Cicero, *De natura deorum*, I, ii, 3–4; *De legibus*, I, x, 28–9; *De amicitia*, V, 20.
[75] A: 'whatsoever'.

by which they made themselves his proper Subjects, as thir homage and present sent by *Ehud* testify'd. To the third, that he had special warrant to kill *Eglon* in that manner, it cannot bee granted, because not expressd; tis plain that he was raysed by God to be a Deliverer, and went on just principles, such as were then and ever held allowable, to deale so by a Tyrant that could no[76] otherwise be dealt with. Neither did *Samuel* though a Profet, with his own hand abstain from *Agag*; a forren enemie no doubt; but mark the reason. *As thy Sword hath made women childless*;[77] a cause that by the sentence of Law it self nullifies all relations. And as the law is between Brother and Brother, Father and Son, Maister and Servant, wherfore not between King or rather Tyrant and People? And whereas *Jehu* had special command to slay *Jehoram*[78] a successive and hereditarie Tyrant, it seems not the less imitable for that; for where a thing grounded so much on natural reason hath the addition of a command from God, what does it but establish the lawfulness of such an act. Nor is it likely that God who had so many wayes of punishing the house of *Ahab* would have sent a subject against his Prince, if the fact in it self, as don to a Tyrant, had bin of bad example. And if *David* refus'd to lift his hand against the Lords anointed,[79] the matter between them was not tyranny, but privat enmity, and *David* as a privat person had bin his own revenger, not so much the peoples.[80] But when any tyrant at this day can shew to be the Lords anointed, the onely mention'd reason why *David* withheld his hand, he may then but not till then presume on the same privilege.

Wee may pass therfore hence to Christian times. And first our Saviour himself, how much he favourd Tyrants, and how much intended they should be found or honourd among Christians, declares his mind not obscurely; accounting thir absolute autority no better then Gentilism, yea though they flourish'd it over with the splendid name of Benefactors;[81] charging those that would be his Disciples to usurp no such dominion; but that they who were to bee of most autoritie among them, should esteem themselves Ministers and

[76] A: 'not'.

[77] 1 Sam. 15:33.

[78] 2 Kings 9:1–2.

[79] 1 Sam. 24:6, 26:9.

[80] M.'s gloss on David's refusal to kill Saul has several likely sources: e.g., the Geneva Bible's marginal annotations on 1 Sam. 24:6 [24:5 in the AV] and 26:9; Christopher Goodman, *How superior powers oght to be obeyd of their subjects* (Geneva, 1558), pp. 138–9, 140; *An abridgment of the late remonstrance*, sig. B1v. Cf. *E*, III, 587.

[81] Luke 22:25.

Servants to the public. *Matt.* 20.25. *The Princes of the Gentiles exercise Lordship over them*, and *Mark* 10.42. *They that seem to rule*, saith he, either slighting or accounting them no lawful rulers, *but yee shall not be so, but the greatest among you shall be your Servant.*[82] And although hee himself were the meekest, and came on earth to be so, yet to a Tyrant we hear him not voutsafe an humble word: but *Tell that Fox Luc* 13.[83] [So farr we ought to be from thinking that Christ and his Gospel should be made a Sanctuary for Tyrants from justice, to whom his Law before never gave such protection.] And wherfore did his Mother the Virgin *Mary* give such praise to God in her profetic song, that he had now by the comming of Christ *Cutt down Dynasta's or proud Monarchs from the throne*,[84] if the Church, when God manifests his power in them to doe so, should rather choose all miserie and vassalage to serve them, and let them stil sit on thir potent seats to bee ador'd for doing mischief. Surely it is not for nothing that tyrants by a kind of natural instinct both hate and feare none more then the true Church and Saints of God, as the most dangerous enemies and subverters of Monarchy, though indeed of tyranny; hath not this bin the perpetual cry of Courtiers, and Court Prelats? whereof no likelier cause can be alleg'd, but that they well discern'd the mind and principles of most devout and zealous men, and indeed the very discipline of Church, tending to the dissolution of all tyranny. No marvel then if since the faith of Christ receav'd, in purer or impurer times, to depose a King and put him to death for Tyranny, hath bin accounted so just and requisite, that neighbour Kings have both upheld and tak'n part with subjects in the action. And *Ludovicus Pius*,[85] himself an Emperor, and Son of *Charles* the great, being made Judge, *Du Haillan* is my author,[86] between *Milegast* King of the *Vultzes* and his Subjects who had depos'd him, gave his verdit for the Subjects, and for him whom they had chos'n in his room. Note here that the right of electing whom they please is by the impartial testimony of an Emperor in the people. For, said he, *A just Prince ought to be prefer'd before an unjust, and the end of goverment before the prerogative.* And *Constantinus Leo*,[87] another Emperor, in the *Byzantine* Laws saith, *that*

[82] Mark 10:43–4. Luke 22:26. [83] Luke 13:32. [84] Luke 1:52 (The Magnificat).

[85] Louis the Pious, Holy Roman emperor, 814–40.

[86] M. (*CB*, I, 454–5) notes the story (but not the quotation) from Girard, *L'histoire*, p. 248: 'qu'un Prince iuste doit estre preferé à un qui ne l'est pas, & que plus doit servir l'integrité d'un homme au commandement d'un Estat, que la prerogative'.

[87] Leo III, Byzantine emperor, 717–41.

the end of a King is for the general good, which he not performing is but the counterfet of a King.[88] And to prove that som of our own Monarchs have acknowledg'd that thir high office exempted them not from punishment, they had the Sword of St. *Edward*[89] born before them by an officer who was call'd Earle of the Palace, eev'n at the times of thir highest pomp and solemnities, to mind them, saith *Matthew Paris*,[90] the best of our Historians, that if they errd, the Sword had power to restraine them. And what restraint the Sword comes to at length, having both edge and point, if any *Sceptic* will doubt,[91] let him feel. It is also affirm'd from diligent search made in our ancient books of Law,[92] that the Peers and Barons of England had a legal right to judge the King: which was the cause most likely, for it could be no slight cause, that they were call'd his Peers, or equals. This however may stand immovable, so long as man hath to deale with no better then man; that if our Law judge all men to the lowest by thir Peers, it should in all equity ascend also, and judge the highest. And so much I find both in our own and forren Storie, that Dukes, Earles, and Marqueses were at first not hereditary, not empty and vain titles, but names of trust and office,[93] and with the office ceasing, as induces me to be of opinion, that every worthy man in Parlament, for the word Baron imports no more, might for the public good be thought a fit Peer and judge of the King; without regard had to petty caveats, and circumstances, the chief impediment in high affaires, and ever stood upon most by circumstantial men. Whence doubtless our Ancestors who were not ignorant with what rights either Nature or ancient Constitution had endowd them, when Oaths both at Coronation, and renewd in Parlament would not serve, thought it no way illegal to depose and put to death thir tyrannous Kings. Insomuch that the Parlament drew up a charge against *Richard the second*,[94] and the

[88] Johann Leunclavius, *Juris Graeco-Romani* (Frankfurt, 1596), II, 83 (second pagination): 'Finibus Principi propositus est omnibus benefacere, quapropter & benefactoris nomine ornatur. Ita ut si quando de beneficentia quippiam remiserit, ex antiquorum sententia, adulterari videatur Principis nota & character.'

[89] M. (*CB*, I, 447), notes from Speed's *Historie* (London, 1623) that the sword of King Edward the Confessor (1042–66) was called Curtana. See p. 212.

[90] M. refers directly to Matthew Paris (a source for Holinshed and Speed), *Historia major* (London, 1640), p. 421: 'in signum quod . . . si oberret, habeat de jure potestatem cohibendi'. See p. 212.

[91] A: 'will needs doubt'.

[92] M. probably has in mind Andrew Horne, *La somme appelle mirroir des iustice: vel speculum iusticiariorum* (London, 1642), p. 9 (Chapter 1, section 2).

[93] M. (*CB*, I, 473) extracts this point from Girard, *L'histoire*, pp. 163, 316.

[94] M. (*CB*, I, 455) refers to Holinshed, *Chronicles*, III, 512.

Commons requested to have judgement decree'd against him, that the realme might not bee endangerd. And *Peter Martyr* a Divine of formost rank, on the third of *Judges*[95] approves thir doings. Sir *Thomas Smith* also a Protestant and a Statesman, in his Commonwelth of *England*,[96] putting the question whether it be lawfull to rise against a Tyrant, answers that the vulgar judge of it according to the event, and the lerned according to the purpose of them that do it. But far before these days, *Gildas* the most ancient of all our Historians, speaking of those times wherein the Roman Empire decaying quitted and relinquishd what right they had by Conquest to this Iland,[97] and resign'd it all into the peoples hands, testifies that the people thus re-invested with thir own original right, about the year 446, both elected them Kings, whom they thought best (the first Christian Brittish Kings that ever raign'd heer since the Romans) and by the same right, when they apprehended cause, usually depos'd and put them to death.[98] This is the most fundamental and ancient tenure that any King of *England* can produce or pretend to; in comparison of which, all other titles and pleas are but of yesterday. If any object that *Gildas* condemns the Britans for so doing, the answer is as ready; that he condemns them no more for so doing, then hee did before for choosing such, for saith he, *They anointed them Kings, not of God, but such as were more bloody then the rest.* Next hee condemns them not at all for deposing or putting them to death, but for doing it over hastily, without tryal or well examining the cause,[99] and for electing others wors in thir room. Thus we have heer both domestic and most ancient examples that the people of Britain have depos'd and put to death thir Kings in those primitive Christian times. And to couple reason with example, if the Church in all ages, Primitive, Romish, or Protestant, held it ever no less thir duty then the power of thir Keyes, though

[95] M. (*CB*, I, 455–6) quotes from a discussion (provoked by the story of Ehud) of whether it is lawful for subjects to rise against their princes in Peter Martyr, *In librum iudicum D. Petri Martyris Vermilii commentarii doctissimi*, first published in 1561 (Geneva, 1565, fo. 60b).

[96] M. (*CB*, I, 454) cites the relevant passage from Sir Thomas Smith, *The commonwealth of England* (1583, and many subsequent editions), Book I, chapter 5. See p. 198.

[97] Cf. *HB*, V, 126–7.

[98] Cf. *HB*, V, 140.

[99] M. read *De excidio & conquestu Britanniae epistola* by Gildas (*c.* 516–570) in Jerome Commelin, ed., *Rerum Britannicarum* (Heidelberg, 1587), p. 11[9]: 'Ungebantur reges non per Deum, sed qui ceteris crudeliores extarent: & paulo post ab unctoribus non pro veri examinatione trucidabantur'.

without express warrant of Scripture, to bring indifferently both King and Peasant under the utmost rigor of thir Canons and Censures Ecclesiastical, eev'n to the smiting him with a final excommunion, if he persist impenitent, what hinders but that the temporal Law both may and ought, though without a special Text or precedent, extend with like indifference the civil Sword, to the cutting off without exemption him that capitally offends. Seeing that justice and Religion are from the same God, and works of justice ofttimes more acceptable. Yet because that some lately, with the tongues and arguments of Malignant backsliders, have writt'n that the proceedings now in Parlament against the King, are without precedent from any Protestant State or Kingdom,[100] the examples which follow shall be all Protestant and chiefly Presbyterian.[101]

In the yeare 1546. The *Duke of Saxonie*,[102] *Lantgrave of Hessen*,[103] and the whole Protestant league raysd op'n Warr against *Charles the fifth* thir Emperor, sent him a defiance, renounc'd all faith and allegeance towards him, and debated long in Councel whither they should give him so much as the title of *Cæsar. Sleidan. l.* 17.[104] Let all men judge what this wanted of deposing or of killing, but the power to doe it.

In the yeare 1559. The Scotch Protestants claiming promise of thir Queen Regent[105] for libertie of conscience, she answering that promises were not to be claim'd of Princes beyond what was commodious for them to grant, told her to her face in the Parlament then at *Sterling*, that if it were so, they renounc'd thir obedience; and soon after betook them to Armes. *Buchanan Hist. l.* 16.[106] certainly when allegeance is renounc'd, that very hour the King or Queen is in effect depos'd.

In the yeare 1564. *John Knox* a most famous Divine and the reformer of *Scotland* to the Presbyterian discipline, at a general

[100] See p. 47.
[101] This sentence marks the transition from the confirmation to the refutation.
[102] Duke Maurice of Saxony (1521–53).
[103] Philip, Landgrave of Hesse (1504–67).
[104] M. (*CB*, I, 499) summarizes the event from Sleidan, *Commentarii*, fo. 296b.
[105] Mary of Guise, widow of James V and mother of Mary, Queen of Scots.
[106] Buchanan, *Historia*, fo. 190b: 'Cum illi subiicerent supplices, ut quae saepenumero promisisset, in memoriam revocaret: respondit fidem promissorum a principibus exigendam, quatenus eam praestare commodum eis videretur. Ad haec, illi subiecerunt, se ergo omne obsequium, & parendi necessitatem ei renunciare'.

Assembly maintaind op'nly in a dispute against *Lethington*[107] the Secretary of State, that Subjects might & ought execute Gods judgements upon thir King; that the fact of *Jehu* and others against thir King having the ground of Gods ordinary command to put such and such offenders to death was not extraordinary, but to bee imitated of all that preferr'd the honour of God to the affection of flesh and wicked Princes;[108] that Kings, if they offend, have no privilege to be exempted from the punishments of Law more then any other subject; so that if the King be a Murderer, Adulterer, or Idolator, he should suffer, not as a King, but as an offender;[109] and this position he repeates again and again before them. Answerable was the opinion of *John Craig* another learned Divine, and that Lawes made by the tyranny of Princes, or the negligence of people, thir posterity might abrogate, and reform all things according to the original institution of Common-welths.[110] And *Knox* being commanded by the Nobilitie to write to *Calvin* and other lerned men for thir judgement in that question, refus'd; alleging that both himself was fully resolv'd in conscience, and had heard thir judgements, and had the same opinion under handwriting of many the most godly and most lerned that he knew in Europe; that if he should move the question to them againe, what should he doe but shew his own forgetfulness or inconstancy.[111] All this is farr more largely in the Ecclesiastic History of *Scotland l.* 4. with many other passages to this effect all the Book over; set out with diligence by Scotchmen of best repute among them at the beginning of these troubles, as if they labourd to inform us what wee were to doe, and what they intended upon the like occasion.

And to let the world know that the whole Church and Protestant State of *Scotland* in those purest times of reformation were of the same beleif, three years after, they met in the feild *Mary* thir lawful and hereditary Queen, took her prisoner yeilding before fight, kept her in prison, and the same yeare depos'd her. *Buchan. Hist. l.* 18.[112]

And four years after that, the Scots in justification of thir deposing Queen *Mary*, sent Ambassadors to Queen *Elizabeth*, and in a writt'n

107 William Maitland of Lethington (*c.* 1528–73), though a Protestant, remained loyal to Mary.

108 M. closely paraphrases John Knox, *The historie of the reformation of the church of Scotland; containing five Books* (London, 1644), p. 390.

109 Knox, *Historie*, p. 392.

110 Knox, *Historie*, pp. 395–6.

111 Knox, *Historie*, p. 397.

112 See Buchanan, *Historia*, fos. 221b, 22[2]b–223a.

Declaration alleg'd that they had us'd toward her more lenity then shee deserv'd, that thir Ancestors had heretofore punish'd thir Kings by death or banishment; that the Scots were a free Nation, made King whom they freely chose, and with the same freedom unkingd him if they saw cause, by right of ancient laws and Ceremonies yet remaining, and old customs yet among the High-landers in choosing the head of thir Clanns, or Families; all which with many other arguments bore witness that regal power was nothing else but a mutual Covnant or stipulation between King and people. *Buch. Hist, l.* 20.[113] These were Scotchmen and Presbyterians; but what measure then have they lately offerd, to think such liberty less beseeming us then themselves, presuming to put him upon us for a Maister whom thir law scarce allows to be thir own equal? If now then we heare them in another strain then heretofore in the purest times of thir Church, we may be confident it is the voice of Faction speaking in them, not of truth and Reformation. [Which no less in *England* then in *Scotland*, by the mouthes of those faithful witnesses commonly call'd Puritans, and Nonconformists, spake as clearly for the putting down, yea the utmost punishing of Kings, as in thir several Treatises may be read; eev'n from the first raigne of *Elizabeth* to these times. Insomuch that one of them, whose name was *Gibson*, foretold K. *James*, he should be rooted out, and conclude his race, if he persisted to uphold Bishops.[114] And that very inscription stampt upon the first Coines at his Coronation, a naked Sword in a hand with these words, *Si mereor in me, Against me, if I deserve*,[115] not only manifested the judgement of that State, but seem'd also to presage the sentence of Divine justice in this event upon his Son.][116]

In the yeare 1581. the States of *Holland* in a general Assembly at

[113] *Historia*, fo. 243a: 'Nam tot Reges a nostris maioribus morte, vinculis, exilio punitos enumerare nihil est opus . . . Gens enim Scotorum cum ab initio libera esset, Reges eo iure sibi creavit, ut imperium populi suffragiis eis mandatum, si res posceret, eisdem suffragiis adimere possent. Eius legis multa ad nostram usque aetatem remanserunt vestigia. Nam & in circumiectis insulis, & in plaerisque continentis locis, in quibus fermo priscus, & instituta haeserunt, is mos in phylarchis creandis adhuc servatur . . . ex quibus facile apparet, regnum nihil aliud esse, quam mutuam inter populos, & Reges stipulationem.'

[114] The warning to James VI of Scotland (later James I of England) was made in 1586. What M. says is appropriated from the margin of 'A Survey of Presbytery' appended to Sir Thomas Aston, *A remonstrance, against presbitery* (n.p., 1641), sig. I4: '*Gibson* threatned King *Iames*, that as *Ieroboam* he should be rooted out, and conclude his race, if he maintaind Bishops'.

[115] See p. 12.

[116] I.e., Charles I.

Coláiste Mhuire Gan Smál
379192
Luimneach

the *Hague*, abjur'd all obedience and subjection to *Philip* King of *Spaine*; and in a Declaration[117] justifie thir so doing; for that by his tyrannous goverment against faith so many times[118] giv'n & brok'n he had lost his right to all the Belgic Provinces; that therfore they depos'd him and declar'd it lawful to choose another in his stead. *Thuan. l.* 74.[119] From that time, to this, no State or Kingdom in the world hath equally prosperd: But let them remember not to look with an evil and prejudicial eye upon thir Neighbours walking by the same rule.[120]

But what need these examples to Presbyterians, I mean to those who now of late would seem so much to abhorr deposing, when as they to all Christendom have giv'n the latest and the liveliest example of doing it themselves. I question not the lawfulness of raising Warr against a Tyrant in defence of Religion, or civil libertie; for no Protestant Church from the first *Waldenses*[121] of *Lyons*, and *Languedoc* to this day but have don it round, and maintain'd it lawful. But this I doubt not to affirme, that the Presbyterians, who now so much condemn deposing, were the men themselves that deposd the King, and cannot with all thir shifting and relapsing, wash off the guiltiness from thir own hands. For they themselves, by these thir late doings have made it guiltiness, and turn'd thir own warrantable actions into Rebellion.

There is nothing that so actually makes a King of *England*, as rightful possession and Supremacy *in all causes both civil and Ecclesiastical*: and nothing that so actually makes a Subject of *England*, as those two Oaths of Allegeance and Supremacy observ'd *without equivocating, or any mental reservation*.[122] Out of doubt then when the King shall command things already constituted in Church, or State, obedience is the true essence of a subject, either to doe, if it be lawful, or if he hold the thing unlawful, to submitt to that penaltie which the Law imposes, so long as he intends to remaine a Subject. Therfore

[117] I.e., the *Edict of the States General* of July 1581 renouncing allegiance to Philip II of Spain.

[118] A: 'so oft'n'.

[119] M. (*CB*, I, 455) summarizes these events from de Thou, *Historiarum*, III, 513.

[120] End of the refutation, start of the peroration.

[121] M.'s source of information (*CB*, I, 379) about the Waldensian church was Peter Gilles, *Histoire ecclesiastique des eglises reformees* (Geneva, 1644). Cf *Sonnet* 15; *E*, III, 513–4; *Likeliest Means*, VII, 291.

[122] From the oath drafted by James I and included in 'An Act for the better discovering and repressing of Popish recusants' (1606).

when the people or any part of them shall rise against the King and his autority executing the Law in any thing establish'd civil or Ecclesiastical, I doe not say it is rebellion, if the thing commanded though establish'd be unlawful, and that they sought first all due means of redress (and no man is furder bound to Law) but I say it is an absolute renouncing both of Supremacy and Allegeance, which in one word is an actual and total deposing of the King, and the setting up of another supreme autority over them. And whether the Presbyterians have not don all this and much more, they will not put mee, I suppose, to reck'n up a seven years story fresh in the memory of all men. Have they not utterly broke the Oath of Allegeance, rejecting the Kings command and autority sent them from any part of the Kingdom whether in things lawful or unlawful? Have they not abjur'd the Oath of Supremacy by setting up the Parlament without the King, supreme to all thir obedience, and though thir Vow and Covnant bound them in general to the Parlament, yet somtimes adhering to the lesser part of Lords and Commons that remaind faithful, as they terme it, and eev'n of them, one while to the Commons without the Lords, another while to the Lords without the Commons?[123] Have they not still declar'd thir meaning, whatever thir Oath were, to hold them onely for supreme whom they found at any time most yeilding to what they petition'd? Both these Oaths which were the straitest bond of an English subject in reference to the King, being thus broke & made voide, it follows undenyably that the King from that time was by them in fact absolutely depos'd, and they no longer in reality to be thought his subjects, notwithstanding thir fine clause in the Covnant to preserve his person, Crown, and dignity, set there by som dodging Casuist with more craft then sincerity to mitigate the matter in case of ill sucess and not tak'n I suppose by any honest man, but as a condition subordinat to every the least particle that might more concerne Religion, liberty, or the public peace. To prove it yet more plainly that they are the men who have depos'd the King, I thus argue. We know that King and Subject are relatives, and relatives have no longer being then in the relation; the relation between King and Subject can be no other then regal autority and subjection. Hence I inferr past their defending, that if the Subject

[123] M. reminds the Presbyterians of their willingness at times to vote with the Independents in either house from Jan. to Oct. 1648.

who is one relative, take away the relation, of force he takes away also the other relative; but the Presbyterians who were one relative, that is to say Subjects, have for this sev'n years tak'n away the relation, that is to say the Kings autority, and thir subjection to it, therfore the Presbyterians for these sev'n years have remov'd and extinguishd the other relative, that is to say the King, or to speak more in brief have depos'd him; not onely by depriving him the execution of his autoritie, but by conferring it upon others. If then thir Oaths of subjection brok'n, new Supremacy obey'd, new Oaths and Covnants tak'n, notwithstanding frivolous evasions, have in plaine termes unking'd the King, much more then hath thir sev'n years Warr not depos'd him onely, but outlaw'd him, and defi'd him as an alien, a rebell to Law, and enemie to the State. It must needs be clear to any man not avers from reason, that hostilitie and subjection are two direct and positive contraries; and can no more in one subject stand together in respect of the same King, then one person at the same time can be in two remote places. Against whom therfore the Subject is in act of hostility we may be confident that to him he is in no subjection: and in whom hostility takes place of subjection, for they can by no meanes consist together, to him the King can be not onely no King, but an enemie. So that from hence we shall not need dispute whether they have depos'd him, or what they have defaulted towards him as no King, but shew manifestly how much they have don toward the killing him. Have they not levied all these Warrs against him whether offensive or defensive[124] (for defence in Warr equally offends, and most prudently before hand) and giv'n Commission to slay where they knew his person could not be exempt from danger? And if chance or flight had not sav'd him, how oft'n had they killd him, directing thir Artillery without blame or prohibition to the very place where they saw him stand? Have they not [Sequester'd him, judg'd or unjudgd, and] converted his revenew to other uses, detaining[125] from him [as a grand Delinquent,] all meanes of livelyhood, so that for them long since he might have perisht, or have starv'd? Have they not hunted and pursu'd him round about the Kingdom with sword and fire? Have they not

[124] Parliamentary casuists in the earlier stages of the Civil War had disclaimed the right to depose the king or even to resist him (his evil counsellors were a different matter), and maintained that their campaign was defensive and not offensive.

[125] A: 'and detain'd'.

formerly deny'd to Treat with him,[126] and thir now recanting Ministers preach'd against him, as a reprobate incurable, an enemy to God and his Church markt for destruction, and therfore not to be treated with? Have they not beseig'd him, & to thir power forbidd him Water and Fire, save what they shot against him to the hazard of his life? Yet while they thus assaulted and endangerd it with hostile deeds, they swore in words to defend it with his Crown and dignity; not in order, as it seems now, to a firm and lasting peace, or to his repentance after all this blood; but simply, without regard, without remorse, or any comparable value of all the miseries and calamities sufferd by the poore people, or to suffer hereafter through his obstinacy or impenitence. No understanding man can bee ignorant that Covnants are ever made according to the present state of persons and of things; and have ever the more general laws of nature and of reason included in them, though not express'd.[127] If I make a voluntary Covnant as with a man, to doe him good, and he prove afterward a monster to me, I should conceave a disobligement. If I covnant, not to hurt an enemie, in favour of him & forbearance, & hope of his amendment, & he, after that, shall doe me tenfould injury and mischief, to what he had don when I so Covnanted, and stil be plotting what may tend to my destruction, I question not but that his after actions release me; nor know I Covnant so sacred that withholds me from demanding justice on him. Howbeit, had not thir distrust in a good cause, and the fast and loos of our prevaricating Divines oversway'd, it had bin doubtless better not to have inserted in a Covnant unnecessary obligations, and words not works of a supererogating Allegeance to thir enemy; no way advantageous to themselves, had the King prevail'd, as to thir cost many would have felt; but full of snare and distraction to our friends, usefull onely, as we now find, to our adversaries, who under such a latitude and shelter of ambiguous interpretation have ever since been plotting and contriving new opportunities to trouble all again. How much better had it bin, and more becomming an undaunted vertue, to have declar'd op'nly and boldly whom and what power the people were to hold Supreme; as on the like occasion Protestants have don before, and many conscientious men now in these times have more then once besought the Parlament to doe, that

[126] I.e., in the resolution to 'make no further addresses or applications to the King' or to receive any passed by the Commons and Lords on 3 and 15 Jan. 1648.

[127] For a similar attitude to covenants see *DDD*, II, 245.

they might goe on upon a sure foundation, and not with a ridling Covnant in thir mouths, seeming to sweare counter almost in the same breath Allegeance and no Allegeance; which doubtless had drawn off all the minds of sincere men from siding with them, had they not discern'd thir actions farr more deposing him then thir words upholding him; which words made now the subject of cavillous interpretations, stood ever in the Covnant, by judgement of the more discerning sort, an evidence of thir feare, not of thir fidelity. What should I return to speak on, of those attempts for which the King himself hath oft'n charg'd the Presbyterians of seeking his life, when as in the due estimation of things, they might without a fallacy be sayd to have don the deed outright. Who knows not that the King is a name of dignity and office, not of person: Who therfore kills a King, must kill him while he is a King. Then they certainly who by deposing him have long since tak'n from him the life of a King, his office and his dignity, they in the truest sence may be said to have killd the King: nor onely by thir deposing and waging Warr against him, which besides the danger to his personal life, sett him in the fardest opposite point from any vital function of a King, but by thir holding him in prison,[128] vanquishd and yeilded into thir absolute and *despotic* power, which brought him to the lowest degradement and incapacity of the regal name. I say not by whose matchless valour[129] next under God, lest the story of thir ingratitude thereupon carry me from the purpose in hand, which is to convince them that they, which I repeat againe, were the men who in the truest sense killd the King, not onely as is prov'd before, but by depressing him thir King farr below the rank of a subject to the condition of a Captive, without intention to restore him, as the Chancellour of *Scotland*[130] in a speech told him plainly at *Newcastle*, unless hee granted fully all thir demands, which they knew he never meant. Nor did they Treat or think of Treating with him, till thir hatred to the Army that deliverd them, not thir love or duty to the King, joyn'd them secretly with men sentenc'd so oft for Reprobats in thir own mouthes, by whose suttle inspiring they grew madd upon a most tardy and improper Treaty.[131] Whereas if the whole bent of thir

[128] Charles I surrendered to the Scots in May 1646.
[129] I.e., the Army.
[130] John Campbell, first earl of Loudon (1598–1663).
[131] The Treaty of Newport between Charles and the parliamentary commissioners in the Isle of Wight, Sept.–Nov. 1648.

actions had not bin against the King himself, but [only] against his evil counselers,[132] as they faind, & publishd, wherfore did they not restore him all that while to the true life of a King, his office, Crown, and Dignity, when he was in thir power, & they themselves his neerest Counselers. The truth therfore is, both that they would not, and that indeed they could not without thir own certain destruction; having reduc'd him to such a final pass, as was the very death and burial of all in him that was regal, and from whence never King of *England* yet reviv'd, but by the new re-inforcement of his own party, which was a kind of resurrection to him. Thus having quite extinguisht all that could be in him of a King, and from a total privation clad him over, like another specifical thing, with formes and habitudes destructive to the former, they left in his person, dead as to Law, and all the civil right either of King or Subject, the life onely of a Prisner, a Captive and a Malefactor. Whom the equal and impartial hand of justice finding, was no more to spare then another ordnary man; not onely made obnoxious to the doom of Law by a charge more then once drawn up against him, and his own confession to the first Article at *Newport*,[133] but summond and arraign'd in the sight of God and his people, curst & devoted to perdition worse then any *Ahab*,[134] or *Antiochus*,[135] with exhortation to curse all those in the name of God that made not Warr against him, as bitterly as *Meroz*[136] was to be curs'd, that went not out against a Canaanitish King, almost in all the Sermons, Prayers, and Fulminations that have bin utterd this sev'n yeares by those clov'n tongues of falshood and dissention; who now, to the stirring up of new discord, acquitt him; and against thir own disciplin, which they boast to be the throne and scepter of Christ, absolve him, unconfound him, though unconverted, unrepentant, unsensible of all thir pretious Saints and Martyrs whose blood they have so oft laid upon his head: and now againe with a new sovran anointment can wash it all off, as if it were as vile, and no more to be reckn'd for, then the blood of so many Dogs in a time of Pestilence: giving the most opprobrious lye to all the acted zeale that for these

[132] A: 'evill Councel'.

[133] On 25 Sept. 1648, Charles provisionally withdrew his objection to its preamble which stated that Parliament had been forced to 'undertake a war in their just and lawful defence'. Cf. *E*, III, 451; *Readie & Easie Way* and *Brief Notes*, VII, 417, 481.

[134] 1 Kings 16:29–33.

[135] See 1 Macc. 1–6 in the Apocrypha for Antiochus IV Epiphanes, overthrown by Mattathias and his son Judas Maccabaeus.

[136] Judges 5:23.

many yeares hath filld thir bellies, and fed them fatt upon the foolish people. Ministers of sedition, not of the Gospel, who while they saw it manifestly tend to civil Warr and blood shed, never ceasd exasperating the people against him; and now that they see it likely to breed new commotion, cease not to incite others against the people that have sav'd them from him, as if sedition were thir onely aime, whether against him or for him. But God, as we have cause to trust, will put other thoughts into the people, and turn them from giving eare or heed to these Mercenary noisemakers,[137] of whose fury, and fals prophecies we have anough experience; and from the murmurs of new discord will incline them to heark'n rather with erected minds to the voice of our Supreme Magistracy, calling us to liberty and the flourishing deeds of a reformed Common-wealth; with this hope that as God was heretofore angry with the Jews who rejected him and his forme of Goverment to choose a King, so that he will bless us, and be propitious to us who reject a King to make him onely our leader and supreme governour in the conformity as neer as may be of his own ancient goverment; if we have at least but so much worth in us to entertaine the sense of our future happiness, and the courage to receave what God voutsafes us: wherein we have the honour to precede other Nations who are now labouring to be our followers. For as to this question in hand what the people by thir just right may doe in change of goverment, or of governour, we see it cleerd sufficiently; besides other ample autority eev'n from the mouths of Princes themselves. And surely they that shall boast, as we doe, to be a free Nation, and not have in themselves the power to remove, or to abolish any governour supreme, or subordinat, with the goverment it self upon urgent causes, may please thir fancy with a ridiculous and painted freedom, fit to coz'n babies; but are indeed under tyranny and servitude; as wanting that power, which is the root and sourse of all liberty, to dispose and *œconomize* in the Land which God hath giv'n them, as Maisters of Family in thir own house and free inheritance. Without which natural and essential power of a free Nation, though bearing high thir heads, they can in due esteem be thought no better then slaves and vassals born, in the tenure and occupation of another inheriting Lord. Whose goverment, though not illegal, or intolerable, hangs over them as a Lordly scourge, not as a free goverment; and

[137] A: 'turn them from looking after these fire-brands'.

therfore to be abrogated.[138] How much more justly then may they fling off tyranny, or tyrants; who being once depos'd can be no more then privat men, as subject to the reach of Justice and arraignment as any other transgressors. And certainly if men, not to speak of Heathen, both wise and Religious have don justice upon Tyrants what way they could soonest, how much more milde & human then is it, to give them faire and op'n tryal? To teach lawless Kings, and all who[139] so much adore them, that not mortal man, or his imperious will, but Justice is the onely true sovran and supreme Majesty upon earth. Let men cease therfore out of faction & hypocrisie to make out-cries and horrid things of things so just and honorable. [Though perhaps till now no protestant State or kingdom can be alleg'd to have op'nly put to death thir King, which lately some have writt'n,[140] and imputed to thir great glory; much mistaking the matter. It is not, neither ought to be the glory of a Protestant State, never to have put thir King to death; It is the glory of a Protestant King never to have deserv'd death.] And if the Parlament and Military Councel doe what they doe without precedent, if it appeare thir duty, it argues the more wisdom, vertue, and magnanimity, that they know themselves able to be a precedent to others. Who perhaps in future ages, if they prove not too degenerat, will look up with honour, and aspire toward these exemplary, and matchless deeds of thir Ancestors, as to the highest top of thir civil glory and emulation. Which heretofore, in the persuance of fame and forren dominion, spent it self vain-gloriously abroad; but henceforth may learn a better fortitude, to dare execute highest Justice on them that shall by force of Armes endeavour the oppressing and bereaving of Religion and thir liberty at home: that no unbridl'd Potentate or Tyrant, but to his sorrow for the future, may presume such high and irresponsible licence over mankinde, to havock and turn upside-down whole Kingdoms of men, as though they were no more in respect of his perverse will then a Nation of Pismires. As for the party calld

138 Cf. Cicero, *Philippics*, VIII, iv, 12: 'Quae causa iustior est belli gerendi quam servitutis depulsio? in qua etiamsi non sit molestus dominus, tamen est miserrimum posse, si velit.'

139 A: 'all that'.

140 Possibly a reference to S., *DR*, p. 15: 'Sed quis unquam audivit, quis legit, haereditarium regem legitimum, regnum possidentem, Christianum, Reformatum, accusatum a suis subjectis, causam capitis dicere coactum, condemnatum, securi percussum?' Even if Shawcross is right about the second edition of *Tenure* being in print by Oct. 1649 this need not exclude the possibility that M. had seen *DR* which was published *no later* than mid-Nov. 1649. See p. 69.

Presbyterian, of whom I believe very many to be good and faithfull Christians, though misledd by som of turbulent spirit, I wish them earnestly and calmly not to fall off from thir first principles; nor to affect rigor and superiority over men not under them; not to compell unforcible things, in Religion especially, which if not voluntary, becomes a sin; nor to assist the clamor and malicious drifts of men whom they themselves have judg'd to be the worst of men, the obdurat enemies of God and his Church: nor to dart against the actions of thir brethren, for want of other argument, those wrested Lawes and Scriptures thrown by Prelats and Malignants against their own sides, which though they hurt not otherwise, yet tak'n up by them to the condemnation of thir own doings, give scandal to all men, and discover in themselves either extreame passion, or apostacy. Let them not oppose thir best friends and associats, who molest them not at all, infringe not the least of thir liberties; unless they call it thir liberty to bind other mens consciences, but are still seeking to live at peace with them and brotherly accord. Let them beware an old and perfet enemy, who though he hope by sowing discord to make them his instruments, yet cannot forbeare a minute the op'n threatning of his destind revenge upon them, when they have servd his purposes. Let them, feare therfore if they be wise, rather what they have don already, then what remaines to doe, and be warn'd in time they put no confidence in Princes[141] whom they have provok'd, lest they be added to the examples of those that miserably have tasted the event. Stories can informe them how *Christiern* the second, King of *Denmark* not much above a hundred yeares past, driv'n out by his Subjects, and receav'd againe upon new Oaths and conditions, broke through them all to his most bloody revenge; slaying his chief opposers when he saw his time, both them and thir children invited to a feast for that purpose. How *Maximilian* dealt with those of *Bruges*,[142] though by mediation of the *German* Princes reconcil'd to them by solem and

[141] Ps. 146:3, 'Put not your trust in princes'. The Geneva Bible has the same text but adds in the margin: 'That God may have the whole praise. Wherin he forbiddeth all vaine confidence'.

[142] M. (*CB*, I, 457) noted the axiom that rulers who have had their power taken away can never be trusted again from de Thou's detailed discussion (*Historiarum*, III, 423–4) of the cases of Christian II of Denmark (1513–23), Maximilian I, Holy Roman emperor (1493–1519), and Charles IX of France (1560–74). Maximilian was humiliated when the citizens of Bruges revolted in 1485 and he reduced them to subjection in 1490.

public writings drawn and seald. How the massacre at *Paris*[143] was the effect of that credulous peace which the French Protestants made with *Charles* the ninth thir King: and that the main visible cause which to this day hath sav'd the *Netherlands* from utter ruin, was thir final not beleiving the perfidious cruelty which, as a constant maxim of State, hath bin us'd by the Spanish Kings on thir Subjects that have tak'n Armes and after trusted them; as no later age but can testifie, heretofore in *Belgia* it self, and this very yeare in *Naples*.[144] And to conclude with one past exception, though farr more ancient, *David*[, whose sanctify'd prudence might be alone sufficient, not to warrant us only, but to instruct us,] when[145] once he had tak'n Armes, never after that trusted *Saul*, though with tears and much relenting he twise promis'd not to hurt him.[146] These instances, few of many, might admonish them both English and Scotch not to let thir own ends, and the driving on of a faction betray them blindly into the snare of those enemies whose revenge looks on them as the men who first begun, fomented and carri'd on, beyond the cure of any sound or safe accommodation, all the evil which hath since unavoidably befall'n them and thir King.

I have somthing also to the Divines, though brief to what were needfull; not to be disturbers of the civil affairs, being in hands better able and more belonging to manage them; but to study harder, and to attend the office of good Pastors, knowing that he whose flock is least among them hath a dreadfull charge, not performd by mounting twise into the chair with a formal preachment huddl'd up at the odd hours of a whole lazy week, but by incessant pains and watching *in season and out of season*,[147] *from house to house*[148] over the soules of whom they have to feed. Which if they ever well considerd, how little leasure would they find to be the most pragmatical Sidesmen of every popular tumult and Sedition? And all this while are to learn what the true end and reason is of the Gospel which they teach; and what a world it differs from the censorious and supercilious lording over conscience. It would be good also they liv'd so as might perswade the people they hated covetousness, which worse then heresie, is idolatry; hated

[143] M. (*CB*, I, 466) notes from de Thou (*Historiarum*, II, 805, 806) how Admiral Coligny, the chief spokesman of the Huguenots, was deceived in the prelude to the massacre of St Bartholomew's Eve, 24 Aug. 1572.

[144] The Neapolitan rebellion against Spanish rule in 1647 was crushed in April 1648.

[145] A: 'after'.

[146] I Sam. 19:6, 26:21.

[147] 2 Tim. 4:2.

[148] Acts 20:20.

pluralities and all kind of Simony; left rambling from Benefice to Benefice, like rav'nous Wolves seeking where they may devour the biggest. Of which if som, well and warmely seated from the beginning, be not guilty, twere good they held not conversation with such as are: let them be sorry that being call'd to assemble[149] about reforming the Church, they fell to progging and solliciting the Parlament, though they had renounc'd the name of Priests, for a new setling of thir Tithes and Oblations; and double lin'd themselves with spiritual places of commoditie beyond the possible discharge of thir duty. Let them assemble in Consistory with thir Elders and Deacons, according to ancient Ecclesiastical rule, to the preserving of Church-discipline, each in his several charge, and not a pack of Clergiemen by themselves to belly-cheare in thir presumptuous Sion,[150] or to promote designes, abuse and gull the simple Laity, and stirr up tumult, as the Prelats did, for the maintenance of thir pride and avarice. These things if they observe, and waite with patience, no doubt but all things will goe well without their importunities or exclamations: and the Printed letters which they send subscrib'd with the ostentation of great Characters[151] and little moment, would be more considerable then now they are. But if they be the Ministers of Mammon in stead of Christ, and scandalize his Church with the filthy love of gaine, aspiring also to sit the closest & the heaviest of all Tyrants, upon the conscience, and fall notoriously into the same sinns, wherof so lately and so loud they accus'd the Prelates, as God rooted out those [wicked ones] immediatly before, so will he root out them thir imitators: and to vindicate his own glory and Religion, will uncover thir hypocrisie to the op'n world; and visit upon thir own heads that *curse ye Meroz*, the very *Motto* of thir Pulpits, wherwith so frequently, not as *Meroz*, but more like Atheists they have blasphem'd[152] the vengeance of God, and [traduc'd] the zeale of his people.[153] [And that they be not what they goe for, true Ministers of the Protestant doctrine, taught by those abroad, famous and religious men, who first reformd the Church, or by those no less zealous, who withstood corruption and the Bishops heer at home, branded with the name of Puritans and

149 The Westminster Assembly of Divines (composed of 121 divines, 10 peers, 20 MPs, and Scots commissioners) first met to frame a church settlement on 1 July 1643.

150 From 1647–59 the Presbyterians' London provincial assembly met at Sion College, Cripplegate St.

151 I.e., on the title pages of their tracts.

152 A: 'mock'd'.

153 A ended here. For M.'s comments on what he added see *DS*, IV, 661–2.

Nonconformists, wee shall abound with testimonies to make appeare: that men may yet more fully know the difference between Protestant Divines, and these Pulpit-firebrands.

Luther.

Lib. contra Rusticos apud Sleidan. l. 5.[154]

Is est hodie rerum status, &c. *Such is the state of things at this day, that men neither can, nor will, nor indeed ought to endure longer the domination of you Princes.*

Neque vero Cæsarem, &c. *Neither is Cæsar to make Warr as head of Christ'ndom, Protector of the Church, Defender of the Faith; these Titles being fals and Windie, and most Kings being the greatest Enemies to Religion. Lib: De bello contra Turcas. apud Sleid. l.* 14.[155] What hinders then, but that we may depose or punish them?

These also are recited by *Cochlæus* in his *Miscellanies* to be the words of *Luther*, or some other eminent Divine, then in *Germany*, when the Protestants there entred into solemn Covnant at *Smalcaldia*.[156] Ut ora ijs obturem &c. *That I may stop thir mouthes, the Pope and Emperor are not born but elected, and may also be depos'd as hath bin oft'n don.*[157] If *Luther*, or whoever els thought so, he could not stay there; for the right of birth or succession can be no privilege in nature to let a Tyrant sit irremoveable over a Nation free born, without transforming that Nation from the nature and condition of men born free, into natural, hereditary, and successive slaves. Therfore he saith furder; *To displace and throw down this Exactor, this Phalaris, this Nero, is a work well pleasing to God;*[158] Namely, for being such a one: which is

[154] M. quotes from Book v, 'Against the peasants', in Sleidan, *Commentarii*, fo. 75a: 'Is autem est hodie rerum status, ut hunc vestrum dominatum homines nec possint nec velint, neque sane debeant ferre diutius'.

[155] From Book 14, 'Of the war against the Turks', in *Commentarii*, fos. 225a–b: 'Neque vero Caesarem his verbis ad bellum excitandum esse, tanquam sit orbis Christiani caput, ecclesiae protector, fideique defensor: nam eiusmodi titulos esse falsos atque ventosos . . . quod plaerique reges ac principes, verae doctrinae sint hostes acerbissimi'.

[156] The Schmalkaldic League was an alliance of Protestant rulers and cities formed in 1531.

[157] Johann Cochlaeus, *In causa religionis miscellaneorum* (Ingolstadt, 1545), fo. 49b: 'Atque ut ora eis obturem ex iure ipsorum saeculari, Papa & Caesar non nati sed electi sunt Principes, qui possunt deponi, id quod propter eorum malefacta saepe factum est'.

[158] Cochlaeus, *Miscellaneorum*, fo. 49a: 'Hunc ergo Moab, Agag, Achab, Phalarim ac Neronem ex sedibus deturbare, summum est beneplacitum Deo'. The half-mythical Phalaris, tyrant of Acragas (Agrigentum), *c.* 570–554 BC, executed his victims in a hollow brazen bull in which he later met his own fate. Cf. *PSD*, IV, ii, 795.

a moral reason. Shall then so slight a consideration as his happ to be not elective simply, but by birth, which was a meer accident, overthrow that which is moral, and make unpleasing to God that which otherwise had so well pleasd him? certainly not: for if the matter be rightly argu'd, Election much rather then chance, bindes a man to content himself with what he suffers by his own bad Election. Though indeed neither the one nor other bindes any man, much less any people to a necessary sufferance of those wrongs and evils, which they have abilitie and strength anough giv'n them to remove.

Zwinglius. tom. 1. *articul.* 42.

Quando vero perfidè, &c. *When Kings raigne perfidiously, and against the rule of Christ, they may according to the word of God be depos'd.*[159]

Mihi ergo compertum non est, &c. *I know not how it comes to pass that Kings raigne by succession, unless it be with consent of the whole people.* ibid.[160]

Quum vero consensu, &c: *But when by suffrage and consent of the whole people, or the better part of them, a Tyrant is depos'd or put to death, God is the chief leader in that action.* ibid.[161]

Nunc cum tam tepidi sumus, &c. *Now that we are so luke warm in upholding public justice, we indure the vices of Tyrants to raigne now a dayes with impunity; justly therfore by them we are trod underfoot, and shall at length with them be punisht. Yet ways are not wanting by which Tyrants may be remoov'd, but there wants public justice.* ibid.[162]

Cavete vobis ô tyranni. *Beware yee Tyrants for now the Gospell of Jesus Christ spreading farr and wide, will renew the lives of many to love innocence and justice; which if yee also shall doe, yee shall be honourd. But if yee*

[159] The title of Article 42 of *Opus articulorum sive conclusionum*, in Huldreich Zwingli, *Operum D. Huldrichi Zwingli* (Zurich, 1581), I, fo. 84a: 'Quando vero perfide & extra regulam Christi egerint, possunt cum deo deponi.'

[160] Zwingli, *Operum*, I, fo. 84b: 'Miho ergo compertum non est, unde hoc cit, ut regna per successiones & quasi per manus posteris tradantur, nisi hoc publico totius populi consensu fiat.'

[161] Zwingli, *Operum*, I, fo. 85a: 'Quum vero consensu & suffragiis totius, aut certe potioris partis multitudinis tyrannus tollitur, deo fit auspice.'

[162] Zwingli, *Operum*, I, fo. 85a: 'Nunc quum tam tepidi sumus in tuenda iustitia publica, sinimus ut impune vitia tyrannorum hodie regnent. Merito ergo ab illis conterimur, & tandem cum illis luimus. Non ergo desunt viae per quas tyranni tollantur, sed deest publica iustitia.'

shall goe on to rage and doe violence, yee shall be trampl'd on by all men. ibid.[163]

Romanum imperium imò quodq; &c. *When the Roman Empire or any other shall begin to oppress Religion, and wee negligently suffer it, wee are as much guilty of Religion so violated, as the Oppressors themselvs.* Idem Epist. ad Conrad. Somium.[164]

Calvin on Daniel. c. 4. *v.* 25.

Hodie Monarchæ semper in suis titulis, &c. *Now adays Monarchs pretend alwayes in thir Titles, to be Kings by the Grace of God; but how many of them to this end onely pretend it, that they may raigne without controule; for to what purpose is the grace of God mentiond in the Title of Kings, but that they may acknowledge no Superiour? In the meane while God, whose name they use, to support themselves, they willingly would tread under thir feet. It is therfore a meer cheat when they boast to raigne by the grace of God.*[165]

Abdicant se terreni principes, &c. *Earthly Princes depose themselves while they rise against God, yea they are unworthy to be numberd among men: rather it behooves us to spitt upon thir heads then to obey them. On Dan*: *c.* 6. *v.* 22.[166]

Bucer on Matth. c. 5.

Si princeps superior, &c. *If a Sovran Prince endeavour by armes to defend transgressors, to subvert those things which are taught in the word of*

[163] Zwingli, *Operum*, I, fo. 85a: 'Cavete vobis, o tyranni, Evangelium enim Iesu Christi late sparsum vitam multorum innovabit, ut innocentiae & iustitiae plurimi studeant. Cui si & vos studueritis, summo honore vos prosequentur: sin furere & vim facere perrexeritis, omnium pedibus conculcabimini.'

[164] Zwingli to Conrad Sam and Simpert Schenk, 18 Aug. 1530, in *Operum*, I, fo. 413b: 'Romanum imperium, imo quodque imperium, ubi religionem sinceram opprimere coeperit, & nos illud negligentes patimur, iam negatae aut contemptae religionis non minus rei erimus, quam ill ipsi oppressores'. Sam (or Som) and Schenk were supporters of Zwingli at Ulm and Memmingen.

[165] Jean Calvin, *Praelectiones in librum prophetiarum Danielis* (Geneva, 1561), fo. 51a: 'Hodie Monarchae semper in suis titulis hoc obtendunt, se esse Reges, & Duces, & Comites Dei gratia: sed quam multi falso nomen Dei praeterunt in hunc finem, ut sibi asserant summum imperium? Quid enim valet saepe in Regum & Principum titulis Dei gratia? nempe ne agnoscant superiorem, quemadmodum dicunt. Interea libenter Deum, cuius clypeo se protegunt, calcarent pedibus: tantum abest, ut serio reputet se habere eius beneficio ut regnent.'

[166] Calvin, *Praelectiones*, fo. 78a: 'Abdicant enim se potestate terreni Principes dum insurgunt contra Deum,: imo indigni sunt qui censeantur in hominum numero. Potius ergo conspuere oportet in ipsorum capita, quam illis parere.'

God, they who are in autority under him, ought first to disswade him; if they prevaile not, and that he now beares himself not as a Prince, but as an enemie, and seekes to violate privileges and rights granted to inferior Magistrates or commonalities, it is the part of pious Magistrates, imploring first the assistance of God, rather to try all ways and means, then to betray the flock of Christ, to such an enemie of God: for they also are to this end ordain'd, that they may defend the people of God, and maintain those things which are good and just. For to have supreme power less'ns not the evil committed by that power, but makes it the less tolerable, by how much the more generally hurtful.[167] Then certainly the less tollerable, the more unpardonably to be punish'd.

Of *Peter Martyr* we have spoke before.[168]

Paræus in Rom. 13.

Quorum est constituere Magistratus, &c. *They whose part it is to set up Magistrates, may restrain them also from outragious deeds, or pull them down; but all Magistrates are set up either by Parlament, or by Electors, or by other Magistrates; They therfore who exalted them, may lawfully degrade and punish them.*[169]

Of the Scotch Divines I need not mention others then the famousest among them, *Knox*, & his fellow Labourers in the reforma-

[167] Bucer's comment on Matt. 5:39 ('But I say unto you, That ye resist not evil'), *Enarrationes*, fo. 55a: 'Et si princeps superior haec armis exigat, & evertare quae iuxta Dei verbum docentur & instituta sunt, conetur, debent illum, exponendo quam simplicissime veritatis causam, orandoque ne a Christo velit depellere, quos adducere illi eum deceat, a proposito suo impio avocare. Sique nihil effecerint, & ille iam non principem, sed hostem, & quidem Dei sese exhibet, contraque ab ipso rite concessa confirmataque inferioribus principibus, & Rebuspublicis iura grassari quaerit: pii principis & magistratus partes erunt, invocato in primis consilio & auxilio Dei, omnia tentare prius, quam huiuscemodi hosti Dei, prodere gregem Christi, adeo ut citius animam suam, quam filios Dei illi cedant. Sunt enim & ipsi in hoc constituti, ut mala a populo Dei depellant, & quae bona ac salutaria sunt, defendant. Tum suprema potestate fungi, adeo non elevat mala, quae ab illa designantur, ut hoc ipso nulla sint minus ferenda, quia nulla nocentiora.'

[168] See p. 22.

[169] M. quotes from David Paraeus, *In divinam ad romanos S. Pauli apostoli epistolam, commentarius*, in *Operum theologicorum* (Frankfurt, 1628), II, [306]: 'Quorum est constituere magistratus, eorum etiam est enormiter grassatores cohercere, aut tollare, si non desistant grassari contra Deum, & contra rempublicam. Constituuntur autem vel per senatum, vel per alios magistratus. Ergo hi recte faciunt, cum cohercent aut tollunt grassatores.' On the same page, Paraeus argues that there is no real difference between foreign and domestic tyrants.

tion of *Scotland*; whose large Treatises on this subject, defend the same Opinion. To cite them sufficiently, were to insert thir whole Books, writt'n purposely on this argument. *Knox Appeal*; and to the Reader; where he promises in a Postscript[170] that the Book which he intended to set forth, call'd, The second blast of the Trumpet, should maintain more at large, that the same men most justly may depose, and punish him whom unadvisedly they have elected, notwithstanding birth, succession, or any Oath of Allegeance. Among our own Divines, *Cartwright* and *Fenner*, two of the Lernedest, may in reason satisfy us what was held by the rest. *Fenner* in his Book of *Theologie* maintaining, That *they who have power, that is to say a Parlament, may either by faire meanes or by force depose a Tyrant*, whom he defines to be him, that wilfully breakes all, or the principal conditions made between him and the Common-wealth. *Fen. Sac: Theolog. c.* 13.[171] and *Cartwright* in a prefix'd Epistle[172] testifies his approbation of the whole Book.

Gilby de obedientiâ. p. 25. & 105.[173]

Kings have thir autoritie of the people, who may upon occasion reassume it to themselves.

Englands Complaint against the Canons.

The people may kill wicked Princes as monsters and cruel beasts.

Christopher Goodman of Obedience.[174]

When Kings or Rulers become blasphemers of God, oppressors and murderers of thir Subjects, they ought no more to be accounted

[170] See 'Iohn Knoxe to the Reader', in Knox, *Appellation* (Geneva, 1558) pp. 77b–78a.

[171] In Chapter 13 of *Sacra theologia* (1585), after defining the tyrant without title, Dudley Fenner goes on to define the tyrant by practice (p. 186); 'Exercitio tyrannus est qui consulte, pacta reipub. omnia, vel praecipua pessundat. Hunc tollunt vel pacifice vel cum bello, quia ea potestate donati sunt, ut regni Ephori, vel omnium ordinum conventus publicus.'

[172] Thomas Cartwright's prefatory epistle (unpaginated) addresses Fenner as 'ornatissimo & charissimo'.

[173] The next two garbled references to 'Gilby' and 'Englands Complaint' result from M. following the misattribution to them in Aston's *Remonstrance* of quotations actually from John Ponet's *Short treatise of politike power* (1556). See S. Miller, 'Two references in Milton's *Tenure of Kings*', *Journal of English and Germanic Philology*, 50 (1951), pp. 320–5.

[174] M. quotes accurately from the 1558 Geneva edition of Goodman's *Superior powers*.

Kings or lawfull Magistrates, but as privat men to be examind, accus'd, condemn'd and punisht by the Law of God, and being convicted and punisht by that Law, it is not mans but Gods doing, *C.* 10. *p.* 139.

By the civil laws a foole or Idiot born, and so prov'd shall loose the lands and inheritance wherto he is born, because he is not able to use them aright. And especially ought in no case be sufferd to have the goverment of a whole Nation; But there is no such evil can come to the Common-wealth by fooles and idiots as doth by the rage and fury of ungodly Rulers; Such therfore being without God ought to have no autority over Gods people, who by his Word requireth the contrary. *C.* 11. *p.* 143, 144.

No person is exempt by any Law of God from this punishment, be he King, Queene, or Emperor, he must dy the death, for God hath not plac'd them above others, to transgress his laws as they list, but to be subject to them as well as others, and if they be subject to his laws, then to the punishment also, so much the more as thir example is more dangerous. *C.* 13. *p.* 184.

When Magistrates cease to doe thir Duty, the people are as it were without Magistrates, yea worse, and then God giveth the sword into the peoples hand, and he himself is become immediatly thir head. *p.* 185.

If Princes doe right and keep promise with you, then doe you owe to them all humble obedience: if not, yee are discharg'd, and your study ought to be in this case how ye may depose and punish according to the Law such Rebels against God and oppressors of thir Country. *p.* 190.

This *Goodman* was a Minister of the *English* Church at *Geneva*, as *Dudley Fenner* was at *Middleburrough*, or some other place in that Country. These were the Pastors of those Saints and Confessors who flying from the bloudy persecution of Queen *Mary*,[175] gather'd up at length thir scatterd members into many Congregations; wherof som in upper, some in lower *Germany*, part of them settl'd at *Geneva*; where this Author[176] having preachd on this subject to the great liking of certain lerned and godly men who heard him, was by them sundry

[175] Mary Tudor, Queen of England, 1553–58, during whose reign a Catholic reaction took place which earned her the title 'Bloody Mary'.

[176] The rest of the paragraph paraphrases William Whittingham's preface to *Superior powers*, pp. 4–5.

times & with much instance requir'd to write more fully on that point. Who therupon took it in hand, and conferring with the best lerned in those parts (among whom *Calvin* was then living in the same City) with their special approbation he publisht this treatise, aiming principally, as is testify'd by *Whittingham* in the Preface, that his Brethren of *England*, the Protestants, might be perswaded in the truth of that Doctrine concerning obedience to Magistrates. *Whittingham in Prefat.*

These were the true Protestant Divines of *England*, our fathers in the faith we hold; this was their sense, who for so many yeares labouring under Prelacy, through all stormes and persecutions kept Religion from extinguishing; and deliverd it pure to us, till there arose a covetous and ambitious generation of Divines (for Divines they call themselves) who feining on a sudden to be new converts and proselytes from Episcopacy, under which they had long temporiz'd, op'nd thir mouthes at length, in shew against Pluralities and Prelacy, but with intent to swallow them down both; gorging themselves like Harpy's[177] on those simonious places and preferments of thir outed predecessors, as the quarry for which they hunted, not to pluralitie onely but to multiplicitie: for possessing which they had accusd them thir Brethren, and aspiring under another title to the same authoritie and usurpation over the consciences of all men.

Of this faction diverse reverend and lerned Divines, as they are stil'd in the Phylactery[178] of thir own Title page, pleading the lawfulnes of defensive Armes against this King, in a Treatise call'd *Scripture and Reason*,[179] seem in words to disclaime utterly the deposing of a King; but both the Scripture and the reasons which they use, draw consequences after them, which without their bidding, conclude it lawfull. For if by Scripture, and by that especially to the *Romans*, which they most insist upon, Kings, doing that which is contrary to Saint *Pauls* definition of a Magistrat, may be resisted, they may altogether with as much force of consequence be depos'd or punishd.

[177] I.e., harpies: mythological monsters with the face and body of a woman and the wings and claws of a bird.

[178] A phylactery is a small vellum box containing four texts from Deuteronomy and Exodus worn by Jews at morning prayer as a sign of strict obedience. For M. it symbolizes the ostentatious display of righteousness. Cf. the Sonnet 'On the new forcers of conscience under the Long Parliament'.

[179] *Scripture and reason pleaded for defensive armes: or, the whole controversie about subjects taking up armes* (14 April, 1643).

And if by reason the unjust autority of Kings *may be forfeted in part, and his power be reassum'd in part, either by the Parlament or People, for the case in hazard and the present necessitie*, as they affirm *p.* 34, there can no Scripture be alleg'd, no imaginable reason giv'n, that necessity continuing, as it may alwayes, and they in all prudence and thir duty may take upon them to foresee it, why in such a case they may not finally amerce him with the loss of his Kingdom, of whose amendment they have no hope. And if one wicked action persisted in against Religion, Laws, and liberties may warrant us to thus much in part, why may not forty times as many tyrannies, by him committed, warrant us to proceed on restraining him, till the restraint become total. For the ways of justice are exactest proportion; if for one trespass of a King it require so much remedie or satisfaction, then for twenty more as hainous crimes, it requires of him twentyfold; and so proportionably, till it com to what is utmost among men. If in these proceedings against thir King they may not finish by the usual cours of justice what they have begun, they could not lawfully begin at all. For this golden rule[180] of justice and moralitie, as well as of Arithmetic, out of three termes which they admitt, will as certainly and unavoydably bring out the fourth, as any Probleme that ever *Euclid*,[181] or *Apollonius*[182] made good by demonstration.

And if the Parlament, being undeposable but by themselves, as is affirm'd, *p.* 37, 38, might for his whole life, if they saw cause, take all power, authority, and the sword out of his hand, which in effect is to unmagistrate him, why might they not, being then themselves the sole Magistrates in force, proceed to punish him who being lawfully depriv'd of all things that define a Magistrate, can be now no Magistrate to be degraded lower, but an offender to be punisht. Lastly, whom they may defie, and meet in battell, why may they not as well prosecute by justice? For lawfull warr is but the execution of justice against them who refuse Law. Among whom if it be lawfull (as they deny not, *p.* 19, 20.) to slay the King himself comming in front at his own peril, wherfore may not justice doe that intendedly, which the

[180] M. alludes both to an arithmetical rule enabling one to find the fourth term in a proposition and to a scriptural precept: 'as ye would that men should do to you, do ye also to them likewise' (Luke 6:31).

[181] The geometrical propositions of Euclid (328–283 BC) were regarded as classic examples of logical demonstrability.

[182] Apollonius of Perga (*c.* 262–190 BC), known as the 'great geometer'.

chance of a defensive warr might without blame have don casually, nay purposely, if there it finde him among the rest. They aske *p.* 19. *By what rule of Conscience or God, a State is bound to sacrifice Religion, Laws and liberties, rather then a Prince defending such as subvert them, should com in hazard of his life.* And I ask by what conscience, or divinity, or Law, or reason, a State is bound to leave all these sacred concernments under a perpetual hazard and extremity of danger, rather then cutt off a wicked Prince, who sitts plotting day and night to subvert them: They tell us that the Law of nature justifies any man to defend himself, eev'n against the King in Person: let them show us then why the same Law, may not justifie much more a State or whole people, to doe justice upon him, against whom each privat man may lawfully defend himself; seing all kind of justice don, is a defence to good men, as well as a punishment to bad; and justice don upon a Tyrant is no more but the necessary self-defence of a whole Common wealth. To Warr upon a King, that his instruments may be brought to condigne punishment, and therafter to punish them the instruments, and not to spare onely, but to defend and honour him the Author, is the strangest peece of justice to be call'd Christian, and the strangest peece of reason to be call'd human, that by men of reverence and learning, as thir stile imports them, ever yet was vented. They maintain in the third and fourth Section,[183] that a Judge or inferior Magistrate, is anointed of God, is his Minister, hath the Sword in his hand, is to be obey'd by St. *Peters* rule,[184] as well as the Supreme, and without difference any where exprest: and yet will have us fight against the Supreme till he remove and punish the inferior Magistrate (for such were the greatest Delinquents) when as by Scripture, and by reason, there can no more autority be shown to resist the one then the other; and altogether as much, to punish or depose the Supreme himself, as to make Warr upon him, till he punish or deliver up his inferior Magistrates, whom in the same terms we are commanded to obey, and not to resist. Thus while they, in a cautious line or two here and there stuft in, are onely verbal against the pulling down or punishing of Tyrants, all the Scripture and the reason which they bring, is in every leafe direct and rational to inferr it altogether as lawful, as to resist them. And yet in all thir Sermons, as hath by others bin well noted, they went much furder. For Divines, if ye observe

[183] *Scripture and Reason*, pp. [33]–4, 36–7.

[184] 1 Pet. 2:13–14.

them, have thir postures, and thir motions no less expertly, and with no less variety then they that practice feats in the Artillery-ground. Sometimes they seem furiously to march on, and presently march counter; by and by they stand, and then retreat; or if need be can face about, or wheele in a whole body, with that cunning and dexterity as is almost unperceavable; to winde themselves by shifting ground into places of more advantage. And Providence onely must be the drumm, Providence the word of command, that calls them from above, but always to som larger Benefice, or acts them into such or such figures, and promotions. At thir turnes and doublings no men readier; to the right, or to the left; for it is thir turnes which they serve cheifly; heerin only singular; that with them there is no certain hand right or left; but as thir own commodity thinks best to call it. But if there come a truth to be defended, which to them, and thir interest of this world seemes not so profitable, strait these nimble motionists can finde no eev'n leggs to stand upon: and are no more of use to reformation throughly performd, and not superficially, or to the advancement of Truth (which among mortal men is alwaies in her progress) then if on a sudden they were strook maime, and crippl'd. Which the better to conceale, or the more to countnance by a general conformity to thir own limping, they would have *Scripture*, they would have *reason* also made to halt with them for company; and would putt us off with impotent conclusions, lame and shorter then the premises. In this posture they seem to stand with great zeale and confidence on the wall of *Sion*; but like *Jebusites*,[185] not like *Israelites*, or *Levites*: blinde also as well as lame, they discern not *David* from *Adonibezec*:[186] but cry him up for the Lords anointed, whose thumbs and great toes not long before they had cut off upon thir Pulpit cushions. Therfore he who is our only King, the root of *David*, and whose Kingdom is eternal righteousness, with all those that Warr under him, whose happiness and final hopes are laid up in that only just & rightful kingdom (which we pray incessantly may com soon, and in so praying wish hasty ruin and destruction to all Tyrants) eev'n he our immortal King, and all that love him, must of necessity have in abomination these blind and lame Defenders of *Jerusalem*; as the soule of *David* hated them, and forbid them entrance into Gods House, and his own. But as to those

[185] See 1 Sam. 5:6.

[186] Judges 1:6, 'but Adoni-bezek fled; and they pursued after him, and caught him, and cut off his thumbs and his great toes'.

before them, which I cited first (and with an easie search, for many more might be added) as they there stand, without more in number, being the best and chief of Protestant Divines, we may follow them for faithful Guides, and without doubting may receive them, as Witnesses abundant of what wee heer affirme concerning Tyrants. And indeed I find it generally the cleere and positive determination of them all, (not prelatical, or of this late faction subprelatical) who have writt'n on this argument; that to doe justice on a lawless King, is to a privat man unlawful, to an inferior Magistrate lawfull: or if they were divided in opinion, yet greater then these here alleg'd, or of more autority in the Church, there can be none produc'd. If any one shall goe about by bringing other testimonies to disable these, or by bringing these against themselves in other cited passages of thir Books, he will not only faile to make good that fals and impudent assertion of those mutinous Ministers, that the deposing and punishing of a King or Tyrant, *is against the constant Judgement of all Protestant Divines*,[187] it being quite the contrary, but will prove rather, what perhaps he intended not, that the judgement of Divines, if it be so various and inconstant to it self, is not considerable, or to be esteem'd at all. Ere which be yeilded, as I hope it never will, these ignorant assertors in thir own art will have prov'd themselves more and more, not to be Protestant Divines, whose constant judgement in this point they have so audaciously bely'd, but rather to be a pack of hungrie Church-wolves, who in the steps of *Simon Magus*[188] thir Father, following the hot sent of double Livings and Pluralities, advousons, donatives, inductions, and augmentations, though uncall'd to the Flock of Christ, but by the meer suggestion of thir Bellies, like those Priests of *Bel*,[189] whose pranks *Daniel* found out; have got possession, or rather seis'd upon the Pulpit, as the strong hold and fortress of thir sedition and rebellion against the civil Magistrate. Whose friendly and victorious hand having rescu'd them from the Bishops thir insulting

[187] M. edits the ministers' contention in *A serious and faithfull representation*, p. 11: 'And consonant to the tenor of the Scriptures herein, hath always been the constant judgement and doctrine of Protestant Divines both at home and abroad, with whose Judgements we do fully concurre; disclaiming, detesting and abhorring the wicked and bloody Tenents and Practices of Jesuites, (the worst of Papists,) concerning the opposing of lawfull Magistrates by private Persons, and the murthering of Kings by any, though under the most specious and colourable pretences'.

[188] Acts 8:9–25.

[189] M. refers to the priests who deceive the worshippers in the Apocryphal Bel and the Dragon.

Lords, fed them plenteously, both in public and in privat, rais'd them to be high and rich of poore and base; onely suffer'd not thir covetousness & fierce ambition, which as the pitt that sent out thir fellowlocusts,[190] hath bin ever bottomless and boundless, to interpose in all things, and over all persons, thir impetuous ignorance and importunity.]

THE END.

[190] See Rev. 9:2–3, and the marginal comment in the Geneva Bible: 'Locustes are false teachers, heretikes, and worldlie suttil Prelates . . . which forsake Christ to mainteine false doctrine'.

Joannis MiltonI
ANGLI
PRO
Populo Anglicano
DEFENSIO
Contra *Claudii Anonymi*, aliàs
SALMASII
DEFENSIONEM REGIAM.

Editio correctior & auctior, ab Autore denuo recognita.

LONDINI,

Typis *Neucombianis, Anno Dom. 1658.*

A DEFENCE OF THE PEOPLE OF ENGLAND
by JOHN MILTON, an Englishman
in reply to
A DEFENCE OF THE KING
by Claudius Anonymous, alias SALMASIUS

PREFACE

I am afraid that if I am as lavish of words but empty of matter in defending the people of England as most people have thought Salmasius was in his defence of the king, I may seem to have deserved the name of a defender who is at the same time most verbose and most absurd. But still, no-one thinks he must be so much in a hurry in dealing with any commonplace subject as not to be in the habit of using an introduction that is at least appropriate to the worth of the task he has undertaken. If I do not omit an introduction in speaking of a matter that is almost the most important of all, nor glance over it too briefly, I hope for my part that I will attain more or less two goals, which I greatly wish. One is that I should in no way fail, as far as lies within my power, this most celebrated cause which is most worthy of being remembered by all ages. The other is that while I should criticize emptiness and excess in my opponent, I should nevertheless be judged to have avoided them myself.

For I will tell of things that are neither trivial nor commonplace: of how a most powerful king, who had crushed the laws and beaten down religion, and was ruling in accordance with his own caprice, was at last conquered in war by his own people who had served a long term of slavery; then how he was handed over into custody; and then when he showed absolutely no reason for them to hope for better of him either by words or by deeds, he was finally condemned to death by the highest council of the kingdom, and struck by the axe before the very door of the palace.[1] I will also tell (something which will be of

[1] I.e., the Banqueting House of Whitehall.

much use in lightening men's minds of a great superstition) under what law, particularly that of the English, this judgement was made and executed; and I shall easily defend my very brave and honest countrymen, who have deserved outstandingly well of all the citizens and peoples of the world, from the most wicked calumnies of slanderers, whether of our country or from abroad, and especially from the slanders of this most empty sophist who behaves like the leader and chief of the rest. For when did the majesty of any king seated upon his lofty throne ever shine out so brightly as that of the English people gleamed forth on the occasion when they shook off that old superstition, which had long prevailed, and entangled in his own laws and drenched beneath a flood of judgement the very king (or rather the man who had turned from their king to their enemy), who alone of mortals claimed impunity for himself by divine right; and were not afraid of inflicting upon him, when found guilty, the same punishment which he would have inflicted upon anyone else?

But why do I proclaim these deeds as done by the people, when they almost speak out for themselves, and bear witness everywhere to the presence of God? For, whenever it is most pleasing to his infinite wisdom, he generally casts down proud and unbridled kings who elevate themselves above human bounds, and often overturns them entirely along with their whole house. It was at his clear command that we were suddenly roused to reclaim the safety and liberty which we had almost lost; he was the leader we followed; and it was with respect for his divine footsteps, which were imprinted everywhere along the journey, that we entered upon a path that was not dark, but bright, distinctly shown and laid open to us by his guidance.

If it were merely by my diligence, such as it is, and by my own powers alone that I would hope to be able to explain all these things in a worthy enough way, and to hand them down as records that all generations and nations would perhaps read, I would be quite wrong. For what speech could be so majestic and splendid, what talent so exceptional as to be equal to undertaking this burden? For when a man can scarcely be found in so many generations who can set down the actions of illustrious men or states excellently, can anyone believe that he can in any words or style comprehend these glorious and marvellous deeds – deeds not of men but clearly of an all-powerful God?

The highest men in our commonwealth have brought it about by their influence that I should undertake this duty, and have decided this task (which is certainly second only in importance) should be given to me: to defend those acts which they had performed with great glory under the leadership of God against envy and slander, over which steel and the machinery of war has no power, with another kind of weapon. Their judgement I think is indeed a great honour to me, that *I* was the man who, by their votes, in preference to the rest,[2] should perform this unregrettable task for the exceptionally brave liberators of my country. And moreover from my early youth I had been fired by those enthusiasms myself which kept on urging me, if not to *do* the best deeds, at least to *praise* them.[3]

Yet, distrusting these supports, I resort to divine aid: and I invoke God, best and greatest, giver of all gifts; that as successfully and as piously as our most distinguished leaders to freedom broke the king's haughtiness and uncontrolled tyranny in battle, then extinguished them at last by a memorable punishment; and with as little trouble as I recently took as one of many to refute and dispose of the king himself when he rose again, so to speak, from the dead, and, in that book which was published after his death,[4] tried to sell himself to the people with new subtleties and artificial verbal devices – now may I as successfully and truly disprove and dispel the impudence and lies of this foreign declaimer.

Since he *is* a foreigner and, although he denies it a thousand times, a grammarian – yet he is not content with the wages which he earns by this title, and has preferred to be a great busybody. It is not with a commonwealth alone that he has dared to meddle, but with a foreign one as well, though he brings to the matter neither discretion nor judgement, nor anything else that so great a judge should certainly have, apart from his arrogance and his grammar. And certainly if he had produced these things which he has now written in Latin, such as it is, amongst the English and in our own language, I believe there would scarcely be anyone who judged the effort was needed to reply, but would partly disdain them as trite and demolished by now with repeated refutations, and partly reject them as tyrannical and abomin-

[2] I.e., of the Council of State, 8 Jan. 1650. It was rumoured that John Selden had prepared a reply independently. See Gui Patin to Dr Charles Spon, May 1650, *Lettres de Gui Patin* (1846), II, 17–18, and Henry Hammond to Gilbert Sheldon, Jan. 1651, in 'Illustrations of the State of the Church during the Great Rebellion', *The Theologian and Ecclesiastic*, VII (1849), p. 147.

[3] Cf. *Church-Government*, I, 812.

[4] I.e., *Eikon Basilike*.

able, hardly to be endured by the most worthless slave – even if he himself was on the side of the royalists. But now when our opponent swells up with his mighty page among foreigners, who are quite ignorant of our affairs, they, as they are getting an incorrect understanding of our affairs, must indeed be fully informed. He should be treated in his own manner (since he is motivated by such a desire to speak ill of others), in his own manner and method, I say.

If anyone should happen to wonder why, then, we have suffered him to flit about for so long unharmed, and exulting and inflated by the silence of us all, I certainly don't know about others, but for myself I can boldly say that I would not have needed long to seek out or track down words and arguments with which I might defend so good a cause, had I only had leisure and health which could indeed bear the labour of writing. Since even now I have quite limited strength, and am forced to apply myself to this bit by bit with difficulty and break off almost every hour, when it is a matter which I ought to have pursued with uninterrupted composition and attention.

For this reason, if I am not granted sufficient ability to celebrate my most outstanding fellow countrymen, the preservers of their fatherland, with a proclamation worthy of their praises, whose immortal deeds already shine brightly throughout the whole world, yet I hope it will not be difficult for me to defend and deliver them from the insolence of this troublesome grammarian and the ravings of his professorial tongue. For nature and laws would be in a very bad way if slavery were noisy and liberty mute, and if tyrants should have people to speak for them, while those who can vanquish tyrants should have none. It would be sad if this very reason, which we have by the gift of God, should not supply arguments much more for men's preservation, liberation and, as far as nature goes, equality with each other, than for their oppression and complete ruin beneath the rule of one man. And so let us approach this most noble cause, happy in this certain confidence that on the other side stand cheating, deceit, ignorance and barbarism; on this side with us stand light, truth, reason and the studies and learning of all the best ages.

Well then, enough by way of introduction, and since our business is with critics, let us see first what is presented by the title of such an elegant volume: 'A Defence of the King, for Charles I to Charles II'.[5]

[5] Salmasius, *Defensio regia, pro Carolo I. ad serenissimum Magnae Britanniae regem Carolum II. filium natu majorem, heredem & successorem legitimum. Sumptibus Regiis* (1649).

It is a mighty task indeed that you take upon yourself, whoever you are – to defend a father to his son: it would be a wonder if you didn't win your case! But I call you forth, though you lie concealed – formerly under a false name, and now under none at all – Salmasius, to another court and other judges, where you will perhaps not hear those 'Bravos' and 'Well dones' which you usually chase after so desperately in your own literary exercise ground.

But why this royal defence to the son who is now king? There is no need of a torturer, we have the confession of the defendant: he says 'at the royal expense'.[6] O you mercenary and expensive orator! So you wouldn't write a defence for Charles the father, who was in your opinion an excellent king, for Charles the son, who is the poorest one, except at the royal expense? But you have, old fox that you are, wished not to be a laughing-stock also, in saying 'a king's defence'; for, as you have sold it, it is no longer yours but is now rightfully 'a king's defence' – indisputably bought for one hundred jacobuses,[7] a huge price, from an absolutely destitute king. For it is not of unknown matters that I speak. I know who brought those gold pieces to your house, who came with that small money purse embroidered with coloured glass beads; I know who saw you stretching out your greedy hands, with the appearance indeed of embracing the king's chaplain,[8] who was sent with the gift, but really to embrace the gift itself; and by receiving this one fee alone almost totally to empty the king's treasury.

But behold the man himself; the doors creak, the actor comes forth upon the stage:

> Pay attention and notice in silence
> So you may learn what the Eunuch wants for himself.[9]

For whatever it is, he enters in a more elevated attitude than usual. 'A horrible message has recently struck our ears, but more our minds, with a terrible wound, about a parricide committed in England in the character of a king by a wicked conspiracy of sacrilegious men.' Surely that horrible message of yours must either have had a much longer sword than the one that Peter drew,[10] or those ears of yours

[6] I.e., *Sumptibus Regiis*.
[7] *Jacobaeis*: the sovereign, first minted in James I's reign and hence known as the jacobus.
[8] I.e., Dr George Morley (1597–1684), later bishop of Worcester and then Winchester.
[9] Terence, *Eunuchus*, Prologue, 44–5.
[10] When Christ was arrested: Matt. 26:51. Mark 14:47. Luke 22:50. John 18:10.

must have been very long-eared, if it could strike them with a wound at such a distance: for it could not even offend ears that were not obtuse. For what harm is done to you people, which of you is hurt, if we punish with death our enemies and opponents, be they commoners or nobles or kings?

But give over these matters, Salmasius, which have nothing to do with you: for I also have a 'horrible message' to send about you, and if it does not strike with a more terrible wound all the grammarians' and critics' ears, provided they have refined and learned ones, I shall be amazed: and the message is 'of a parricide committed' in Holland 'in the character' of Aristarchus[11] by the 'wicked' barbarism of Salmasius; in that you, a great critic indeed, hired 'at the king's expense' to write a royal defence, not only moved to pity the mind of no-one who was not a fool with a most disgusting exordium, which is most like the nonsense and dirges of mourning women hired for the funeral, but straightway at the end of the first sentence roused laughter among those who had hardly read it, because of your manifold impropriety of speech. For what, I ask, is the meaning of 'to commit parricide in the character of a king', what is the meaning of 'in the character of a king'?[12] What style of Latin ever used such an expression unless you are telling us by chance of some pseudo-Philip[13] who put on the character of a king to commit some parricide in England? This word, I think, has fallen from your mouth with greater truth than you fancied. For a tyrant, just like a player king indeed, being only a ghost and mask of a king, is not a true king.

However, you will be punished for the Franco-Latin mistakes of this kind with which you everywhere abound, not so much by me (for I haven't the leisure) as by your own fellow grammarians themselves. To them I give you over to be ridiculed and flogged.

Far more terrible is this fact: that what was decreed by our highest magistrates concerning the king you say was committed by 'a wicked conspiracy of sacrilegious men'. You scoundrel! Is this what you call the acts and decrees of a recently most powerful kingdom, which is

11 Aristarchus of Samothrace (*c.* 217–215 to 145–143 BC), literary scholar of the Alexandrian school, known as *grammatikotatos*.

12 *in persona Regis*: M. exploits the possible meanings of *persona* from 'mask' through to 'individual'.

13 I.e., Andriscus, a pretender who claimed to be Philip, son of Perseus (king of Macedon, 179–168 BC); finally defeated in 148 BC.

now an even more powerful republic? About its deeds, not even a king could up till now be brought to pronounce or publish in writing anything more grave.

Deservedly therefore have the most mighty states of Holland, true offspring of those who were once the liberators of their country, condemned to darkness by their edict this defence of tyranny,[14] most destructive to the liberty of all peoples. And as for the actual author of it, every free state ought to debar him or throw him out of its territories, and especially that which supports by its payment so thankless and so offensive an enemy of the commonwealth. Of that commonwealth, just like ours, he attacks the very foundations and causes; and moreover by one and the same effort he tries to weaken and overthrow them both, he cuts to pieces with abuse the most outstanding defenders of liberty there under the shelter of our names. Think it over now amongst yourselves, most illustrious States General of the United Netherlands, and consider in your hearts, who has urged on this advocate of royal power to write, who recently began to act the king among you, what plans, what attempts, what commotions at length resulted throughout Holland, what would now be – how slavery and a new master had been made ready for you and that liberty of yours, defended by the weapons and toils of so many years – how nearly obliterated it would now have been among you, had it not breathed again by the most timely death recently of a rash young man.[15]

But that fellow of ours goes on with his bombast, and invents marvellous tragedies: 'Whoever this unspeakable talk reached' (undoubtedly the news of Salmasius' parricidal barbarism), just as if they had been touched by a thunderbolt, suddenly 'their hair stood on end with horror and their voice stuck in their throat'. The natural philosophers may hear this and learn it now for the first time – that hair stands on end because of being struck by a thunderbolt! But who does not know that poor and cowardly spirits are struck with amazement at any great deed or talk, and then most show themselves the idiots that they have been all along? Some 'did not hold back their tears', I believe they were some 'court ladies' or any others softer than these; amongst them Salmasius himself too has become Salmacis by

[14] Holland and West Friesland issued an edict suppressing *DR* on 17 Jan. 1650.
[15] I.e., William II, Stadtholder of Orange (and son-in-law of Charles I); died 6 Nov. 1650, aged 24.

some modern metamorphosis, and with this artificial fountain of tears of his, made ready at night, attempts to soften manly hearts. So I give warning and order to watch out

> – lest disreputable Salmacis should weaken anyone with
> waves of evil power.
> Lest when he came as a man, he should leave thence effeminate,
> and suddenly grown soft at the waves' touch.[16]

'In fact, the more bravely spirited' (for I suppose he cannot even name the brave and spirited except with disgusting affectation) 'burned with such a flame of indignation that they could hardly control themselves.' We don't care a bit for those madmen; we are used to driving off and putting to flight those threatening men of yours with the true courage that has control over itself. 'No-one surely did not call down curses upon the instigators of such a crime.' But their voice, as you were just saying, 'stuck in their throat'; and I wish that it had stuck there right up to this day, if you want this to be taken to apply simply to our exiles – and we have it also on excellent authority that nothing is more frequently on their lips than curses and imprecations, which are certainly to be abominated by all good men, but not feared. Of the others, it is hardly credible that, when the news of the execution of the king's punishment had arrived there, anyone was found, especially amongst a free people, so born to slavery as to harm us in word or count our deed as a crime. But rather that all right-thinking men said everything good about it – or rather, gave thanks to God for having produced so glorious and distinguished an example of justice, and one which could be such a salutary example to the remaining kings.

And as for those 'savage and steely-hearted'[17] people who lament the 'miserable and marvellous slaughter' (of someone or other) along with their jingling speaker, the most frigidly boring 'after the name of king was formed and famed in the world' – I bid them to lament again and again. But meanwhile what boy just out of school, or young brother from any cloister you would like to name, would not have declaimed much more fluently, or rather in better Latin, on this fall of a king than this royal orator? But it would be too absurd if I were to pursue precisely the inarticulate ravings of this man at such a length

[16] Ovid, *Metamorphoses*, IV, 285–6, 385–6. Salmacis, the nymph of the Carian fountain, was united in one body with Hermaphroditus, son of Hermes and Aphrodite.

[17] Cf. Tibullus, *Elegies*, I, 10, 2.

throughout the whole volume. Yet I would gladly do it (since his pride and haughtiness, as they say, is inflated beyond measure), if he did not protect himself behind such a great, inelegant, ill-ordered bulk of a book, and, just like that soldier in Terence, lurk behind the front ranks;[18] a clever plan indeed, so that even the most eager person might get tired of noting all the details, and be finished off by boredom before he could contradict them. But at this point I wanted to give some example of him at least in this prelude, so to speak, and to give sagacious readers a taste of the man right from the outset, so that in this hors d'oeuvre consisting of a single page, we may try out how elegantly and splendidly he will entertain us with the rest of his dishes; to see how many absurd puerilities he will have piled up throughout the whole work, when he has set them so thickly where it was least fitting – at its very head.

From here on I easily pass over all the nonsense he chatters and the harangues on paper that is destined to wrap up mackerels;[19] however as far as our affairs are concerned, I do not doubt that what has been published and proclaimed on the authority of parliament will have more weight with all right-minded and sensible people abroad than the slanders and lies of one utterly shameless little man, who was hired for a price by exiles from our country, enemies to our native land, and who has not hesitated to scrape and throw together onto paper every outright falsehood he hears, whenever any one of those to whom he had hired out his services dictates or spreads idle gossip.

And so that all may clearly understand how he has no scruples as to what he writes, true or false, holy or unholy, no other witness will need to be called by me than Salmasius himself. He writes in his *Apparatus contra primatu papae* that:

> there are very important reasons why the church ought to return from episcopacy, to the apostolic institution *of elders*;[20] from the episcopacy there was brought into the church an evil far greater than those schisms which were feared earlier; that plague which came out of it to invade churches sank the whole body of the church beneath wretched tyranny; or rather it put kings and

[18] Terence, *Eunuchus*, 781. For M.'s justification of this jibe, see *PSD*, IV, ii, 726.

[19] *scombris: scomber* (mackerel) was a traditional insult among Roman poets. Cf. *DS*, IV, 580.

[20] *ad Apostolicam* presbyterorum *institutionem*: M. interpolates 'presbyterorum' (also adding the emphasis) into his quotation from S., *Librorum de primatu papae, pars prima, cum apparatu accedere de eodem primatu Nili & Barlaami tractatus* (Leyden, 1645), p. 169.

> princes themselves beneath the yoke; greater benefit would pour back into the church by the abolition of the whole hierarchy, rather than that of its head alone, the pope, p. 196.[21] The episcopacy together with the papacy could be removed to the greatest benefit of the church. With the removal of the episcopacy, the papacy itself would fall, on the grounds that it was founded upon it, p. 171. There are particular reasons why it should be removed in those kingdoms which have already renounced the papacy.

He does not see:

> why the episcopacy should be retained there. A reformation does not seem complete which has been left unfinished in this particular. No reason or probable cause can be adduced why once the papal supremacy is removed, the episcopacy either ought to or can be retained, p. 197.

Although he wrote this and much more four years before, now he is so false and shameless that he dares in this place seriously to accuse the parliament of England because 'they voted that the episcopacy was not only to be cast out of the house of lords, but also wholly cast off'.[22] Yes, and he even advises and defends the episcopacy itself, using the same proofs and reasons that in that previous book of his he had refuted with great force; namely 'that bishops are necessary, and to be kept at all costs in case a thousand destructive sects and heresies should sprout forth in England'. O sly turn-coat! Are you so unashamed as to act inconstantly even in religious matters and – I had almost said – to betray the church, whose most holy ordinances you seem to have defended with all that noise, so that whenever it was convenient for you, you could all the more ridicule and subvert those very institutions?

It is concealed from nobody that when the houses of parliament were burning with the desire to reform our church after the example of other churches, and had decided to abolish the episcopacy totally, first the king intervened, then made war upon us chiefly for that reason; this at last turned to his own destruction. Go now and boast that you are the defender of a king, you who, so that you may zealously defend the king, now openly betray and attack the cause of the church

[21] p. 196: 1658. 1651Q and 1651F give the correct reference.

[22] Charles I assented to the bill excluding the bishops from the Lords on 13 Feb. 1642; the ordinance for abolishing archbishops and bishops was passed on 9 Oct. 1646.

which was undertaken by yourself: with its heaviest reprimand you should now be marked out.

But about the constitution of our commonwealth. Since you, a trifling foreign teacher, set aside your chests and book boxes stuffed full of nonsense that you would have done better to put into order, and prefer to cause a stir in a foreign commonwealth and be odious, I make this brief reply to you, or rather to someone more sensible than you: that this constitution is what our time and dissensions allow; that it is not such as to be wished, but such as the persistent discords of wicked citizens allow it to be. But if a commonwealth which is in difficulties with factions, and protects itself with weapons, concerns itself with the healthy and sound part only,[23] and neglects or excludes the rest, whether they are commoners or aristocrats, it is certainly just enough; even though it has refused to have more to do with king and nobles, taught by its own sufferings.

But to rail at that 'supreme council' and even at the 'president of the council' – truly you are absurd; for that council, which is a figment of your dreams, is not supreme, but set up by the authority of parliament for a certain time only, consisting of about forty men of its number, of whom anyone can be president by the votes of the rest.[24] Moreover it has always been quite customary that parliament, which is our senate, should appoint fewer men, chosen from their number, as often as seemed good. To them the power has been granted of meeting in one place wherever they wished and of holding, so to speak, some smaller senate. To these same people most serious matters have often been committed and entrusted so that they might be settled more quickly and in greater calm; the care and charge of the fleet, army, treasury, in short all the functions of peace or war. Whether this is called a 'council' or anything else, it is perhaps new as a word, but ancient in reality, and without it no commonwealth at all can be correctly administered.

But concerning the execution of the king and the revolution[25] amongst us – stop shouting, stop spewing out that venom of your

[23] *sanae et integrae . . . partis.*

[24] M. outlines the provisions of the Act for Constituting a Council of State for the Commonwealth of England, 13 Feb. 1649.

[25] *conversione: conversio* ('a turning round', 'revolution') would not have had quite its modern meaning, but could refer to any – especially cyclical – change: the restoration of Charles II in 1660 was also, without any paradox, a 'revolution'. Cf. *AR*, II, 493, 539; *HB*, V, 1.

bitterness,[26] until I can show in separate chapters 'by what law, by what right, by what judgement' those actions have been taken, and come to close combat. If however you insist upon 'by what right, by what law', I shall say, by that law which God himself and nature sanctified, so that all things which were for the safety of the commonwealth should be considered lawful and just.[27] Such formerly was the reply wise men made to such as you.

You charge us with 'having abolished laws that had been settled throughout so many years'; you don't say whether they were good or bad; nor if you did say would you deserve a hearing, for our laws, Olus,[28] what have they to do with you? I wish they had abolished more of the laws and of the hair-splitting lawyers. They would have consulted the interests more rightly indeed both of the christian cause and of the people. You gnash your teeth because 'the Manii,[29] the sons of the earth, who were hardly noble at home, and hardly known to their own countrymen, should have believed they could do these actions'. You should have remembered what not only the scriptures but also the lyric poet teaches you:

> God has the power to change the places of the lowest
> and the highest and reduce the famous man,
> bringing forth the unseen . . .[30]

Consider this also; out of those who you say are 'hardly noble', some yield to none of your side or kind in nobility; others who are their own ancestors by their hard work and virtue take the road to true nobility, and can be compared with any of the noblest at all: moreover they prefer to be called 'sons of the earth' (at least it is their own) and to work energetically at home than by doing without land and home, and selling smoke as you do, a man of no substance, a knight made of straw, to sustain hunger in a foreign land, at the bidding and in the pay of masters. Believe me, you ought rather to be driven away from this foreign tour of yours back to your relations and family, except that you understand this one thing: you know how to rattle off certain worthless lectures and trash at such a great price among foreigners.

You censure the fact that our magistrates 'receive the dregs of the all the sects'. Why should they not receive them? Those whom it is the

[26] Cf. Cicero, *De amicitia*, xxiii, 87.
[27] A variation on the famous maxim, *salus populi suprema lex esto*. See Cicero, *De legibus*, III, iii, 8.
[28] Cf. Martial, *Epigrams*, VII, 10.
[29] Cf. Persius, *Satires*, VI, 56ff.
[30] Horace, *Odes*, I, 34.

church's right to eject from the company of the faithful, it is not the magistrates' right to drive from the state, provided that they have not sinned against the civil laws.[31] Men first gathered to form a state so that they might lead a life safely and freely without suffering violence or injuries; to form a church so as to live piously and religiously. The former institution has its laws, the latter its teaching, quite separate: hence throughout the whole christian world over so many years, war is sown from the seeds of war – because the magistracy and the church confuse each other's duties. Because of this also we do not endure popery at all. For we realise that it is not so much a religion as a priestly tyranny under the guise of religion, adorned with all the spoils of civil power, which it has seized for itself contrary to the very teaching of Christ.

As for 'Independents' – such people as are imagined by you alone – none have ever been seen amongst us, except only those who, since they do not recognize that there are assemblies and synods above each individual church, feel with you that all of them, as members of the hierarchy, or indeed the very trunk, should be uprooted. Hence the name of Independents has prevailed among the common people.

As for the future, I see you act so that you may stir up against us not only the hatred of all kings and monarchs but also most savage war. Once King Mithridates, although for a different reason, tried to stir up all kings against the Romans, alleging almost the same false accusations: that the Romans had a plan to overthrow all kingdoms, that nothing human or divine stood in their way, that from the beginning they had got nothing that was not won by weapons, that they were robbers, particularly enemies of kingdoms; these things Mithridates wrote to King Arsaces.[32]

But as for you who speak the most childish rhetoric in that schoolroom of yours – what great confidence has raised your self-estimation so far as to imagine that you could stir up any king, even one still a boy, to war by your exhortations and, though you don't wish to be seen at it, 'by sounding the battle signal on your trumpet' – especially from that mouth of yours that is so feeble and offensive that I believe that not even the Homeric mice,[33] if you had been the trumpeter,

[31] A constant belief for M., most comprehensively discussed in *A Treatise of Civil Power*.

[32] Mithridates VI, Eupator Dionysus. The letter is appended to Sallust, *Histories*.

[33] M. refers to the *Batrachomyomachia*, a mock-epic on a battle between the frogs and the mice, formerly attributed to Homer. See *C*, II, 757.

would ever have made war upon tadpoles? So far am I from fearing any war or danger for us, most cowardly man, which you can kindle among foreign kings by that raving and at the same time silly eloquence of yours – you who, in jest surely, lay accusations against us before them that 'we treat kings' heads' like 'balls, play with crowns like hoops, care no more for imperial sceptres than fools' staffs topped with heads'. But meanwhile, most foolish head, you are yourself most worthy of topping a fool's staff – you who think kings and princes are persuaded to go to war by such childish arguments.

Then you cry upon all peoples, who will never hear what you say, I know that well enough. You call even those wicked and barbarous dregs of the Irish to the aid of the king's party – this is one thing which can be taken as an indication of how wicked you are, and how mad, how you outdo almost all mortals in impiety, boldness and frenzy, since you do not hesitate to beg the loyalty and help of an accursed race,[34] from whose impious society, drenched with the blood of so many completely innocent citizens, even the king himself always shrank shuddering – or pretended to shudder. And as for that treachery, that cruelty which he strove with greatest effort to conceal, as far as he could, and to put far from him – you, you most worthless of two-legged creatures, fear neither God nor men in openly taking that up of your own accord. Come then, gird yourself up now to defend the king with the Irish as supporters and allies.

You take care at first (a precaution that is necessary, upon my word) in case anyone should suspect you are going to snatch away all praise for eloquence from Tully perhaps or Demosthenes; and you announce in the preface that 'you don't think it good that you should behave in the manner of an orator'. Truly you are not stupidly wise – what you can't do, you don't think you ought to do. But for you to behave as an orator (who that knows you well enough, ever expected it?) you who neither do nor can bring into the light anything painstaking, anything clear, anything that savours of wisdom, but like a second Crispinus, or that little Greek Tzetzes,[35] don't take trouble over how right it is, provided that you write a lot; nor if you do take trouble, have the power to accomplish it.

[34] For M.'s references to the Irish as murderous and barbaric, see *Church-Government*, I, 798; *O* and *E*, III, 308, 580.

[35] Plotius Crispinus, whose garrulity Horace sneers at, *Satires*, I, i, 20; Johannes Tzetzes (12th century), a captious and copious Byzantine scholar.

'This case', you say, 'will be tried, with the whole world listening and, so to speak, sitting in judgement.' This is so very agreeable to us that we wish to be granted now an opponent, not hot-headed and unskilful such as you are, but wise and intelligent.

When you conclude, you are quite tragic – or rather Ajax the Chastiser himself:[36] 'These men's injustice, impiety, treachery, cruelty, I will cry out to heaven and earth, and the doers themselves I will hand over to posterity convicted, and the accused I will prosecute to the end.' O little flowers of rhetoric! So you, without wit, without talent, a crier and a hair-splitter, born only to pull good writers apart or transcribe them, do you think you can produce anything of your own which will live, you whom a later age, believe me, will drag away and consign to oblivion together with your completely useless writings? Except that this royal defence of yours shall turn out to owe something perhaps to its own reply, so that after being long neglected and lulled to sleep, it may be taken in hand again. And this I would ask the most illustrious States of Holland: that they should let it be at once sent from their treasury – for it is not a treasure – and roam where it wishes. For if I make it plain to all with what idleness, ignorance and falsehood it is stuffed, then the more widely it is spread about, the more stringently in my opinion indeed it is suppressed. Now let us see how he will 'prosecute the accused to the end'.

[36] *Ajax ipse Lorarius*: M. refers ultimately to the deranged Ajax of Sophocles (*Ajax*, 1–133) who, taking some sheep for Agamemnon and his men, slaughtered them with his whip. But in 1646 S. used the same story in his *Grallae*, p. 150, to deride an opponent of Nicholas Vedelius, and then devoted the whole of the first chapter of his *Grallator furens* (1647) to elaborating this. See, however, *C*, II, 729.

CHAPTER I

You empty windbag of a man, Salmasius – you have gained much in pride perhaps and much in arrogance from the fact that the king of Great Britain is indeed defender of the faith and you are the defender of the king. For myself, I will grant the aforesaid titles respectively to the king and to you because of the equal right and desert: since truly the king defended the faith and you defended the king in such a manner that each of you seems rather to have overturned his own cause. This I shall show throughout the whole of the following, and particularly in this first chapter.

You had indeed said on the twelfth page of your preface, that 'so good and just a cause ought not to be adorned with rhetorical colouring; for to tell the story simply, as it happened, is to defend the king'. So since in the whole of this chapter, in which you had promised that narration would be simple, you neither tell the story simply as it happened, nor refrain from adorning it with rhetorical colourings, surely, if we abide by your opinion, the king's cause will be neither good nor just. However, you must beware of assuming for yourself what nobody grants you – the ability to tell any story in oratorical fashion – since in the telling you can sustain neither the parts of an orator nor an historian, nor even that of an advocate but, like some pedlar with his skill in calling his wares around the market place, you kept on rousing great expectations about yourself in your introduction, as if for the next day's advertisement; not so you might at last tell the story you promised, but so you might sell those wretched colourings and pots full of rouge to as many readers as possible.

For when you are 'about to speak about the deed, you feel yourself surrounded and terrorized by so many marvels of novelty that you don't know what to relate first, what next and what last'. This is a simple tale? I will tell you what the matter is. First of all you feel yourself terrorized by the many marvels of your own lies, next you feel that completely empty head of yours not only 'surrounded' but driven round and round by so many trifles and so many absurdities that what ought to be said 'first, what next, what last' at any time, you not only do not know now, but never have known previously. 'Amongst the difficulties which occur in expressing the enormity of so unbelievable a crime, this one thing presents itself as easy to say and it must be repeated again and again', to wit 'that the sun itself never looked upon another more atrocious deed'. The sun has looked upon many things, good schoolmaster, which Bernard did not see.[1] But you may bring up the sun again and again and you will certainly have done in your wisdom something which not our crimes but the chilliness of your defence will most violently demand.

'The origin of kings', you say, 'began with the new sun'. May the gods and goddesses, Damasippus,[2] grant you a solstice in which you may warm yourself since you cannot stir a foot without the sun. May no-one say perhaps that you are a doctor who remains in the shade. But upon my word, you are still in darkness since you do not distinguish a father's right from a king's. And when you have called kings fathers of their country, you believe that you have persuaded people at once by this metaphor: that whatever I would admit about a father, I would straightway grant to be true of a king. A father and a king are very different things. A father has begotten us; but a king has not made us, but rather we the king. Nature gave a father to people, the people themselves gave themselves a king; so people do not exist because of a king, but a king exists because of the people. We endure a father, even a fretful and harsh one; we endure a king also. But we do not also endure a father who is a tyrant. If a father kills his son, he will pay the penalty with his life: why will a king not likewise be subject to the same most just law if he has destroyed the people, that is to say his own sons? Especially so that while a father cannot stop being a father, a king can easily stop being either a father or a king. But if it is 'from the nature of the deed' as you say that judgement

[1] St Bernard (1091–1153), Abbot of Clairvaux, was famed for his wisdom, hence the proverbial saying to which M. refers: *Bonus Bernardus non videt omnia.*

[2] See Horace, *Satires*, II, 3, 16.

should be made, I tell you, you foreigner who are a complete stranger to our affairs, I, an eye-witness and a native, tell you that we 'removed from our midst' a king who was neither 'good' nor 'just' nor 'merciful', nor 'reverent' nor 'dutiful' nor 'peace-making', but one who had been an enemy for almost ten years; not a father of his country, but its destroyer.

'This is often done' you confess, for you do not dare to deny it, 'but not by protestants to a protestant king.'[3] If indeed a king can be called protestant who in a letter written to the pope had called him Most Holy Father,[4] and who was always fairer to papists than to the orthodox. And since he was such, he is not the first even of his own family who has been removed 'from our midst' by protestants. What! Was not his grandmother Mary stripped of her kingdom and compelled to go into exile, and finally beheaded by protestants while not even the Scottish protestants reacted unfavourably?[5] In fact, if I say they supported it, I would not be lying.

But in a time where there is such a scarcity of protestant kings, we have no reason to wonder that nothing of this sort has happened – that one of them was put to death. But just you dare to deny that one may drive out a wicked king or a tyrant from his kingdom or punish him with any punishment according to his deserts (which is in accordance with the opinion of even the highest theologians who have been the very founders of the reformation of the church)!

You grant how very many kings have perished by a bloody death, this one 'by the sword', that 'by poison', another in the filth 'of a prison' or 'by a noose'. But of all ways, it seems to you the most pitiable, and monstrous that a king was brought to trial, 'compelled to plead a capital case, condemned and struck by the axe'. Tell me, you utter fool, whether it is not more humane, more fair, more suitable to the laws of all states to place a defendant for whatever charge on trial, to give him the opportunity to defend himself, to put him, when he is condemned by law, to a death that he has deserved, so that the condemned may be given time to repent or to compose himself, rather than immediately he has been apprehended, without the case having been heard, to slaughter him like a sheep? How rare is the accused

[3] See pp. xix, 33.

[4] The form of address used by Charles in replying to a letter of 20 Apr. 1623 from Pope Gregory XV.

[5] See pp. 23–5, 228.

who, if the choice is given him, would not prefer to be punished in the former way rather than the latter?

So if this method of punishment is considered more moderate when used by a king against his people, why is the same method not believed to be more moderate when used by a people against their king, and even more welcome to the king himself? You preferred the king to be killed secretly and without witnesses, either so that no memory should remain of the wholesome nature of such a good example or so that the consciousness of such a glorious deed should have avoided the light and to have had laws and justice itself by no means in its support.

Then you heighten the matter by saying that it was not in the uproar or the factional strife of the nobles, or in the frenzy of rebels, soldiers or people, not from hatred, nor fear, nor eagerness to rule, nor blind impulse of mind, but by planning and design that they accomplished the crime they had long meditated. O you deserved indeed to turn from being a lawyer into a grammarian! You who, from the accidents of a case, as they say, which in themselves have no force, commence scolding when you have not yet proved whether the deed should be judged either as faulty or praiseworthy. Now see how easily I will attack you: if the deed was fair and fitting, the authors are the more greatly to be praised because they were occupied by no sentiments but acted for the sake of virtue alone. If it was difficult and burdensome, they are the more greatly to be praised because they acted not on blind impulse but by planning and design. However I would rather believe that these things were done by divine instigation, whenever I recall to mind the unexpected eagerness of spirit, the firm agreement with which the whole army, which a great part of the populace had joined, from almost all counties in the kingdom, with one voice,[6] demanded punishment for the king himself as the author of all their ills. Whatever it was, whether you consider the magistracy or the people, no-one ever attempted with a more elevated spirit and a calmer one (which even their adversaries confess) so outstanding a deed that was so worthy even of heroic ages. And by this deed they made famous not only laws and jurisdiction which were restored henceforth to mortals on a fair basis, but justice itself, and rendered

[6] M. is emphatic about the extent of popular support in *DS*, IV, 633–4. Petitioning by the regiments and others first reached a peak in mid-Nov. 1648 with a further wave after the Purge.

her more glorious henceforth and greater than before, after this famous judgement.

Now we have exhausted nearly the third page of this chapter, but that plain story which he promised has nowhere made an appearance. He complains that we inculcate that 'whenever a king rules in a burdensome and hateful manner, he can be with impunity stripped of his kingdom. They have deduced from this doctrine', he says, 'that if they had had a king who was better in a thousand respects, they would not have saved his life.' See the sharpness of the man; for I am eager to know from you how this follows, unless you grant to us that a king who was better in a thousand ways than ours would rule in a burdensome and hateful manner. From here you have lowered yourself to a position where you make the man you defend worse in a thousand ways than those kings who rule in a burdensome and hateful manner; that is the most savage perhaps of all tyrants. Good luck to you kings with so vigorous a defender!

Now he begins his narrative. 'They tortured him with a variety of torments.' Name them. 'They transferred him from prison to prison.' And they might do so freely, since from being a tyrant he had become an enemy captured in war. 'Often changing his guards' – so that they shouldn't change sides themselves. 'Sometimes showing him hope of liberty, sometimes even of restoring him by making an agreement.' See how it was not a deed previously meditated by us, how we had not long seized upon 'opportunities and ways' of rejecting the king. Those things which we demanded from him long before when he was almost the victor – and, unless they were granted, no liberty, no safety were to be hoped for by the people – these same things we requested from him as a captive, humbly, not once but rather three times and more[7] – and just so often we received a denial. When no hope was left of the king, there was passed that noble decree of parliament, that no demands should be sent thenceforth to the king[8] – beginning not from the time when he began to be a tyrant but from the time when he began to be incurable.

Afterwards however some of the number of parliamentarians adopted new plans for themselves, and, having gained a suitable occasion, moved that proposals again be sent to the king:[9] with the same wick-

[7] I.e., at Newcastle (July 1646) and Hampton Court (Aug. 1647), and in the Four Bills sent to the Isle of Wight (Dec. 1647). Cf. *E*, III, 527.

[8] I.e., the Vote of No Addresses. See p. 29.

[9] In May–July 1648.

edness and madness indeed as the Roman senate showed once when, though they were loudly contradicted by Marcus Tullius together with all honest men, they moved that ambassadors be sent to Antony.[10] With the same outcome too, had it not been decided by immortal God to hand *them* over to slavery, but to deliver *us* to liberty. For when the king had granted nothing more than he had done before which might truly incline towards a firm peace settlement, they still decided that they were satisfied by the king. And so the sounder part,[11] when it saw itself and the commonwealth betrayed, implored the loyalty of the army who are most brave and faithful to the commonwealth. In such a situation indeed, this alone occurs to me – something which I would not wish to say: that our troops showed better sense than our parliamentarians[12] and ensured the safety of the commonwealth by their weapons when the others had almost condemned it by their votes.

Then he relates a lengthy story in doleful terms, but so clumsily that he seems to be begging rather than stirring up sorrow. It pains him that 'in such a way as no king ever did, the king should endure capital punishment', though he had often asserted that no king ever endured capital punishment at all. Do you, fool, usually compare method with method when you don't have fact to compare with fact? 'He endured capital punishment', he said, 'like a robber, like a murderer, like a parricide, like a traitor, like a tyrant.' Is this defending the king or is it not really making a much more severe judgement upon the king than that which was made by us? Who has so suddenly seduced you to declare yourself on our side? He complains that 'masked executioners cut off the king's head'. What do you do with this man? He complained earlier 'about parricide committed in the character of a king', now he complains that it was committed in the mask of an executioner![13]

Why should I go through the rest, some things completely false, some trifles 'about fights and kicks' of common soldiers, and how freedom 'to see the corpse was rated at fourpence' – stories which proclaim the ignorance and petty-mindedness of our frigidly boring

[10] M. refers to the senate debates of Jan. 43 BC, discussed by Cicero in the fifth and sixth *Philippics*.
[11] *Pars itaque sanior*.

[12] *patres conscriptos*: the formula *patres* (*et*) *conscripti* referred to either the official list of senators, and hence the senate as whole, or the union of two kinds of senator – patrician and plebeian.

[13] *in persona carnificis*: continuing the word-play on *persona*.

grammarian; certainly they can make no reader a whit sadder. It would have been better, upon my word, for Charles the son to have hired one of that herd of jesters who sing their sad songs to the crowd at a crossroads, rather than to have employed this orator (mournful, will I call him, or most laughable?) to lament the misfortune of his father; one so foolish and tasteless that not even from his tears could the least grain of salt be squeezed.

Now he ceases to relate the story; and what he does next, it is very hard to say. So muddy and irregular is the flow of his writing; now he roars, now he gapes, he uses no method at all in his volubility, and repeats the same thing ten times which could be nothing but base even when said only once. And certainly I don't know whether some unrehearsed trifles spoken by any chatterbox, such as he had chanced to pour out in little verses, standing on one foot, would not have been much more worthy to be written on paper – so very unworthy do I think they are of a serious reply.

I pass over the fact that he praises as 'protector of religion' a king who made war upon the church, so that he might retain the bishops, tyrants and enemies of religion, in the church. But what man could preserve 'the purity of religion', when he himself had been enslaved by those most impure traditions and ceremonies of the bishops? I would wish you to enumerate the errors 'of the sects' in truth, to whom you say 'licence is granted to hold their sacrilegious meetings', which even Holland does not grant: meanwhile no-one is more sacrilegious than you who take upon yourself the worst freedom of all – that of perpetual slander. 'They could not harm the commonwealth more seriously than by removing its master.' Learn, slave, learn, scoundrel, that unless you remove the master, you remove the commonwealth: it is private things, not those of the public, that have a master.[14] 'But they persecute with the greatest injustice the pastors who hate their deed.' In case anyone chances not to know what sort those pastors are, I will tell you briefly. They are the same men who had preached both in their words and their writings that the king should be resisted by warfare; who had not left off cursing unceasingly, as was done to Meroz,[15] all those who had not supplied this war

[14] *privata res est, non publica quae dominum habet*: M. is exploiting the original meaning of *respublica* as 'things of the public' (or, as in English, 'the common weal' and 'commonwealth'), not subject to individual ownership (*dominium*).

[15] See p. 36.

either with weapons or money or forces; who raved on in sacred gatherings that war had been undertaken not against a king, but against a tyrant worse than any Saul or Ahab, even one that out-Nero'd Nero himself. After the removal of the bishops and priests whom they used most violently to abuse under the name of pluralists and absentees, they began by rushing into their most distinguished benefices, some into two, some into three, as quickly as possible: from this there is no-one who does not see how shamefully those deservedly elevated pastors neglect their own flocks.[16] No restraint, no respect for religion could check them, mad with lust and frenzy, until before the church, the worst place for notoriety, they themselves burned with the same infamy which they had shortly before branded upon the priests. Now because their greed is not yet satisfied, because their spirit is made restless from ambition and accustomed to stirring up crowds and hating peace, they do not stop preaching sedition against the magistrates who now exist – something which they had done before against the king – saying now that he was a pious king and indeed cruelly removed; this man whom just now they themselves had handed over, abominably accursed, to be stripped of all royal authority and pursued by a holy war, into the hands of parliament as if by God's will. They now say that the sects indeed have not been rooted out. This is certainly a most absurd thing to ask from magistrates, who have never by any means or method up till now had the power to root out greed and ambition (the two most ruinous heresies in the church) from the rank and division of the pastors themselves.

The sects which they abuse in our country I know are obscure; those which they follow are notorious and far more dangerous to the church of God. The leaders of these were Simon Magus and Diotrephes.[17] Yet we are so far from persecuting these men, utterly wicked though they are, that we indulge them too much, though they are involved in factions and plotting an overthrow every day.

It offends you now, being a Frenchmen and a vagabond, that the English are 'more ferocious than their own hounds',[18] as your doglike

[16] *suos greges quam turpiter negligant pastores isti merito egregii*: M. plays on *grex* (flock) and *egregius* (picked out of the flock, distinguished).

[17] See Acts 8:9 and 3 John 9 for Simon, who 'bewitched' people into thinking he was 'some great one', and Diotrephes, who loved 'preeminence'.

[18] The first of S.'s repeated allusions to the English as 'Molossian' hounds. See Lucretius, *De rerum natura*, V, 1063.

eloquence has it, and have no concern for 'the lawful successor and heir' of the kingdom, none for 'the king's youngest son', none for 'the Queen of Bohemia'.[19] You shall answer yourself, not I. 'When the form of a commonwealth is changed from a monarchy into something else, the succession is not granted among the guardians of the changed government', *Apparat. de primatu.*[20] 'A very small section of one kingdom', you say, 'brought about all these changes throughout three kingdoms' – and they were worthy indeed, if this were true, to have power over the rest, as men do over women. 'These are the men who presumed to change the ancient government of the kingdom into another which belongs to many tyrants' – rightly indeed and successfully so. You cannot blame them without being at once most disgracefully a barbarian and solecist not only in morals, but also in syntax,[21] you shame among grammarians.

'The English will never wash out this stain.' Rather you, though you yourself are the blot and truly the stain of all learned men, yet will never have the power to stain the fame and eternal glory of the English who, with such greatness of mind as has scarcely been heard of in any record, struggled out of and overcame not only armed enemies, but the inwardly hostile – that is, superstitious – opinions of the mob, and created for themselves in general the title of Deliverers thereafter amongst all peoples, after daring, as a people, a deed which amongst other nations is thought to spring only from heroic virtue.

What 'the protestants and ancient christians' did or would have done at this juncture, I will tell you later when I discuss the case with you in its rightful place, so as not to labour under your fault of outdoing in loquacity all idlers and Battuses.[22] You ask how you will reply 'to the Jesuits' in our cause. Mind your own business, deserter; be ashamed of your own deeds, since the church is ashamed of you, who after having recently so boastfully and ferociously attacked the supremacy of the pope and the bishops, have now become the sycophant of the bishops. You confess that 'some protestants', whom you do not name (I however will name them, since you say they 'are

[19] I.e., Elizabeth, daughter of James I, who married Frederick V, the Elector Palatine in 1613.

[20] S., *De primatu*, p. 127.

[21] S., *DR*, p. 23, had written 'regimen regni antiquum in alium qui . . .' where neuter pronouns fail to agree with masculine nouns.

[22] See Ovid, *Metamorphoses*, II, 688 for the story of Battus, turned into stone for failing to keep secret Mercury's theft of Apollo's cattle.

far worse than the Jesuits'; Luther for certain, Zwingli, Calvin, Bucer, Paraeus, along with many others) have asserted that a tyrant 'must be removed'. 'But the question of who is a tyrant should be referred to the judgement of the wise and learned. But who indeed were these men? Were they wise or learned or renowned for virtue or notable for their nobility?' I entreat that a people who feel the yoke of slavery heavy on their necks, may be so wise, so learned and so noble that they know what should be done to their tyrant, even if they do not send to canvass either foreigners or grammarians. But not only the parliaments of England and Scotland have declared in the most expressive words and actions, but almost all the people of both realms have agreed that this man was a tyrant, until because of the tricks and deceits of the bishops they divided afterwards into two factions. What if it pleases God that, just as those who are made sharers in the light of the gospel, so those who fulfil his decrees against the most powerful kings of this world, are not the many wise, or learned or powerful or noble men? So that by means of those who are not, he may destroy those who are; so that no flesh may boast in his presence.[23]

And who are you to scold at this? A learned man? You who seem to have worn out the pages of gleanings, lexicons and glossaries right up to old age, rather than to have read through good authors with judgement or benefit, so that you go on about nothing except manuscripts and variant readings and dislocated and faulty passages; you show you have drained off not even a tiny drop of substantial learning. Are you a wise man? You who are accustomed to dispute about the most detailed details and to wage a pitiful war; who insult now astronomers, now doctors, who should be trusted in the exercise of their own skill, when you yourself are unskilled in and ignorant of these professions; who, if anyone should try to forestall you in the trivial glory of having restored a single word or letter in any copy, would lay him under prohibition of fire and water, if you could. And yet you are angry and snarl because everyone calls you a grammarian. You call Dr Hammond, who was recently the most principally beloved chaplain of this king, in some trivial book a 'good-for-nothing' because he had called you a grammarian.[24] I believe you would have hurled this same insult

[23] Cf. 1 Cor. 1:26–9.

[24] *in libro quodam nugatorio nebulonem appellas, quod is te Grammaticum appellavisset*: Henry Hammond had called S. 'that *learned Grammarian*' in *Of the power of the keyes: or, of binding and loosing* (London, 1647), pp. 21ff. S. replied by calling Hammond *nebulo* in

at the king himself and withdrawn this whole defence, if you had heard that he approved of his chaplain's judgement about you.

Now see how I, one of those Englishmen whom you often dare to call 'frenzied, unlearned, unknown and wicked', scorn and mock you. For it would be most unworthy of them if the very English nation should take any public notice of you, you worm. Although you twist and turn upwards, downwards or in every direction, you are nothing but a grammarian. Rather as if you had proclaimed to some god or other a wish more stupid than that of Midas himself;[25] whatever you touch, except when you commit grammatical errors, is grammar. Whoever 'from those dregs of the common people' whom you harass (for truly I will not disgrace those aristocrats of ours to whose wisdom, virtue and nobility their celebrated deeds bear enough witness, by being willing to compare you to them or them to you) – whoever, I say, out of those dregs of the common people has persuaded himself of only just this: that he was born not for the benefit of kings, but for God and his country, should be judged much more learned indeed than you, much wiser, much more honest and useful for every life. For he is learned without letters, you are lettered without learning – you who understand so many languages, run through so many volumes, write so many things, and yet are still a sheep.

Specimen confutationis animadversionum Desiderii Heraldi (Leyden, 1648), p. 19. See L. Miller, 'Milton, Salmasius and Hammond: the history of an insult', *Renaissance & Reformation*, IX (1973), pp. 108–15.

[25] Midas was a legendary Phrygian king; Dionysus granted him his wish that all he touched might turn to gold.

CHAPTER II

The argument that Salmasius had said was 'indisputable', when concluding the above chapter, was that 'a thing actually is as it is believed to be, when all men unanimously have the same opinion about it'. His assertion of this, however, was utterly false when referring to 'a matter of fact'. But I now, as I am about to discuss the right of kings, will be able to twist it round with full truth upon himself.

For he defines a king as 'one who has supreme power over his kingdom, responsible to no-one but God, who is allowed to do whatever he pleases, who is free from the restrictions of the laws' (if indeed something could be said to be defined when it is made infinite on the earth). And I will prove completely the opposite, not using my own testimonies and reasonings alone, but his own also: that no race or people who are indeed of any account (for it is not necessary to go into all the barbarous areas), that no race, I say, ever granted laws or power of this kind to their king 'that he should be free from the restrictions of the laws, that he should be allowed to do what he pleases, that he should judge all, but be judged by none'.

And I certainly do not think that anyone of any race (except for Salmasius alone) ever displayed such a servile spirit as to maintain that all the inhuman crimes of tyrants were the rights of kings. The majority of those amongst us who most strongly supported the king always abhorred this disgraceful belief. Rather it is easy to detect that even Salmasius himself, before he had been corrupted by bribery felt quite otherwise about these matters, as is shown by other previous writings. So servile in nature and spirit are these words that they do not seem to have been written by a free man in a free state – still less in that most celebrated commonwealth and most famous academy of Holland,[1] but in some workhouse or slave market auction block.

For if what pleases a king is allowed by the right of kings (which that utterly hideous Antoninus Caracalla, though persuaded by Julia his step-mother through incest,[2] did not at once dare to believe) there really is no-one, nor ever was, who ought to be called a tyrant. For even though he violated all divine and human rights, yet nevertheless, as a king, he will be guiltless because of the right of kings. For what sin has that most just of men committed? He has used his right against his subjects. A king can commit against his subjects no wrong so horrible, so cruel, and so mad that anyone can complain or protest that it exceeds the limits of the right of kings.

Do you judge that 'the right of kings has its origin in the right of nations, or even rather that of nature', you beast? For why shall I call you a man when you are so unfair and inhumane to all the race of men, and when you try so hard to degrade and debase all the human race who most resemble God, by asserting that those savage and ungentle masters which at one time the fanaticism, at another the crime or the ignorance of certain people, or in the last place treachery has imposed upon races, have been provided and imposed by mother nature who is most gentle? Having rendered them now much more fierce by this impious doctrine, you not only set them on to tread upon all mortals, and after this trample them in a more wretched fashion, but strive by the right of nature, by the right of kings, even by the very laws of the people, to arm them against the people. Nothing can be at once more stupid and more wicked than this. You are worthy indeed who, contrary to Dionysius of old,[3] have changed yourself from a grammarian into a tyrant. Not that by this you may be granted that royal freedom of doing badly to someone else, but that other right – of dying badly. In this way alone, like the celebrated Tiberius shut up on Capri,[4] destroyed by your own hand, you may every day feel that you are dying.

[1] I.e., the university of Leyden. See *CB*, I, 380.

[2] Marcus Aurelius Antoninus, known as Caracalla, was emperor from 211 till his assassination in 217. For this apocryphal anecdote see Spartianus, 'Vita Caracalli', *Historia Augusta*, X, 2.

[3] Dionysius I, tyrant of Syracuse (*c.* 430–367 BC) noted for his misuse of words and his literary pretensions. Cf. M.'s allusions in 'Of that sort of Dramatic Poem which is called Tragedy', prefixed to *Samson Agonistes*, and *AR*, II, 495.

[4] Tiberius, Roman emperor, 14–37. Retired to Capri, never to return to Rome again, in 26. Cf. Satan's account of Tiberius' retirement in *Paradise Regained*, IV, 90–97.

But let us examine a little more exactly just what is that right of kings. 'So the whole East' you say 'has decided, so the West.' I shall not repeat to you what Aristotle and Marcus Cicero, most sagacious authors if any others are, have written – the former in the *Politics*, the latter in his speech *De provinciis* – that the peoples of Asia easily endure servitude, but that the Jews and Syrians have been born to it.[5] I confess that only a few people want their freedom or are able to make use of it, a few who are wise indeed and great souled. By far the greatest portion prefers fair masters – masters indeed, but fair ones. As for enduring unjust and intolerable ones, God has never been so hostile to the whole human race, nor has any people ever been so wholly abandoned by all hope and counsel that they of their own accord imposed this necessity and the harshest law of all over themselves and their children.

You bring forward first 'the words of the king in Ecclesiastes famous for his wisdom'.[6] And so we too call forth the law of God. The matter of the king we will consider later, as from this we shall better understand his opinion. Let God himself be heard, Deut. 17: 'when you have come into the land, which the Lord God gives to you, and will say, I will set over me a king just like all the races which are around me'[7] – a passage which I would wish all people to notice again and again, as here, at the testimony of God himself, the decision has always lain in the power of all peoples and nations to employ the form of commonwealth which they choose, or to change this to another form. God clearly says this concerning the Hebrews; concerning other nations he does not deny it. God has decided then that the form of a commonwealth is more perfect than that of a monarchy as human conditions go, and of greater benefit to his own people: since he himself set up this form of government. He granted a monarchy only later at their request and then not willingly. But if they clearly wanted a king, so God might show that he left it freely to the people whether the commonwealth was administered by one person or more – as long as it was managed justly – he set up laws for the future king also, in which he was warned against 'increasing his number of horses, wives or riches' so that he might understand that he had himself no power over others, since he could decide nothing about himself outside the law. And so he was ordered to write out in full 'all the precepts of that

[5] See p. 11. [6] I.e., Solomon. [7] Deut. 17:14.

law' also in his own hand, and when they were written out 'to observe them so that his mind should not be exalted beyond his brothers'. From this it is apparent that the king as well as the people was bound by these laws.

The writings of Josephus are much in this vein. He was an apt interpreter of the laws of his race, most excellently versed in his own nation's form of government, and preferable to a thousand other swindling rabbis, *Antiquitat.* Bk. 4: 'Αριστοκρατία μὲν οὖν κράτιστον, etc. 'An aristocracy', he says, 'is the best form of government; and do not seek another form of government, for it is enough to have God set over you. But if such a great lust for a king has seized you, let him set more store by the laws and God than his own wisdom; and let him be obstructed if he is eager to become more powerful than is advantageous to your state'.[8] This and more did Josephus write upon this passage in Deuteronomy.

Another authority is Philo Judaeus, a weighty author, a contemporary of Josephus, and most learned in the law of Moses, upon the whole of which he wrote with an extensive commentary. When he interprets this chapter of the law in his book concerning the creation of the prince,[9] he releases the king from the laws upon no other terms than those upon which any enemy can be said to be released from the restrictions of the laws. τοὺς ἐπὶ λύμῃ καὶ ζημίᾳ τῶν ὑπηκόων, etc. 'Those who', he says, 'acquire great power for themselves to the destruction and ruin of the people should not be called kings but enemies; as they do things which enemies do who should not be conciliated by any peace. For those who do harm under the guise of governing are worse than open enemies. For it is easy to drive off the latter, but the wickedness of the former is not easy to discover.'

So when they are discovered, what stands in the way of their being treated as enemies? Thus in the second book of the *Allegories of the Law* he says 'a king and a tyrant are opposites'; and then, 'a king not only commands, but also obeys'.[10]

These points are true, someone will say. A king ought indeed to observe the laws most carefully; but if he does wrong, by what law should he be punished? By the same law, I say, as the rest; for I find

[8] Josephus, *Jewish Antiquities*, IV, 223. M.'s opposition between Josephus and the rabbis is a false one since Josephus incorporates rabbinical materials in his work.

[9] Philo Judaeus, *De specialibus legibus*, IV, 185.

[10] Philo Judaeus, *Legum allegoria*, III (not II), 79–80.

no exceptions. There is no written law about the punishment of priests nor even about that of the lowest magistrates. All of them, since no law has been written about their punishment, could certainly with equal right and reason claim impunity for all their crimes; yet none of them has ever claimed this, nor do I think anyone would be granted it on these grounds.

So far we have learned from the actual law of God that a king ought to obey the laws; and not exalt himself above the rest who are also his brothers. Now let us see whether Ecclesiastes offers any other advice, Ch. 8, v. 1 etc. 'Observe the command of the king; or at least because of the oath of God, do not go from his sight in disquiet; do not persist in an evil cause, for he will do whatever he wishes. Where the word of the king is, there is the power and who may say to him "What are you doing?"' It is well enough known that in this place Ecclesiastes is giving precepts, not to the sanhedrin nor to the senate, but to each private citizen.[11] He orders him to observe the commands of the king, at least because of the oath of God; but who swears to obey a king unless the king in turn has sworn to obey the laws of God and of his native land? So the Reubenites and Gadites promised their obedience to Joshua, Josh. 1: 'as we were obedient to the word of Moses, so will we be to you, so long as God is with you, as he was with Moses'.[12] You see their express condition. Hear Ecclesiastes himself elsewhere, Ch. 9: 'the soft words of wise men ought rather to be heeded than the shouting of one who rules amongst fools'. What further advice does he give? 'Do not persist in an evil cause, for he will do whatever he wishes'; he will certainly do it against evil men who persist in an evil cause, as he is armed with the authority of the laws; for he can act with leniency or severity, as he wishes. Nothing here sounds tyrannical, nothing which a good man may fear. 'Where the word of a king is, there is the power; and who may say to him "What are you doing?"'[13] And yet we read of a man who said to a king not only 'What have you done?' but even 'You have done something foolish', 1 Sam. 13.[14] But Samuel is out of the ordinary. I reply to you with your own statement made below, p. 49: you say, 'What was out of the ordinary in Saul or David?' In the same way I say, what in Samuel? He was a prophet: and so are those today who act by his example; for they act by the will of

[11] *privato*: M. almost invariably uses the term *privatus* to refer to the private citizen or person in contradistinction to the magistrate.

[12] Joshua 1:17.

[13] Eccles. 9:17, 8:3–4.

[14] 1 Sam. 13:13.

God, either 'expressed' or 'innate', which even you yourself grant below, p. 50.

So Ecclesiastes wisely in this passage advises private citizens not to contend with the king: for usually a struggle even with a rich man, with anyone powerful, is harmful. So what then? Shall the aristocracy, shall all the other magistrates, shall the whole people, whenever the king is pleased to rave, not even dare to gape? Shall they not stand in the way of a stupid, wicked, raging man who is contriving ruin for all good men, shall they not go to meet him lest he first destroy all things human and divine, lest he riot with plunderings and burnings and slaughters throughout all the lands of the kingdom, being so 'free from the restrictions of the laws that he may do what he pleases'? O knight from the slave auctions of Cappadocia![15] Every free nation (if you will ever after this dare to set foot in a free nation) ought to cast you out to the ends of the earth like a monstrosity needing to be sent away, or given over as a candidate for slavery to the mill, under the solemn pledge that if they should release you from there, they should grind instead of you themselves beneath some tyrant,[16] and him a complete fool. For what could be said or borrowed from others so savage or ridiculous which does not apply to you?

But proceed: 'The Israelites, when asking God for a king, said they wished to be governed by him under the same right as all the other nations which employed this method of government. But the kings of the east used to rule with supreme right and unrestricted power, as Virgil testifies:

> Not so do Egypt and great Lydia,
> The peoples of Parthia and the Median Hydaspes
> Observe a king.'[17]

Firstly what does it matter to us what kind of king the Israelites wanted for themselves? Especially since God was angry, not only because they wanted a king on the pattern of the nations and not his own law, but clearly because they desired a king at all? Then, it is not credible that they asked for an unjust king or one freed from the restriction of the laws, since they could not bear Samuel's sons when they were restricted by laws, and sought refuge in a king only out of

[15] Cf. Martial, *Epigrams*, X, 76, 5.
[16] Cf. Terence, *Andria*, 199.
[17] S., *DR*, pp. 29–30; Virgil, *Georgics*, IV, 210–12.

their greed. Finally what you quote from Virgil does not prove that the kings of the east rule 'with absolute power'. For those bees in Virgil, who are more observant of their kings than even the Egyptians and the Medes, yet by the testimony of the same poet:

Spend their time under mighty laws[18]

therefore not beneath kings who are freed from the restrictions of all law. But see how little ill-will I have for you. Though most people consider you are a worthless wretch, I will show that you have only put on the borrowed mask of a worthless scoundrel. In your *Apparatus ad primatum Papae* you say that certain learned men of the Council of Trent[19] made use of the example of bees to prove the pope's supremacy. From them you, with equal wickedness, have taken this borrowing. And so the reply that you made to them when you were honest, now that you have become a worthless wretch, you will make to yourself and with your own hand drag off the mask of the scoundrel. 'There is a commonwealth of bees and thus do natural philosophers term it: they have a king but a harmless one. He is a leader rather than a tyrant, he does not beat, nor nip, nor kill his subject bees.'[20] So it is no wonder if they respect him so. Upon my word, it was bad luck when you made contact with those bees; for although they may be Tri-dentine,[21] they show you to be a drone.

However Aristotle, a most careful writer about politics, affirms that the kind of monarchy in Asia, which he also calls barbaric, was κατὰ νόμον, that is, according to law, *Pol.* 3.[22] Moreover, although he enumerates five kinds of monarchy and writes that four were government according to the law and by the vote of the people, yet he says they were tyrannical because so much power had been given to them, although it was by the will of the people. But the Spartan kingdom seems most properly to be a kingdom because all power was not in the hands of a king. The fifth sort, which he calls παμβασιλείαν,[23] is that to which alone he attributes what you write is the right of all kings – that they should rule as they please: where in the world or at what

[18] Virgil, *Georgics*, IV, 154.

[19] The Council of Trent met to reform the church, 1545–63.

[20] S., *De primatu*, p. 211.

[21] *Tridentinae*: M. is punning on Tridentine as 'of Trent' and 'three-toothed'. For the less pointed usage, 'Trentine', see *E*, III, 511.

[22] Aristotle, *Politics*, III, 14 (1285a).

[23] παμβασιλεία: defined by Aristotle (1285b) as a form of kingly rule where one man controls a city or nation in the manner of a household.

time it ever held good, he does not say, nor does he seem to have made mention of it for any other reason than to show it is silly, unjust and most greatly tyrannical.

You say that Samuel, when he was discouraging them from electing a king, set forth 'to them the right of kings'.[24] Where did he derive it from – from the law of God? But that law has shown, as we have seen, a very different right of kings. Or was it from God himself speaking through Samuel? But he disapproved of it, blamed it, considered it a fault: so the prophet set forth not a right of kings granted by God, but a most vicious manner of ruling, seized by the pride of kings and their lust for power. It was not what kings ought to do, but what they wanted to do; for he showed the people the manner of a king, just as previously he had shown the manner of priests, the sons of Eli, in the same word (which you, p. 33, by a solecism even in Hebrew, call משפת):[25] Ch. 2, v. 13, 'The manner of those priests with the people was this'. Clearly wicked, hateful and tyrannical: and so that manner was by no means a right, but a wrong.

So too the ancient fathers have explained this passage. One will serve me as the image of many, Sulpicius Severus, a contemporary of Jerome and dear to him, and, in the opinion of Augustine, a man of great learning and wisdom. He in his sacred history says that Samuel is setting forth to the people the despotism of kings and pride of power.[26] Certainly the right of kings is not despotism and pride; but, on the testimony of Sallust, the right and power of kings which were granted for the preservation of freedom and the advancement of the commonwealth, turn into pride and despotism.[27] The same interpretation of this passage is given by all orthodox theologians, lawyers and most rabbis, as you could have learned from Sichardus.[28] For none of

[24] *jus illis regium*: S., *DR*, p. 33, bases his account of the *ius* (right) of kings on the more extreme account of kingship in 1 Sam. 8:11–18.

[25] *Hebraico etiam soloecismo* משפת: the last character (from the right) should be *tet* and not *tav*. In either case the word can be transliterated as *mishpat*. M.'s discussion – maintaining, against S., that *mishpat* here should be taken to mean manner or custom (as in 1 Sam. 2:13) and not right – is based on Wilhelm Schickard, *Mishpat ha-Melekh, Jus Regium Hebraeorum e Tenebris Rabbinicis Erutum & Luci Donatum* (Strasburg, 1625), pp. 64–5: '. . . voculam משפט (*vers.* 11.) non judicium sed *consuetudinem* interpretantur, quo sane significatu saepius etiam reperiri constat, ut 1. Sam. 2. 13.'

[26] Sulpicius Severus, *Historia sacra* (Leyden, 1635), p. 56 (I, 32): see M., *CB*, I, 440.

[27] Sallust, *Bellum Jugurthinum*, XXXI, 26.

[28] See Schickard, *Jus Regium*, pp. 54–66 (Theorem VII: 'Neque enim legibus omnino solutus erat'), esp. p. 65. Cf. *CB*, I, 460.

the rabbis has said that the absolute right of kings is dealt with in this passage. You yourself later on, Ch. 5, p. 106, complain that 'not only Clement of Alexandria[29] but all are mistaken here' and you alone of all of them have hit the nail on the head. Now it is truly either some impudence or stupidity, in opposition to all, especially the orthodox, to turn the manners of kings, completely condemned by God himself, into the right of kings; and to defend them under the honourable pretext of right, though you still confess that that right too often exists in plundering, injuries, violence and insults.

Or was anyone ever so much *sui juris* that he might seize, drive, overthrow and confuse all things? Or did the Latin writers, as you affirm, 'ever say that these things were done by anyone by virtue of his own right'? In Sallust, Gaius Memmius, a tribune of the people, had said, when attacking the pride and unpunished crimes of the nobility: 'to do whatever you like without fear of punishment, that is to be a king'.[30] This pleased you, and at once you count it as profit, vainly indeed if you had been a little awake. Did he here assert the right of kings? Or did he not rather rebuke the listlessness of the people, for allowing the nobles to domineer over them without fear of punishment, and for now, once again, enduring those customs of kings which, by exercising their own right, their ancestors had driven together with the king himself from their territory? You ought to have consulted Marcus Tullius at least. He would have taught you to interpret Sallust, and Samuel too, more correctly. He in his oration *Pro Rabirio* says 'none of us is ignorant of the customary ways of kings; these are the commands of kings; mark and obey my words'. And he quotes other passages of this kind from the poets in the same place which call it not the right but the customary way of kings, and he says we ought to read and examine these, not 'only to gain pleasure, but also to learn to look out for them and escape'.[31] You see how badly Sallust has punished you, when you thought you had brought him, who is most hostile to tyrants, forward as a supporter of your right of tyrants. Believe me, the right of kings seems to be tottering and even hastening its own downfall when, like a sinking man, it clutches like this at the weakest straws there are, and tries to hold itself up by those

[29] St Clement of Alexandria (*c.* 150 to *c.* 211–16), expounded the superiority of Christian to Greek and pagan philosophy.
[30] Sallust, *Bellum Catilinae*, VI, 7.
[31] Cicero, *Pro C. Rabirio Postumo*, XI, 29.

witnesses and examples which drive on more violently to destruction one who would sink later perhaps in some other way.

'The supreme right', you say, 'is that of causing the supreme harm.[32] This holds good, most particularly in the case of kings, who, when they employ their supreme right, perform those actions of which Samuel says the right of kings consists.' A pitiful right which, now that you are brought to extremities, you cannot further defend except by calling it supreme harm! It is called supreme right when someone chases after legal formulas, lingers almost upon the individual letters of the law, and does not preserve its justice or interprets a written law too artfully and maliciously, from which Cicero says arose that well-known proverb. But since it is certain that all right flows from the fountain of justice, it inevitably follows that you are wicked when you say it is the right of a king 'for a king to be unjust, unfair, violent and a robber and such as they customarily were' who were worst, and this is what 'the prophet recommended to the people'. For what right, whether extreme or slack, written or not written, can exist for the purpose of committing crimes?

In case it comes into your mind to grant this about others but deny it about a king, I have someone I may set against you, and I think a king who freely owns that the kind of right of kings you are talking about is hateful both to himself and God: Ps. 94, 'Shall the throne of hardships be linked with you, of one who frames trouble by law?'[33] Do not therefore do God this most frightful injury, as to say that he taught that the wickednesses and evil deeds of kings are the right of kings, since he teaches that it is for this very reason that he abominates association with wicked kings – that they are accustomed to create all annoyance and troubles for their people under the guise of the right of kings. Do not falsely accuse the prophet of God: while you think you have him in this passage as an instructor of the right of kings, you do not present us with the true Samuel but, like the famous witch,[34] you call forth an empty ghost – although I believe that even that Samuel from hell would not have been such a liar as not to have said that what you called the right of kings was rather tyrannical lack of self-restraint.

We read of right granted to crime and you say that 'it was the less

[32] For this maxim, see Cicero, *De officiis*, I, X, 33.

[33] Ps. 94:20.

[34] I.e., the Witch of Endor (1 Sam. 28:7–25) who brought up Samuel from the dead to advise Saul.

good kings that used to employ the right of freedom[35] they were granted'. But I have proved that this right was introduced by you for the destruction of the human race and was not granted by God. It remains to show that it comes from the devil, which will appear more clearly below. You say 'this freedom grants the power, if you wish' and your excuse is that you have Cicero as the authority on this right. I never regret quoting your evidence; for you yourself usually destroy your case by means of your own witnesses. So hear the words of Cicero in 4. *Philip.*: 'What reason for waging war is more just than to drive off slavery? In this situation, even though the master is not troublesome, yet it is most wretched that he has the power to be so if he wants.'[36] Has the power by force, that means; for if Cicero were speaking about a right he would be contradicting himself, and from a just reason for war be making an unjust one. So what you describe is not a right of kings but the harmfulness, force and violence of kings.

You pass from the king's freedom to that of the private citizen: 'a private citizen may lie and be ungrateful'. And so may kings; what do you achieve by this? May kings therefore plunder, murder and rape with impunity? What difference does it make to the gravity of the injury whether a king or robber or enemy from some other place murders the people, plunders and enslaves them? By the same right certainly, we ought both to drive the one and the other out, as the enemy and plague of human society, and punish them. Or rather with more justice, the king, because he has been exalted by so many favours and honours from us and is betraying the public safety entrusted to him under oath.

You grant at last that 'laws were granted by Moses, according to which that king, to be chosen at some time or other, ought to rule, although they are different from that right which Samuel put forward'. This doubly conflicts with your previous assertion; for whereas you had put the king in a position that was totally unrestricted by laws, now you say he is restricted. Then you set up the systems of right of Moses and Samuel as contradictory to each other, which is silly.

'But', says the prophet,[37] 'you will be slaves to the king.' Supposing that I did not deny that they were slaves, yet they were not slaves by royal right, but perhaps by the usurpation and injustice of a very great

[35] *licentiae jure*: S., *DR*, p. 31.

[36] Cicero, *Philippics*, VIII (not IV), iv, 12. See p. 33.

[37] 1 Sam. 8:17.

number of kings. For the prophet had forewarned them that that stubborn request would become their punishment, not by the right of kings but because of their own deserts. But truly if a king may do what he pleases because he is unrestricted by laws, certainly a king will be far more than a master, and his people lower than the lowest of all slaves. For a slave, even when foreign-born, had the law of God as his protector against a harmful master. A whole people, a free nation indeed, shall have no protector on earth and no law, in which they may have refuge when harmed, distressed and plundered; they were liberated from slavery under Egyptian kings only so that they might be handed over to one of their own brothers to be crushed by a harsher slavery if he should please. Since this is in agreement neither with God's law nor reason, no-one can doubt that the prophet expounded the ways, not the right, of kings, nor exactly the ways of all kings, but of the majority.

You come down to the rabbis, and you bring forward two with the same bad luck as before: for that chapter about a king in which Rabbi Joses repeatedly said the right of kings was contained, is obviously the one in Deuteronomy,[38] not Samuel. For Rabbi Judah has said very rightly indeed, and contrary to your statement, that the one in Samuel is concerned only so far as to inspire fear in the people.[39] For it is pernicious for something to be named and taught as a right which is clearly an injustice, unless it perhaps be called a right improperly. With this also is concerned verse 18: 'and you will cry out on that day because of your king, but the Lord will not heed you'; certainly that punishment was awaiting the obstinate who wished that a king be given to them, contrary to the will of God.

And yet these words do not prevent them from being able to try prayers or anything else. For if the people might cry to God against the king, they might without doubt also enter upon every other honourable means of freeing themselves from the tyrant. For who, when he is oppressed by some evil, calls to God in such a way as to neglect everything else which is his duty, being fallen only to idle prayers?

[38] It is S., *DR*, p. 33, who raises – though only to dismiss – the possibility that R. Joses is here referring to the less extreme account of kingship in Deut. 17, and M. merely seizes on his suggestion.

[39] M. throws S.'s own quotation from R. Judah (*DR*, p. 33: also Schickard, *Jus Regium*, p. 64) back at him.

But however it is, what has this to do with the right of kings, what to do with our right? We never asked for a king against the will of God, nor received one as his personal gift, but exercising the right of nations, without God's command or prohibition, we set one up according to our laws. This being the case, I do not see why it should not be attributed to our praise and virtue to have cast off our king, since it was counted as a crime for the Israelites to have asked for one. This the event itself also has confirmed; for, when we had a king, we prayed against him – and at last God heeded us and freed us; but those who, when they did not have a king, urgently requested one from God, he commanded to be slaves, until on returning from Babylon they reverted to their old form of government.

Then you open your Talmud school, but this also is tried out with bad luck. For in your wish to show that a king should not be judged, you exhibit from the codex of the sanhedrin 'that the king neither is judged nor judges'.[40] But this conflicts with the request of that people, who kept asking for a king so he might act as a judge: you are eager to patch this up – but in vain – by saying it ought to be understood as concerning the kings that reigned after the captivity in Babylon. But look, here you have Maimonides, who 'sets up this difference between the kings of Israel and of Judah: for David's posterity judge and are judged'.[41] He concedes neither function to the Israelites. You get in your own way, for you quarrel with yourself or with your rabbis; you plead my cause. This, you say, 'didn't apply to the first kings' because it is said, verse 17, 'You will be his slaves'; by customary practice indeed, not by right; or, if by right, as a punishment for asking for a king, although they did not suffer it perhaps beneath this or that individual king, but under the majority – which does not concern us. But you don't need an opponent, you are always such an opponent to yourself. For you relate, in support of my side, how first Aristobulus, and afterwards Jannaeus, surnamed Alexander,[42] received that right of kings not from the sanhedrin, the guardian and intepreter of right, but gradually took it upon themselves and usurped it, though the senate struggled against them. To please them, that pretty story of the chief men of the sanhedrin being 'struck lifeless by Gabriel' was devised, and this splendid right, upon which you seem chiefly to rely

[40] Tractate Sanhedrin 19a: M. quotes from S., *DR*, p. 34.
[41] For Maimonides, M. quotes S., *DR*, p. 35.
[42] Rulers of Judaea: see pp. 138–9.

(that is, that 'a king is not to be judged') you confess[43] has been raised up out of that tale worse than an old woman's, namely rabbinical.

But that the kings of the Hebrews 'could be judged and even be condemned to a beating'[44] Sichardus informs us at length from the books of the rabbis. It is to him that you owe all these points, and yet you do not blush to cry out against him. Moreover we read that Saul himself submitted to judgement according to lot, even to the death, together with his son Jonathan, and obeyed his own edict himself.[45] Uzziah also, when he was thrown out of the temple by the priests under a judgement of leprosy, just as if he was one of the common people, submitted and ceased to hold the kingship.[46] What if he had refused to leave the temple, to relinquish the magistracy and live separately, and had asserted that right of kings unrestricted by the law? Do you think the Jews and the priests would have suffered their temple to be defiled, their laws violated and the whole people endangered by infection? So shall the laws have power against a king afflicted by leprosy and have none against a tyrant? Who is so mad or foolish as to think that, while care has been taken and provision made under the laws so a diseased king should not harm the people by contagion, if a wicked, unjust, cruel king should plunder, torture, and kill the people, and overturn the state from its foundation, no remedy has been devised by the laws for these far graver ills?

But 'no example can be brought forward of any king who has been called into court and endured the judgement of death.' But Sichardus answers that most sensibly by saying that it is just as if someone should argue in this manner: the emperor has never been summoned before an elector; so if the Elector Palatine should appoint a day for the emperor's appearance, the emperor is not bound to respond in court, although the Golden Bull instructs that Charles IV submitted himself and his successors to this judicial examination.[47]

Why do we wonder if, given the corrupt state of the people, kings have been so far indulged, when so many private citizens, either because of their wealth or favouritism, gain impunity even for most serious crimes? And that ἀνυπεύθυνον, that is, 'to be dependent on

[43] M. exploits S.'s own admission, *DR*, p. 36: 'sed hae nugae sunt & fabulae Rabbinicae'.

[44] *judicari posse, atque etiam ad verbera damnari*: see Schickard, *Jus Regium*, p. 56: 'sed ajunt ordinario judicio Reges ob transgressionem leges potuisse conveniri, & ad verbera damnari . . . consensu totius antiquitatis Ebraeae confirmatum fuit.'

[45] 1 Sam. 14:37–45.

[46] 2 Kings 15:5.

[47] Schickard, *Jus Regium*, pp. 62–3. The Golden Bull was issued at the Diet of Metz, Dec. 1356.

nobody, to be accountable to no mortal', which you say is most proper to royal majesty, Aristotle, *Pol.* 4, ch. 10, asserts is quite tyrannical and no way to be tolerated in a free nation.[48] But you produce Antony, a most terrible tyrant, destroyer of the Roman republic (a suitable authority indeed!) as a proof that it is not just to demand from a king an account of his actions: and yet when setting out against the Parthians, Antony summoned to him Herod, who was accused of murder, to plead his case. And it is believed that he would have punished even a king, had not the king bribed him with gold.[49] So Antony's assertion of royal power and your 'royal defence' have flowed forth from the same spring.

But not without reason you say, 'for kings hold their kingship not from another but have received it and derive it from God alone'. Say which ones if you please? For I deny that there ever existed kings of this kind. For the first king, Saul, if the people had not wanted a king, even despite the opposition of God, would never have been king; and although he was proclaimed king at Mizpah, yet he lived almost as a private citizen, following the herd of his father until he was created king a second time by the people at Gilgal.[50] What of David? Although he was anointed by God, was he not anointed again by the tribe of Judah in Hebron, then by all the Jews, but only after an agreement was made beforehand? 2 Sam. 5, 1 Chron. 11.[51] But an agreement binds kings, and confines them within defined limits. Solomon sat, you say, 'on the throne of the Lord, and pleased all men', 1 Par. 29.[52] So it was something even to have pleased the people! Jehoiada made Jehoash king but he struck up an agreement at the same time between the king and people, 2 Kings 11.[53] I admit that those kings, as well as the rest of David's descendants were established both by God and by the people. All the rest, anywhere in the world, I assert, have been established by the people alone; you must show that they were established by God – except in that sense alone in which all things, both the greatest and the smallest, are said to be performed and established by God.

48 Aristotle, *Politics*, IV, 10 (1295a).

49 Josephus, *Jewish Antiquities*, XIV, 303, 327. Herod the Great (*c.* 73–4 BC) had originally been nominated king of the Jews by Antony. Cf. *Paradise Regained*, II, 423–5.

50 1 Sam. 10:24, 11:15.

51 2 Sam. 5:3. 1 Chron. 11:3.

52 *super solium Domini, et cunctis placuit*: this differs from the Junius-Tremellius text of 1 Chron. 29:23, but agrees with the Vulgate version as used by S., *DR*, p. 39.

53 2 Kings 11:17.

And so the throne of David by some special right is called the throne of Jehovah; the thrones of other kings are Jehovah's not otherwise than everything else. This you ought to have learned from the same chapter, verses 11, 12: 'Yours are all things in heaven and earth, yours is the kingdom, Lord, riches and glory stem from your sight, might and power' etc.[54] And this is so often said, not so that kings may swell with pride, but so they may be warned that though they think themselves gods, yet is there God above them to whom they owe all their possessions. Thence is easily understood that doctrine of the Essenes[55] and poets that kings 'exist at God's will and are from Jove'. [For King Solomon himself considers that even lesser magistrates also, namely judges, are from the same God, Pro. 8. 15, 16; and Homer thinks they are from the same Jove, Iliad. α.

> —— δικάσπολοι, οἵτε θέμιστας, judges, who the laws
> Πρὸς Διὸς εἰρύαται —— guard, from Jove.[56]

And][57] all we men certainly are likewise from God, and are the race of God. So this universal right of God does not take away the people's right. Moreover all other kings, who have not been named such by God, have received and derive their kingship from the people alone, to whom they are bound to be accountable. And, although the crowd usually flatter their kings, yet the kings themselves, whether good, like Sarpedon in Homer, or bad like those tyrants in the Lyrist, recognize this.

> Γλαῦκε τίη δὴ νῶι τετιμήμεσθα μάλιστα, etc.
> Glaucus, why are we treated with the greatest honour
> in Lycia, and all men look upon us as Gods?

He answers himself: 'because we outshine the rest in bravery; therefore let us fight bravely', he says, 'so the Lycians may not accuse us of cowardice'.[58] By this speech he intimates both that kingly honours are received from the people and that an account of the conduct of war must be rendered to the people. But bad kings, to strike fear into the people, announce publicly that God is the author of royal power: but in their private prayers, they respect no other deity than Fortune. Relevant is that famous passage of Horace:

[54] 1 Chron. 29:11–12.
[55] The Essenes, with the Pharisees and Sadducees, formed the three main Jewish sects; said by Josephus to be the most rigorously ascetic.
[56] Homer, *Iliad*, I, 238–9.
[57] 1658.
[58] Homer, *Iliad*, XII, 310ff.

> You the rough Dacian, you the roving Scythians fear,
> and the mothers of barbarian kings, and
> tyrants clad in purple,
> lest with unlawful foot you cast down
> the firm-standing column, lest the mass of the people
> rouse to arms those slow to arms
> and break their power.[59]

So if kings today rule through God, it is also through God that peoples claim their own liberty, since all things are done by God and through God. Both things Scripture also testifies equally – both that through him kings rule, and through him they are cast down from their throne (though we perceive that both are done far more often by the people than by God). And so the right of the people, like that of the king (whatever that may be), is from God. Whenever a people have created a king without some visible sign from God, they can by the same right of theirs cast the king out. To depose a tyrant is clearly a more divine action than to set him up; and more of God's divinity is seen in a people when they renounce an unjust king, than in a king who oppresses an innocent people. Rather the people judge harmful kings by the authority of God; for God has arrayed his favourites in this very honour, Ps. 149, that while they celebrate Christ their king with praises, the kings of nations (who are all tyrants according to the gospel) 'they should fetter with chains and exercise upon them the written law'[60] even though they boast that they are unrestricted by all written right and laws. No-one should be so stupid and so wicked as to believe that kings, who are almost the most worthless of mortals, are valued so highly in God's estimation that the whole world hangs upon and is governed by their nod; so that for their sakes and on their account, the so to speak divine human race is to be considered as having the same place and number as all the dumb and most worthless animals.

Come now, for to prevent you having nothing to say, you bring into our midst Marcus Aurelius,[61] on the grounds that he supports tyrants. But it would have been better for you not to have touched Marcus Aurelius. I do not know whether he said that God alone is the judge of princes. Xiphilinus certainly, whom you cite on αὐταρχία, says

[59] Horace, *Odes*, I, 34, 9–17.
[60] Ps. 149:8–9.
[61] Marcus Aurelius Antoninus, Roman emperor, 161–80.

περὶ αὐταρχίας ὁ Θεὸς μόνος κρίνειν δύναται.[62] But I do not agree that αὐταρχίαν there is synonymous with monarchy – and the oftener I read what goes before, the less I think so. For any reader would wonder how that strange opinion, suddenly grafted onto the rest, coheres with it, or what it means; especially since Marcus Aurelius, the best of emperors, dealt with the people, as Capitolinus reports, just as they are dealt with beneath a free state.[63] But no-one doubts that the right of the people was at that time supreme. The same emperor, in the first book of his autobiography,[64] professes that he revered Thrasea, Helvidius, Cato, Dion, Brutus,[65] who were all tyrannicides, or strove after that glory, and proposed to himself a form of republic in which all affairs might be governed by just laws and equal right. And in the fourth book he says that not he but the law is master. He recognized too that all things belong to the senate and people: 'we', he says, 'are so far from having anything that belongs to us that we live in your house'. Such Xiphilinus has to say.[66] So far was Marcus Aurelius from appropriating anything to himself by the right of kings. When he was dying, he recommended his son to the Romans to be ruler upon the condition that he should be worthy:[67] and so he did not exhibit that absolute and imaginary right to rule – as if handed down through God's hands – termed, in short, αὐταρχία.

However you say that 'all the records of Greeks and Romans are full of examples': but they are nowhere to be seen; 'full too are those of the Jews', and yet you add that 'the Jews were mostly less favourable to royal power'. Rather you have found and will find that the Greeks and Romans were much less favourable to tyrants. So too the Jews, if that book of Samuel in which he, 1 Sam. 10, had described the rights of kingship were extant. This book, so the doctors of the Hebrews have reported, was torn apart or burnt[68] by kings so that

[62] 'Concerning αὐταρχία, God alone is able to judge': S., *DR*, p. 40, is citing the eleventh-century epitome by Xiphilinus of Dio Cassius, *Roman History*, LXXII, 1, 14. Autarchy (αὐταρχία) is usually taken to mean absolute rule or despotism.

[63] Capitolinus, 'Vita M. Antonini', *Historia Augusta*, XII, 1.

[64] Marcus Aurelius, *Meditations*, I, 14.

[65] Thrasea Paetus and his son-in-law Helvidius Priscus were noted first-century republicans; Cato Uticensis (95–46 BC) opposed Julius Caesar; Dion (*c.* 408–354 BC) drove Dionysius II out of Syracuse; Marcus Junius Brutus (85–42 BC) was a leader of the conspiracy to assassinate Caesar.

[66] Xiphilinus, 'Epitome of Book LXXII'.

[67] Dio Cassius, *Roman History*, LXXII, 33, 2.

[68] 'Then Samuel told the people the manner of the kingdom, and wrote *it* in a book, and

they might exercise tyranny over their subjects with greater impunity.

Look round now to see if you can catch hold of some straw. It finally occurred to you to twist King David's words, Ps. 17, 'Let my judgement come forth from your presence':[69] so, says Barnachmoni, 'no man judges a king but God'.[70] And yet it seems more likely that David wrote this when he was harried by Saul and did not even refuse to be judged by Jonathan, although then already anointed by God; 'if there is injustice in me, kill me yourself', he says, 1 Sam. 20. Then like anyone else who is falsely accused by men, he calls upon the judgement of God. This is revealed by what follows: 'your eyes see what is right, since you have searched my heart' etc.[71] What has this to do with a king's judgement or that of a court? Certainly people most undermine and demolish the right of kings when they reveal that it is supported by and built on such treacherous foundations.

Behold at last that trite argument, the prize of our native courtiers: 'Against you alone have I sinned', Ps. 51, 6.[72] As if indeed King David when doing penance in grief and tears, lying on the earth in sackcloth and ashes, humbly begging mercy from God, thought at all about the right of a king when he said this, when he judged that he was hardly worth the right of a slave. Did he despise in comparison with himself all the people of God, his own brothers, so far as to think that he could not be sinning against them by committing murders, adulteries and robbery? Far be such pride from so holy a king – and such shameful ignorance of himself or his neighbour. So 'against you alone have I sinned' is undoubtedly to be understood as 'against you chiefly'. However this may be, certainly the words of the psalmist and expressions laden with emotion are in no way suited to explicate right, nor should they be dragged into that use.

But 'he was not summoned to court and did not plead a capital charge in the presence of the sanhedrin.' So be it: for how could

laid *it* up before the LORD', 1 Sam. 10:25. M. again agrees with Schickard, *Jus Regium*, p. 66: 'Samuelis tractatus, quem . . . de Jure Regio scripsit, adhucdum superesset, facile omnis haec liticula dirimeretur. At putant combustum esse'.

69 Ps. 17:2.

70 For Barnachmoni, M. again quotes from S., *DR*, p. 40 (see also Schickard, *Jus Regium*, p. 65).

71 1 Sam. 20:8.

72 *Tibi soli peccavi*, Ps. 51. 6.: M.'s text and numbering (51:4 in AV) agrees with the Vulgate as given by S., *DR*, p. 40 (and also by Schickard, *Jus Regium*, p. 65, whose gloss is similarly incredulous: 'Ergo nemini mortalium rationem reddere debeo, nec contra subditos peccare potero!').

something be found out when it was done so far without witnesses and so secretly that for some years perhaps (such are court secrets) scarcely more than one or two seem to have been privy to it: 2 Sam. 12,[73] 'you have done this secretly'. Then, what if the sanhedrin should be slow even in punishing private citizens? Will anyone advance as proof from this that they should not be punished? But the reason is not obscure. He had condemned himself: v. 5, 'Guilty on a capital charge is the man who has done this'. At once the prophet rejoined to this: 'You are that man.' In the prophet's judgement also, he was guilty on a capital charge. But God by his own right and with extraordinary mercy towards David, absolved the king both from his sin and the sentence of death itself which he had pronounced against himself: v. 13, 'you will not die'.

Now you rave against some bloodthirsty advocate or other and spend the utmost effort upon the task of refuting his peroration:[74] let him see to this himself, I am fulfilling the task which has been set me – to complete it in as few words as possible. Certain things however I cannot pass over, first your remarkable contradictions: on p. 30 you have this, 'the Israelites do not beg for an unjust king, a violent man and a plunderer, and such as those kings usually were who were worst.' But on p. 42 you rail at the advocate because he had declared that the Israelites asked for a tyrant.[75] 'Did they prefer', you say, 'to rush headlong from the frying pan into the fire – that is, to try out the savagery of the worst tyrants rather than endure the wicked judges to whom they had by now grown used?' First you say that the Hebrews preferred tyrants to judges, now that they preferred judges to tyrants and 'wanted nothing less than a tyrant'. So from your own material the advocate will reply to you; for according to you every king is by right of kings a tyrant.

What follows is good, that 'the supreme authority then rested in the people, because they rejected judges and chose a king'.[76] You will remember this when I ask you for it again. You deny that 'God in his anger bestowed upon the Israelites a king as a tyrant or punishment, but as a beneficial and good thing.' Yet this is easily refuted. For why should they cry out against the king whom they had chosen, except

[73] 2 Sam. 12:12.

[74] I.e., John Cook.

[75] Cook, *King Charls his case*, p. 8.

[76] *authoritatem in populo maximam tunc fuisse, quod judices repudiarunt, regem optarunt*: M. repeatedly returns to this passage from *DR*, p. 42.

because royal power was an evil thing; not in itself indeed, but because most often, just as the prophet[77] warns here, it turns into pride and domination. If I do not satisfy you in this, recognize your own written agreement and blush. *Apparat. ad primatum papae*: 'God in his anger gave them a king, offended at their sin of refusing to have God as their king. So the church, as if in punishment for its offence because it had abandoned the pure worship of God, has been given over to the more than kingly rule of one mortal monarch.'[78] So if your comparison holds good, either God gave a king to the Israelites as a punishment, and as an evil thing, or gave a pope to the church for its good and as a good thing. What is more unreliable than this man, what more mad? Who would trust this man in the least important affair, when in such a great matter he sets no store by what he asserts and later denies it. You affirm, p. 29, that 'the king is unrestricted by the laws among all nations: such was the judgement of the East and of the West'. But on p. 43, 'all kings of the east were κατὰ νόμον [lawful] and legitimate; moreover the Egyptian kings were restricted by the laws in the greatest and smallest matters' – when at the beginning of the chapter you promised you would prove the following: that all kings are 'unrestricted by laws, that they give laws, but do not receive them'. For my part I am not angry with you, for either you are mad or you are on my side. This surely is attacking, not defending; this is making fun of a king. If you are not, certainly that phrase of Catullus fits you very squarely,[79] but the other way round; for you are as much the worst patron of all as anyone was ever the best poet. Surely, unless that dullness in which you say the advocate is 'sunk' has blinded you instead, now you will feel you 'have become brutish' yourself.

Now you confess that 'to all kings of nations also laws have been given; yet not so that they are restricted by them out of fear of judgement and capital punishment'. This you have shown neither from scripture, nor from any author worthy of credit. So hear this in few words: to grant civil laws to those who are not restricted by laws is stupid and silly; to punish all others, but to give impunity for all crimes merely to one man, when the law excepts no-one, is quite unjust. These two things never happen to wise legislators, much less God. But so that all may see that you in no way prove from the

[77] I.e., Samuel. [78] S., *De primatu*, p. 230. [79] See Catullus, 49.

writings of the Hebrews what you had undertaken to prove in this chapter, you confess of your own accord that there are among teachers, 'those who deny that a king other than God ought to have been acknowledged by their ancestors, but was given as a punishment'. With their opinion I agree.

For it is not fitting nor worthy for a man to be king unless he far excels all the rest. When many men are equal, as the majority are in every state, I think that power should be granted on an equal basis and to all in turn: but who does not think that it is quite unworthy for all to be slaves to their equal, or to one who is quite often their inferior and very frequently a fool? Nor does it 'act as a recommendation of royal government' that Christ took his origin from kings, any more than it acts as a recommendation of very bad kings that they had Christ for a descendant. 'The Messiah is a king': we acknowledge, we rejoice and we pray that he may come as quickly as possible, for he is worthy, and no-one is like him or able to follow him. Meanwhile royal government, which has been entrusted to unworthy and undeserving people, as most commonly happens, is rightly considered to have brought more bad than good upon the human race. Nor does it follow directly that all kings are tyrants. But let us suppose that it did: I grant you this in case you think me too obstinate. Now you use what I have granted. 'These two implications follow', you say: 'God himself would have had to be called king of tyrants, and indeed would be the greatest tyrant himself.' If one of these implications does not follow, there certainly does follow that circumstance which almost always follows from your whole book – that you perpetually contradict not only the scriptures, but yourself, since in the sentence immediately above you had said that 'one God is king of all things, which he himself also created.' But he also created both tyrants and demons; and so in your opinion he is their king too.

On your second conclusion I spit, and wish that blasphemous mouth of yours might be closed up, as you are asserting that God is the greatest tyrant, if he is called king and master of tyrants, as you yourself so often say.

But you do not help the cause of the king much more, when you point out that Moses also 'was a king with supreme power'. For he indeed might have been, or anyone else, so long as he was one who could 'refer to God' our affairs, as did Moses, Exod. 18.19. But not even Moses, although he was, so to speak, God's intimate, was allowed to do as he pleased to God's people. For what does he say? 'This people came to me', he says, 'to consult God'; not therefore to receive Moses' commands. Then Jethro takes up the matter: 'act the part of this people towards God, and impress upon them the laws of God'.[80] And Moses, Deuteronomy 4.5: 'I have taught you statutes and judgements, as God has commanded me.' Hence he is said to have been 'loyal in all God's house,' Num. 12.[81] And so the king of the people was Jehovah; Moses was, as it were, only an interpreter of Jehovah the king. So you must be wicked and sacrilegious if you dare, unbidden, to transfer this supreme power from God to man, which Moses himself did not hold in supremacy but only by proxy and as intermediary beneath the presiding spirit of God. Your pile of wickedness is also increased by the fact that you say here that Moses was a king with supreme power, when in *Apparatus ad Primatum*, p. 230, you said that 'together with seventy elders he ruled the people; and was the leader of the people, not their master'. So if he was king (as he certainly was, and the best of kings), and that, as you say yourself, with 'power that was clearly supreme and royal', and yet he was not master nor did he rule the people alone, then on your authority it necessarily follows that kings, although endowed with supreme power, are not yet masters with royal and supreme right, nor ought to rule the people alone, how much less according to their own pleasure?

Now with what shamelessness indeed do you falsely fabricate a command of God 'concerning the appointment of a king over them as soon as they entered the holy land', Deut. 17.[82] For you cunningly leave out what precedes: 'when you say, I will set a king over me.' And now remember what I will now ask you to give me back; when you said, p. 42, that 'the people were endowed then with the most unlimited power'.

Now again you will decide for yourself whether you mean to be frenzied or impious. 'Since God', you say, 'determined so long before the kingly government that needed to be set up, as being the best form of government for that people, how will these matters be reconciled? The prophet opposed it; God acted in such a manner with the prophet as if he did not wish it.' He sees himself ensnared, he sees himself obstructed; wait now and see with that great malice against the prophet, and impiety towards God he seeks to remove the

Coláiste Oideachais Mhuire Gan Smál
Luimneach

[80] Exod. 18:19–20. [81] Num. 12:7. [82] Deut. 17:14.

obstruction from his way: 'it must be considered in these circumstances', he says, 'that it was Samuel whose sons were then the judges of the people, and the people rejected them because of their corrupt judgements. So Samuel did not wish his sons to be cast out by the people. God, to oblige his prophet, hinted that he was not very pleased with what the people desired.' Say in one word, wretch, what you are saying in circumlocutions. Samuel deceived the people, and God, Samuel. Not the advocate, then, but you are the 'frenzied' and 'insane' one, who, to honour a king only, pays no respect to God. Does Samuel seem to you the type to have placed his sons' greed and ambition before the safety or goodwill of his country; who would have tricked the people when they were seeking a right and beneficial course with such crafty and such sly advice; who would have spoken false teachings instead of true ones? Does God seem to you the type to oblige anyone in so disgraceful an affair or act insincerely with the people? So either the right of kings was not what the prophet expounded to the people, or that right, by the testimony of God and the prophet, was evil, burdensome, violent, useless and costly to the commonwealth; or lastly, which it is sacrilege to say, both God and the prophet wished to deceive the people.

For in many places God attests that he was very much displeased because they had asked for a king, ver. 7: 'not you but me have they scorned, lest I should reign over them, to judge by those deeds by which they have abandoned me and worshipped strange gods',[83] clearly as if it seemed some kind of idolatry to ask for a king who demands that adoration and honours almost divine be accorded him. Surely the man who sets over him an earthly master, who is above all laws, is near to erecting a strange god for himself; a god at any rate not often reasonable but more often brutish and bestial, since reason has been corrupted. So 1 Samuel 10.19, 'you have rejected your God, who himself preserves you from all your hardships and afflictions, since you have said to him, "set a king over us" '; and, chap. 12.12, you asked for a king 'when the Lord is your king'; and, ver. 17, 'see that your evil is truly great in the sight of the Lord, in asking for a king for yourselves'. And Hosea speaks contemptuously of the king, Ch. 13. 10, 11: 'Where is your king? Let him now preserve you in your cities. Where are your protectors? Since you said, give me a king and

[83] 1 Sam. 8:7.

nobles, I gave you a king in my anger.' Hence that hero Gideon, who was greater than a king, said 'I will not be master over you, nor shall my son be master over you, but your master will be the Lord', Jud. 8[84] – clearly as if he had been teaching at the same time that it was not for a man to be master over men but for God alone. Hence Josephus calls the commonwealth of the Hebrews, in which God alone held sovereignty, θεοκρατίαν [a theocracy], in opposition to Apion, an Egyptian grammarian and an abusive one, like you.[85] The people, at last recovering their senses, complain in Isaiah 26.13 that it had been disastrous for them to have had masters other than God. All these passages are the proof that a king had been given to the Israelites as a result of God's anger.

When you tell the story of the tyrant Abimelech – who is there that you do not move to laughter? It is said of him that when he was killed it was partly by a stone thrown by a woman, partly by the sword of his armour-bearer.[86] 'God rendered evil to Abimelech. This history', you say, 'most powerfully proves that God alone is the judge and punisher of kings.' Rather, of tyrants, worthless men and bastards, if the following holds good: whoever, by right or wrong, seizes a tyranny, shall acquire royal right at once over the people and escape punishment; immediately weapons shall fall from the magistrates' hands and thenceforth they will not dare to murmur. But what if some great robber should die like this in war, would God therefore be the only punisher of robbers? What if he had been condemned under the law at the hand of the executioner. Would God have rendered evil to him any the less? You have nowhere read that their judges also were prosecuted under the laws; yet you of your own accord admit, p. 4, that 'in an aristocracy even the prince, if he does some wrong, can and ought to be judged'. Why not likewise a tyrant in a kingdom? Because God rendered evil to Abimelech. But so too did that woman, and so too did the armour-bearer, over both of whom he made a display of having royal right. What if a magistrate had done so? Does he not bear the sword of God for the very purpose of rendering evil to the evil?

After this 'most powerful' proof drawn from the death of Abimelech, he turns as is his manner to words of invective; nothing but 'dirt' and 'mud' pours from his mouth; and of those things which he promised he would prove, he has proved none, either from sacred

84 Judges 8:23. 85 Josephus, *Contra Apion*, II, 165. 86 See Judges 9:53–4.

books or from the rabbis. For he has not shown either that a king is free from laws, nor why, if he commits a crime, he alone of mortals should not be punished. Rather he entangles himself in his own witnesses and shows by his own efforts that the opinion which is the opposite of his own is truer.

And when he makes too little progress with proofs, he tries to stir up hatred against us by the most terrible accusations of all, as if the best and most innocent king had been cruelly removed. 'Was Solomon', he says, 'a better king than Charles I?' There are those, to confess the truth, who have not hesitated to liken his father James to Solomon and indeed to prefer him for his distinguished birth. Solomon was the son of David; and he was Saul's musician first. James was the son of the earl of Darnley who caught David the musician (after he had entered the chamber of his wife the queen by night) with the door bolted, and not long after killed him, as Buchanan relates.[87] So James was more illustrious in birth and often called a second Solomon, although whether he was the son of David the musician, that story has left up in the air, to be guessed by readers. But to compare Charles with Solomon – I don't see how it could have entered your head. For that Charles whom you elevate with so many praises – his obstinacy, greed, cruelty to and savage domination of all good and honest men, his wars, burnings, plunderings and innumerable murders of wretched citizens – even while I write this, his own son Charles is confessing and lamenting on that public seat of penitence in Scotland in the midst of the people: moreover he is resigning that royal right of yours.[88]

But if you take such great delight in parallels, let us compare Charles with Solomon. Solomon 'began his reign' with the execution 'of his brother' which was most well deserved: Charles, with his father's funeral. I do not say 'murder' (although all indications of poison were beheld on his father's body), for suspicion of this rested upon Buckingham.[89] Yet Charles, though this man was the murderer of the king and of his father, not only freed him of all guilt in the

[87] Buchanan, *Historia*, fos 210a–b, tells the story of David Rizzio, secretary to Mary, Queen of Scots, killed by the earl of Darnley because of his alleged adultery with her.

[88] On 16 May 1650 Charles signed a humiliating declaration acknowledging the failings of his parents.

[89] The allegation that George Villiers, Duke of Buckingham (1592–1628), the former favourite of James I, had poisoned him was frequently made. Cf. *E.* III, 351–2, and Cook, *King Charls*, p. 12.

presence of the highest council of the realm, but lest that matter be wholly subjected to the examination of parliament, dissolved the sitting.[90] Solomon 'oppressed the people with the heaviest taxes': but he spent it on the temple of God and public buildings, Charles on extravagance. Solomon was enticed by a huge number of wives to the worship of idols; Charles by one wife. Though Solomon was enticed into trickery, it is not read that he enticed others; Charles enticed others not only by the richest rewards of a corrupt church, but also compelled them by edicts and ecclesiastical decrees to set up altars hateful to all protestants and worship crucifixes painted on the wall, overhanging the altars. But not even for this was 'Solomon condemned to die by the people'. Nor, I say, does it follow from that that he ought not to have been condemned by the people. For many things could have happened on account of which this did not at that time seem expedient to the people. The people certainly revealed what was their right not long after, both in words and deeds: when ten tribes expelled Solomon's son;[91] and if he had not hastened to fly, it is to be believed that they would have actually stoned to death a king who had only threatened them.

[90] June 1626.
[91] I.e., Rehoboam, see 1 Kings 12:18, and cf. *E*, III, 382–3.

CHAPTER III

It has now been sufficiently argued and demonstrated that kings after Moses were, at the command of God, bound by all laws just as the people were, and that no exemptions from the laws are found in scripture. So it is quite false, and said without authority and reason, that kings 'could do with impunity what they wanted' or that 'they could not be punished by the people' and accordingly that 'God has reserved their punishment to his own tribunal'. Let us see whether the gospel advises what the law did not advise, and did not command either. Let us see whether the gospel, that divine proclamation of liberty, sentences us to slavery under kings and tyrants, from whose lawless power the old law, though it also taught some kind of slavery, did free the people of God.

Your first proof you take from the character of Christ – but who does not know that he took on the character not only of a private citizen but even of a slave so we might be free? Nor is this to be understood merely of internal freedom and not of civil liberty. For how strange are those words which Mary, mother of Christ, uttered in prophecy of his coming – 'he has scattered the proud in the thought of their own hearts, he has dragged down rulers from their thrones, he has exalted the humble'[1] – if his coming rather strengthened tyrants on the throne and subjected all christians to their most savage rule. By being born, serving and suffering under tyrants, he has himself obtained all honourable liberty for us. As Christ has not removed from us the ability to endure slavery with calmness if it is necessary, so

[1] Luke 1:52.

too he has left us with the ability to aspire honourably to liberty, but has granted the latter in greater measure. Hence Paul, 1 Cor. 7, decides thus, not only of evangelical but also of civil liberty: 'Have you been summoned, since you are a slave? Do not heed it, but if you can be made free, enjoy it rather. You have been bought at a price, do not be the slaves of men.'[2] It is in vain therefore that you exhort us to slavery by the example of Christ, who at the price of his own slavery strengthened civil liberty too for us: and in our place he took upon himself the form of a slave, but he never lost the heart of a liberator. From this I will show you that he taught far differently about the nature of the right of kings than the doctrine you teach. For you are a teacher (strange in a republic!) not of the right of kings but the right of tyrants and decide that if any nation has drawn a tyrant by lot, whether by heredity or conquest or by chance, it is enslaved not only by necessity, but also by religious obligation.

But as usual I will employ your own testimonies against you. Christ asked Peter, when certain Galilean money collectors were demanding double drachmas of him, Mat. 17, from whom kings of the earth received taxes or presents – from their own sons or from strangers? Peter answered him, 'from strangers'. So, said Christ, 'the children are free; but for fear we should offend them, give something to them for me and for yourself'.[3] This passage engages the commentators in various debates, as to whom these double drachmas were paid. Some say to the priests for the sanctuary, others to Caesar: I think it was paid to Herod, who embezzled the revenue of the temple. For Josephus relates that various taxes which were exacted by Herod and his sons, were finally remitted by Agrippa.[4] But this tax, though small in itself, when joined to many others, was heavy: and those of which Christ speaks here must have been heavy; otherwise, even under the republic, poor people were only counted by the head and not taxed. And so from this Christ took the opportunity of accusing Herod's injustice, being under his rule. The rest of the kings of the earth (if they do indeed desire to be called fathers of their country) do not usually command excessively heavy taxes from their sons, that is, their own citizens, but from foreigners, especially when these have been subdued in war. But Herod on the contrary would oppress not foreigners but his sons. However this may be, whether you grant that

[2] 1 Cor. 7:21–3. [3] Matt. 17:24–7.

[4] Josephus, *Jewish Antiquities*, XIX, 6. Agrippa I, king of Judaea, 41–4.

'sons' here is to be understood as the king's own subjects or the sons of God,[5] that is the faithful and christians in general, as Augustine understands it, it is absolutely certain that if Peter was a son and therefore free, we also are free, on the authority of Christ, either as citizens or as christians. So it is not the right of kings to exact excessively heavy taxes from sons and free men. For Christ testifies that he paid, not because he had to, but so that he should not, as a private citizen, cause trouble for himself by offending those who were making the demand; since he knew that he had a far different duty and service to fulfil in that course of his life. So while Christ denied that it was the right of kings to impose excessively heavy dues upon freemen, certainly he even more clearly denies that it is the right of kings to plunder, ravage, murder and torture their own citizens and especially christians. Since he seems to have discussed the right of kings elsewhere too in this manner, certain people began to suspect that he did not consider the licence of tyrants as the right of kings. For it was not for nothing that the Pharisees tested out his mind with questioning of this kind. When they were about to interrogate him concerning the right of kings, they said that he cared for no-one, and did not respect the character of men; and it was not for nothing that he grew angry when this kind of inquiry was proposed to him, Mat. 22.[6] What if someone wished to approach you insidiously and seize on your words, to elicit from you what would be to your harm, question you about the right of kings under a king? Would you grow angry with anyone who questioned you about this? I don't suppose! Hence then observe that his opinion about the right of kings was not agreeable to kings.

The same point is to be gathered most clearly from his answer, by which he seems to repel his examiners from him rather than instruct them. He asks for a coin of the tribute. He says, 'Whose image is this?' 'Caesar's.' 'Render then to Caesar the things that are Caesar's, and the things that are God's to God.' Rather, who does not know that those things which belong to the people should be given back to the people? Render to all men what you owe them, says Paul, Rom. 13.[7] So not all things are Caesar's. Our liberty is not Caesar's, but is a birthday gift to us from God himself. To give back to any Caesar what we did not receive from him would be most base and unworthy of the

[5] *filios Dei*: habitual Augustinian usage.
[6] Matt. 22:15–21.
[7] Rom. 13:7.

origin of man. For if upon beholding the face and countenance of a man, someone should ask whose image is that, would not anyone freely reply that it was God's? Since then we belong to God, that is, we are truly free and on that account to be rendered to God alone, surely we cannot, without sin and in fact the greatest sacrilege, hand ourselves over in slavery to Caesar, that is to a man, and especially one who is unjust, wicked and tyrannical?

Meanwhile he leaves open what things are Caesar's and what God's. But if this coin was the same as that double drachma customarily paid to God, as it certainly was later under Vespasian,[8] then indeed Christ has not lessened the controversy, but complicated it; since it is impossible to render the same thing at the same time to God and Caesar. But he showed what things were Caesar's; that coin of course, stamped with the image of Caesar. So what profit do you gain from this, apart from a denarius, either for Caesar or yourself? For either Christ gave Caesar nothing but that denarius, and asserted everything else was ours, or if he gave to Caesar all money inscribed with Caesar's name, now in contradiction with himself, he will give almost all our property to Caesar; as he declared openly, both in his own name and that of Peter, that they did not pay to kings a mere double drachma out of obligation. In short the reasoning you rely on is weak; for coins bear the portrait of the prince, not to show that it is his property but to show that it is valid, and so that nobody may dare to tamper with a coin marked by the prince's portrait. But if an inscription alone had the power to establish right of kings, kings would immediately make it so that all our property belonged to them, merely by writing their names on it.[9] Or if all our possessions already belong to them, which is your belief, that coin was not to be rendered to Caesar because it bore Caesar's name or portrait, but because it was already Caesar's before by right, even if it was not stamped with any portrait. From this it is clear that Christ in this passage wanted not so much to remind us so obscurely and ambiguously of our duty towards kings or Caesars, as to prove the wickedness and malice of the hypocritical Pharisees. Moreover when the Pharisees reported to him at another time that Herod was preparing an ambush against his life, did they get a humble or submissive reply from him to take back to the tyrant? Rather he said, 'go and tell that fox',[10] implying that

[8] Vespasian, Roman emperor, 69–79.

[9] For a similar exegesis, see *T*, II, 643.

kings do not plot against their own citizens by right of kingship, but in the manner of a fox.

'But he submitted to death beneath a tyrant.' And how could he possibly, except under a tyrant? 'He suffered death under a tyrant'; so he might be a witness and defender of all the absolutely unjust acts of royal right! You are an extraordinary reckoner of morals indeed! And Christ, although he made himself a slave to free us, not to put us under the yoke, still behaved in this manner; and did not yield anything to royal right except what was just and good.

Now let us come at length to his teaching about this matter. The sons of Zebedee, who aimed at the greatest authority in the kingdom of Christ, which they imagined would soon be on earth, were reproved in this way by Christ, so that he might at once impress upon all christians what kind of right of magistrates and civil power he wanted to set up amongst them. 'You know', he said, 'that the princes of nations are rulers over them, and great men exercise authority over them; but it will not be so amongst you. Rather let whoever wishes to be great amongst you be your attendant; and whoever wishes to be first among you, be your slave.'[11] Unless you were mentally deranged, could you have believed this passage illustrates your side of the case, and that by these arguments you win us over to consider our kings as masters of all? May we meet with such enemies in war, who stumble into the camp of the enemy as you usually do, as if into their own camp, blindly and without arms (although we know well enough we can conquer them even when they are armed). In your madness you are always accustomed, like this, to set out what is most hostile to your cause as if it lent it the strongest support. The Israelites kept asking for a king 'such as all those nations had'. God advised them against it, using many words which Christ has summarized briefly in this speech: 'you know that princes of nations are rulers over them'. Yet when they asked for one, God gave them a king, although he was angry. Christ, so that the christian people should in no way ask for one to be their ruler, like the other nations, prevented them with the warning, 'among you it will not be so'. What could be said more clearly than this? Amongst you there will not be this proud rule of kings, even though they are called by the plausible title of Euergetes[12]

[10] Luke 13:32.

[11] Matt. 20:25–7.

[12] *Euergetae*: from the Greek, εὐεργέτης (well-doer or benefactor), sometimes adopted as a title by Hellenistic kings.

and benefactors. But whoever wishes to become great among you (and who is greater than the prince?) 'let him be your attendant': and whoever wishes to be 'first' or 'prince' (Luke 22)[13] 'let him be your slave'. And so that advocate whom you rail at was not wrong, but had Christ as his authority, if he said that a christian king is the servant of the people,[14] as every good magistrate certainly is. But a king will either be no christian at all, or will be the slave of all. If he clearly wants to be master, he cannot at the same time be a christian.

Moreover Moses, who instituted a law that to some extent authorized slavery, still did not rule proudly over the people, but himself bore the burden of the people; and carried the people in his bosom, as a nursing father does a sucking infant, Num. 11.[15] Moreover a nursing father is a slave. Plato instructed that magistrates should be termed not masters, but deliverers and helpers of the people; the people not slaves, but sustainers of the magistrates, since they are the ones who provide food and wages for the magistrates even under kings.[16] The same people Aristotle calls guardians and attendants of the laws.[17] Plato calls them both attendants and slaves. The apostle indeed calls them ministers of God,[18] which does not at all hinder them however from being those of both laws and people. For the laws as much as the magistrates are for the good of the people.

And yet you keep crying that this is 'the opinion of the rabid hounds of England'. I would certainly not consider the English to be hounds, except for the fact that you, mongrel, bark at them with such base yapping: the lord of St Loup,[19] please God, the holy wolf indeed, complains that the hounds are rabid. Once upon a time St Germain, whose colleague was that famous St Loup of Troyes, by his authority deprived the unchaste king in our country, Vortigern, of his realm.[20] And so St Loup spurns such as you, the master not of a holy wolf but of one that is famished and thievish, more despicable than that master of vipers in Martial.[21] You have at home also a barking Lycisca[22] yourself, who rules over you most pitilessly, though you are the ruler of the wolf, and makes a din about your titles and opposes you in a

[13] Luke 22:25.
[14] Cook, *King Charls*, p. 24.
[15] Num. 11:12.
[16] Plato, *Laws*, IV, 715.
[17] Aristotle, *Politics*, III, 16 (1287a).
[18] Rom. 13:4.
[19] S.'s estate was at St Loup in France.
[20] Cf. *HB*, V, 136–41.
[21] Martial, *Epigrams*, I, 41, 7.
[22] *Lycisca*: the name of a bitch in Virgil (*Eclogues*, 3, 18) and Ovid (*Metamorphoses*, 3, 220).

loud voice. Therefore it is no wonder that you wish to thrust royal domination upon others, since you are yourself so slavishly accustomed to endure feminine rule at home. And so whether you are a master of the wolf, and have a she-wolf as your mistress, or are a wolf yourself or a werewolf, I assert that you must be the sport of the English hounds. But now I have no leisure to hunt wolves; and so after having got out of the woods, let us return to the king's highway.

You who recently wrote against all primacy in the church, now 'call Peter prince of the apostolic crown'. Who can trust you, little man, when your principles are so fluid? What of Peter? 'Be subject to all human ordinance for the sake of the Lord; whether to the king as one above you or to governors as those who are sent by him for the punishment of wrong-doers and the praise of those who do well; since thus is the will of God.'[23] Peter wrote this not only for private persons, but also for strangers who were scattered and dispersed throughout most of Asia Minor, who in those places where they were living had no right except that of hospitality. Do you think that the same thing befits inhabitants, freemen, nobles, meetings, assemblies and parliaments of native citizens in their own country as befits scattered foreigners in a strange land? Or that the same befits private citizens in their own land, as it does senators and magistrates, without whom not even kings can exist? But imagine it was natives, imagine it was not private persons but the Roman senate itself for whom these things were written. What do you gain from this, since no precept, which has some reason joined to it, usually binds or has the ability to bind anyone beyond the reason for the precept? 'Be subject', ὑποτάγητε, that is, if you consider the root meaning of the word, be subordinate or legally subject, for, ἡ γὰρ τάξις νόμος, says Aristotle, 'law is order'.[24] 'Be subject for the sake of the Lord.' Why? Because both a king and a governor are appointed by God to punish wrong-doers and praise those who act well. 'Since this is the will of God.' That is, that we should yield to such as are described here; there is no word in this place about others. You see how very well established is the reason for this precept. He adds, v. 16, 'as free men' – therefore not as slaves. What if the tables are turned, and the rulers rule with the torture and destruction of good men, the impunity and praise and reward of wrong-doers? Shall we be subject forever, not only all private persons,

[23] 1 Pet. 2:13–15.

[24] Aristotle, *Politics*, 1287a.

but the nobility, all the magistrates, lastly the parliament itself? Is the ordinance not said to be that of men? So why shall human power have the strength to appoint what is good and advantageous for men, but not have the strength to remove what is bad and destructive to the same people? But that king to whom they are commanded to be subject was Nero, the tyrant at Rome at the time. So we must be subjects even to tyrants? But I say it is doubtful whether Nero or Claudius was emperor at that time,[25] and those who are ordered to be subjects were foreigners, scattered about, and private citizens, not consuls, praetors or the Roman senate.

Now let us get to Paul (since you believe that you are allowed a freedom concerning the apostles which you do not wish to allow us concerning kings, so that at one moment you can grant primacy to Peter, and at another snatch it away). Paul says this to the Romans, Ch. 13:[26] 'Let every soul be subject to the powers above it; for there is no power except from God; the powers that be are ordained by God.' He writes this to the Romans not as does Peter to foreigners, who are scattered about, but yet rather to private citizens and common people. He also writes so that he may hold forth most splendidly on the whole reason, origin and end of governing a republic. By this the true and separate reason for our obedience should also shine forth more clearly, unconnected with all slavery. 'Let every soul', that is, each man, 'be subject.' What the apostle propounds in this chapter, Chrysostom has sufficiently explained: ποιεῖ τοῦτο δεικνὺς, etc., 'he does this', he says, 'to show that Christ did not introduce his laws to overthrow the common government, but to establish it more firmly'. Not therefore so that by setting Nero or any other tyrant above all law and punishment he might establish a most cruel empire of one man over all mortals. 'And so that he might teach at the same time that superfluous and useless wars should not be undertaken': he does not therefore condemn wars undertaken against a tyrant, who is an internal enemy of his country, and for that reason most dangerous. 'At that time there spread about people's gossip exposing the apostles as rebels and insurrectionists, as if they did and said everything to overthrow the common laws. These people's mouths the apostle has now stopped.'[27] So the apostles have not written defences of tyrants, which

[25] Nero, Roman emperor, 54–68; Claudius, Roman emperor, 41–54.
[26] Rom. 13:1.
[27] Chrysostom, *Homilies* (23, on Romans), *NPN*, XI, 511.

you do, but did such things and taught such things as were suspected by all tyrants and therefore rather needed defence and some commentary from them.

We saw from Chrysostom what the apostle's purpose was. Now let us examine his words: 'Let every soul be subject to the powers above it.' However he does not set out what these are. For he did not intend to do away with the rights and constitutions of all nations and surrender everything to one man's inclinations. Certainly every excellent emperor has always acknowledged the authority of the laws and of the senate as far superior to his own authority. Likewise among all nations except barbarians right has always been quite sacred. Hence Pindar, in Herodotus, said that νόμον πάντων βασιλέα, the law was king over all;[28] Orpheus in his hymns calls it the king not only of mortals but even of immortals: 'Αθανάτων καλέω καὶ θνητῶν ἁγνὸν ἄνακτα Οὐράνιον νόμον. –[29] He gives the reason: Αὐτὸς γὰρ μοῦνος ζώων οἴηκα κρατύνει, 'For the law alone holds the government of living things.' Plato in the *Laws* says that τὸ κρατοῦν ἐν τῇ πόλει, the law is that which ought to have the greatest power in a state.[30] In his letters he praises very highly that state where the law is both ruler and king of men, and men are not tyrants over the law.[31] The same is the opinion of Aristotle in the *Politics* and Cicero in the *Laws*, that laws rule over magistrates just as magistrates rule over the people.[32] And so since, in the judgement of the wisest of men and by the constitutions of the most sagacious states, the law has always been considered the highest and supreme power, and the teaching of the gospel does not conflict with reason or with the right of nations, certainly that man will be most truly subject to the powers above him who obeys whole-heartedly the laws and magistrates who govern the state according to the laws.

So he teaches this subjection not only to the people but to kings also; who are in no way above the laws. 'For there is no power except from God' – that is, no form of government, no lawful manner of ruling men. The most ancient laws were also once ascribed to the authority of God; for the law is, as Cicero says in *Phil.* 12, 'none other than right reason drawn from the power of the gods, commanding

[28] Herodotus, *Histories*, III, 38.

[29] 'I call heavenly law the holy king of immortals and mortals': *Hymns*, LXIV, in *Orphica* (Leipzig, 1885), pp. 91–2.

[30] Plato, *Laws*, IV, 715.

[31] Plato, *Letters*, VIII, 354C.

[32] Aristotle, *Politics*, 1287a; Cicero *De legibus*, III, 1, 2.

what is honourable, and forbidding the opposite'.[33] So from God comes the establishment of magistrates so that by their government the human race might live beneath laws: but the freedom to choose this or that form of government, these or those magistrates, has always been in the power of the free nations of men. Hence Peter calls both kings and governors ἀνθρωπίνην κτίσιν, a human creation; and Hosea says, Ch. 8, 'They establish kings, but not by my will; they put princes in command whom I do not know of.'[34] For in the state of the Hebrews alone, where they could consult God in various ways, the nomination of a king had to be referred to God by law: all we other nations have received no command of this kind from God. Sometimes either the very form of government, if it is faulty, or those men who hold the power, come from men and the devil, Luke 4:[35] 'To you I will give all this power; for it was handed over to me, and I give it to whoever I wish.' Hence he is called the prince of this world; and, Apocalyp. 13, the serpent gave to the Beast his power and his throne and great authority.[36] Therefore it is necessary that St Paul be understood to mean not any powers, but lawful ones of the kind also described below; it is necessary that he be understood to mean the powers themselves, not always the men who hold command. Hence Chrysostom speaks clearly: 'What are you saying', he says, 'has then every prince been appointed by God? I say not: for the apostle speaks not about any single prince but about the position itself. He does not say, there is no prince except for God, but that there is no power.'[37] So Chrysostom. 'But the powers that be are ordained by God.' So the apostle means lawful ones to be understood here; for an evil and faulty thing, since it is disorderly, cannot possibly be ordained and be at the same time faulty. For this places two contraries together – order and disorder.

'But the powers which be' you interpret as if it were said 'which now are', so you can more easily prove that the Romans ought to have obeyed Nero who, as you think, then 'reigned'; clearly you must pardon us! For you may think as badly as you wish of the English Commonwealth, but you will have of necessity to grant that the English ought to assent to it, since it 'now is' and 'is ordained' by God, as once Nero's empire was. For Nero no less than Tiberius had

[33] Cicero, *Philippics*, XI (not XII), xii, 28.
[34] 1 Pet. 2:13. Hos. 8:4. [35] Luke 4:6. [36] Rev. 13:2.
[37] Chrysostom, *Homilies* (23, on Romans), *NPN*, XI, 511.

seized 'by his mother's arts a power that in no way belonged to him',[38] in case you reply that it was gained legally. So that you yourself are the more wicked, a reviser of your own teaching when you wish for the Romans to have been subject to the power which then was, and the English not to be subject to the power which now is. But no two things in this world are more directly opposed to each other than your extreme wickedness is almost always opposed to itself. What then will you do, wretch? With this keenness of yours you have clearly ruined the young king; for upon your own opinion, I will torture you to confess that this power in England which now is has been ordained by God, and then that all Englishmen within the boundaries of the same commonwealth ought to be subject to the same power. So wait, critics, and keep your hands off, this is a new emendation by Salmasius on the epistle to the Romans; he has discovered that it should not be rendered the powers which are, 'but which now exist'; so he might show that all ought to have been subject to the tyrant Nero who was then emperor indeed.

But, my good man, ληκύθιον ἀπώλεσας, you have destroyed your own pitcher.[39] As you destroyed the king just then, so now you have done the same to this pretty emendation. The epistle which you say was written under Nero, was written under Claudius, an honest prince and not a bad man: this learned men have completely proven by the surest arguments;[40] also five years under Nero were most praiseworthy, whence this argument so often impressed upon us, which is in the mouths of many and has imposed upon many – that a tyrant must be obeyed because Paul exhorted the Romans to be subject to Nero – is found to be the crafty fabrication of some ignoramus.

'He who resists the power', that is, the legal one, 'resists God's ordinance.' This precept binds even kings who resist the laws and the senate. But in truth he who resists a corrupt power, or resists one who destroys and overturns a power that is not corrupt, surely he does not resist God's ordinance? In your right mind, I believe, you would not say so. The following little verse removes all doubt that the apostle speaks here about lawful power only; for he explains by definition, in case anyone can be mistaken and thence go chasing silly theories, who are the magistrates that are the ministers of this power, and why he

[38] See Suetonius, *Nero*, 9.
[39] See Aristophanes, *Frogs*, 1200ff.
[40] See Louis Cappel, *Historia Apostolica illustrata* (Geneva, 1634), pp. 76–7.

exhorts us to be subjects: 'Magistrates are not a terror to good works but to bad; good men shall gain praise from this power; a magistrate is a minister of God, given us for our good; it is not in vain that he carries a sword, one to avenge anger upon him who does evil.'[41] Who denies, who refuses, except the wicked, to subject himself freely to a power or a minister of a power of this kind? And not only to avoid the 'anger' and offence, or from fear of punishment, but also 'for the sake of conscience'.

For without magistrates and civil government, no commonwealth, no human society, no life can exist. But if any power or magistrate acts in a fashion contrary to this, neither the former nor the latter has been properly ordained by God. Thence subjection is neither owed or taught to such a power or magistrate, nor are we prevented from any sensible resistance to them, for we will not be resisting the power or the magistrate, which is here excellently depicted, but a robber, a tyrant, an enemy. If he is to be called a magistrate, however, just because he holds power, because he can seem to be ordained by God to punish us, under such conditions the devil too will be a magistrate.

Certainly there is only one true definition of one thing: so if Paul here defines a magistrate, which he does indeed with precision, he could not by the same definition and in the same words be defining a tyrant – a thing quite totally the reverse. Hence it is most certainly to be gathered that he wished us to be subject only to a man whom he himself defined and described as a magistrate, not to the tyrant, his opposite. 'For this reason you pay taxes';[42] he adds a reason to his command. Hence Chrysostom says, 'why do we give taxes to the king? Is it not as if we are paying hire to one to watch over us, for our care and protection? But we would have paid him nothing, if we had not come to know from the beginning that such superintendence was useful for us.'[43] Therefore I will repeat what I said above; since this subjection is not asked of us absolutely, but only with the addition of a reason, the reason which is added will be the true rule of our subjection: when we are not subjects under that reason, we are rebels; when we are subjects without that reason, we are slaves and cowards.

'But the English', you say, 'are far from being free, because they are evil men, they are criminals.' I do not wish to make mention of the faults of the French, although they live beneath kings, nor to make too

[41] Rom. 13:3–4. [42] Rom. 13:6.
[43] Chrysostom, *Homilies* (23, on Romans), *NPN*, XI, 513.

many excuses for the English; but I say that their shameful acts are such as they learned under kings, so to speak, in Egypt, and they have not been able to unlearn them straightaway while in the desert, although under the rule of God. But there is good hope of the majority; not to begin here high commendation of those excellent men who are most saintly and strive after the truth. Amongst us, I believe, there is no smaller number of them than in the countries where you think there are most of such men. But 'a heavy yoke is placed upon the English'. What if it is placed upon those who were striving to place the yoke upon the rest of the citizens, or upon those who were deservedly subdued? For the rest, I think, do not take it badly, now the treasury is drained by the civil wars, to sustain their own liberty at their own expense.

Now he sinks back to his rabbis who peddle trifles. He says that a king is not bound by the laws, yet proves from them that a king 'may be guilty of *lèse-majesté* if he allows his right to be diminished'. And so a king will be bound and not bound, a defendant and not a defendant: for so frequently is he used to contradicting himself that contradiction herself seems to be twin-sister to this man.

But God, you say, gave many kingdoms in slavery to Nebuchadnezzar. I confess that he did so for a certain time, Jeremiah 27.7. Show that he delivered the English over into slavery to Charles Stuart even for the least half an hour. That he allowed them to be in such a position, I would not deny, but I never heard that he delivered them over to it. Or if God gives people into slavery whenever a tyrant is more powerful than his people, why may he not likewise be said to set them free whenever a people are more powerful than their tyrant? Shall the tyrant claim his tyranny as something received from God and we not claim our liberty likewise from him? There is no evil in the state which God does not send upon it, Amos 3:[44] hunger, pestilence, sedition, the enemy – which one of these will the state not repel from it with all its strength? It will do so, certainly, if it can, although it knows that these were sent upon it by God himself – unless he himself should order otherwise from heaven. Why will it not equally rightly get rid of tyrants, if it is stronger? Or are we to believe that the uncontrollability of this one man is sent from God for the harm of all, rather than the self-control of the whole state for the good of all? Far

[44] Amos 3:6.

from states, far from every assembly of free-born men be the stain of a doctrine that is so stupid and so destructive, and which completely wipes out all civil society, and thrusts the whole human race, on account of one or two tyrants, down almost to the condition of four-footed animals: since tyrants, if they are lifted up above all law, will hold equal right and power over both the species of beasts and of men.

I pass over now those stupid dilemmas, to wallow in which you invent someone's quotation that 'that supremacy means that of the people', even if I do not hesitate to affirm that all the authority of a magistrate begins with the people. Hence Cicero in the *Pro Flacco*: 'Those most wise and saintly ancestors of ours decided that those things should be ordered and forbidden which the common people approved and the people ordered.'[45] Hence Lucius Crassus, the eminent orator, and leader of the senate at that time, whose cause he was then pleading with the people: 'Do not', he said, 'allow us to be slaves to anyone except all of you, to whom we can and must be so.'[46] For although the senate governed the people, yet the people had delivered over to the senate that power of directing and ruling itself. Hence we read that majesty was formerly attributed to the Roman people more often than to kings. Likewise Marcus Tullius in the *Pro Plancio*: 'For it is the condition of a free people and especially of this people, who are the leader and master of all nations, to be able by voting to give or take away from anyone what it wishes. Our part is to bear the will of the people calmly: if we do not esteem honours highly, we do not need to serve the people; but if we do seek them, we must not grow tired of begging for them.'[47] Should I fear to call the king the slave of his people when the Roman senate, the master of so many kings, professed itself the slave of the people? This is true, you will say, in a democracy; for the *Lex Regia* had not yet transferred the power of the people to Augustus and his successors.[48] Then look at Tiberius whom you say was 'a tyrant, several times over', as he truly

[45] Cicero, *Pro Flacco*, VII, 15.

[46] Lucius Licinius Crassus, consul 95 BC and admired by Cicero as an orator and constitutionalist: see *De oratore*, I, lii, 225.

[47] Cicero, *Pro Plancio*, IV, 11.

[48] *nondum enim lex regia potestatem populi in Augustum, et successores ejus transtulerat*: the *lex regia* (or *lex de imperio*) was the law by which the emperor was invested with his *imperium*. The status of the only (partially) surviving example – the so-called *lex de imperio Vespasiani* (69) – is unclear.

was. Yet when he was called master by someone, even after that royal law was passed, as Suetonius relates, Tiberius officially declared that he should not call him so any more because it was an insult. Do you hear? That tyrant considered it an insult to him to be called master. Likewise he said in the senate, 'I say now and have said often at other times, senators, that a good and beneficial prince, whom you have endowed with such great and free power ought to serve the senate and often all the citizens and most commonly individuals too; and I do not repent that I said it. I have considered, and still consider, you good and just and well-disposed masters.'[49] And you will not gain any benefit if you say these things were made up by him, as he was most cunning in the art of hypocrisy; for who wishes to seem what he ought not to be? Hence it was not only Nero's custom, as Tacitus writes, but also that of the other emperors, to do homage to the people in the Circus.[50] On this Claudian, VI *Cons. Honorii.*:

> O how much mysterious power over the people is gained by the appearance of Empire in person, and how greatly the dignity of one repays that of the other, when the royal purple does homage to the mob crowding the tiers of the Circus, and with one accord from that hollow valley rising to the sky resounds the din of the crowd as it is paid homage.[51]

By this homage, what else were the Roman emperors doing except confessing that the whole people, even after the *Lex Regia*, were their masters?

And that is what I suspected right at the beginning, that you have spent more effort on turning over glossaries and in grandly publishing certain wearisome trifles, than on careful, earnest reading through of good authors. As you are not even lightly tinged with the wisdom of the ancient masters, you think that a matter which has been made perfectly well known by the opinions of the most outstanding philosophers and the words of the most sensible leaders in the state is absolutely new and dreamed only 'in mad fits of enthusiasts'. Come now, take that Martin the shoemaker and William the tanner whom you so despise, as your colleagues and initiators in ignorance: although they will be able to teach you and solve those utterly stupid

[49] Suetonius, *Tiberius*, 27, 29.
[50] Tacitus, *Annals*, XVI, 4.
[51] Claudian, *De sexto consulatu Honorii*, 611ff.

riddles. 'Are the people to be slaves in a democracy, when a king is a slave in a monarchy; and is it the whole or only a part of the people?' So when they have played the part of Oedipus to you, you may be the Sphinx to them and go headlong to misfortune;[52] otherwise I see there will be no end to your sillinesses and riddles.

You ask, 'When the apostle names kings, are we, by them, to understand the people?' Paul instructs that prayers should be made for kings, 1. Timothy 2.2; but he had instructed before that prayers should be made for the people, v. 1. But there are some, both among kings and among the people, for whom we are even forbidden to pray. May I not punish by law a man for whom I may not pray? What prevents it? But 'when Paul wrote this, the very worst men were emperors'. This is false also; for Ludovicus Capellus proves by most infallible arguments that this letter too was written under Claudius.[53] When Paul makes mention of Nero, he calls him not a king but a 'lion', that is a savage beast, out of whose mouth he rejoices that he was snatched, 2. Tim. 4.[54] And so for kings, not for beasts, 'we should pray, so that we may lead a peaceful and quiet life', yet 'with all piety and respectability'. You see that it is not so much of kings here, as of peace, piety and respectability too that account should be taken. But what people would not prefer to lead a life 'harassed, restless', warlike, honourable, protecting themselves and their children (it does not matter whether it is against a tyrant or an enemy), rather than lead beneath an enemy or tyrant a life that is not only equally harassed and restless but also shameful, slavish and dishonourable? Listen to the opinion of the Samnites in Livy who had tried out both conditions: they had rebelled, because peace was worse for slaves than war for freemen.[55] Rather listen to your own words; for I summon you yourself as witness again and again now – not to make you important but so all may observe how two-faced and self-contradictory you are, and how you are merely the paid slave of a king. 'Who', you say, 'would not prefer to endure the dissensions that often arise from the rivalry of nobles under an aristocracy, than certain wretchedness and ruin stemming from a single monarch who is accustomed to rule in a tyrannical manner? The Roman people preferred that to be the condition of their republic, however much it was shaken by discords,

[52] The Sphinx committed suicide after Oedipus solved the riddle. See *E*, III, 413; *Paradise Regained*, IV, 572–5.

[53] Cappel, *Historia*, p. 74.

[54] 2 Tim. 4:17.

[55] Livy, *Ab urbe condita*, X, 23, 14.

rather than the intolerable yoke of the caesars. A people who have preferred the condition of monarchy to avoid sedition, when they found by experience that the evil which they wanted to avoid was the lesser of the two, often seeks to return to its previous condition.'[56] These and more such are your own words in that dissertation about bishops produced under the assumed name of Walo Messalinus, p. 412 – against Petavius the Jesuit, though you yourself are more of a Jesuit and the worst of that crew.

What the holy scripture has established about this matter, we have seen, and do not repent having investigated it with all diligence. Thence it will perhaps not be worth the effort of searching out the opinion of the ancient fathers through so many huge volumes. For if they assert anything which scripture has not produced, we rightly reject their authority, great though it may be. But the quotation you produce from Irenaeus – that 'kings are appointed by God's command suitable to those who are governed by them at that time' – scripture quite clearly conflicts with this.[57] For though God had indicated openly that judges were more suitable for ruling his people than kings, he still left it all to the people's will and judgement, so that they might if they wished change the form of government beneath nobles, which was more suited to them, for the worse one beneath kings. We read also that often a bad king was given to a good people, and vice versa a good king to a bad people. And so it is for the wisest men to ascertain what is most fitting and useful for the people. For it is agreed that the same form of government does not suit every people nor the same people all the time, but sometimes this form, sometimes that one, accordingly as the virtue and industry of the citizens sometimes increases and sometimes diminishes.[58] But whoever removes from a people their power of choosing for themselves the form of government they want, removes for certain that in which civil liberty is almost wholly rooted.

Then you cite Justin Martyr's offer of compliance to the Antonines, best of emperors;[59] who would not have offered it to them, so distinguished and moderate as they were? 'But', you say, 'how much

[56] Walo Messalinus (Salmasius), *De episcopis ac presbyteris contra D. Petavium Loiolitam, dissertatio prima* (Leyden, 1641), p. 412. See *Church-Government*, I, 781.

[57] S., (*DR*, p. 62) quotes Irenaeus, *Against heresies*, V, 24, 3.

[58] See *CB*, I, 420.

[59] M. (*CB*, I, 437) himself cited the 'Pro Christianis Defensio II ad Antoninum Pium' from Justin Martyr, *Opera* (Paris, 1615), p. 64.

worse christians are we today? They bore a prince of a different religion.' Of course, since they were private persons and far inferior in strength. 'Now, indeed, papists will not bear a protestant king', nor 'protestants a papist one.' You indeed act sensibly – so you show yourself to be neither a papist nor a protestant. You act generously also; for you lavishly grant of your own accord what we have not asked for now, that all christians today clearly agree in this matter which you alone oppose with remarkable boldness and wickedness, which is also most unlike those fathers whom you praise; for they were writing defences on behalf of christians to pagan kings, while you are doing so on behalf of a king who was a most wicked papist, to christians and protestants.

Many ideas you next cite vainly from Athenagoras,[60] and many from Tertullian, which have already been said much more clearly and plainly by the apostles themselves. Tertullian however is very far from agreeing with you, who wish a king to be master: this you either did not know or else wickedly concealed. For he, a christian, dared to write to a heathen emperor in his *Apologeticum* that an emperor ought not to be called lord. 'Augustus', he said, 'who shaped the empire, did not wish even to be called lord, for this is a title belonging to God: I will of course call the emperor lord, but only when I am not compelled to call him lord in God's place. For the rest I am a free man to him; my Lord is God alone, etc.' And in the same work: 'How is he who is father of his country also its master?'[61] Now rejoice in Tertullian whom you would have certainly done better to leave alone. 'But he calls those who killed Domitian parricides.' He calls them so rightly; for he was killed by a plot of his wife and slaves, by Parthenius, and by Stephanus who was guilty of stealing money.[62] But if the senate and people of Rome had judged Domitian an enemy, as they judged Nero previously and were searching for him to put him to death; if they had punished him according to ancestral custom, do you think Tertullian would have called them parricides? Rather if he had done so, he would have been worth putting to death himself; as you are now worthy of the gallows. The same answer will suit Origen[63] as Irenaeus.

[60] Athenagoras was a second-century Greek philosopher who converted to, and became an apologist for, christianity.

[61] See p. 11.

[62] Domitian, Roman emperor, 81–96. See Suetonius, *Domitian*, 17.

[63] Origen (*c.* 186–253) was one of the most eminent of the Church Fathers.

Athanasius says that it is impious to call the kings of the earth before human tribunals.[64] Who said this to Athanasius? For I hear no word of God in this. And so I shall believe emperors and kings, who confess that this is false for themselves, rather than Athanasius. Then you bring in Ambrose (who became a bishop after being a proconsul and a catechumen) with his ignorant, not to say flattering, interpretation of those words of David, 'against you alone have I sinned'.[65] Ambrose wished all others to be subject to the emperor, so that he himself might subject the emperor to himself. For how proudly and with what more than popish pride, he treated the emperor Theodosius at Milan, judged him guilty himself of the slaughter at Thessalonica and prevented his entry into the church; and how then he showed himself a raw beginner in gospel doctrine – all this is known to all.[66] When the emperor cast himself down at his feet, he ordered him to leave the church-porch; when he had at last been restored to the church, and after he had made offerings, and was standing at the altar, he drove him outside the railings with these words: 'O emperor, access to the inner places is only granted to priests and the others may not touch them.' Was this a preacher of the Gospel, or a priest of Jewish rites? Yet he (such are the arts of almost all churchmen) set the emperor as a master over the rest, that he himself might be master of the emperor. And so with these words he drove Theodosius back, as it were, to be his subject: 'you are emperor over your fellow-men and fellow-slaves. For there is only one master, king and creator of all things.'[67] Fine indeed! This truth which the slyness and flattery of bishops kept obscure, the hastiness of temper of one man and, to speak more gently, his ignorant zeal brought to light.

To Ambrose's ignorance you join your own ignorance or heresy, in explicitly denying that 'under the old covenant there was remission of sins through the blood of Christ, at the time when David confessed to God that he had sinned against him alone', p. 68. The orthodox believe that not except by the blood of the lamb slaughtered from the beginning of the world was there ever any remission of sins. I do not

[64] S., *DR*, p. 67, quotes Athanasius, *Sermo de Cruce et Passioni Domini.*

[65] S., *DR*, p. 68, quotes Ambrose, *Letters*, LI, i.

[66] Theodosius I (the Great), emperor of the East, 378–95, submitted to Ambrose (*c.* 340–97), bishop of Milan, in 390. Cf. *CB* and *R*, I, 432, 607; *E*, III, 587.

[67] The usual reference is to Theodoret, *Ecclesiastical History*, V, 17, but M.'s Latin in fact conforms to Epiphanius Scholasticus, *Historia Ecclesiastica Tripartita*, IX, 30. For a possible allusion to Epiphanius, see *AR*, II, 518.

know whose disciple you are, you new heretic; certainly that disciple of the great theologian whom you violently criticize was not wandering far from the truth when he said that anyone of the people could by equal right with David have cried upon God with these words, 'against you alone have I sinned'.

Then you make a display of Augustine,[68] and produce some old clerics from Hippo. The quotations of Augustine which are adduced by you do not stand in our way. For why should we not admit with the prophet Daniel,[69] that God changes eras, gives kingdoms and takes kingdoms away, yet by the agency of men. If God alone gave a kingdom to Charles, he also took it away from Charles and gave it to the nobles and people. If you say that our obedience should have been exhibited to Charles for that reason, you must say that it ought now to be exhibited to our magistrates. For you grant yourself that God gave to our magistrates also the same power as he gives to evil kings 'to punish the people's sins'; and so no-one, by your opinion, except God can remove from their office our magistrates, who have equally been set up by God. And in this way, as usual, you turn your own sword-point against yourself, with your own hand, you are your own assassin; nor with harm, since you have advanced to that pitch of wickedness and shamelessness, of stupidity and madness, that you yourself assert that those people whom you prove by so many arguments should not be harmed by a finger, should instead be pursued in war by all their subjects. You say that Ishmael the murderer of Gedaliah, the prefect, was called a parricide by Jerome – and deservedly; for he killed the ruler of Judaea, a good man, without any cause.[70] The same Jerome on Ecclesiastes says that that teaching of Solomon, 'Observe the voice of the king', agrees with the teaching of Paul.[71] And he should be praised indeed because he expounded that passage with more moderation of spirit than did the rest of his contemporaries.

'You will not come down to later times after Augustine, to seek out the opinion of doctors.' Yet so all may understand that you can lie more easily than remain silent (if you still have any supporters of your point of view), straight after one sentence you do not restrain yourself from coming down to Isidore of Seville, Gregory of Tours, Otto of

68 St Augustine (354–430), bishop of Hippo.

69 Dan. 2:21.

70 See Jer. 41:2.

71 M. echoes S.'s quotation, *DR*, p. 71, from Jerome's commentary on Ecclesiastes.

Friesing[72] – even into the heart of barbarism. If only you had known how worthless their authority is in our eyes, you would not have adduced here their obscure evidence by lying.

You readers wish to know why he dares not come down to the present time, why he hides himself, why he suddenly vanishes? I will tell you: he sees that all the most eminent teachers of the protestant church there are will be his most bitter opponents. Let him only put it to the test and he shall feel how easily I shall rout and destroy him – though he struggles and collects all his forces into one mass – by bringing out into the battle line Luthers, Zwinglis, Calvins, Bucers, Martyrs and Paraeuses; I will set against you even your Leyden friends, whose university, whose most flourishing state, once the dwelling place of freedom, in short whose springs and streams of a liberal education could not wash away that slavish rust and inborn barbarism of yours. Since you have not one orthodox theologian on your side – you may name one at your leisure – stripped of all protestant support, you do not blush to flee for refuge to the Sorbonne: a college which you know quite well is totally devoted to popish doctrine and has no authority among the orthodox. So we deliver so wicked a champion of tyranny to the Sorbonne to be swallowed up;[73] we do not wish so cheap a slave to be ours, who denies that 'the whole people are the equal of the most lazy king'. In vain you strive to offload and transfer to the pope what all free nations, every religion, all the orthodox take to themselves and adopt as their own. The pope indeed was the first originator of this most shameful doctrine of yours when he with his bishops was insignificant and had little power. By these means at length, he gradually gained great wealth and great power and himself ended as the greatest of all tyrants. Yet all tyrants he bound most firmly to himself, when he persuaded the peoples, whose minds he had long held crushed beneath superstition, that they could not repeal the power of kings however bad unless he released them from their oath of allegiance. But you avoid orthodox writers and, by pleading that an opinion was introduced by the pope which is common to and very well known by themselves, try to bring unpopularity upon the truth. If you did not do it craftily, it would be seen that you are neither papist nor protestant,

[72] Isidorus Hispalensis, bishop of Seville, 602–36; Gregory of Tours, 538–94; Otto, bishop of Friesing, and twelfth-century chronicler of Frederick I (Barbarossa).

[73] *Sorbonae igitur absorbendum*: M.'s pun reflects his longstanding hostility to the Sorbonne.

but some kind of half-barbarian Edomite Herodian, who worships and adores any most fierce tyrant[74] as if he was the Messiah sent down from Heaven.

You say 'you have shown this from the teaching of the fathers of the first four centuries, which alone should be considered evangelical and christian'. Shame has deserted this man; how many things were said and written by them which Christ and the apostles would neither have taught nor approved? How many things in which all protestants disagree with the fathers? But what have you shown from the fathers – 'that evil kings too are appointed by God'? Suppose that they are appointed, as all evils too are in some way appointed by God: 'therefore they have God alone as judge, they are above the laws, by no law written or unwritten, natural or divine can they be brought to trial by their subjects or before their own subjects'. Why? Certainly no law forbids it, none exempts kings: all reason and right and divine law commands that all who sin should be punished without distinction. Nor have you brought forward any law written or unwritten, natural or divine which forbids it. So why may not kings also be punished? 'Because even bad ones are appointed by God.' Shall I say that you are more worthless than stupid and an idiot? You must be very wicked to dare to disseminate a completely destructive doctrine among the mob, and very stupid to rely most heavily upon such silly reasoning. God said, Isaiah 54, 'I have created the killer to destroy';[75] so a killer is above the laws; investigate this and turn it over as much as you like, you will find the conclusion the same either way.

For the pope too is appointed by God in the same way as a tyrant, and granted for the punishment of the church, as I have shown above from your own writings also. Yet 'because he has raised his primacy to an intolerable pinnacle of power, not unlike a tyranny', you assert that 'both he and his bishops should be removed with a better right than they were appointed', *Wal. Mes.*, p. 412. You say that the pope and bishops, although appointed by God in anger, should be removed from the church because they are tyrants; you say that tyrants should not be removed from the commonwealth because they have been appointed by God in anger. Truly absurd and irrational: for while the pope cannot harm the actual conscience (which alone is his realm) of someone against his will, you cry that he who can in reality not be a

[74] For '*Herodian* flatterers' see *T*, II, 644.

[75] Isa. 54:16.

tyrant must be removed as being a most burdensome tyrant. But the true tyrant, who holds our life and property in his power, you contend that he should by all means be borne in the commonwealth. These statements of yours when compared with each other betray you as so ignorant and so childish, whether you argue true or false, that your fickleness, ignorance, rashness, and thoughtlessness can lie concealed from nobody thereafter.

But another reason suggests itself: 'Human affairs would seem upside down' – and all the better, for it would be all up with human affairs if matters which are at their worst should always stay in the same place. I say for the better, for the king's authority would return to the people, from whose will and votes it came in the first place and was conferred on one of their number: power would by a very fair law pass from the one who did the injury to the one who suffered the injury, since a third party amongst men could not be suitable; for who would bear a foreigner to judge him? All men would be equally bound by the laws, and nothing can be more just than that. There would be no mortal God. Whoever sets up one such among mankind is no less wicked towards the commonwealth than towards the church.

Again I would use your own weapons against you. You say that 'it is the greatest heresy to believe that one man sits in Christ's seat: these two marks are the sign of the antichrist, infallibility in spiritual matters, and omnipotence in temporal ones', *Apparat. ad Primat.*, p. 171. Are kings infallible? Why should they then be omnipotent? Or if they are so, why are they less destructive to civil affairs than the pope to spiritual ones? Does God truly not look after civil affairs? If not, surely he does not prevent us from doing so. If he does, he wishes the same reformation to happen in the commonwealth as in the church; especially if it has been ascertained that infallibility and omnipotence assigned to one man are the same causes of all evils in both. For in civil matters God has not taught such patience that the commonwealth should endure every most savage tyrant, but the church should not. Rather he has taught the contrary: and he has left the church indeed with no weapons apart from patience, innocence, prayers and the teaching of the gospel. Into the hands of the commonwealth and all magistrates at once he has handed not patience but laws and a sword, the avenger of wrongs and violence. Hence the perverted and absurd nature of this man endures either wonderment or laughter; as in the church he is Helvidius and Thrasea and a clear tyrannicide, so in the commonwealth he is the common slave and attendant of all tyrants.

If his opinion holds good, not only we have rebelled who have rejected our kings, but all protestants also who have rejected the pope as master, against the will of their kings.

But for a long time now he has lain felled by his own weapons. For such is the man that – only let his opponent's hand not fail – he himself supplies an abundance of weapons against himself: and no-one furnishes handles more convenient for refuting or ridiculing himself. One will quicker leave off flogging him through actual fatigue than he of offering his back.

CHAPTER IV

Perhaps you think, Salmasius, that you have won great favour from kings and have obliged all the rulers and masters of the world with this royal defence. But if they were to judge their own advantage and interest by the criterion of truth rather than that of your flatteries, they would hate no-one worse than you, and drive off and keep no-one further away from themselves. For in raising the power of kings immeasurably above the laws, by the same means you remind almost all nations of their slavery, which they had not suspected. You also drive them the more violently into suddenly shaking off that sluggishness in which they idly used to dream they were free men, by reminding them of something they didn't realize: that they were the slaves of kings. And they will judge the power of kings to be the less bearable to them the more successfully you persuade them that such unlimited power grew not as the result of their own sufferance of it, but that it originated from the beginning with its present nature and extent just because of the right of kings. So you and this defence of yours, whether you convince the people or whether you don't, will needs be destructive, deadly and accursed for all kings hereafter. For if you convince the people that the right of kings is all-powerful, they will no longer bear a monarchy; if you do not convince them, they will not endure kings who obtain such illegal power as if it were theirs by right.

If those kings who are undecided about this matter will listen to me and let themselves be bounded by the laws, then instead of the uncertain, weak and violent power which they now possess, full of cares and fears, they will preserve for themselves a completely stable, peaceful and long-lasting one. If they should despise this advice, which is so healthy for themselves and their kingdoms, merely because of its author, let them know that it is not so much mine as that of a very wise king of old. For Lycurgus,[1] the Spartan king who sprang from an ancient line of kings, saw that his neighbours who ruled Argos and Messena had each turned their rule into a tyranny, and that this had been equally destructive to themselves and to their states. So as to look to the well-being of his country at the same time as keeping the office of king in his own family as long as possible, he shared his power with the senate and made the ephors' power against the king himself similar to that of censors – to consolidate his rule. By doing this he handed down a very stable kingdom to his descendants for many generations. Or, as others will have it, the restraint of Theopompus,[2] who ruled over Sparta more than one hundred years after Lycurgus, was such that he set the popular power of the ephors above his own. By this deed he boasted that he had firmly established his kingdom and had left it to his sons much greater and longer-lasting.

Today's kings would have here an example to imitate that was certainly not undistinguished – one that was even an excellent authority for perfectly safe advice. For no law has ever decreed – or ever could decree – that all men should suffer one man as a master who was above the laws. For that law which overturns all laws cannot itself be a law. And so when the laws reject you as a subverter and murderer of all laws, you try in this chapter to renew the fight with precedents. So let us try out precedents: for often precedents give plainer instruction in matters where the laws are silent and in their silence merely give hints. We will begin with the Jews, who were best advised about God's will. 'Later', as you put it, 'we will come down to the christians.' But we will make an earlier beginning, from the time when the Israelites, who had somehow become subject to kings, cast off that yoke of slavery from their necks.

The king of Moab, Eglon, had conquered the Israelites in war.[3] He had settled the seat of his power among them in Jericho. He did not

[1] Lycurgus: legislator, traditionally credited with founding the Spartan constitution, possibly in the ninth century BC.

[2] Theopompus: ruler of Sparta (eighth century BC), sometimes proposed (e.g., by Plutarch) as originator of the ephorate.

[3] Judges 3:12–20. See pp. 17–19.

despise the divine, for when mention was made of God, he rose from his throne. The Israelites had served Eglon for eighteen years. They had sent a gift to him not as if he was their enemy but as if he was their own king. However, while they were publicly giving him a present as their king, they killed him by treachery as an enemy.

Truly Ehud who killed him is believed to have done it by the advice of God. What could be a better recommendation for a deed of this kind? For God usually encourages men to do deeds that are honourable and praiseworthy, not unjust, treacherous and cruel. But nowhere do we read that he had an express command from God. 'The sons of Israel cried to the Lord' – and so did we. The Lord brought forth a saviour for them – and so he did for us. Eglon, from their neighbour became a member of the household, and from their enemy became their king. Our king became our enemy, so he was not a king; for in no way can anyone be a citizen of the state if he is an enemy to it. Antony was not considered a consul nor Nero an emperor after each was judged an enemy by the senate. As Cicero very clearly points out in his fourth *Philippic* about Antony: 'If Antony is a consul, Brutus is an enemy; if Brutus is the preserver of the state, Antony is an enemy. Who thinks Antony is consul unless they are robbers?'[4]

By equal justice, I say who but a country's enemies think a tyrant is a king? So whether Eglon was a foreigner and Charles a native matters little since each was an enemy and a tyrant. If Ehud slaughtered Eglon justly, we have justly punished Charles. Yes, and that hero Samson, though even his countrymen blamed him – Judg. 15, 'Did you not know that the Philistines rule over us?'[5] – yet made war alone on his masters and killed not one but many of his country's tyrants at one stroke, whether at the instigation of God or of his own courage.[6] And he made prayers beforehand to God to help him.[7] So it didn't seem impious but pious to Samson to kill his masters, the tyrants of his country, when the majority of the citizens did not decline to be slaves.

But David the king and prophet refused to kill Saul, the anointed of God. Not that we are necessarily obliged to refuse to do whatever David refused. David refused as a private person. Will it be necessary

[4] Cicero, *Philippics*, IV, iii, 8; iv, 9.

[5] Judges 15:11.

[6] *sive Dei, sive propriae virtutis instinctu occidit*: for a similar refusal to be explicit about motivation, see *Samson Agonistes*, 1545–7, 1637–8.

[7] Judges 16:28–30.

that a council, a parliament, a whole nation refuses it at once? David refused to kill his enemy by treachery; shall a magistrate then refuse to punish a criminal by law? David refused to kill a king; shall the senate then refuse to punish a tyrant? David had a religious scruple about killing one anointed by God; so then shall a nation have scruples about condemning to death their own anointed, especially one who was smeared with the blood of citizens and who had blotted out that unction whether sacred or civil by such long enmity?

Indeed kings whom God anointed through his prophets or fixed on by name for a definite task, like Cyrus once, Isa. 44,[8] these I acknowledge as the anointed of the Lord; the rest I judge to be the anointed either of the people or the soldiers or only of their own faction. But you will never induce me to grant you that all kings are the anointed of the Lord, and say that for this reason they are above the laws and should not be punished for any crimes whatsoever. And why?

David forbade himself and certain private persons to raise their hands against the anointed of God. But God himself forbade kings, Ps. 105, to touch his anointed,[9] that is, his people. He put the anointing of his people before the anointing, if there was any such thing, of kings. Then shall it not be permissible to punish the faithful if they have committed any crime against the laws? It nearly came about that King Solomon put to death the anointed of God, the priest Abiathar;[10] and he didn't spare him because he was the anointed of God, but because he had been his father's friend. So if the Lord's religious and civil anointing could not deliver from punishment the highest priest, who is mostly also the highest magistrate, why should merely civil anointing deliver a tyrant? 'But Saul also was a tyrant and worthy of death.' So be it: but it will not follow from this that David was worthy or suitable to kill King Saul in any place without the authority of the people or the order of magistrates. So was Saul really a tyrant? I wish you would say so, even though you said above, Ch. 2, p. 32, that 'he was not a tyrant but a good and chosen king'. Is there any reason now why any informer or forger should be marked with a brand in public while you miss out on the same mark of shame, since they usually practice their deceptions in better faith indeed than you usually write and treat even matters of the greatest importance? So Saul, if that suits your turn, was a good king. But if that is less

[8] Isa. 44:28. [9] Ps. 105:14–15. [10] 1 Kings 2:26.

expedient for you, suddenly he won't be a good king, but a tyrant. And this is certainly no wonder. For while you so impudently pander to tyrannical power, what else do you do but make good kings all into tyrants? But in truth David, although he did not wish to kill the king his father-in-law for many reasons which have no bearing on our case, yet to defend himself did not hesitate to gather forces, to seize or besiege Saul's cities; and he would even have held the town of Keilah against Saul with a garrison, had he not known the townspeople were badly disposed towards him.[11] What if Saul had besieged the city, put up ladders against the walls and had been willing to be the first to climb up – do you think David would at once have cast down his weapons and betrayed all his men to an anointed enemy? I trust not. Why wouldn't he have done what we have done? For in having promised copious aid to the Philistines, the enemies of his country, when he was compelled by the necessity of his interests, he did against Saul what I believe we should never have done against our tyrant. I am ashamed and for a long time have been tired of your lies. You falsely say it is a doctrine of the English 'that enemies should be spared rather than friends' and accordingly that 'they ought not to have spared their king because he was a friend'. Whoever heard this before it was made up by you, you greatest liar amongst men? Yet we pardon it: to be sure, there was missing from this chapter that most choice (and trite) highlight of your speech that had now been brought five times (and before the end of the book, ten times) out of your little pots and perfume jars, namely that the English 'are fiercer than their own hounds'. It is not so much that the English are fiercer than their own hounds, as that you are hungrier than any mad dog, since you with your tough insides can bear to return again and again to that old cabbage which you have so often vomited up.

David, finally, ordered the Amalekite to be put to death as (for so he pretended himself) the killer of Saul.[12] Here there is no likeness either in the deed or in the actors. But, unless David appeared to have gone over to the Philistines and become part of their army and for that reason strove the more carefully to remove from himself all suspicion of hastening on the king's death, there was no reason, in my opinion at least, why he should treat that man so badly who announced that he had with a convenient blow finished off the king who was already

[11] 1 Sam. 23:1–12.

[12] 2 Sam. 1:13–15.

dying, and dying uncomfortably. The same deed in Domitian's case (who similarly condemned Epaphroditus to death because he had helped Nero to kill himself) is condemned by all.[13] Then with a new impudence – with regard to a man whom you had just called a tyrant and 'one chased by an evil spirit' – you consider it no longer enough to call him the anointed of the Lord, but 'the Lord's Christ'. So cheaply do you hold the name of Christ that you are not afraid to bestow so holy a name as that even upon a tyrant possessed by the devil.

I come now to that instance in which whoever does not see that the right of the people is older than the right of the king must be blind. On the death of Solomon, the people held a meeting at Sichem about making his son king.[14] Rehoboam set out for this place as a candidate, so he might not seem to claim the kingdom as his inheritance nor to possess a free people like his father's cattle. The people put forward the conditions of his future rule. The king asks for three days to be given him to consider the matter. He consults the elders. They give him no advice about royal right but tell him to win over the people with indulgence and promises, since it was in their power to make him king or pass him over. Then he consults his peers who had been brought up with him from boyhood. They, stirred up by some gadfly like Salmasius, thunder nothing but royal right and urge him to threaten whips and scorpions. Rehoboam replied to the people according to the counsel of the latter. And so the whole of Israel seeing that the king 'hearkened not to them' at once testified to their own freedom and the right of the people openly with free voices. 'What share do we have in David? To your tents, Israel. Now look after your house yourself, David.' Then when Adoramus was sent to them by the king, they pelted him with stones and perhaps would have made an example of the king as well had he not fled with the greatest speed. He raises a huge army to bring the Israelites back under his control. God prevents it. 'Do not go up', he says, 'do not fight against your brothers, the sons of Israel, for this thing has been done by me.' Now consider: before, the people were wanting a king. That displeased God. Now the people do not want Rehoboam as their king. Not only does God allow this to be within the people's power but forbids and stops the king making war in that cause: and he teaches

[13] Suetonius, *Domitian*, 14.

[14] 1 Kings 12:1–24.

that those who had rebelled were not on that account to be called rebels but nonetheless brothers. Now pull yourself together.

All kings, you say, are of God. So the people should not resist even tyrants. On the other hand, I say that the meetings of people, elections, campaigns, votes, decrees are similarly of God, by his testimony here. So even a king in the same way ought not to resist the people, by the authority of the self-same God. For as it is certain that kings today are of God, and as this fact has the power to command the people's obedience, so is it certain that the free assemblies of the people today are also of God and this has the force either to keep kings in line or to get rid of them. Nor for this reason ought they to bring war on a people any more than Rehoboam ought. You ask why then didn't the Israelites revolt from Solomon? Who apart from you would ask such stupid questions when it is agreed that they revolted without punishment from a tyrant? Solomon fell into certain vices, but he did not therefore at once become a tyrant. He compensated for his vices by great virtues and great services to the state. Grant that he had been a tyrant. Often matters are such that the people do not wish to remove a tyrant, often such that they cannot. It is enough that they removed him when they could. 'But Jeroboam's deed was always condemned, and his defection from his religion abominated, his successors always considered rebels.' I read in many places that he was blamed not for his defection from Rehoboam, but from the true worship of God;[15] and I remember that his successors indeed were often called wicked, but nowhere rebels. 'If something is done', you say, 'contrary to right and the laws, right cannot arise from it.' What, I ask you, then will become of the right of kings? In this way you always disprove yourself. 'Every day', you say, 'adulteries, murders, thefts are committed without punishment.' Don't you realize that here you are replying to your own question as to why tyrants so often get off without punishment? 'Those kings were rebels, yet the prophets did not lead the people astray from their obedience.' Why then, wicked and false prophet, do you try to lead the people of England astray from their magistrates, even if they are rebels, in your opinion? 'The faction of English robbers', you say, 'alleges that they were driven on to this crime which they undertook so impiously by I know not what call sent from heaven.' That the English ever alleged this is one of your

[15] 1 Kings 14:7–16.

countless lies and imaginings. But I go on to deal with you by precedents.

Libnah, a very powerful city, revolted from King Joram, because he had abandoned God.[16] So the king revolted, not that city, and it is not branded because of that revolt but, if you consider the added motive, seems rather to be approved. 'Revolts of this kind ought not to be used as examples.' Why then did you promise with so much idle bragging that you would fight it out with me for the whole of this chapter by precedents, when you yourself can bring forward no examples except pure denials which have no force as proofs? And the ones I have brought forward, which are definite and solid, you say ought not to be used as precedents? Who would not hiss you off the stage after arguing like this? You have challenged us with precedents. We have brought forward precedents. What is your answer to that? You turn your back and look for byways to escape.

So I proceed. Jehu killed a king at the command of the prophet. He even saw to the killing of Ahaziah, his own lawful king.[17] If God had not wanted the tyrant to be killed by a citizen, if this had been impious, a bad precedent, why did he order it to be done? If he ordered it, surely it was lawful, praiseworthy and glorious. Yet killing a tyrant was not good and lawful because God ordered it, but God ordered it because it was good and lawful.

Although Athaliah had already been ruling for seven years, the priest Jehoiada did not fear to drive her from the kingdom and slaughter her.[18] 'But', you say, 'she had taken a kingdom she did not own.' Did not Tiberius much later take 'a power in no way belonging to him?'[19] But above you kept affirming that he and other tyrants of that kind, according to the teaching of Christ, should be obeyed. It would be clearly ridiculous if it was lawful to kill a king who had unrightfully acquired royal power, but not one who behaved most badly. But by law she could not rule, being a woman; 'you will set over you a king',[20] not a queen. If it comes to that, then I say: you will set over you a king, not a tyrant. For there is a greater difference between a king, and a tyrant, than a male and a female.

[16] 2 Kings 8:22.
[17] 2 Kings 9:1–27.
[18] 2 Kings 11:15–16. 2 Chron. 23:14–15.
[19] Although Agrippa Postumus, Augustus' surviving grandson, was executed immediately upon Augustus' death in AD 14 (possibly in accordance with Augustus' wishes), the succession of Tiberius was apparently regular. See Tacitus, *Annals*, I, 3–13.
[20] 1 Sam. 8:11.

Amaziah, a cowardly and an idolatrous king, was put to death not by some conspirators, but, which is more probable, by the chiefs and the people. For when he fled from Jerusalem, unaided by anyone, they pursued him as far as Lachish. They are said to have entered upon this plan 'after the time he had abandoned God', and we read that there was no enquiry held by Azariah his son about his father's death.[21] You cite much nonsense again from the rabbis, to set the king of the Jews above the sanhedrin. You do not consider the words of king Zedekiah himself, Jer. 38: 'The king is not the man who has any power against you.'[22] In this way he addresses the chiefs, confessing himself clearly inferior to his own senate. 'Perhaps', you say, 'not daring to deny them anything for fear of sedition.' But how much is that 'perhaps' of yours worth, I ask, when your most positive assertion is not worth a straw? For what is more fickle and changeable than you, what more inconstant? How often have I found you changeable and changing colour, how often in disharmony with yourself, disagreeing with yourself and differing in your opinion?

Again you make comparison between Charles and the good kings of Israel. First you name David as someone to be despised. 'Take David', you say, 'guilty at the same time of adultery and homicide; no such thing with Charles. Solomon, his son, who was commonly called wise.' Who would not consider it improper for the names of the greatest and holiest of men, especially of kings, to be bandied about in this way by a most vile, worthless good-for-nothing? Have you had the effrontery to compare Charles with David; a superstitious king, hardly initiated into christian doctrine, with a most religious king and prophet; a stupid with a very wise one; an un-warlike with a very brave one; a most unjust with a most just one? Can you praise the chastity and self-control of one whom, together with the duke of Buckingham, we know to be covered with every crime? What concern is it of ours to investigate the secret nooks and crannies of his life, when in the open theatre he used to embrace women wantonly, and kiss them, and handle the breasts of maids and matrons, not to speak of the rest. Rather, I advise you, you pseudo-Plutarch,[23] to refrain henceforward from drawing the most foolish parallels of this kind, in case I should

[21] 2 Kings 14:19,21.
[22] Jer. 38:5.
[23] *Pseudoplutarche*: Plutarch's *Lives* consists largely of pairs of biographies, a prominent Greek being followed by a prominent Roman figure.

find it necessary to publish things concerning Charles about which I would otherwise gladly remain silent.

So far it is clear what has been attempted or accomplished against tyrants by the people, and by what right, in those times when God himself was directing the Hebrew commonwealth in person, so to speak, by his will and word. The ages that follow do not guide us by their own authority, but in directing all men by the rule and reason of their ancestors, they only strengthen ours in imitation of them. And so when God, after the Babylonian captivity, had given them no new command about the form of government, although the royal line was not extinct, they returned to the ancient Mosaic form of commonwealth. They resisted Antiochus, king of Syria,[24] to whom they were tributaries, and his governors, because he ordered unlawful acts through the Maccabees, their priests; and they freed themselves by arms; then they granted the principate to the most worthy man, until Hyrcanus,[25] son of Simon, brother of Judas Maccabaeus, despoiled David's tomb and began to keep foreign troops and add a certain royal power to the priesthood. Hence his son Aristobulus[26] was the first to put the crown upon his head. The people did not stir or undertake any action against him; and no wonder, as he only ruled a year. He himself was also seized by a most serious illness, and repented of his crimes and did not cease to wish for his own death until in the middle of making these wishes he expired. His brother Alexander[27] was the next ruler. 'Against him', you say, 'nobody rose, although he was a tyrant.' Oh, you might have lied quite carelessly if Josephus had perished and only your 'Josippus' remained,[28] from whom you produce some useless sayings of the pharisees. And so the matter stands thus: Alexander, since he governed the state badly both in peace and war, although he protected himself with a large mercenary band of Pisidians and Cilicians, still could not restrain the people from almost overwhelming him even in the middle of sacrificing with palm and citrus fronds, as being unworthy of that office. Afterwards, for six

[24] Antiochus IV (Epiphanes), Seleucid king, 175–163 BC, whose policy of Hellenization provoked a revival of Jewish nationalism and a revolt led by the priest, Judas Maccabaeus. Cf. *Paradise Regained*, III, 160–9.

[25] John Hyrcanus I, high priest and ruler, 134–104 BC.

[26] Aristobulus I, assumed the kingship, 104–103 BC.

[27] Alexander Jannaeus, reigned 103–76 BC.

[28] M. follows Josephus, *Jewish Antiquities*, XIII, 372ff., S., *DR*, p. 83, the tenth-century chronicle by Josippus (Josippon, or Joseph Ben Gorion).

years, grievous war was made upon him by almost the whole nation; and when he had killed many thousands of Jews in this and was at last desirous of peace and asked them what they wished to be done by him, they all replied with one voice that he should die; and that they would hardly pardon him even when he was dead. To avert by any means this story which is most inconvenient for you, you have concealed your own most shameful deception with some little pharisaical maxims, when you ought either to have wholly omitted this example or faithfully related the matter just as it had happened, except that, being a crafty old fox and a light-shunner, you trusted your lies far more than your case. Even those eight hundred pharisees, whom he ordered to be crucified, were of the number of those who had taken up arms against him: and they along with the rest bore witness with one voice that they would put the king to death, if he had been defeated in war and come into their power. After her husband Alexander, Alexandra[29] took the kingdom; like Athaliah[30] before, not lawfully (for the laws did not allow a woman to rule, which you yourself have just confessed) but partly by force (for she led an army of foreigners) and partly by influence, for she had gained the favour of the pharisees who had the greatest power amongst the people, by means of this law, that the title of the power would be in her hands while the power itself would be in theirs. Just so in our country recently the Scottish Presbyterians granted Charles the title of king, their price being that they might keep the kingship to themselves.[31] After the death of Alexandra, her sons Hyrcanus and Aristobulus fought for the kingdom.[32] The latter, being the mightier in strength and industry, drove his elder brother from the kingdom. While Pompey was then turning to Syria from the Mithridatic War, the Jews, who thought that they had now obtained a very fair judge of their liberty in Pompey, sent an embassy to him. They renounced both brothers as kings; they complained that they had been enslaved by them. Pompey stripped Aristobulus of his kingdom; he left the priesthood to Hyrcanus and the principate legitimately under the country's custom;[33] thenceforth he was called priest and ethnarch. Again in the

[29] Alexandra Salome, reigned 76–69 BC.

[30] 2 Kings 11:1–3.

[31] M. could be referring either to the 'Engagement' between Charles I and the Scottish commissioners of Dec. 1647 or the 'Treaty' made by Charles II in June 1650.

[32] Aristobulus expelled Hyrcanus who fled to Aretas III of Arabia. Aretas then besieged Aristobulus in Jerusalem, at which point Pompey intervened.

[33] For Pompey (106–48 BC) appointing Hyrcanus, see Josephus, *Jewish Antiquities*, XIV, 73.

rule of Archelaus, son of Herod,[34] the Jews sent fifty ambassadors to Augustus Caesar and made serious charges against the dead Herod and Archelaus. They deprived him of his kingship to the utmost of their ability, and begged Caesar to let the Jewish people exist without kings. Caesar was somewhat moved by their prayers, and appointed him not as a king but simply as an ethnarch. Again in his tenth year the people sent charges of tyranny against him to Caesar through ambassadors. Caesar heard these kindly, summoned him to Rome and when he was condemned by the court sent him to exile in Vienne. Now I would like you to make a reply to me; with respect to those who wished their kings to be charged, condemned and punished, would not they themselves, if they had the power, or if the choice had been given to them, would not they themselves, I say, have condemned them in court and themselves put them to death? Now you do not deny that the people and nobles also quite often took up arms against Roman governors who ruled a province greedily and cruelly. You make up very stupid reasons for this in your usual way: 'they were not yet used to the yoke'. Very likely under Alexander, Herod and his sons! They did not wish 'to make war upon' Gaius Caesar and Petronius.[35] Sensible of them indeed: they were not able to do so. Do you wish to hear their own words? Πολεμεῖν μὲν οὐ βουλόμενοι διὰ τὸ μηδ᾽ ἄν δύνασθαι.[36] What they themselves confess to be due to their own weakness, do you, hypocrite, attribute to religious scruples?

Then with a great deal of effort you accomplish absolutely nothing, while you are proving from the fathers what you had also done before with equal tediousness – that kings must be prayed for. For who denies it in the case of good kings? For bad ones too as long as there is hope; for robbers too and for enemies; not that they should lay waste our fields or kill us with slaughter, but that they may recover their senses. We pray for both; yet who forbids us to punish the one sort by law and the other by arms? I care nothing for your 'Egyptian liturgies'; but that priest who prayed, as you say, that 'Commodus[37] might

[34] Archelaus, son of Herod the Great, reigned over Judaea, Samarcitis and Idumaea, 4 BC–AD 6.

[35] Gaius Julius Caesar Germanicus (Caligula), Roman emperor, 37–41, ordered Publius Petronius, proconsul of Asia and legate of Syria, to erect a statue of the emperor in the Temple.

[36] 'Not wishing to make war because we cannot': Josephus, *Jewish Antiquities*, XVIII, 274.

[37] Commodus, elder son of Marcus Aurelius, and sole emperor 180–92.

succeed his father', in my opinion was not praying at all but calling down the worst evils upon the Roman empire.

You say that 'we have broken our word, pledged more than once in solemn assembly to preserve the authority and majesty of the king'. I wait for you to be more detailed about this matter below; I will meet you again there.

You return to the comments of the fathers. About them hear this briefly: whatever they said and have not confirmed from sacred books, or by some suitable enough reasoning is the same to me as if any other ordinary person had said it. First you bring forward Tertullian, not an orthodox writer, notorious for many errors, so that if he was of your opinion, this would still stand for nothing. But what says he? He condemns riots, he condemns rebellions; we condemn them too, but we do not wish at once to have made a judgement beforehand about all the right of peoples, about the privileges, and resolutions of the senate, and the power of all the rest of the magistrates apart from the king alone. They are speaking about seditions rashly kindled by the madness of the multitude, not about magistrates, not about the senate or parliament summoning the people to lawful arms against tyrants. Hence Ambrose whom you quote: 'Not to fight back, to weep, to groan, these are the protections of a priest, and who is there who can, either alone or among a few, say to the emperor "your law is not approved by me?" Priests are not permitted to say this, shall laymen be permitted to do so?'[38] You see now clearly of whom he speaks here: of priests, of private laymen, not of magistrates. You see, however, with what weak and perverted reasoning he bore his torch in the dissension between the laymen and the priests, also concerning civil laws, that were to occur afterwards.

But since you think we are most hard-pressed and confused by the examples of the early christians, because they, though harassed in all ways, 'did not stir up war against the Caesars', I will show firstly that they could not; then that whenever they could, they did stir them up; finally that even if they did not when they could, those people in other respects were still not worthy that we should take examples from their life and customs in such great matters.

First, as everybody knows, from the time when there was no longer a Roman republic, all the strength of the empire and control of affairs

[38] M. consolidates two quotations by S., *DR*, p. 91, from Ambrose's *Oratio in Auxentium de tradendis basilicis* and *Epistle XXXII*.

reverted to Caesar alone; all the legions were paid by Caesar alone: so that if all the senate to a man, the whole equestrian order, and all the plebeians had attempted an overthrow, they could indeed have exposed themselves to slaughter, and still have accomplished absolutely nothing towards recovering their liberty. For if they chanced to get rid of the emperor, the empire would still have remained. Now truly what could the christians do, who, although innumerable, were still scattered, unarmed, and belonged to the plebeians – generally the lowest class? How large a number of them might one legion have easily kept to obedience? What great leaders often attempted in vain at the cost of their own deaths and the destruction of veteran armies, could those little men, usually part of the common people, hope to be able to see through to the end? About three hundred years from the birth of Christ, more or less twenty years before Constantine, when Diocletian was emperor,[39] only the Theban legion was christian; and on this very count it was slaughtered by the rest of the army in Gaul at the town of Octodurum. 'With Cassius, with Albinus, with Niger' they did not conspire;[40] and does not Tertullian wish it to be set in their favour that they did not pour forth their blood for infidels? So it is agreed that the christians could not have freed themselves from the control of the emperors. And for christians to conspire with others was not all advantageous to them as long as pagan emperors ruled.

But that afterwards christians made war upon tyrants and either defended themselves with weapons or often avenged tyrants' wicked deeds, I will now show. First of all Constantine, when converted to christianity, got rid of his co-emperor Licinius by war when he was oppressing the eastern christians.[41] By this deed he immediately declared that punishment could be inflicted on one magistrate by another since, for the sake of his subjects, he put to death Licinius, who ruled with a right equal to his own, and did not leave the punishment to God alone: for Licinius could have likewise put Constantine to death if Constantine had crushed in these ways the people

[39] Diocletian, emperor of the East from 284 until his abdication in 305.

[40] Avidius Cassius was governor of Syria under Marcus Aurelius, proclaiming himself emperor and being assassinated in 175; Clodius Albinus and Pescennius Niger were proclaimed emperor by their soldiers but were defeated by Septimius Severus (Roman emperor, 193–211) at Issus (194) and near Lyons (197).

[41] Licinius (who had been promoted to emperor of the West at the Conference of Carnuntum in 308) began to revive the persecution of the christians *c.* 320. He was defeated by Constantine in 323, forced to abdicate, and executed in 324.

entrusted to him. So after the matter was referred by God to men, why was not Parliament to Charles as Constantine to Licinius? For the soldiers appointed Constantine, but our laws have made parliament equal to kings, or rather even superior.

The Byzantines resisted Constantius, an Arian emperor,[42] by force of arms for as long as they could; and when Hermogenes was sent with soldiers to drive Paul the orthodox bishop from the church, they made an attack and beat him off, set fire to the house to which he had retreated, and killed him half burned and mangled. Constans threatened war upon his brother Constantius unless he restored to Paul and Athanasius their bishoprics.[43] You see how those most holy fathers, when it was a question of their bishoprics, were not ashamed to stir up a brother to make war upon his own king? Not long after, christian soldiers, who at that time were making emperor whom they wished, killed Constans son of Constantine for ruling dissolutely and proudly, and transferred the empire over to Magnentius.[44] Shall I go on? Those who greeted Julian,[45] who was not yet apostate but a pious and energetic king, as their emperor against the will of Constantius, their real emperor – were they not among those christians whom you set before us as an example? When Constantius, in his letter read aloud to the people, sharply forbade this deed, they all cried out that they had done as their provincial governor, and the army, and the authority of the state had resolved. The same people declared war upon Constantius, and as far as lay in their power, stripped him of his empire and his life.

What about the people of Antioch, men who were notably christian? They prayed, I suppose, for Julian now he had become apostate when they used to approach him openly and revile him with insults, and mock his long beard and bid him make ropes out of it. Do you think they poured forth prayers for the life and safety of a man and then, when the news of his death was heard, proclaimed

[42] *Constantio imperatori Arriano*: 1651Q, 1651F, 1658. After Constantine the Great's death in 337, his three sons Constans (337–50), Constantius II (337–61) and Constantine II (337–40) inherited the empire. Constantius was an Arian and quarrelled with his pro-Nicene brothers: see Theodoret, *Ecclesiastical History*, II, 5. The Yale editor (IV, 415) inexplicably substitutes Constans and then explains M.'s 'error'. Cf. *R*, I, 557; *HB*, V, 115.

[43] Constans restored Athanasius in 346. See Socrates, *Ecclesiastical History*, II, 16.

[44] Constans died in the rebellion of Magnentius in 350. Cf. *HB*, V, 114.

[45] Flavius Claudius Julianus (Julian the Apostate) was proclaimed emperor at Paris in 360; died in 363.

thanksgivings, feasts and public rejoicing? Shall I go on? They say this same man was also killed by a christian fellow soldier. Sozomen, certainly, a writer of ecclesiastical history, does not deny it, but rather praises the person if he had actually done thus: οὐ γὰρ ἀπεικός τινα τῶν τότε στρατευομένων, etc. 'It is no wonder', he says, 'that one of the soldiers thought this to himself; that not only the Greeks but all men up till this age were accustomed to praise tyrannicides, who, for the liberty of all, do not hesitate to seek death; and no-one should criticize this soldier, who was so energetic in the cause of God and religion.'[46] So says Sozomen, a writer of the actual age, a good and holy man. From him we can easily perceive what the remaining good men in that time thought about this matter. Ambrose himself when ordered by the emperor Valentinian the younger to leave the city of Milan,[47] refused to obey, but was fenced around by the people in arms and defended himself and his church against the emperor's officers, and dared to resist the supreme power contrary to what he himself taught. At Constantinople more than once, because of the exile of Chrysostom, a very great rebellion arose against the emperor Arcadius.[48] So I have briefly explained how the ancient christians acted towards tyrants, not only the soldiers, but the people and the fathers of the church themselves, either in resisting, or waging war, or stirring it up right down to Augustine's time, since you are not pleased to go on further. For I remain silent about the fact that Valentinian, son of Placidia, was killed by Maximus, a nobleman, on account of adultery committed with his wife:[49] I do not mention Avitus the emperor[50] also who dismissed his soldiers and abandoned himself to luxury, and was at once stripped of his power by the Roman senate: because these things happened some years after the death of Augustine.

But I grant you all this, pretend that I have set forth none of these matters. Suppose that the old christians obeyed their kings through thick and thin, and did not do or wish to take any action against tyrants, I will now instruct you in what remains of my chapter how

[46] Sozomen, *Ecclesiastical History*, V, 2.
[47] Valentinian II, western emperor, 375–92, supported the Arians against Ambrose.
[48] Arcadius, eastern emperor 383–408, exiled Chrysostom in 404.
[49] Valentinian III, son of Galla Placidia and western emperor 423–55, was killed by supporters of Aetius: Petronius Maximus proclaimed himself emperor, and was murdered, in 455.
[50] Flavius Maecilius Eparchius (Avitus), western emperor, 455–6.

they were yet not people on whose authority we ought to rely, or from whom we can safely seek examples. Already long before Constantine, the christian people had lost much of that primitive sanctity and integrity both of their doctrine and of their customs. After the church, which had been enriched by him with vast wealth, began to fall in love with offices, absolute command, and civil power, at once everything tumbled headlong. First luxury and idleness, then a troop of all heresies and vices, just as if their prisons had somewhere been opened, moved over into the church. Hence envy, hate, discord were overflowing everywhere; at last brothers in that dearest bond of religion were disagreeing with each other just as bitterly as the keenest of enemies. No shame, no respect for duty was left; soldiers and commanders of the forces whenever they pleased themselves now created new emperors, now killed good ones and bad ones alike. What need have I to mention the Vetranniones,[51] and Maximi,[52] what need to mention Eugenius,[53] who were suddenly elevated to power, or Gratian an excellent emperor, or Valentinian the younger who was far from the worst, who were killed by them? These indeed were the acts of soldiers and camp-followers, but also of christians of that age which you say was most evangelical and most to be imitated.

So now hear a few words about the clergy: pastors and bishops and sometimes those fathers whom we admire, each leaders of their own flock, used to fight about a bishopric just as if for a tyranny: now throughout the city, now in the church itself at the very altar, priests and laymen would fiercely contend indiscriminately; they created slaughter and sometimes produced great carnage on both sides. You may remember Damasus and Urcisinus,[54] who flourished at the time of Ambrose. It would take a long time to tell of those riots in Constantinople, Antioch and Alexandria, especially under the leadership and paternity of Cyril whom you praise as a preacher of obedience, when Orestes, the commander of Theodosius, was almost killed by the

[51] Vetrannio was briefly proclaimed emperor when Magnentius rebelled against Constantius II.

[52] In 383, Magnus Maximus staged a revolt in Britain against the emperor Gratian (375–83) and was recognized as western emperor by Theodosius I (allowing Valentinian II to retain Italy and Africa). Maximus was defeated by Theodosius in 388 and put to death. Cf. *HB*, v, 119–20.

[53] When Valentinian II was murdered in Gaul in 392, Eugenius was set up as client emperor by the Franks only to be defeated by Theodosius in 394.

[54] In the schism after the death of Pope Liberius in 366, rival factions consecrated Damasus and Urcisinus (Ursinus) as pope.

monks in that city battle.[55] Now who would not be stunned either at your shamelessness or negligence? 'Up until Augustine', you say, 'and after his time, there is no mention extant in history of any private person, or commander, or any number of conspirators, who have killed their king or fought against him in arms'. I have named from very well-known histories, both private persons and leaders who have slaughtered with their own hands not only bad but even very good kings; whole armies of christians who fought against their own emperors. You adduce the fathers, who either persuade or boast in many words of obedience towards the king; I adduce both the same fathers, and others too, who by no fewer deeds refused obedience even in lawful matters, defending themselves with weapons against the emperor, others who brought wounds by force upon his deputies, others who were competitors for bishoprics and fought amongst themselves in civil wars. It was lawful indeed for christians to fight with christians and citizens with citizens over a bishopric, but unlawful to do the same with a tyrant, over liberty, children and wives, or lives! Who would not be dissatisfied with fathers of this kind?

You bring in Augustine who pronounces that 'the power of a master over slaves and of a king over subjects' are the same thing; I reply that if Augustine has pronounced thus, [he has said things which neither Christ nor his apostles ever said. Since, however, he seems on their authority alone to recommend something which is otherwise quite obviously false, then although he pronounces thus he still does not injure my cause. For when he has spoken thus about a master's power over his slaves, Bk. 19, ch. 14, *De Civitate Dei*, 'In the house of a just man who lives by faith, even those who command serve those whom they seem to command';[56] and if he said the same thing 'about the power of a king over his subjects' as you say, and did not contradict himself, he proclaimed that even kings, especially good ones, really serve those whom they seem to command. Meanwhile concerning the power of a bad king over his subjects and that of a robber over every one he meets, he has certainly proclaimed them the same, Bk. 4, ch. 4. *De Civit. Dei*: 'with the removal of justice, what are kingdoms', except 'great robbers' dens; for what are robbers' dens themselves, except little kingdoms?' See to what end you have derived from Augustine that magnificent right of yours, the royal right of doing

[55] See Socrates, *Ecclesiastical History*, VII, 14.

[56] Cf. *CB*, I, 474.

anything they please; that power of kings is equal with and identical to not that of painters and poets, but that of robbers.][57]

That the three or four remaining pages of this chapter are either pure lies or tedious writings repeated again and again, anyone can discover for himself from the replies which have already been made by me. As for what concerns the pope, against whom you harangue at length without cause, I gladly let you shout about this until you are hoarse. But as for adding such a long-winded argument to catch the ignorant by saying that 'every christian was subject to kings, whether just or tyrannical, until the power of the pope began to be recognized as greater than that of the king, and freed subjects from their oath of loyalty', I have pointed out that this is quite false by bringing forward very many examples 'both up to Augustine and after his age'.

But nor does what you say last, 'that pope Zachary absolved the French from their oath of allegiance', seem to be much more true.[58] François Hotman who was both a Frenchman and a lawyer and a very learned man says in his *Francogallia*, Ch. 13,[59] that Chilperic was not deposed or the kingdom transferred to Pepin by the pope's authority, but proves from very ancient chronicles of the Franks that the whole business was transacted in the great council of the nation in accordance with its original authority. That there was any need at all then for the French to be released from that oath is denied by the records of the French themselves, and by pope Zachary too. For it is related in the records of the Franks, by the testimony not only of Hotman but of Girard,[60] a very well-known writer of that nation's history, that the old Franks had from antiquity saved for themselves all right both to choose and also to depose their kings if they thought fit; and they were accustomed to swear no other oath to the kings they created than that they would vouch for their loyalty and duty to them in this way, if in turn they would at the same time vouch also for what they promised when they were sworn in. So if kings, by badly governing the commonwealth entrusted to them, should break their sworn oath first, there is no need of the pope, as they have themselves

57 1658.

58 M.'s earlier view of the role of Pope Zacharias in the removal of Childeric III in 751 (based on Sigonius, *De regno Italiae* (Frankfurt, 1591), p. 74) was, however, very close to this: see *CB* and *R*, I, 444, 578.

59 M. (*CB*, I, 459, 461) first learned of Hotman from de Thou's summary in *Historiarum*, II, 969.

60 See *CB*, I, 461–2 for the entries from Girard, *L'histoire*, pp. 123, 129, 134.

released the people from their oath by their own treachery. Finally pope Zachary himself, in that letter to the Franks quoted by you, disclaimed for himself and attributed to the people the authority which you say he claimed for himself. For 'if a leader is responsible to the people by whose favour he holds the kingdom, if the people have made a king and can unmake him', which are the words of the pope himself, it is not likely that the Franks would have wished to damage their ancient right by any later oath or ever bind themselves so that they could not always do as their ancestors could – to honour good kings indeed, but depose bad ones – nor vouchsafe to tyrants that loyalty which they thought they only granted to good kings. When the people are bound by such an oath, a king either turned into a tyrant or corrupted by cowardice, releases them by his perjury; justice itself releases them, and so too does the law of nature itself: hence even in the judgement of the pope himself, there was absolutely nothing for the pope to release.

CHAPTER V

I am of the opinion, Salmasius, and always have been, that the law of God agrees exactly with the law of nature, and that therefore if I have shown adequately what appointments have been made by divine law about kings and what actions have been taken by the people of God, both Jewish and Christian, I have shown at the same time and by the same effort what is most suited to the law of nature. Yet because you think that we 'can now be most powerfully refuted by the law of nature', I will now confess of my own accord that what I used recently to think was needless is certainly necessary. So I shall make clear in opposition to your opinion in this chapter that nothing is more consistent with the laws of nature also than that tyrants be punished. If I do not carry my point, I do not refuse to grant you at once that they cannot be punished also by the laws of God.

It is not my plan now to construct a long account about nature and about the origin of political life. For very learned men have treated that subject lengthily both in Greek and in Latin. I myself strive for as much brevity as possible and I take pains in this matter, not so much that I (who would gladly have done without this task), but that you, shall refute and overthrow yourself.

So I shall start with what you set down yourself, and I shall lay it as the foundations of this discussion to be. 'The law of nature', you say:

> is a principle implanted in all men's minds, taking account of the good of all peoples in so far as men are pleased to live together in societies. But it cannot procure that common good unless, as there are people who must be governed, it also arranges people who ought to govern.

Indeed, lest the stronger oppress the weaker, and in this way those whom mutual safety and defence had brought together into one place, violence and wrong would drive apart and compel to return to an uncivilized life. Is this what you meant – even if you said it more wordily? And so 'from the number of those who gathered together', you say,

> certain people must have been chosen as excelling the rest in wisdom or courage, who either by force or by persuasion might hold those who were disobedient to their duty. Often a single person whose virtue and prudence was outstanding could have performed this function. Sometimes several might do it by mutual consultation. However, since one person cannot look after and manage everything, he must share his plans with several people and admit others into the governing body. So whether power be referred to one man or devolves upon the people as a whole, since not all can direct the commonwealth at one time nor one man do all, therefore in reality governing always rests in the hands of several.

And below:

> the principle of government itself, whether it is dispensed by several, or by few, or by one person, is equally natural, since it comes down from the foundations of nature itself, which does not allow one single person to govern so that he does not have any other sharers in rule.

Though I could have gathered this from the third book of Aristotle's *Politics*, I preferred to transcribe as a gathering from you what you stole from Aristotle, as Prometheus did fire from Jupiter, for the overthrow of monarchs and destruction of your own self. For investigate as much as you want the law of nature which has just now been put forward by yourself. You will not find any place for royal right, as you expound that right, in nature nor even any trace of it. 'The law of nature', you say, 'since it arranges who should rule others, had an eye to the good of all peoples.' So not of one person – not of the monarch. And so the king exists on account of the people: therefore the people are stronger than and superior to the king. Since the people are superior to and stronger than the king, there can exist no right of the king by which he, the inferior, can damage the people, the superior, or keep them in slavery. Since a king has no right to do wrong, the right of the people remains supreme by nature. So by the right by which men first shared their counsels and strength for the sake of their mutual defence before the creation of kings; by the right by which for the preservation of the common safety, peace and liberty of all men, they put one or more in charge of the rest; by the same right they might correct or depose the same people whom they had placed because of their virtue and prudence at the head of the rest, or any others that badly manage the state, on account of cowardice, stupidity, dishonesty or treachery: since nature always has regarded and does regard not the power of one man or few men but the safety of all [whatever happens to the power of the one or the few].[1]

Now truly whom do the people choose? You say 'those excelling the rest in wisdom or courage', those indeed who by nature seemed most fit for ruling, 'whose extraordinary virtue and prudence could discharge' that office. So there is no right of succession by nature, no king by nature except he who excels all the rest in wisdom or courage. The rest are kings by force or by faction contrary to nature, since they ought rather to be slaves. For nature gives command to the wisest men over the less wise, not to a bad man over good ones, nor to a fool over wise men. So those who take away command from these men act wholly in a manner befitting the law of nature. Hear in your own words the end to which nature appoints all the wisest men king – so that 'he may keep to their duty those who do not obey' either nature or the laws. But can a man keep others to their duty who neglects, or does not know, or perverts his own?

Tell me now any dictate of nature by which we are ordered not to observe, not to care for, to consider of no account the wisest things in public and civil affairs (though nature herself in matters natural and inanimate, so as not to lose her end, very often brings about great and wonderful things). Show any rule of nature or of natural justice by which lesser defendants ought to be punished, while kings and princes for all evils go unpunished, or rather, while committing the greatest crimes be worshipped, revered and held next to God. You grant that 'the principle of government itself, whether dispensed by many or by a few or by one, is equally natural'. So a king is not by nature more sanctified than nobles or the magistrates of the people, and since you have granted above that they can and ought to be

[1] 1658: this addition may reflect the uncertain state of affairs following the recent death of Cromwell.

punished if they sin, you must admit the same of kings who have been appointed for the same end and benefit. For you say 'nature does not in this way suffer the single self of one man to govern so that he does not have other people to share the command'. So it does not allow a monarch, nor one man to rule so that he holds all the rest slaves to his single command. You who give to the king people to share the command 'so the government always remains in their power', you give him likewise colleagues and equals; you add those who can punish and those who can depose.

So as you always do, while you no longer extol royal power, but only establish it in nature, you destroy it: so I think nothing more unfortunate could happen to kings than to have you to defend them. O unhappy and wretched man, what mist of mind has driven you into this deceit so that you yourself should now unknowingly and with so much effort lay bare and reveal to all your dishonesty and ignorance which until now has long lain hidden and virtually masked, and yourself hire out your services to your own disgrace, and be so diligently devoted to making yourself a laughing stock? What anger of the gods is responsible, in payment of what punishment have you been summoned into the limelight in front of people's eyes, so that with so much pomp you might defend a most disgraceful cause with the greatest of impudence as well as the greatest stupidity, and by so defending it, betray it unwillingly and through ignorance? Who could wish you more desperate and more wretched than you are, when now only imprudence, only folly can save you from being most wretched, if you have rendered the tyrants, whose cause you have undertaken, so much more hateful and detestable to all by your unskilful and stupid defence, contrary to your expectations, as you have attributed to them greatest freedom[2] to do wrong and dominate with impunity, and have roused unadvisedly just so many more enemies against them?

But I return to your self-contradictions. When you committed so great a crime against yourself as to strive to base tyranny in nature, you say that you had first to praise monarchy beyond other methods of government. This, as usual, you cannot undertake without contradicting yourself. One moment having said that 'the principle of government itself, whether by more or by fewer, or by one is equally natural', at the next you are saying 'that which is exercised by one person is of

[2] *licentia.*

these three more natural' – or rather (which you also said recently), 'nature does not allow one single man to govern'. Now reproach whoever you wish with the death of tyrants, since you have cut the throats of all monarchs and also of monarchy itself by your foolishness. But it is not now the place to discuss what is the better form of governing the commonwealth, by one person or by many. Many famous men have indeed praised monarchy, but only if he who is sole ruler is the best man of all and most worthy of ruling. If this does not eventuate, nothing slips more readily than monarchy into that tyranny which is worst.

Now when you say that 'it is modelled on the pattern of one God', who is worthy to hold on earth a power like that of God, except one who is most outstanding beyond all others and is even very like God in his goodness and wisdom? And he, in my opinion at least, can only be that Son of God for whom we wait. As for your thrusting the 'kingdom' again into the category of the family, so as to liken a king to a head of the household: a father certainly deserves the rule of his family, all of whom he either begot or supports: with a king there is nothing of this kind, but most clearly everything is the opposite. Then you propose that we should imitate animals that live in groups, first 'birds' and among them 'bees', since these are birds according to your natural philosophy. 'Bees have a king.' Those of Trent of course – don't you remember? The rest, on your testimony, 'have a republic'. But stop your foolishness about bees, they belong to the muses, and hate beetles like you and, as you see, disprove you. 'Quails live under a quail matriarch.'[3] Lay your snares for your own pelicans; we are not caught by so foolish a bird-catcher.

But now you deal with something that is your concern, not ours: '*Gallus gallinaceus*, the cock', you say, 'rules over both males and females.' How can this happen? Since you yourself, who are Gallic and so they say, only too cocklike, do not rule over your hen, but she rules and exercises kingship over you. So if the cock is the king of many women, you are a slave to your hen and must be not *gallinaceus* but some kind of *Gallus stercorarius* – cock of the dung-heap. As regards books indeed, no-one publishes bigger dungheaps, and you deafen everyone with your crowing over them. This is the only resemblance you have to a cock. Now I promise I will give you many barley

[3] S., *DR*, p. 103. Cf. M.'s sceptical remark in *DDD*, II, 300: 'God gave Quails in his wrath, and Kings in his wrath'.

grains if in turning over this whole dungheap of yours, you show me even one jewel. But why should I give you barley? For you have by scratching looked not for barley, like that honest worthy cock in Aesop, but for gold like that worthless one in Plautus[4] – although the result was unequal to this extent, for you found from it one hundred gold jacobuses, though you deserved more to be cut down with Euclio's club like that wretched bird in Plautus.

But we must move on. 'The same reason, the benefit and safety of all, demands that he who has been once appointed to the government be preserved there.' Who denies it, so long as his preservation is consistent with the safety of all? But who does not see that it is absolutely alien to nature for one man to be preserved to the destruction of all? But you wish at any cost for 'a bad king to be preserved, rather even the worst one, because he does not produce so much harm for the state by governing badly as is created by disasters from the revolts which are roused to remove him'. What does this have to do with the natural rights of kings? Or if nature advises me to allow myself to be plundered by robbers so that I can redeem myself from captivity with all my means rather than be compelled to fight for my life, will you as a result set up a natural right of robbers? Nature persuades people to yield to the violence of tyrants sometimes, to yield to the times. Will you found a natural right of tyrants also upon this forced endurance of the people? The same right which nature gave the people for their own preservation, will you affirm that she also gave to a tyrant to destroy the people? Nature teaches that out of two evils one should choose the lesser and, for as long as it is necessary, to endure it. Or will you conclude that from this there arises a natural right for a tyrant, as perhaps being at the time the lesser evil, to do evil without being punished? Remember at least those things which you yourself formerly wrote about bishops against the jesuit; your words quite the opposite of these here have been quoted by me above in chapter three. There you affirmed that 'seditions, dissensions, discords of nobles and people are a far lighter ill than certain misery and destruction under one monarch who is a tyrant'. And what you affirmed was indeed true; for you were not yet mad, and being not yet gilded with Charles's jacobuses, had not contracted this gold-born royal disease. I should say perhaps, if you were not who you are, that

[4] Plautus, *Aulularia*, 465.

you would be ashamed at length of your most disgraceful transgressions, but for you it is easier to burst apart than blush, as you long ago now lost your modesty to make money.

Did you not remember yourself that the Romans had a most flourishing and glorious republic after the banishment of the kings? Could it happen that you forgot the Dutch? Their republic, after the expulsion of the king of Spain, after wars that were lengthy but successfully waged, bravely and gloriously obtained its liberty and supports you on its stipend, knight grammaticaster – but not so that the Dutch youth may learn from you, you shyster and sophist, to be so unwise as to prefer to return to the slavery of Spain, than be heirs to their fathers' liberty and glory. You may carry off with you that plague of a doctrine of yours to the Riphaean mountains[5] and the icy ocean, where you may as well go to the devil.

Your last example is the English, who cut down Charles the tyrant after he had been taken prisoner in war and found incurable. But 'they spoiled with their quarrels an island that was happy under its kings and floating in luxury'. Rather, when it was almost destroyed by luxury so it might be more tolerant of slavery, they delivered it from slavery. Behold then the editor of Epictetus with Simplicius' commentary,[6] a most severe Stoic, to whom 'an island floating in luxury' seems to be happy! I know well enough that no such lesson proceeded from the porch of Zeno.[7] What does that matter? Shall kings be permitted to do whatever they please, under your teaching, and you yourself, seigneur du Loup, not be permitted to send forth whatever philosophy you please from your brothel, as from some new Lyceum?[8]

But now resume the part you undertook. 'Never under any king was so much blood drained, so many families desolated.' All this may be imputed to Charles, not to the English; as he had first prepared an army of Irish against us, and ordered all the Irish to conspire against the English by his own warrant. By their means he had killed about two hundred thousand Englishmen in the single county of Ulster. Of

[5] *ad Riphaeos ultimos*: a range in northern Scythia.

[6] M. refers to S., *Simplicii commentarius in Enchiridion Epicteti* (Leyden, 1640): Epictetus (*c.* 55–*c.* 135) was a Stoic philosopher whose teachings later influenced Marcus Aurelius.

[7] Zeno (335–263 BC) founded the Stoic school (so called from the Stoa in Athens where he taught).

[8] Translation obscures M.'s punning association of *lupus* (wolf), *lupanar* (brothel), *lukos* (Greek: wolf), and Lyceum (the garden where Aristotle taught; so called from *Lukeios*, a Greek epithet of Apollo whose temple adjoined it).

the rest I say nothing: he had stirred up two armies to destroy the parliament of England and the city of London; he had committed many other hostilities before even one soldier was enlisted by the people or the magistrates to defend the commonwealth.

What doctrine, what law, what religion ever instructed men so that they should prefer to consult their leisure and spare their money, blood and lives rather than go to meet the enemy? For whether foreign or internal, what does it matter, since the destruction of the commonwealth threatens as equally disastrous and bitter whether as a result of the one or the other? All Israel saw that they could not without much bloodshed avenge the Levite's wife who had been violated and killed.[9] Surely they did not therefore consider that they should remain quiet, or refrain from civil war although it should be extremely fierce, nor did they therefore allow one insignificant woman to die unavenged? Certainly if nature instructs us to endure the despotism of a king, even though he is a very bad one, rather than put into danger the safety of very many citizens by recovering liberty, she should instruct likewise not only to endure a king whom you still contend is the only one that should be endured, but also the power of the nobles and of the few; even sometimes a crowd of robbers and rebellious slaves. Fulvius or Rupilius would not have gone into the slave war after the slaughter of the praetorian armies, nor Crassus have gone against Spartacus after the destruction of the consular camp, nor Pompey into war against the pirates.[10] The Romans would have submitted either to slaves or pirates, in case the blood of so many citizens should be shed – at the exhortation of nature no doubt! And so nowhere do you show that 'nature has imprinted this feeling upon nations' or any one of the kind. And yet you do not stop prophesying evil and denouncing divine vengeance upon us, which I hope God may turn upon your prophesying and such as you. We have had vengeance upon one who was a king only in name, but in fact was our bitterest enemy, with the punishment that was due to him; and have atoned for the countless deaths of good countrymen by the punishment of the man responsible.

Now you say that a monarchy is proven to be more natural from the

[9] Judges 20.

[10] Fulvius Flaccus and Publius Rupilius fought in the Slave War in Sicily which was brought to an end in 131 BC; Marcus Licinius Crassus, the triumvir, defeated Spartacus in 71 BC; Pompey used unprecedented powers to destroy the pirates in 67 BC.

fact that 'more nations both now and formerly have adopted monarchy than aristocracy and democracy'. I reply first that this was done without the urging of God or nature. God only reluctantly allowed his people to live beneath the rule of a king. What nature and right reason urges is best perceived from the most prudent nations. The Greeks, Romans, Italians, Carthaginians and many others have preferred because of their own nature a rule of the nobles or people to that of a king; and these nations indeed are a good example of all the rest. Hence Sulpicius Severus relates that 'the name of king has always been hateful to almost all free nations'.[11]

But these things are not now relevant here, nor are the many points which follow, which are repeated over and over by you with empty futility. I hasten to the point, so I may now show by examples what I have proved by reasoning: that it is very particularly in accordance with nature that tyrants should be punished in some way; that all nations have over and over again done this, at the teaching of nature herself. From this your impudence must be proclaimed, and your most disgraceful licence in lying will thenceforward become known to all. First of all you introduce the Egyptians; and certainly who does not see that you play the gypsy throughout all? 'Amongst these people', you say, 'there is nowhere mention of any king killed by the people in uprising, no war brought upon them, or any attempt made by the people to dethrone them.' What then of Osiris,[12] perhaps the first king of the Egyptians? Was he not slain by his brother Typhon and twenty-five other conspirators? And a great part of the people followed them and fought a great battle with Isis and Horus, the king's wife and son? I pass over Sesostris who was almost crushed by his brother through treachery;[13] also Chemmis and Chephren,[14] against whom the people were deservedly hostile, and whom they could not tear apart while alive so they threatened to do it after they were dead. Do you think that those who dared to slaughter their best kings were held back by the light of nature or some religious scruple and kept their hands off their worst kings? Would people who kept threatening to dig up their kings, who were dead and at last harmless,

[11] Sulpicius Severus, *Historia*, p. 56 (I, 32).

[12] Osiris, the chief Egyptian god, was worshipped, as Apis, in the shape of a bull, and slain by Typhon, or Set. Isis was the goddess of the earth and Horus (Orus) of the sun. Cf. *AR*, II, 549.

[13] Sesostris was a mythical ruler and conqueror.

[14] Chemmis (Cheops) and Chephren, famed as builders of pyramids.

from the tomb (a place where even the body of any meanest pauper is usually inviolate) – would such a people fear to punish according to the law of nature kings who were alive and most harmful, if only they had the strength? I know you would affirm these things, however silly they may be. But so you may not dare to affirm them, I will make you speechless.

Know then that many ages before Chephren, Ammosis was king among the Egyptians and was a tyrant as great as the greatest. The Egyptians bore him patiently. You triumph; for this is what you want. But hear what remains, O best and most truthful fellow, for the words of Diodorus are what I quote: μέχρι μέν τινος ἐκαρτέρουν οὐ δυνάμενοι, etc. 'They bore him for some time, though oppressed, because they could in no way resist those who were more powerful.'[15] But as soon as Actisanes, king of Ethiopia, began to wage war against him they took their opportunity and most revolted, and after he had been easily subdued Egypt became part of the kingdom of Ethiopia. You see here that the Egyptians, as soon as they could, took up arms against a tyrant, joined forces with a foreign king to deprive their king and his posterity of the kingdom and preferred a good and moderate king, such as Actisanes, though he was foreign, to a tyrant of their own.

The same Egyptians, with the heartiest consent of them all, conquered Apries the tyrant who commanded mercenary troops in a battle under the leadership of Amasis, and strangled him. They gave the kingdom to Amasis, a noble man. Note this too; Amasis kept honourable watch over the captured king for a time in his own palace; at last at the accusation of the people that he was acting unjustly in supporting his own and their enemy, he handed the king over to the people and they put him to death as aforementioned. So Herodotus and Diodorus say.[16] What more do you seek? Do you think any tyrant would not prefer to end his life by an axe than by the noose? Afterwards when the Egyptians were 'subdued' beneath the Persian empire, you say, 'they were loyal to them', which is utterly false. For they never remained loyal to the Persians, but in the fourth year after

[15] Diodorus Siculus, I, ix, 2.

[16] The pharaoh Apries (589–570 BC) was defeated by Amasis (pharaoh *c.* 569–525 BC) who had been sent to put down a rebellion but was instead set on the throne himself. See Herodotus, II, 161–78; Diodorus Siculus, I, 21–4; 53–8.

they had been subdued by Cambyses,[17] they rebelled. Then when conquered by Xerxes, not much later they revolted from his son Artaxerxes, and adopted a certain Inarus as their king.[18] When conquered with him, they again rebelled and setting up Tachus as king, declared war on Artaxerxes Mnemon.[19] But they were not more faithful to their own king but took the kingdom from the father and handed it over to his son Nectanebus, until at last they were brought back under Persian control again by Artaxerxes Ochus.[20] Even under the Macedonian empire, as far as lay in their power, they showed by their deeds that tyrants should be restrained. They threw down the statues and images of Ptolemy Physco,[21] but could not kill him as he had remarkable power because of his mercenary army. Alexander his son was driven into exile because of the murder of his mother by a popular uprising.[22] Likewise when his son Alexander acted in too insolently despotic a manner, the people of Alexandria dragged him by force out of the palace and killed him in the public gymnasium.[23] They finally expelled Ptolemy Auletes from the kingdom for his many crimes.[24] A learned man cannot be ignorant of such well-known facts as these, and a man ought not to be who professes to teach them, and who demands to be believed in such important matters. So, who would not say it was shameful and most disgraceful that this man, if he is so uncultivated and so unlearned, should with so much infamy to good scholarship conceitedly proclaim himself a most learned man

[17] Cambyses, son of Cyrus the Great, and Persian king 529–521 BC; conquered Egypt in 525 after the death of Amasis.

[18] Xerxes I, Persian king 486–465 BC, had suppressed an Egyptian revolt in 486; succeeded by Artaxerxes I (465–424 BC) who eventually overcame Athenian-backed Egyptian resistance in 454. Cf. *Paradise Regained*, IV, 271.

[19] Artaxerxes II (Mnemon), Persian king 404–358 BC, twice failed to recover Egypt. The Egyptian ruler, Tachos, was removed by his Spartan ally, Argesilaus, who gave the crown to the last pharaoh, Nekhthareb (Nectanebus).

[20] Artaxerxes III (Ochus), Persian king 358–338 BC; reconquered Egypt in 343 at the second attempt.

[21] I.e., Ptolemy VII (Euergetes), Macedonian king of Egypt; joint ruler 170–164 BC; sole ruler, 164–163, and again 145–116. There was a successful revolt against him in 132, though he reconquered Alexandria in 127.

[22] Ptolemy IX (Alexander I), finally installed as ruler by his mother in 107 BC, but suspected of matricide (101) and expelled by military uprising.

[23] Ptolemy X (Alexander II) married his step-mother, Cleopatra Berenice, in 80 BC and murdered her shortly after the wedding; killed by the Alexandrians.

[24] Ptolemy XI (Auletes) succeeded in 80 BC; forced to flee from Alexandria in 58, but restored by the tribune Gabinius Aulus in 55.

and go round after payments from kings and states; or if he is so wicked and lying, should not be branded with some special ignominy and be expelled from the community and society of all learned and of all good men?

After surveying Egypt, let us now examine the Ethiopians, their neighbours. The king, chosen by God as they believe, they worship as a kind of god; yet whenever the priests condemn him, he commits suicide. For in this way, Diodorus testifies,[25] they punish all other evil doers; they do not put them to death themselves, but send an officer and order the guilty to die at their own hand.

Next you come to the Assyrians and Medes and Persians, who most respect their kings: you affirm, against the word of all historians, that 'the right of the king there is united with the greatest freedom of doing anything one pleases'. Firstly Daniel relates how the men drove away King Nebuchadnezzar when he grew too proud and sent him off to the beasts. Their right is not called that of kings, but of the Medes and Persians; that is, the right of the people, and since it was irrevocable it also bound the kings. And so although Darius the Mede most strenuously tried to snatch Daniel from the hands of the satraps, he could not do it.[26] 'People believed then', you say, 'that it was wrong to repudiate a king because he abused that right.' Yet in saying these very words you are so wretchedly insensible, that while you are praising the obedience and self-control of those peoples, you mention of your own accord that the kingdom was snatched from Sardanapalus[27] by Arbaces. But he did not do it alone, but was helped, partly by the priests who were very skilled in law, and partly by the people, and did it chiefly for the reason that he abused his royal right, not with cruelty, but only by luxury and softness. Skim through Herodotus, Ctesias,[28] Diodorus; you will realize that it is quite the contrary of what you say, 'that mostly these kingdoms were destroyed by subjects, not by foreigners': Assyrian kings were removed by Medes, the Medes by the Persians, and in each case by their 'subjects'. You yourself confess that 'Cyrus[29] rebelled and tyrannies were seized in various places in the empire'. Is this what you mean by royal right among the Medes

[25] Diodorus, III, 5–6.
[26] Dan. 5:20–21; 6:8,14.
[27] Sardanapalus, last Assyrian king, died *c.* 626 BC.
[28] Ctesias was a fifth-century BC historian, relied on by Diodorus.
[29] Cyrus the Great (559–529 BC), founder of the Persian empire through defeating Astyages (his overlord), King Croesus and Nabonidus.

and Persians and their reverence for their kings, which you have set up? What Anticyra[30] can heal such a delirium?

You say that 'with what right the Persians ruled is clear from Herodotus'. Cambyses, when he wished to marry his sister, consulted the royal judges, 'men chosen from the people', interpreters of laws, to whom all matters were usually referred. What did they say? They said they could not find a law which bids a brother join with his sister in matrimony, but they had found another one by which a king of Persia may do as he pleases. Firstly if a king was able to do everything by his right, what need was there of another interpreter of the laws apart from the king himself? Those superfluous judges would have stayed anywhere rather than in the palace! Then if the king of Persia might do as he pleased, it is unbelievable that Cambyses, who was most desirous of despotism, should be so ignorant as to enquire of those judges what he might do. So what then? Either they wished 'to humour the king', as you yourself admit, or they feared what he might do to them, as Herodotus says,[31] and pretended that they had found some law that would do, forcing flattery upon the king. In judges and lawyers even in this day and age this is not new. But indeed 'the Persian Artabanus said to Themistocles[32] that there was no law amongst the Persians better than the one in which it had been decreed that the king must be honoured and worshipped'. You are indeed bringing forward an excellent law – one about the worship of kings – which was condemned even by the early fathers; and an excellent person to recommend the law, too, in Artabanus who not much later himself slaughtered Xerxes his king with his own hand. Worthy defenders of kings are the regicides that you advance before us: I suspect you are contriving some plots against kings!

You quote the poet Claudian as a witness to the obedience of the Persians. But I recall to you their histories and annals, which are crammed full of revolts of the Persians, Medes, Bactrians, Babylonians, even the murders of kings. Your next authority is Otanes the Persian, who was himself also the killer of his king Smerdis.[33]

[30] *Anticyra*: name of three ancient towns noted for the production of hellebore, a cure for madness (perhaps with a pun: anti-Cyrus).

[31] Herodotus, III, 31.

[32] Plutarch, *Themistocles*, XXVII.

[33] Smerdis imposed himself as ruler after the death of Cambyses and was killed in a conspiracy led by Otanes: for this and Otanes' speech (hostile to monarchy, as M. says), see Herodotus, III, 79.

When he with his hatred of royal power sets out the injuries and crimes of kings, their breaking of the law, murder of unsentenced men, their rapes, adulteries, you wish this to be called right of kings, and it comes into your mind to slander Samuel again. I have replied above to the matter of Homer, who sang that kings were from Jove: I would believe King Philip's[34] interpretation of the right of kings just as much as Charles's.

You bring forward some quotation then from a fragment of Diotogenes the Pythagorean, but you do not say what kind of king he is speaking of. Hear therefore how he began. All which follows should be referred to this, Βασιλεὺς κ᾽ εἴη ὁ δικαιότατος, etc: 'Let him be king who is the most just; and most just is he who acts most lawfully', for without justice no-one 'could be king, nor is there justice without law'. This is directly in conflict with your right of kings. Ecphantas, who is also quoted by you, philosophizes in the same way, δεῖ δὲ καὶ τὸν εἰς αὐτὰν καταστάντα, etc: 'He who undertakes the kingdom must be by nature most pure and full of the light of truth.' And below, ὁ κατ᾽ ἀρετὰν ἐξάρχων, etc: 'He who rules according to virtue is called, and is, a king.'[35] The man then whom you call king, in the judgement of the pythagoreans is not a king at all. Hear now in your turn Plato in the eighth *Epistle*, Ἀρχὴ γιγνέσθω ὑπεύθυνος βασιλική, etc: 'Let royal power be responsible for rendering an account; let the laws be master both of the other citizens and also of the kings themselves, if they should do anything outside the laws.'[36] I add Aristotle, *Pol.* 3, ἐν μέν τοι ὁμοίοις καὶ ἴσοις οὔτε συμφέρον ἐστίν, etc: 'among people who are similar and equal, it is neither profitable nor just for one man to be master of all, nor for him himself to be the law either where there are no laws, or where there are laws; nor for a good man to be master of good men, or a wicked man master of wicked men'. And, Bk. five, 'the man whom the people do not want, at once is not king, but a tyrant', ch. 10.[37] Look also at Xenophon in the *Hiero*, ἀντὶ τοῦ τιμωρεῖν αἱ πόλεις αὐτοῖς, etc: 'so far are states from punishing the killing of

[34] Philip II, king of Macedon 359–336 BC.

[35] M.'s Latin as well as his Greek conforms to that of one of the parallel Greek and Latin editions of Stobaeus' fifth-century anthology; e.g., 'Admonitiones de Regno, Sermo XLVI', in *Ioannis Stobaei Sententiae, ex Thesauris Graecorum Delectae* (1609), pp. 329 (for Diotogenes) and 333, 334 (for Ecphantas).

[36] Plato, *Letters*, VIII, 355d–e.

[37] Aristotle, *Politics*, III, 17 (1288a); V, 10 (1313a).

tyrants that they bestow great honours upon him who has killed a tyrant, and erect statues of tyrannicides even in the temples'.[38] I will add as an eyewitness Marcus Tullius in the *Pro Milone*: 'The Greeks grant the honours of gods to those men who have killed tyrants: what have I seen myself in Athens, and in the other cities of Greece, what religious rites instituted to such men, what songs, what poems? They are consecrated almost to immortality both in religion and remembrance.'[39] Polybius finally, a most weighty author, in the sixth book of his *Histories*, τότε δὲ ταῖς ἐπιθυμίαις ἑπόμενοι, etc: 'When princes', he says, 'began to gratify their lusts, then the kingdom was turned into a tyranny, and a conspiracy was embarked upon against the lives of the rulers; and the originators of this were not the worst of the citizens but all the most noble and greatest souled.'[40] Though I have much more at hand, I have picked these few examples to taste: for I am overwhelmed with abundance.

From the philosophers you now appeal to the poets; I follow you there most gladly. 'Even Aeschylus alone', you say, 'can teach us that kings in Greece held power subject to no laws, no judgements. He, in the tragedy the *Supplices*, calls the king of the Argives ἄκριτον πρύτανιν, a ruler not liable to judgement.' But know (for all the more I perceive you are reckless and have no judgement wherever you turn), know, I say, that we should not consider what the poet says, but who is speaking in the poet's work and what he says. For different characters are brought on, sometimes good, sometimes bad, sometimes wise, sometimes straightforward, not always speaking what the poet thinks, but what is most suitable to each character. The fifty daughters of Danaus, banished from Egypt, betook themselves to the king of the Argives as suppliants. They beg him to protect them against the violence of the Egyptians who are pursuing them with a fleet. The king replies that he cannot, unless he first communicates the matter to the people:

> Ἐγὼ δ' ἂν οὐ κραίνοιμ' ὑπόσχεσιν πάρος
> Ἀστῶν δὲ πᾶσι τοῖσδε κοινώσας πέρι.[41]

The women, being foreigners and suppliants, fear the unreliable votes of the people and again address the king with more coaxing terms:

[38] Xenophon, *Hiero*, IV, 5.

[39] Cicero, *Pro Milone*, XXIX, 80.

[40] Polybius, *Histories*, VI, 7, 7.

[41] 'I would not make the promise before I have shared these matters with all of the citizens.'

Σύ τοι πόλις, σὺ δὲ τὸ δήμιον,
Πρύτανις ἄκριτος ὤν.

You represent the city and the people, a ruler not to be judged.

Again the king answers:

Εἶπον δὲ καὶ πρὶν, οὐκ ἄνευ δήμον τάδε
Πράξαιμ' ἂν οὐδέπερ κρατῶν ——

I told you before, I would not do this without the people's consent, not even if I could.

And so he refers the whole matter to the people:

Ἐγὼ δὲ λάους συνκαλῶν ἐγχωρίους
Πείσω τὸ κοινόν.[42]

And so the people decree that help should be brought to the daughters of Danaus; whence the words of the old man Danaus in his happiness:

Θαρσεῖτε παῖδες, εὖ τὰ τῶν ἐγχωρίων
Δήμου δέδοκται παντελῆ ψηφίσματα.[43]

Be of good cheer, daughters, the most absolute votes of the natives, in a popular meeting, have decreed well.

If I had not set this out, how rashly this smatterer would have established the law about the right of kings among the Greeks from the mouth of women, and foreigners and suppliants, when both the king himself and the very story teach us quite otherwise.

The same also is taught by Euripides' Orestes who after his father's death, being himself king of the Argives, was summoned into court by the people because of the murder of his mother, and pleaded his own cause and was condemned to death by the votes of the people.[44] That at Athens royal power was subject to the law, the same Euripides bears witness in his *Supplices* also where Theseus, king of Athens, says this:

—— οὐ γὰρ ἄρχεται
Ἑνὸς πρὸς ἀνδρὸς, ἀλλ' ἐλευθέρα πόλις,
Δῆμος δ' ἀνάσσει ——[45]

This city is not ruled by one man, but is free, and the people reign.

[42] 'I will call together the peoples of the area, and persuade them together.'
[43] Aeschylus, *Supplices*, 368–9, 370–1, 398–9, 517–18, 600–1.
[44] See Euripides, *Orestes*, 930–49. Cf. *E*, III, 589.
[45] Euripides, *Supplices*, 404–5.

Thus his son Demophoon, king of the Athenians likewise, says in the same poet's *Heraclidae*:

> Οὐ γὰρ τυραννιδ' ὥστε βαρβάρων ἔχω,
> 'Αλλ' ἢν δίκαια δρῶ, δίκαια πείσομαι.[46]
>
> For I do not rule over them in a tyrannical way as if they were barbarians, but if I do things that are just, justice is done to me in return.

That the right of kings in Thebes in ancient times was just the same, Sophocles bears witness in *Oedipus Tyrannus*. Hence both Tiresias and Creon reply fiercely to Oedipus, the former saying:

> Οὐ γάρ τι σοὶ ζῶ δοῦλος
> I am not your slave.

And the latter:

> Κἀμοὶ πόλεως μέτεστι τῆς δ' οὐ σοὶ μόνῳ.[47]
> I have right in this city too, not you alone.

And then Haemon to Creon in *Antigone*:

> Πόλις γὰρ οὐκ ἔσθ', ἥτις ἀνδρὸς ἔσθ' ἑνός.[48]
> That is no state which belongs to one man.

Now truly everyone knows that the kings of Lacedaemon have often been brought to court and sometimes sentenced to death. [No wonder, when Lycurgus himself, who wrote their laws, could have learned from Homer, whom he had read through attentively, that kings were subject to the same right even in the time of the heroes. In Homer, Achilles did not hesitate, after he had found that Agamemnon himself was the plague of his people who were at that time suffering under a pestilence, in a most crowded meeting of the Greeks, though being himself a king, to submit a king to his own people to be judged with these words:

> Δημοβόρος βασιλεὺς, ἐπεὶ οὐτιδανοῖσιν ἀνάσσεις.
> Ἦ γὰρ ἂν 'Ατρείδη νῦν ὕστατα λωβήσαιο. Iliad. α.[49]
>
> King who devours the people, since you rule over men of no substance, for otherwise, son of Atreus, you would be doing wrong now for the last time.

46 Euripides, *Heraclidae*, 423–4. See p. 12.
47 Sophocles, *Oedipus Tyrannus*, 410, 630.
48 Sophocles, *Antigone*, 737.
49 Homer, *Iliad*, I, 231–2.

The witness that men of all ranks also felt the same way as the heroes about the right of kings can be the chief of lyric poets, Alcaeus. His poems, although most pleasing on their own account, Horace relates were still all the more popular with the people, because they contained the praises of those who had cast tyrants out of their cities:

> The ghosts marvel as both say words worthy of sacred silence, but the rabble, crowded shoulder to shoulder, drink in with more eager ears about battles and the banishment of tyrants: Od. 23.1.2.[50]

I will add to these things Theognis, who has the same opinion. He flourished not so long before the arrival of the Medes in Greece, a time when throughout all Greece many men flourished who were distinguished for their wisdom, and the teachings which he handed down in his verses, he himself professes that he received from wise men:

> Δημοφάγον δὲ τύραννον ὅπως ἐθέλεις κατακλῖναι.
> 'Ου νέμεσις πρὸς θεῶν γίγνεται οὐδεμία.[51]
> Cast down as you please a king who devours the people.
> No anger for this is revealed by the gods.][52]

And these quotations indeed make clear enough what was the ancient right of kings in Greece.

Let us come to the Romans. You return first of all to that statement, made not by Sallust, but by Gaius Memmius in Sallust: 'to do with impunity whatever you like'. This has been answered above. Sallust himself is the authority in clear words for the statement that 'the Romans had a government by law, though a regal name for their government';[53] and when it 'became a tyranny', as you know, they thrust it out. So Marcus Tullius, *In Pisonem*: 'Shall I consider as consul a man who did not consider the senate's existence in the republic? And shall I count as consul a man who does not have that council, without which not even kings could have existed at Rome?'[54] Do you hear – that the king at Rome was nothing without the senate? 'But Romulus had governed the Romans as he pleased, as Tacitus says.'[55] Yes, for they had not been given a firm base of laws, they were

[50] 23.1.2: an error. Horace, *Odes*, II, 13, 29.
[51] Theognis, *Elegies A.*, 1181–2.
[52] 1658.
[53] Sallust, *Bellum Jugurthinum*, XXXI, 9.
[54] Cicero, *In Pisonem*, 10, 23.
[55] S., *DR*, p. 113; see Tacitus, *Annals*, III, 26.

a conflux of refugees rather than a commonwealth. Once upon a time all mortals used to live without laws, when commonwealths did not yet exist. But after Romulus, on the authority of Livy, even though everybody wanted a king as they had not yet experienced the sweetness of liberty, 'yet the supreme power was allowed to the people so that they did not grant more right than they kept back'. The same writer says that 'that right was removed by force' by the caesars.[56] Servius Tullius at first ruled by guile, as if he was a deputy of Tarquinius Priscus. Afterwards indeed he himself referred it to the people, to see if 'they wanted and ordered him to be king'. At last, as Tacitus says, 'he was the ordainer of laws which even the kings obeyed'.[57] Would he have done this wrong to himself and his descendants, if he had thought that the right of kings had before been above the laws? The last of those kings, Tarquinius Superbus 'first relaxed the habit of consulting the senate about everything'.[58] Because of this and other crimes the people annulled the power of King Lucius Tarquinius; they ordered him into exile with his wife and children. This is for the most part from Livy and Cicero, than whom you could not produce other better interpreters of the right of kings amongst the Romans. As for the dictatorship, that was only temporary, never used except in the greatest state crises, and it had to be laid down again within six months.

And what you call the right of the emperors, that was not right but clearly force; a control gained not by any right but that of arms. But, you say, 'Tacitus who flourished under the empire of a single man' wrote thus: 'the gods have granted the supreme authority over affairs to a prince, to subjects there remains the honour of obeying'. And you do not say where it comes from – no doubt because you are conscious of imposing remarkably upon your readers. This indeed I at once smelt out, though I did not at once find that passage. For these are not the words of Tacitus, a good writer, and a firm opponent of tyrants, but are from Tacitus' works and are the words of Marcus Terentius, a certain Roman knight. When he was a defendant on a capital charge, amongst other things which were said by him in fear of death, he flatters Tiberius thus, *Annals* 6: 'The gods have granted you the

[56] Livy, *Ab urbe condita*, I, 17, 2–9; I, 46, 1.

[57] Tarquinius Priscus (616–579 BC) and Servius Tullius (578–535 BC), the fifth and sixth kings of Rome. Tacitus, *Annals*, III, 26.

[58] Tarquinius Superbus, last king of Rome, 534–510 BC. Livy, *Ab urbe condita*, I, 49, 7.

supreme judgement over affairs, to us there remains the honour of obeying.'[59] This you bring forward as if it were the opinion of Tacitus – you who would not reject opinions convenient for you that had been brought forward, not only from a bakery or a barbershop, but from the very torture chamber: so indiscriminately do you rake together everything, either for the sake of showing off, or from consciousness of your feebleness. If you had preferred to read Tacitus himself rather than copy an excerpt from somewhere too carelessly,[60] he would have taught you the origin of that right of emperors. 'After the victory at Actium, when the situation of the state was turned upside down, and there was nothing of our ancient or uncorrupt customs anywhere, all men, stripping off equality, began to observe the orders of a first citizen.' The same author would have instructed you in the third book of the *Annals* whence comes all your right of kings: 'after equality was stripped off, and in place of moderation and modesty, ambition and violence began to advance, tyrants came forth and remained amongst many peoples forever'.[61] You could have learned the same thing from Dio, if your natural superficiality and changeability would allow you to comprehend anything so deep. For he relates, Bk. 53, quoted by you, that it was brought about partly by weapons, partly by the trickery and hypocrisy of Octavian Caesar that emperors were freed from the laws.[62] For while he promised before a public meeting that he would step down from the principate, obey the laws and even the orders of others, for the reason of waging war in his provinces, he always kept legions under his control, and while he pretended to decline power, he gradually seized it. This is not being duly released from the laws, but releasing the bonds of the laws by force, as that gladiator Spartacus could have done; and then claiming for himself the name of prince or emperor or αὐτοκράτορος [autocrat], as if God or the law of nature had made all men and laws subject to him.

Do you wish to investigate a little more deeply the origin of the right of the caesars? Marcus Antonius was made consul on the order of Caesar, who by taking up arms impiously against the republic then held the greatest power. When the Lupercalia[63] was being celebrated

[59] Tacitus, *Annals*, VI, 8.
[60] See *R*, I, 573, for M.'s contemptuous reference to an example of this, Virgilio Malvezzi's *Discourses upon Cornelius Tacitus* (1642).
[61] Tacitus, *Annals*, I, 3–4; III, 26.
[62] Dio Cassius, *Roman History*, LIII, 28.
[63] *Lupercalia*: a pastoral festival celebrated in February and named after the Lupercal, a

at Rome, by a previous arrangement as it seems, Antony placed a diadem upon Caesar's head amidst the groans and lamentations of the people. Then he ordered that it be written in the calendar, on the Lupercalia, that Antony the consul, at the bidding of the people, offered the kingship to Gaius Caesar. Of this matter Cicero writes in the second *Philippic*: 'Was it for this that Lucius Tarquinius was driven out and Spurius Cassius, Spurius Melius and Marcus Manlius were killed, so that many generations later a king should be set up in Rome by Mark Antony, something which is not lawful?'[64] Truly you are worthier even than Antony himself of every terrible torture and eternal disgrace, although don't you be proud about this, for I do not compare you, a most contemptible man, with Antony in any other matter except your crime – you who in these unspeakable Lupercalia of yours have applied yourself to placing not upon the head of one alone, but of all tyrants, a diadem loosed from all laws but never to be loosened by any [you most dissolute Lupercus].[65]

Certainly if one should believe the oracle of the caesars themselves, for so the christian emperors Theodosius and Valens[66] call their own edict, *Cod.* lib. 1, titl. 14, the authority of emperors depends upon the authority of the law. So the majesty of the ruler, even by the judgement or the oracle of the caesars themselves, must be submitted to the laws on which it depends. Hence, when the power of the emperors had grown to maturity, Pliny said to Trajan in his *Panegyric*: 'a tyranny and a principate are different by nature. Trajan fends off and puts from him actual kingship, and occupies the seat of a prince, so there may be no room for a master.' And below: 'All things which have been said by me about other princes relate to this fact – that I may show how our father reshapes and rectifies the customs of the principate that have been corrupted and perverted by long habit.'[67] What Pliny calls the perverted customs of the principate – are you not ashamed to keep on constantly calling the right of kings? But so much in brief about the right of kings among the Romans.

What they did to their tyrants, whether kings or emperors, is com-

sacred grotto on the Palatine hill. The one involving Antony and Caesar took place in 44 BC.

64 Cicero, *Philippics*, II, xxxiv, 87.

65 *Lupercus dissolutissimus*: 1658. S. is (like Antony) a Lupercus, or priest of the Lupercalia, the rites of which may have aimed at the propitiation of a wolf god.

66 *Valens*: 1651Q, 1651F, 1658; should be Valentinian. See p. 13.

67 Pliny, *Panegyrics*, XLV, 3; LIII, 1.

monly known. They expelled Tarquin [, and in the manner of their ancestors even then. For either their neighbour Etruria provided a very ancient example of the expulsion of the tyrant Mezentius from the city of Agylla, or by that story Virgil, the supreme master of the seemly, wished to show Octavian Caesar, who was even then ruling in Rome, with what right kings had existed amongst all nations – and this from very far back in time, *Aeneid*. Bk. 8:

> But tired out at length while he rages unspeakably, the citizens take up arms and surround both him and his house: they slaughter his companions; they hurl fire onto the rooftops. He slipped away amid the carnage and took refuge in the territory of the Rutulians, and was defended by the weapons of Turnus his host. So all Etruria rose up in righteous fury: they demand back the king for execution, in open warfare.[68]

You see here that citizens inflamed with righteous anger, sought the tyrant not only to kill him on sudden impulse, not only expelled him from his kingdom, but asked for him back as a fugitive and exile, for judgement (or rather for execution) by undertaking war].[69]

'But how', you say, 'did they expel Tarquin? Did they summon him to court? Not at all; they shut the gates against him when he came.' Ridiculous fool, what could they do but shut the gates when he was speeding there with part of his troops? What does it matter whether he was ordered into exile or put to death, if only it is agreed that he paid the penalty? The most distinguished men of that age killed Gaius Caesar the tyrant in the senate. This deed Marcus Tullius, himself an excellent man, and publicly named father of his country, celebrated with extraordinary praise in many other places as well as the second *Philippic*. I will quote a few of his words: 'All good men, as far as was in them, killed Caesar; some lacked a plan, others the courage, others the opportunity, none the will.' And below: 'For what action ever, O holy Jupiter, was taken, not only in this city but in all lands, that was greater, that was more glorious, that was more to be commended to the everlasting remembrance of men? In the partnership of this plan I do not decline to be included with the leaders, as it were inside the Trojan horse.'[70]

The famous quotation from Seneca the tragedian can refer both to the Greeks and the Romans:

[68] Virgil, *Aeneid*, VIII, 489–95. For Mezentius, see also *DDD*, II, 327, and *PSD*, IV, ii, 795.
[69] 1658.
[70] Cicero, *Philippics*, II, xii, 29; xiii, 32.

> No victim can be sacrificed in Jupiter's honour more magnificent and sumptuous than an unjust king.[71]

For if you have in mind Hercules, whose opinion this is represented as being, it shows what the greatest men among the Greeks in that age felt: if the poet, who flourished under Nero (and poets generally create something that is almost their own opinion for their best characters), it indicated both what Seneca himself and what all good men, even in the time of Nero, thought should be done to a tyrant, and how pious and how pleasing to the gods they considered tyrannicide to be. So all the best men of Rome, as far as was in them, killed Domitian. Pliny the younger confesses this openly in that *Panegyric* to the emperor Trajan:

> It was pleasurable to beat that proudest of countenances into the ground, to press upon him with a sword, to vent one's rage with axes, so that blood and pain might follow each blow. No-one was so moderate in his joy that it did not seem as good as revenge to look upon the mangled joints, the mutilated limbs and at last the grim and terrible statues cast down and melted in the flames.

And then: 'They cannot love good princes enough, who have not enough hated bad ones.' Then amongst the crimes of Domitian he sets the fact that he slaughtered Epaphroditus, in some way the killer of Nero: 'Has the recent vengeance for Nero been forgotten by our grief? Am I to suppose that one who was avenging Nero's death would allow his reputation and life to be slandered?'[72] Obviously as if he judged it almost a crime not to have murdered Nero, and a very serious crime to avenge his murder.

From this it is clear that all the most outstanding men among the Romans not only killed tyrants in whatever way and whenever they could, but that, like the Greeks formerly, they held that deed as worthy of the greatest praise. For whenever they could not judge a tyrant in his lifetime because they were his inferiors in strength, they would both judge him when he was dead, and condemn him by the Valerian law. For Valerius Publicola, the colleague of Junius Brutus, when he saw that tyrants could not be brought to judgement because they were hemmed round by their own soldiers, proposed a law, under which one could kill them without sentence in any manner, and

[71] Seneca, *Hercules furens*, 922–4. See p. 17.

[72] Pliny, *Panegyrics*, LII, 4; LIII, 2 and 4.

give an account of the deed afterwards.[73] Hence it was with Gaius Caligula, whom Cassius killed with a sword and everybody with their prayers. Valerius Asiaticus, a man of consular rank, not present at the time, still shouted out to his soldiers who were in an uproar because of the emperor's death: 'Would that I had killed him!'[74] The senate at the same time resolved to efface the memory of the caesars and demolish the temples; so far were they from being angry with Cassius. When Claudius later was hailed as emperor by the soldiers, they forbade him by agency of a tribune of the plebs to take on the principate; but the violence of the soldiers prevailed. The senate judged Nero a public enemy, and searched for him so he might be punished after the custom of their ancestors. The form of punishment was that he be stripped and his neck inserted beneath a fork, and his body be whipped to death with rods. See how much more mildly and moderately the English acted with their tyrant, who in many people's opinion had been the author of more shedding of blood than Nero himself! So the senate condemned Domitian after his death. They ordered what they could – that his statues be publicly pulled down and dashed to the ground. Commodus, slain by his own men, was not avenged but judged a public enemy by the senate and people, who searched for his corpse for mutilation. About this matter the senate's resolution is extant in Lampridius: 'Let his honours be taken away from an enemy of his country, let the parricide be drawn, and torn to pieces in the gladiators' stripping room; let the enemy of the gods, the executioner of the senate be dragged on the hook', etc.[75] The same men condemned the emperor Didius Julianus to death in a very crowded senate; and they sent a tribune and ordered him to be killed in the palace.[76] The same people annulled the power of Maximinus,[77] and judged him a public enemy. It is helpful to quote the actual resolution of the senate from Capitolinus: 'The consul put the question: "Senators, what is your pleasure concerning the Maximins?"'

[73] Valerius Publicola (Poplicola), traditionally one of the first consuls (509 BC) to whom was attributed an early law *de provocatione* (appeal), anticipating the *Lex Valeria.* Cf. *E*, III, 590.

[74] See Dio Cassius, *Roman History*, LIX, 30, 2.

[75] Lampridius, 'Commodus', *Historia Augusta*, XVIII, 3.

[76] In 193 Didius Julianus was chosen to succeed Pertinax as emperor by the Praetorian Guard, but, after a switch in its allegiances, was deposed by the Senate and murdered within weeks. See Spartianus, 'Didius Julianus', *Historia Augusta*, VIII, 8.

[77] Maximinus, proclaimed Roman emperor in 235; declared a public enemy and murdered with his son in 238.

The reply was, ' "enemies, enemies, whoever kills them will earn a reward!" ' Do you want to know whether the Roman people and the provinces obeyed Maximinus the emperor or the senate? Hear the words of the same author Capitolinus: 'The senate sends letters' to all the provinces to come to the aid of the common safety and liberty; these letters were heard by everyone. Everywhere the friends, deputies, generals, tribunes, soldiers of Maximinus were killed: few cities kept their allegiance to the public enemy.[78] Herodian relates the same thing.[79] What more need I say about the Romans?

Let us now see what the right of kings was like at that time among the neighbouring nations. Amongst the Gauls, their king, Ambiorix, confesses 'that his power was such that the multitude had no less right over him than he over the multitude'. So he was judged no less than judging. Likewise King Vercingetorix was charged with treason by his own people; Caesar relates these things when writing his *Gallic War*.[80] Nor was 'the power of the Germanic kings infinite or free: the chiefs take resolutions about minor matters, and everyone about more important ones. The king or prince is heeded more because of the weight of his persuasion than by his power of ordering; if his opinion has displeased them, they reject it with a murmur.'[81] So Tacitus. You indeed now concede that what you lately cried out was absolutely unheard of was done frequently – that without doubt 'fifty Scottish kings have either been expelled or imprisoned or killed, certain ones even having been publicly executed'. Since it has been done repeatedly in Britain itself, why do you, corpse-bearer of tyrants, who carry them out at night like paupers, cry out about it with so much lamentation as an unspeakable and unheard of thing?

You go on to exalt the piety of the Jews and Christians towards their tyrants, and sow a harvest of lies from lies, which I have now so often disproved. Just now you were widely praising the obedience of the Assyrians and Persians, and now you enumerate their rebellions; and after you had said shortly before that they never rebelled, now you bring forward many reasons why these same people have so often rebelled! Then you return to your story of the king's execution which had been long interrupted, so that if you had not then perchance taken enough care to be foolish and ridiculous, you would do so now.

[78] Capitolinus, 'Maximini Duo', *Historia Augusta*, XVII, 4; XXIII, 2–7.
[79] Herodian, *History*, VIII, v, 8–9.
[80] Julius Caesar, *De bello Gallico*, V, 27, 3.
[81] Tacitus, *Germania*, 11.

You tell how he was 'led through the limbs of his court'.[82] What you mean by the limbs of his court I eagerly desire to know! You survey the disasters of the Romans when they changed from a kingdom into a republic, in which I have shown above that you make a lie of your own words most shamefully. You who used to point out in your work against the jesuit that 'there were only seditions beneath aristocracies and democracies, but destruction was certain under a tyrant', now – O most empty and corrupt of mankind – do you dare to say that 'because their kings had formerly been ejected they drained the cup of the evils that rose from their seditions, as punishment?' Indeed because King Charles afterwards presented you with one hundred jacobuses; this was why the Romans paid for the expulsion of their kings.

But it went badly with the murderers of Julius Caesar. Indeed if ever any tyrant were to be spared, I would wish it to be he: for although he rushed a kingship upon the republic somewhat too violently, yet he was perhaps most worthy of kingship:[83] not that I would think that on this account anyone should have paid the penalty for killing Caesar more than Gaius Antonius,[84] Cicero's colleague, did for killing Catiline. Afterwards when he was condemned for other crimes, as Cicero says in the *Pro Flacco*, 'Catiline's tomb was decorated with flowers.' For supporters of Catiline were exultant, 'kept on saying that then Catiline's deeds were just', to stir up hatred against the rest who had destroyed Catiline.[85] These are the skills of wicked men, by which they may deter the most outstanding men from punishing tyrants and often too from punishing the most wicked criminals. I might say in return, with ease, how often matters have gone well and prosperously for the killers of tyrants, if anyone could establish anything certain from the outcome of events.

You object that 'the English did not execute their hereditary king, as tyrants are generally sacrificed, but as robbers and traitors are'. First I do not know what heredity should contribute to impunity for crimes: that it confers any it is hardly possible for a wise man to believe. Then in what you refer to as 'barbaric cruelty' one should

[82] *per aulae suae membra ductum*: S., *DR*, p. 118. M. is quibbling about *membrum* ('limb' or, metaphorically, 'part').

[83] Like Cicero (*Philippics*, II, xliv, 116), M. is prepared to acknowledge Caesar's remarkable gifts.

[84] Gaius Antonius Hybrida, elected consul with Cicero in 63 BC; not present at Pistoria in Jan. 62 when his army defeated Catiline.

[85] Cicero, *Pro Flacco*, XXXVIII, 95.

praise rather the leniency and moderation of the English. Though to be a tyrant contains within it all kinds of impieties, robberies, treasons and treacheries towards the country, they considered it sufficient to exact no more serious a punishment from the tyrant than they usually exact from any simple robber or common traitor.

You hope that 'some Harmodiuses and Thrasybuluses[86] will rise up who, by the slaughter of my countrymen, will make sacrifice to appease the dead spirits of the tyrant'. But you will sooner lose courage and will end a life worthy of yourself by hanging, you who deserve to be cursed by all good men, before you see Harmodiuses making an offering of the blood of Harmodiuses to a tyrant. For it is very likely that that end will come upon you, and who could prophesy more correctly about such a criminal as you? The other thing is impossible. You mention thirty tyrants who rebelled under Gallienus.[87] What if one tyrant attacks another: will all then who oppose a tyrant or destroy him be tyrants themselves? You will not persuade people of this, you slave-knight; nor he who is your authority, Trebellius Pollio,[88] almost the most obscure of historians. 'If any emperors were judged public enemies by the senate', you say, 'faction did it, not right.' You recall to our memory what created emperors; it was faction and violence and, to speak more clearly, the madness of Antony, not right, that made them so they themselves first rebelled against the senate and people of Rome. 'Galba',[89] you say, 'paid the penalty for rising up against Nero.' Say also what penalty Vespasian paid who did the same against Vitellius.[90] 'So much difference', you say, 'was there between Charles and Nero, as between those English butchers and the Roman senators of that time.' Arrant rogue, by whom it is blame to be praised, and great praise to be blamed! Only a few sentences back, when writing about this very thing, you were saying that 'the senate under the emperors was an assembly of slaves in togas'; now you say that same 'senate was an assembly of kings'. If this is so, what

[86] Harmodius, Athenian tyrannicide who (with Aristogiton) slew Hipparchus in 514 BC; Thrasybulus opposed the oligarchy of the Four Hundred at Athens in 411 BC and helped overthrow the Thirty Tyrants in 404–403.

[87] Gallienus, Roman emperor, 253–67, who dealt with a multiplicity of invasions and uprisings.

[88] Trebellius Pollio, the supposed author of 'Tyranni Triginta' in the *Historia Augusta*.

[89] Galba, Roman emperor, 68–69, successfully rose against Nero but was assassinated seven months later.

[90] I.e. none. Vitellius, Roman emperor, AD 69, succumbed to the forces of Vespasian who went on to reign prosperously for ten years.

prevents kings, on your authority, being slaves in togas? Blessed are kings in this eulogist! Amongst men there is none more wicked, amongst four-footed beasts none more senseless – unless I may say that it is his own peculiarity that no-one brays more learnedly.

You want the parliament of England to be more like Nero than the Roman senate. This malignant itch of yours for cobbling together the most inept comparisons compels me to correct you; and how like Charles was to Nero, I will show. 'Nero', you say, 'killed his own mother' with a sword. Charles did the same with poison to his father who was also the king. For to pass over other proofs, he who snatched from the clutches of the laws the duke who was charged with the poisoning, cannot but have been guilty himself too. Nero killed many thousands of christians; Charles many more. There were some, on the testimony of Suetonius, who praised Nero after his death, who missed him, who for a long time 'decorated his tomb with spring and summer flowers' and predicted all sorts of evils for his enemies:[91] and there are some who miss Charles with the same madness, and exalt him with the highest praises, of whom you, gallows-knight, lead the company.

'The English soldiers, more fierce than their own hounds, set up a new and unheard of tribunal.' Behold that most pointed metaphor or proverb of Salmasius, which has now been rammed in six times, 'more fierce than their own hounds'; come, orators and you schoolmasters, pluck if you are wise this most elegant little flower, of which Salmasius is so very fond. Entrust to your notes and chests the cosmetic of this most eloquent man, so it won't perish. Has your madness so used up your words that you are forced like a cuckoo to croak the same ill-omened song over and over again? What sort of monstrosity shall I call this? Madness, as the stories go, turned Hecuba into a dog;[92] it turns you, lord of St Loup, into a cuckoo!

Now you begin with fresh inconsistencies. Above, p. 113, you had asserted that 'the prince was freed from laws, not of compulsion' only, but 'of direction; that there are none at all by which he is restricted'. Now you say that you will speak 'below of the difference between kings, in so far as some have had lesser power and others greater in ruling'. You wish to prove 'that kings could not be judged or condemned by their subjects, by an argument' which you yourself call

[91] Suetonius, *Nero*, 57.

[92] See Ovid, *Metamorphoses*, XIII, 399–427.

'most strong' – in reality a most stupid one; you say 'there was no other difference between judges and kings: but yet the Jews kept asking for kings out of weariness and hatred of judges'. Perhaps you think that because they could judge and condemn those judges for bad behaviour in office, they were led by weariness and hatred of them to demand kings who they could not punish or force into line for violating all laws? Who except for you generally argues so stupidly? So it was for some other reason than to have a master superior to the laws that they asked for a king; to guess now what that was is not relevant: whatever it was, both God and his prophet have testified that it was done without sensible counsel. Again you now threaten with the bitterest strife your rabbis, from whom you asserted above that you had proved that a king of the Jews could not be judged, because they have related that a king can be both judged and beaten: which is clearly the same as if you had confessed you then had made up all that you said you'd proved from the rabbis. At last you come down to contriving affected little debates about the number of Solomon's stables, and how many 'mangers he had for his horses', forgetting the king's defence.

At last from a stable boy you return to being a knight, who preaches about virtue and preaches the same thing endlessly in different words, or rather the sort of monster you were before, a ranting cuckoo. For you complain that 'in these later generations the force of order has been slackened and its rule corrupted' – because *one* tyrant, freed from all laws, is not permitted to slacken all order and corrupt the manners of all with impunity! This doctrine, you say, 'the Brownists[93] among protestants' introduced. Thus Luther, Calvin, Zwingli, Bucer and all the most famous orthodox theologians were in your judgement Brownists. The English endure your abuse the more patiently, when they hear you ranting against the most outstanding doctors of the church and in effect the whole protestant church with almost the same insults.

[93] *Brunistae*: followers of Robert Browne (1550?–1633?), earliest separatist from the Church of England.

CHAPTER VI

After the law of God and nature has been disturbed by you in vain and most badly handled, from which you have gained nothing apart from the shame of ignorance as well as wickedness, I don't see what you then can advance in this royal cause apart from trifles. But although I hope that I should have fully satisfied all good and learned men and this most noble of causes also, even if I should put an end to my answer at this point, still in case others should meanwhile think that I have evaded the variety and sharpness of your argument rather than your immoderate prolixity, I will go on as far as you wish. But I shall be so brief that it may easily appear that after having done all which, if not the dignity, at least the urgency of the cause required, I am now only gratifying the expectation or even curiosity of some people.

'From here on', you say, 'another and greater rank of arguments will rise before me.' Is there a greater rank of arguments than that which the law of God and nature supplied? Bring help, Lucina,[1] Mt Salmasius is in labour.[2] Not for nothing did he become the wife of his wife. Mortals, await some monstrous birth. 'If he who is and is called king could be accused before another power, this must be altogether greater than royal power; but that which is set up as greater must truly be called and be royal. For royal power must be defined in this way: as the power which is highest in the state and unique; and above which no other is recognized.' O truly a mouse brought forth by a mountain and a ridiculous one at that! Bring help, grammarians, to this gram-

[1] Lucina was the Roman goddess of childbirth.

[2] *parturit Mons Salmasius*: alludes to Ovid, *Ars Poetica*, 139; 'Parturiunt montes, nascetur ridiculus mus.'

marian in labour. It is all up – not with the law of God or nature, but with the dictionary!

What if I should answer you in this way? Let names give way before realities. It is not our business to be cautious of the name, as we have got rid of the reality. Let others who love kings care about this. We enjoy our liberty. You would take away a reply that was certainly not unfair. But so that you may understand that I am dealing with you in all matters on a good and equal footing, I will reply not according to my own opinion alone, but that of the best and wisest of the men of old, who judged that both the name and power of kings could perfectly coexist with the greater power of laws and the people. In particular Lycurgus, a man most famous for wisdom, when he wished most to provide for the interests of royal power, as Plato tells us, could find no other way of preserving it, than by making the power of the senate and the ephors, that is of the people, greater than that of the king in his own country. Theseus in Euripides' play felt the same thing. Although he was king of Athens, yet after setting free the Athenian people to his own great glory, he not only raised the power of the people above that of the king but left the kingdom none the less in that state to his own descendants. Thus Euripides in the *Supplices* brings him on speaking like this:

> Δῆμον κατέστησ' ἀυτὸν εἲς μοναρχίαν
> 'Ελευθερώσας τήνδ' ἰσόψηφον πόλιν.
>
> I have made the people themselves into the monarchy, freeing this city which has an equal right in voting.

And again to the Theban herald:

> Πρῶτον μὲν ἤρξω τοῦ λόγου ψευδῶς ξένε
> Ζητῶν τύραννον ἐνθάδ', οὐ γὰρ ἄρχεται
> 'Ενὸς πρὸς ἀνδρὸς, ἀλλ' ἐλευθέρα πόλις,
> Δῆμος δ' ἀνασσει——[3]
>
> Firstly you began your speech, stranger, with a false address, in asking for the ruler here: for this city is not ruled by one man but is free, and the people reign.

This was what he said; although he both was, and was called, king in that city. The godlike Plato bears witness also in his eighth *Epistle*: 'Lycurgus introduced the senate and the power of the ephors, τῆς

[3] Euripides, *Supplices*, 352–3, 403–6.

βασιλικῆς ἀρχῆς σωτήριον, a means of saving the power of the king. And by this means that power was preserved throughout so many centuries in great honour. After law became mistress, she became king of men.' But the law cannot be king unless there is someone who, if the occasion should come about, can act in accordance with the law against the king also. Thus to the Sicilians he recommends royal power with limitations, ἐλευθερία γιγνέσθω μετὰ βασιλικῆς ἀρχῆς, etc: 'Let there be freedom along with royal power; let royal power be ὑπεύθυνος, responsible for giving an account of its actions. Let the law rule kings also if they do anything illegal.'[4] Finally, Aristotle says in the third book of his *Politics*, 'In the state of Sparta, there seems to be the best example of a monarchy, amongst those monarchies which are governed by law': but all forms of monarchy, he says, were governed by law apart from one which he calls παμβασιλείαν, and he does not mention that such a thing ever existed anywhere.[5] And so Aristotle felt that such a monarchy as the Spartans had is most properly of all called, and is, a monarchy; therefore he could not deny that such a king was no less properly called and was a king, when nevertheless the people were above the king. So many great writers have guaranteed on their honour the safety of the title and the substance of kingship to the king, even where the people keep the highest power in their own hands for cases of need, though they don't usually exercise it. Don't let such a narrow mind as yours be so fearful for the perfection of grammatical details – that is of words – so that rather than have the order of your glossary disturbed or harmed in any way, you would be willing to betray the liberty and commonwealth of all men. Know too from now on that names are subordinate to things, not things to names. Thus you will have more wisdom and you will not 'go on to infinity', which you fear. 'So it was in vain that Seneca thus describes those three kinds of constitutions.' Let Seneca go on in vain so long as we are free men; unless I am mistaken, we are not the kind of people whom Seneca's flourishes will reduce to slavery. Seneca, however, even though he says that the highest power rests with a single person, still says that 'it belongs to the people',[6] and it is plainly entrusted to the king for the welfare not the destruction of all; and it has not been bestowed by the people as a possession but merely for his use. 'Then it is not by the

[4] Plato, *Letters*, VIII, 354b, 355d.

[5] Aristotle, *Politics*, III, 14 (1285a–b).

[6] Seneca, *De beneficiis*, VII, iv, 2.

will of God that kings now rule, but by that of the people.' As if indeed God does not rule people so that the people hand over rule to whomever God wishes! In the *Institutes* themselves, the Emperor Justinian openly acknowledges that the caesars began to rule from the point when 'by the *lex regia* the people granted to them and vested in them all their own authority and power'.[7]

But how long shall I go on rehashing those points of yours which I have by now so often disproved? Once again – something which shows your rude and uncivilized nature and your most offensive character – although you are a foreigner and a stranger, you poke inquisitively into the affairs of our commonwealth which has nothing to do with you. Come here then, as is fitting for such a great busybody, with a remarkable grammatical mistake. 'Whatever', you say, 'those profligate men say, *are*[8] meant to deceive the people.' Wicked man, was this the reason that you, an outlawed grammarian, were desirous of interfering with our commonwealth, so that you might fill us up with your grammatical mistakes and barbarisms? But tell us how we have deceived the people. 'The form of government which they have set up is not democratic[9] but military.' This indeed was what that band of deserters hired you for with a paltry sum and ordered you to write: so it is not you, who babble about things which you don't understand at all, but those who hired you for a price who need an answer. Who 'threw the lords out of parliament? Was it the people?' Indeed it was the people! And by doing that, they threw off an unbearable yoke of slavery from their necks. Those very soldiers, by whom you say this was done, were not foreigners, but our countrymen and a majority of the people, and they did it with the consent and by the desire of almost all the rest of the people, and supported by the authority of parliament also. 'Was it the people', you say, 'who maimed the commoners of the lower house, by putting some of the members to flight, etc?' It was the people, I say. For why should I not say that the action of the better, that is the healthier, part[10] of the government, in which resides the true power of the people, was the act of the people. What if the majority in parliament should prefer to

[7] *lege regia populus iis et in eos omne imperium suum, et potestatem concessit*: slightly adapted from Justinian, *Institutes*, I. 2.6.

[8] *Quicquid ... illi perditi homines dicunt, ad populum decipiendum pertinent*: from S., *DR*, p. 133, where *quicquid* (singular) and *pertinent* (plural) do not agree.

[9] *popularis*.

[10] *pars potior, id est sanior*.

be slaves, and to offer the commonwealth for sale – should not the minority be allowed to prevent this and keep their liberty, if it lies in their power? 'But the officers did this with their soldiers.' Then thanks are due to the officers, because they did not fail the commonwealth, but drove back the unruly workmen and shopkeepers of London who shortly before, just like the lowest dregs who supported Clodius,[11] had besieged the house of parliament itself. And will you therefore call the chief and proper right of parliament which is to look out for the liberty of the people before all else either in peace or in war 'a military despotism'? But it is no wonder that this is said by traitors who have dictated to you what you say. For thus that most corrupt faction of Antony and his followers once used to call the Roman senate, when it went to war against the enemies of the country, 'Pompey's Camp'.[12] Now I am truly glad that your side resent the very brave general of our army, Cromwell, because he – surrounded by a happy crowd of friends, attended by the fair favour of the people, and also the prayers of all good men – undertook the Irish War,[13] which was most pleasing to God. For after hearing later on of his many victories, I now believe that they have wasted away from spite.

I pass over much long-winded rubbish of yours about the soldiers of Rome. Who does not see that what follows is most remote from the truth? 'The power of the people', you say, 'ceases to exist when that of a king begins to exist.' By what law does that come about? For it is generally agreed that almost all kings of nations everywhere receive from the people a rule which is handed over to them under certain conditions: if the king should not abide by them, pray tell us why should that power, which was only held in trust, not return to the people as well from a king as from a consul or from any other magistrate? For when you talk about 'the public safety demanding it', you are speaking absurdities; since the means to ensure safety are wholly the same, whether 'that power is returned to the people' from a king, or from nobles or triumvirs who are wrongly using the authority which has been handed over to them. However you grant yourself that it can be returned to the people from all officers whatsoever, the king alone excepted. Certainly if a people in their right mind did not give

[11] Publius Clodius, rabble-rouser who colluded with Catiline and (until 56 BC) Caesar, and was bitterly opposed by Cicero.
[12] See Cicero, *Philippics*, XIII, xi, 26.
[13] Cromwell's campaign in Ireland included brutal triumphs at Drogheda and Wexford.

power over themselves to the king or any magistrates except for the common welfare of everybody only, there can be no reason why for quite opposite reasons, to prevent the destruction of all, they could not take away the power they had given as well from a king as from other magistrates. Might it not be taken away from one even more easily than from many? And to give power over oneself to any mortal other than upon trust would be the height of madness; nor is it believable that any people since the beginning of the world – at least any people which was its own master – has been so wretchedly foolish that it either surrendered all power utterly or after having entrusted it to its magistrates recalled it to itself without the weightiest reasons. But if disturbances, if civil wars arise from this, certainly no right arises from this for a king to retain by force that power which the people claim back as their own. Hence it comes about that it must be attributed to the wisdom of the people, not to the right of the king, and it is surely something that we do not deny 'that the ruler should not be changed lightly'. But it in no way follows that therefore it should never happen or for absolutely no reason. And you have not yet produced any proof or brought forth any right of kings showing that a people who are all in agreement ought not to deprive an unsuitable king of his kingdom, if only this can be done, as it has been done so often in your country of France also, without upheaval and civil war. And so the welfare of the people is the supreme law,[14] not the welfare of a tyrant, and for this reason the law should benefit the people against a tyrant, not the tyrant against a people. But you have dared to overthrow so sacred, so venerable a law with your juggler's tricks; you have wished the law which is supreme amongst men and most beneficial to the people to have effect only in granting impunity to tyrants. Since we English are so often according to you 'enthusiasts' and 'inspired' and 'prophets', may you, I say, know as a result of my prophecy, that God and men threaten to avenge so great a crime upon you: and yet the subjection of the whole human race to tyrants, which is doing as much as you could to condemn them to the lions, is in itself so monstrous a sin as to be in part its own vengeance upon you, and will pursue you sooner or later with its furies wherever on earth you run to and wherever you roam, and will hunt you into a madness even worse than that in which you now rave.

[14] See p. 62.

I come now to your other argument which is no better than the former one: if the people may take back their power, 'there would be no difference between a popular and a royal constitution, except for the fact that in the latter single rulers are appointed, in the former many'. What if there was no other difference? Would the commonwealth receive any harm from that?[15] But look at some other differences brought forward by yourself, 'of time and succession' to be sure, 'since popular magistrates are generally chosen annually', while kings, unless they commit some crime, last forever – and for the most part the succession runs in the same family. So let them differ amongst themselves or not differ, for I am not at all concerned about those minutiae. On this point they certainly agree: that in both cases, whenever it matters to the commonwealth, the people can call that power, which they had handed over to another for the public welfare, back to themselves without injustice for the same reason. 'But by the *lex regia*, so called in Rome, which is mentioned in the *Institutes*, the Roman people granted to its chief, and vested in him, all its own authority and power.' Certainly – compelled by the force of the caesars who under the honourable pretext of law sanctioned what was merely their own violence. This I have discussed above – a thing which the lawyers themselves do not disguise in treating this passage of the *Institutes*. Therefore what was not granted lawfully and by the will of the people is undoubtedly revocable. But yet it is most reasonable that the Roman people did not transfer any other power to the chief citizen than they had before granted to their own magistrates: that is, a lawful and revocable power, not a tyrannical and senseless one. Therefore the caesars received the power of the consul and the tribune – but no-one assumed that of dictator after Julius. They were even accustomed to honour the people in the Circus – as I have mentioned above in the words of Tacitus and Claudian. But as 'many private citizens have once upon a time sold themselves into another's slavery, so can a whole people'. O you knight from a jail, you slave-dealer! Eternal shame even to your own native country! You are so disgusting a keeper and a public pimp of slavery that even the lowest band of slaves on any sale platform ought to curse and spit at you! Certainly if a people had delivered themselves to kings in this way, the

[15] *nunquid inde respub. detrimenti caperet?*: alludes to the formula by which power was conferred on the consuls; *ne quid res publica detrimenti capiat.*

kings too might deliver the same people to any other master of all or sell them off at a price. And yet it is agreed that a king cannot even sell off the inheritance of the crown. Therefore he who holds the grant from the people only of the use and enjoyment of the crown (as it is said) and the royal inheritance[16] – shall he be owner of the people itself? Not if you were a knight holed through with both ears pierced,[17] not if you stood forward with gypsum-whitened feet would you be so much the cheapest of all the slaves as you now are, being the author of so shameful an opinion as this. Go on and exact the penalties for your crimes unwillingly from yourself, as you are now doing. Finally you stammer out a lot about the right of war which is out of place here. For Charles did not conquer us in war; and his ancestors, even though they had done so most successfully, have yet renounced that right you speak of time and again; nor however have we ever been so thoroughly conquered that we did not swear allegiance to them while they in turn swore allegiance to our laws. When Charles had notably violated these laws, after we had been first provoked by him himself – call him an ancient conqueror or a present-day lying king – we completely vanquished him in war: but in accordance with your own opinion, 'what is gained by war passes into the ownership of him who has acquired it'. And so hereafter be as wordy as you wish on this point, be what you have been not long ago about Solinus, a horse-trainer in the style of Pliny,[18] the most wordy of all babblers. But whatever prattle you speak next, whatever disturbance you make, whatever quotes you may take from the rabbis, whatever hoarse shout you may make right to the end of this chapter, know that you have sweated with all this labour no longer for the sake of the conquered king, but to help us against the king, who are by God's aid his conquerors.

[16] See p. 11 for the king as usufructuary. [17] A mark of slavery: see Exod. 21:6.

[18] The *Collectanea* (or *Polyhistor*, as revised in the sixth century) of Gaius Julius Solinus (*c.* 200), based largely on Pliny, was edited with an extensive commentary by S., *Plinianae exercitationes in Caii Julii Polyhistora* (Paris, 1629). See *DS*, IV, 569.

CHAPTER VII

On account of two inconveniences which are indeed very great, and in your consideration very heavy, you said in the previous chapter that the power of the people was not greater than that of the king: since, if you conceded that, another name would have to be found for a king, the term king having been transferred to the people. Also certain divisions of your political system would be disordered: one of these would be an expense for your dictionary; the other the Cross for your politics. I have answered these so that some account might be taken, first of our own safety and liberty, and then even of your system of naming and politics. Now you say 'it is to be fully proven by other considerations that a king cannot be judged by his own subjects, and of these reasons this will be the most powerful and convincing: that a king does not have an equal in his kingdom'. What are you saying? A king does not have an equal in his kingdom? Then what are those twelve most ancient peers [of the king][1] of France? Are they fables and trifles [of Turpin's]?[2] Are they so called in vain and as a mockery? Take care of speaking this insult to those leading men of France. [Or is it because they are equal to each other? As if indeed out of the whole French nobility only twelve were equal to each other; or that for this reason it should be judged fit to call them peers of France.][3] But if they are not in reality peers of the king [of France because, along with him, they manage the commonwealth with equal right and coun-

[1] 1651Q: omitted in 1651F, 1658.

[2] 1658. Turpin (eighth century) was the supposed chronicler of the deeds of Charlemagne and Roland.

[3] 1651F: further revised in 1658.

sel],[4] watch out in case your glossary, which is the only thing that interests you, is not more mocked in the kingdom of France than in our Commonwealth.

Come then, make it clear that there is no equal of a king in his own kingdom. 'Because', you say, 'the people of Rome, after the expulsion of the kings, set up two consuls not one; so that if one committed a fault, he could be controlled by his colleague.' Anything more silly could hardly be imagined. So why did one of the consuls keep the *fasces* with him, not both, if one had been appointed to control the other? What if both also had conspired against the republic? Would the situation have been better than if the Romans had given no colleague to a single consul? But it is agreed that both consuls and all magistrates ought always to have obeyed the senate, whenever the senators and people decided it was in the interests of the commonwealth. [For this point I have Marcus Tullius as a most credible witness in his speech *Pro Sestio*.[5] From him at the same time hear a very short description of the Roman state, which he used to say was 'very wisely set up' and that all good citizens ought to know it, which is what I say too. 'Our ancestors, since they had removed the power of the kings, created annual magistracies, so that they might set the council of the senate forever over the commonwealth: and elections were made to this council by the whole people; and entry into that supreme rank should be open to the hard work and virtue of all citizens. They placed the senate as guardian, protector and champion of the commonwealth: they decided that the magistrates would employ the authority of this rank and be, so to speak, ministers of this most weighty council.']⁶

The decemvirs[7] could serve as an illustrious example. They were endowed with the supreme power of the consuls, yet the authority of the senators reduced them all to order at the same time, even when they struggled against it. We read that even some consuls, before they had laid down their magistracy, were judged public enemies and arms were taken up against them: for no-one would count a man to be consul if he was making war. So war was waged against Antony the consul, by the authority of the senate. In this he was conquered and

[4] 1651F: further revised in 1658.

[5] Cicero, *Pro Sestio*, LXV, 137.

[6] 1651F: retained in 1658.

[7] *Decemviri*: the ten patricians to whom power was granted when the Roman constitution was suspended in 451 BC.

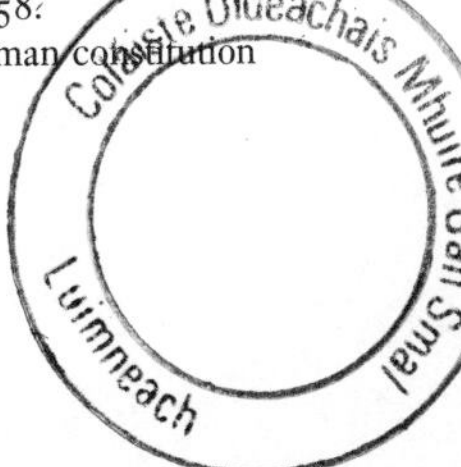
Coláiste Oideachais Mhuire Gan Smál
Luimneach

would have paid the penalty of death, except that Octavian Caesar,[8] who was striving after empire, entered into a plan with him to overthrow the republic.

Now your statement that 'it is appropriate to kingly majesty for command to lie in the hands of a single person' is no less slippery, and is immediately refuted by you yourself. For 'the judges of the Hebrews held power one at a time and for the whole length of their life. Scripture also calls them kings; and yet by the great sanhedrin' they were judged. So it is plain that in wishing to be thought to have said everything, you say almost nothing except contradictions. I ask then what form of government you call it when two or three emperors at once controlled the Roman empire – do you think they were emperors, that is, kings, or aristocrats, or a triumvirate? Or truly will you say that the Roman empire under Antoninus and Verus, Diocletian and Maximian, Constantine and Licinius was not one empire?[9] Now those 'three kinds of government' of yours are imperilled by your own arguments, if they were not kings: if they were, then it is not special to royal power that it should be in the hands of one person. 'If one of these', you say, 'should commit a wrong, the others can report on him to the people or the senate, so he may be accused and condemned.' Then do not they – the people, or the senate to whom that other one reports – judge? So if you allow yourself any belief, there was no need of one colleague to judge the other. Alas, what a defender you are, clearly to be pitied if you were not rather to be cursed! So open to blows from every direction than if anyone happened to want to aim at you as a game, to strike you pointedly in any place, I believe that he could hardly miss even at random.

You state that it is 'ridiculous for a king to wish to appoint judges over him, by whom he may be condemned to death'. But I set against you Trajan, who was not ridiculous but the best of emperors. When he gave the dagger to Saburanus, captain of the praetorian guard, as the emblem of his power (as the custom was), he repeatedly warned him in these words: 'Receive this sword on my behalf, if I act rightly;

[8] Octavian (63 BC–AD 14) established his claim to power by defeating Antony in 31 BC. He received the title Augustus (henceforth conferred on all emperors) in 27 BC.

[9] When Antoninus (i.e., Marcus Aurelius) succeeded in 161 he immediately petitioned the Senate to appoint Lucius Verus (130–69) as Augustus (the first time the principate was shared on a collegiate basis). Diocletian promoted Maximian to Augustus in 286; they both abdicated in 305. Constantine disputed Licinius' promotion to Augustus in 308 and eventually overthrew him in 323.

but if otherwise, rather use it against me because it is less lawful for the governor of all things to go astray.' So say Dion and Aurelius Victor.[10] You see how the excellent emperor set up a judge over him, even if he was not an equal. This same speech Tiberius might perhaps have made out of hypocrisy and empty talk; but he would be almost a criminal who thought that Trajan, an excellent and most holy man, did not say from the heart what he thought was true and right and lawful. How much more righteously then did he obey the senate clearly out of consideration for his duty, when he might not have obeyed them, being their superior in strength; and he confessed that they were superior in right. Pliny in his *Panegyric* says about him:[11] 'The senate both asked and ordered you to take up your fourth consulate. This is the word of command, not of flattery, believe your own obedience;' and shortly after, 'this indeed is your object: to recall and restore our liberty'. What Trajan thought of himself, the senate similarly thought of Trajan, and thought that their authority was in fact supreme; for they who could command an emperor could also judge him. So the emperor Marcus Aurelius, when Cassius, the prefect of Syria, tried to snatch the kingship from him,[12] offered himself to the judgement of either the senate or the people of Rome; ready to give up the kingdom if they thought it good. Now truly who can judge and set up the right of kings more rightly or well than from the very mouths of the best kings?

Indeed by the law of nature every good king always considers the senate or the people his equals and betters. But since a tyrant is by nature the lowest of all men there is no-one who cannot be judged his equal and superior if he has more strength. For just as men formerly reached under the leadership of nature from force to laws, so where laws are set at nothing, with the same leader too, there must necessarily be a return to force. 'To think this', says Cicero, *Pro Sestio*,[13] 'is part of good sense; to do it, part of courage; and both to think and do it is truly the perfect crowning glory of virtue.' Let this remain then in nature, to be shaken by no skills of parasites, that be a king good or bad, the senate and people are his superiors. This you also confess yourself, when you say that royal power passed from the people to the king. For the power that they have given to the king, by nature and by

[10] See p. 12.

[11] Pliny, *Panegyrics*, LXXVIII, 1 and 3.

[12] Avidius Cassius was assassinated three months after he proclaimed himself emperor in AD 175.

[13] Cicero, *Pro Sestio*, XL, 86.

a kind of virtue or, so to speak, virtually, even when they have given it to another, they still hold themselves. For natural causes which produce any effect in this way through some excellence, retain more of their virtue than they impart; nor do they drain themselves dry by imparting. You see, the closer we approach nature, the more evidently does the power of the people extend above that of the king.

It is also agreed that the people, if only free choice is left them, never grant their power to a king absolutely and as a possession, nor by nature can do so; but only do so for the sake of public safety and liberty. And when the king ceases to care for this, it is understood that the people have given nothing at all, because they only gave it for a certain end, on the advice of nature herself; and if neither nature nor the people can attain this end, what they granted will be no more valid than any void bargain or treaty. By these considerations it is more firmly proven that the people are superior to the king. Hence this argument of yours 'most powerful and strong, that a king cannot be judged because he does not have an equal in his kingdom, or a superior', dissolves away. For you assume what we by no means grant.

'In a popular state', you say, 'a magistrate appointed by the people can be punished by them for a crime; in an aristocracy, the nobles by their colleagues; but it is monstrous that a king in his own kingdom may be forced to be on trial for his life.' What else do you now conclude but that those who set up a king over them are the most wretched and stupid of all people? But why, I ask, can a people not punish a guilty king as well as a popular magistrate or the nobles? Or do you think that all peoples who live under kings have been so desperately in love with slavery that when they were free, they preferred to be slaves, and put themselves completely and wholly under the mastery of one man, who was often evil, and often foolish, so that they left themselves against a master, who might be most cruel if such fell to their lot, no protection for their safety or refuge in the laws or in nature itself? Why then do they lay down conditions when kings first enter their office, why even give them laws to rule by, or is it to allow themselves to be more despised and ridiculous? Would a whole people so degrade themselves, abandon themselves, fail themselves, as to place all their hope in one man, who was almost the most empty of them? Why likewise do kings swear to do nothing against the law? So wretched mortals, of course, may learn to their own very great ill that only kings may perjure themselves without punishment! This is what these unspeakable inferences of yours go to show:

> If a king who is elected has promised something even upon oath – when if he had not promised this, perhaps he would not have been taken on – and if he refuses to stand by the agreement, he cannot be judged by the people. Moreover, if he swore to his subjects at his election that he would administer justice according to the laws of the realm and if he does not do it, they will be freed from their oath of allegiance, and he will *ipso facto* leave off power, but the penalty must be exacted by God, not by men against the transgressor.

I have transcribed these words, not for their elegance, for they are most unpolished; nor because they need any further refutation, for they refute themselves, explode and condemn themselves by their most overt falsity and baseness; but I have done it so that I might recommend you to kings for your outstanding merits: so they, amongst all those duties at court, may mark some position of standing or office fit for you. For while some manage the accounts, some are bearers of the cup, [some of the dishes,][14] some masters of the revels, you will most conveniently indeed be their master of perjuries. You will not be the arbiter of royal elegance, [like the famous Petronius,][15] for you are too ignorant, but the supreme arbiter of treachery. But so that all may admit that the greatest stupidity is united in you with the greatest wickedness, let us weigh up a little more carefully those splendid assertions which you have just made: 'A king', you say, 'even if he swore to his subjects at his election that he will rule according to the laws', and if he does not do it, 'they will be freed from their oath of allegiance and he will *ipso facto* leave off power' yet cannot be deposed or punished by them. Why a king, I ask, less than a popular magistrate? Because under that kind of government the people do not transfer all their power to the magistrate. Then do they to a king, to whom they deliver rule over themselves for no longer than he wields it well? And so a king, who is sworn to observe the laws, can be deposed or punished as guilty just like a popular magistrate. For you cannot make further use of that all-powerful argument that all power has

[14] 1658.

[15] 1658. Petronius Arbiter, the *arbiter elegantiae* (arbiter of taste) at Nero's court, committed suicide in 66 AD. See Tacitus, *Annals*, XVI, 18, and cf. *AR*, II, 518.

been transferred to the king, because you yourself have stumbled unawares through your own devices.

Learn now 'another most powerful and invincible reason why subjects' cannot judge 'their king: because he is freed from the laws, because the king alone sustains all the laws'. Since I have so frequently proved this to be completely false, even this invincible reason of yours, along with the former one, falls to nothing. However if a king is sometimes not punished for some personal crimes such as rape, adultery and the like, it happens not so much because of the clemency as the long-suffering of the people lest more disorder comes upon the people from the death of the king and the alteration in affairs, than good from the revenge of one or two. When in truth he begins to be burdensome and insufferable to all, then indeed all nations have always believed it lawful to kill a tyrant, condemned or uncondemned, in any way they can. Hence Marcus Tullius in his second *Philippic* about the murderers of Caesar:[16] 'These men first attacked with their swords not a man striving for kingship but one who was already king: which deed in itself is splendid and godlike, and has been set before us for imitation.' How unlike him you are!

'Homicide, adultery, injury – these are not royal crimes, but those of private people.' Hurray, parasite! You have deserved well of all the pimps and villains of the court by this utterance. O how elegantly you at once play the parasite and by the same means the pimp! 'A king who is an adulterer can rule well, and the same with one who is a murderer, and for that reason he ought not to be deprived of life because with his life he is stripped also of his kingdom. But it was never approved by human and divine laws that a double punishment should be exacted for one crime.' Foul and disreputable speech! By this same reasoning, neither popular magistrates nor the nobles, in case they be afflicted with double punishment, nor even a profligate judge or senator, ought to pay any penalties of death. For with their lives they are also deprived of their magistracy.

As you strive to take from the people and confer upon the king power, so with majesty too; a delegated and transferred majesty if you like, but certainly you cannot take away their primary majesty, just as you cannot their primary power. You say 'a king cannot commit treason against his people; but a people can against their king'. And

[16] Cicero, *Philippics*, II, xliv, 114.

yet a king is a king simply on account of the people, not the people on account of the king. So the whole people or the majority[17] must always have more power than the king. You say no, and make calculations: 'he has more power than any single individual, any two, any three, any ten, any hundred, and thousand, and ten thousand'. So be it. 'Than more than half the people.' I do not contradict that. 'What if half of the other half is added, will he still not have more power?' By no means!

Go on; why do you take away the abacus, most skilful logician, or do you not understand arithmetical progression? He changes methods, and asks: 'whether the king along with the nobles has more power?' Again I say no, Vertumnus,[18] if by the nobles you mean lords; since it can happen that no-one amongst them is worthy of the name of noble. It quite often happens too that there are many more among the commoners who outdo lords in virtue and wisdom; and when to these is added the majority or better part of the people,[19] I should not be afraid to say that they represent the whole people. 'But if the king does not have more power than all the people, then he will be king only of single individuals, not of all taken together.' Correct, unless they have wished it. Now balance up your accounts; you will find that you have lost your principal by unskilful computation.

'The English say that the right of majesty by its origin and nature resides in the hands of the people; this in truth is to bring on the overthrow of all states.' Even of aristocracy and democracy? Indeed you speak believably: what about a gynocracy too, a state in which they say you are nearly beaten up at home, would not the English do you a kindness, O man of very little courage? But you have hoped for this in vain. For it is most justly ordered that you who desire to impose tyranny upon all men abroad, yourself at home serve out a most disgraceful and hardly masculine slavery.

'We must instruct you', you say, 'in what we wish to mean by the name of "people".' There are very many things in which you should be instructed further, for you seem to be profoundly ignorant of those matters which concern you more nearly, and never to have learned, nor even to have been able to understand anything except the

[17] *pars major.*

[18] *Vertumnus*: Etruscan god associated with the seasons and hence changeability. Cf. '*Vertumnian* distinctions and evasions', *T.* II, 675.

[19] *pars populi major vel potior.*

alphabet. But this you think you know, that we mean by the name of people only the common people because 'we have abolished the house of lords'. But that is the very thing which shows we include under the term people all citizens of any rank whatsoever, since we have established a single supreme house of commons only, in which the lords too, as part of the people, not for themselves alone as before but for those constituencies by which they have been elected, have the lawful right to vote.

You then inveigh against the common people, saying that 'being blind and dull, it does not have the skill of ruling; nothing is more puffed up, empty, changeable and inconstant'. All these things suit you very well; and of the lowest rabble indeed are even true, but not likewise of the middle sort. Of their number are the men who are almost the most sensible and skilful in affairs. As for the rest, luxury and opulence on the one hand, poverty and need on the other, generally divert them from virtue and the study of statesmanship.

You assert that there are now 'several ways of establishing kings who owe nothing to the people on this score', and firstly those 'who hold their kingdom by inheritance'. But truly those nations must be slaves and born to slavery who acknowledge such a master, to whom they believe they have fallen by inheritance without their own consent: certainly they cannot be considered as citizens or freeborn or free men; nor can be judged to have any commonwealth; but rather must be counted among the goods and possessions, so to speak, of their master and his son and heir. For as to right of ownership, I do not see how they differ from slaves and cattle. Secondly you say, 'a man who made a kingdom for himself by warfare cannot acknowledge the people as the source of the power he has extended or usurped'. But we are not talking now about a conquering, but a conquered king; what a conqueror can do, we will discuss elsewhere, you must stick to this.

But whereas you so often attribute to a king the ancient right of the head of the household, so that you may seek from there 'an example of the absolute power in kings', I have now frequently shown that it is totally different. That Aristotle too, whom you make much ado about, would have taught you the same thing even at the beginning of his *Politics*, if you had read it. There he says that they judge badly who think there is very little difference between a head of household and a king. 'For a kingdom is different from a household not only in number but in kind.'[20] For after villages grew into town and cities, that royal right of the household gradually vanished and ceased to be recognized. Hence Diodorus writes, Bk. 1, that kingdoms in ancient times were not given to the king's sons, but to those who had done the greatest services to the people.[21] And Justin says:[22] 'In the beginning, the government of affairs, races and nations was in the hands of kings. They were exalted to the pinnacle of this majesty, not by gaining popular support, but for a moderation approved among good men.'

Whence it is quite clear that in the very beginning of nations, paternal and hereditary government very soon gave way to virtue and the people's right. This is the origin of royal power, and the most natural reason and cause. For it was for that very reason that men first came together, not so that one might abuse them all, but so that when one injured another, there should be law and a judge between men, whereby the injured might be protected or at least avenged. When formerly men were scattered and dispersed, some eloquent and wise man led them into civil life;[23] you say 'chiefly with the following plan: that he might have power over them when he had gathered them together'. Perhaps you mean Nimrod, who is said to have been the first tyrant:[24] or this is your wickedness alone, which could not fall to those great men of old of lofty souls, a fiction of yours alone, related by no-one, as far as I know, before you; since it is revealed by the memorials of all the ancients that those first founders of cities had in view the advantage and safety of human kind, not their own benefit and mastery.

One thing I cannot pass by, with which I believe you wished to adorn the rest of this chapter like some mosaic inlay: you say 'if a consul had had to come to court before he had left office, a dictator must have been created for this', though you said at the beginning 'for that reason a colleague was given to him'. So your statements always match each other, and declare on almost every page how whatever you say or write is of no importance. 'Under the ancient Anglo-Saxon kings', you say, 'the common people never used to be summoned to the councils of the realm'. If any of our people had asserted this, I could have convinced him of his error without much trouble; I am less concerned at this foreign assertion of yours, wandering in mind about

[20] Aristotle, *Politics*, I, 1 (1252a).
[21] Diodorus Siculus, I, 43, 6.
[22] M. Junianus Justinus (Justin), *Epitoma historiarum philippicarum Pompei Trogi*, I, 1, 1.
[23] Cf. Cicero, *De inventione*, I, 2.
[24] See Gen. 8:8–10.

our affairs. And this is approximately what you have held about the common right of kings. I omit the many things remaining, for you are accustomed to most frequent digressions, as they are either supported on no foundation or are beside the point: for I do not take pains to seem your equal in loquacity.

CHAPTER VIII

If you had published your opinion about the the general right of kings without abuse of anyone, Salmasius, even though you did it during this revolution[1] among the English, but while you were employing your freedom of writing, there was no reason why any Englishman should be enraged by you, nor would you have gained any less in asserting the opinion which you support. For if this is a command both of Moses and of Christ, 'that all men should be subject to their kings whether good or bad, be they Spanish, French, Italian, German, English, Scots', which you asserted above (p. 127), yet what concern was it of yours, an unknown foreigner, to stammer out our laws, and to wish to lecture upon them to us from the professional chair, as if they were your own papers and miscellanies, when you had previously (and verbosely) instructed us that our laws ought to give way, whatever they were, to the laws of God.

Now it is generally enough agreed that it is not so much by your own wish that you have applied your mind to the royal cause, as because you have been hired, partly for payment (a very large one too, considering the resources of the man who hired you) and partly by hope of some greater reward, to mangle with your notorious pamphlet the English, who trouble none of their neighbours and manage their own affairs by themselves. Were this not so, is it credible that anyone would be so shameless or insane as not to hesitate, though he was a distant stranger, to plunge himself gratuitously into our affairs and even attach himself to a party? For what harm does it do you how the

[1] *mutatione*: like *conversio*, *mutatio* ('a changing, altering') could be used of any cyclical event.

English control their own affairs? What do you want for yourself, Olus, what are you looking for? Do you have nothing at home to concern you? Would that you had the same cares as that most famous Olus in the epigram, and perhaps you have; certainly you deserve them. Or did that wife who spurs you on, who is said to have urged you on when you yourself were already running to write this to please the exiled Charles, did she predict for you perhaps greater commissions in England and I don't know what fees on Charles's return? But know this, wife–husband, that there is no room in England for a wolf or for the master of a wolf. Hence it is no wonder that you have so often poured out such great rage upon our hounds. Why not return to those illustrious titles of yours in France, and first to that starved dominion of St Loup, then to that sacred council of the Most Christian King.[2] You are too far distant abroad from your native country for a councillor. But she, as I see clearly, misses neither you nor your counsels, not even when you went back a few years ago and began to smell out and pursue a cardinal's kitchen:[3] she is right, by God, she is right and can easily allow you, you effeminate Frenchman,[4] with your male wife and desks stuffed full of emptiness, to roam about until you find, somewhere in the world, a grant lavish enough for a horse-riding grammarian or illustrious Hippo-critic, if any king or state has a mind to bid a very high price for a wandering teacher on sale. But here am I to bid for you, and we shall now see at once whether you are saleable or not, and for what price.

You say 'the parricides persist in saying that the constitution of the realm of England is a mixed one, not purely royal.' Under Edward VI, our countryman Thomas Smith, a good lawyer and a statesman, whom you do not say was a parricide, persists in saying the same thing, practically at the beginning of the book which he wrote about the commonwealth of England.[5] And he asserts that it is not only true of our commonwealth, but of almost all such – and this on the basis of Aristotle's opinion; otherwise no government can stand. But since you would believe it to be a sin, so to speak, to say anything without contradictions, you shamefully repeat those former arguments of

[2] I.e., of France.
[3] Cardinal Richelieu, chief minister of Louis XIII, had offered a post to Salmasius in 1640.
[4] *semivirum Gallum*: M. plays on *gallus* as a Frenchman, a cock, and a priest of Cybele (whose rites involved castration). Cf. *PSD*, IV, ii, 821.
[5] See p. 22.

yours that are now quite forlorn. You say that 'there neither is nor ever was any nation which did not mean by the name of king that power which is less than God alone, and which had God alone as its judge'; and yet a little later you admit 'the name of king was once given to powers and magistrates of the kind who did not have full and free right, but one depending upon the will of the people', like 'the chief magistrates of the Carthaginians, the judges of the Hebrews, the kings of the Spartans' and, finally, 'Aragon'. You agree with yourself prettily enough, don't you?

Then you survey five sorts of monarchy out of Aristotle, of which only one possessed the right which you say is common to all kings. About this more than once now it has been said that no example of it has existed, either as quoted from Aristotle or anywhere else. The other four he clearly shows were both fixed by laws and subject to them. The first of these was the kingdom of the Spartans, and it was most greatly deserving of the name kingdom in his opinion, out of the four which were fixed by law. The second was foreign to the Greeks, lasting only because it was fixed by law and had the consent of the people. But without their consent, every king at once will not be a king but a tyrant, if he retains the kingdom against the will of the people – on the testimony of the same Aristotle, Bk. 5.[6] The same must be said about the third type of king, which he calls Aesymnetes, elected by the people, and generally for a specific time and specific purposes, such as were the dictators virtually among the Romans. The fourth kind is those who ruled in heroic times, upon whom for their outstanding merits the kingship was conferred by the people of their own accord, but still fixed by the laws; nor indeed did these men retain the kingdom except by the consent of the people. He says that these four kinds of kingship differ from tyranny in nothing more than that the rule is in the one case at the consent of, and in the other against, the will of the people. The fifth kind of kingship finally, which is called παμβασιλεία and entails supreme power, such as you wish to be the right of all kings, is clearly condemned by the philosopher as neither advantageous, nor just, nor natural, unless it be that a people could endure a kingship of this kind, and bestow it upon those who far outshine all others in virtue. These things are accessible to everyone in the third book of the *Politics*.[7]

[6] Aristotle, *Politics*, V, 10 (1313a).

[7] Aristotle, *Politics*, III, 14 (1285a).

But you, I believe, so you might seem for once clever and flowery, were passionately eager to compare 'these five kinds of monarchy to the five zones' of the world; 'between the two extremes of royal power, three other more temperate kinds seem to be interposed, like those which lie between the torrid and frigid zones'. Dear life! What beautiful comparisons you always produce for us! So you soar speedily off from here to the frigid zone, to which you yourself condemn the kingdom of 'absolute power'. After your arrival there it will be twice as frigid. We meanwhile await from you, our new Archimedes,[8] that marvellous globe which you describe in which there are two extreme zones, one torrid, the other frigid, and three temperate zones in the middle!

'The kings of the Spartans', you say, 'could lawfully be hurled into chains, but it was not lawful to put them to death.' Why not? Is it because when Agis was condemned to death, the officers of the law and foreign soldiers, shocked by the novelty of the case, judged it unlawful to put the king to death? And the Spartan people took his death badly indeed, not because it was a king who had been put to death but because he was a good man and popular with them, and had been hemmed round with judgement by a faction of wealthy men. So too Plutarch: 'Agis was the first king who was put to death by the ephors.'[9] In these words he only relates, not what it was lawful to do, but what was actually done. For it is childish to believe that those who can bring a king to trial or even to imprisonment cannot put him likewise to death.

Now at last you gird yourself up to face the right of English kings. You say 'there was always one king of England'. You say this because you had just said 'a king is not a king unless he is the one and only ruler'. But if this is so, some indeed who I used to believe were kings of England, were really not so. For to leave out many of the Saxon kings who had either sons or brothers as partners in government, it is known that Henry II, of Norman descent, ruled along with his son.[10]

You say, 'Let them show any kingdom under the control of a single person who has not been given absolute power, though the power is in some kingdoms more relaxed, in others tighter.' You show an

[8] Archimedes (*c.* 287–212 BC), greatest of the ancient mathematicians and geometers.
[9] Plutarch, *Agis and Cleomenes*, XIX, 6; XXI, 3.
[10] The son (d. 1183) of Henry II (1154–89) was crowned in June 1170 and used the style *rex Anglorum*.

absolute power that is relaxed, ass; is not absolute power supreme power? How then can it be both supreme and relaxed? Whatever kings you admit have a relaxed power, I will easily prove not to have absolute power, and therefore to be inferior to a people free by nature, which is both itself its own lawmaker and able either to tighten or relax the power of the king.

Whether the whole of Britain once owed obedience to kings is uncertain. It is more likely that, according to the demands of circumstances, they used now this, now that form of government. Hence says Tacitus: 'The Britons once owed obedience to kings, now they are drawn by their chieftains into factions and parties.'[11] Abandoned by the Romans, they were for about forty years without kings:[12] and so the 'perpetual kingship', which you uphold, did not exist in antiquity; and I positively deny that it was hereditary. Both the succession of kings and the way of making them proves this. For the people's approval is sought in clear words: 'Do you wish to consent to having him as king?'[13] Just as if, in the Roman way, he had said: 'Do you wish and order this man to rule?'[14] This would be unnecessary if the kingdom were hereditary by right.

But among kings usurpation very often counts for right. You strive to base upon the right of war the royal right of Charles who was so often conquered in war. William, surnamed 'the Conqueror', indeed subjugated us. But those who are not strangers to our history know that the resources of the English were not so weakened in that one battle of Hastings that they might not have easily renewed the war. But they preferred to accept a king than to endure a victor and a tyrant. And so they gave their sworn oath to William, to keep faith with him. William likewise gives his oath to them at the altar to behave in turn towards them in all respects like a good king. When he broke his word, and the English again took up arms, he himself, mistrusting his own strength, swore again on the gospels to observe the ancient laws of England.[15] So if afterwards he wretchedly oppressed the English, he did it not by right of war but by right of perjury. It is certain moreover that many ages ago now the conquered and the

[11] Tacitus, *Agricola*, XII.

[12] See p. 22.

[13] *consentire vultis de habendo ipsum regum?*: the coronation oaths of Edward II (French), Richard II (English) and Henry IV (Latin) were frequently cited in pamphlets.

[14] *vultis, jubetis hunc regnare?*: M. refers to the *petitio consulatus* or candidature for consulship. Cf. *E*, III, 461.

[15] See p. 10.

conquerors united to become one race; so that that right of war, if any ever existed, must have long now become obsolete. His own dying words, which I report copied from the Caen book, a most trustworthy source, remove all doubt. 'I appoint no-one', he says, 'as the heir of the kingdom of England.'[16] By this speech that right of war and at the same time that of heredity were bewailed and buried along with the dead William himself.

I see now that you have acquired an office at court, which I foretold would happen; you have surely become supreme royal treasurer and superintendent of court cunning. Hence you seem to write what follows by virtue of your office, magnificent sir. 'If any of the previous kings have been forced to abate any of their right, that cannot hinder a successor from claiming it again for himself.' You give a timely warning; and so if at any time our ancestors have lost any of their right through idleness, will that hinder us, their posterity? If they were indeed willing to pledge themselves to slavery, they certainly were not able to pledge us, who will always have the same right of freeing ourselves as they had of handing themselves over to slavery to anyone whatsoever.

You wonder 'how it happens' that 'a king of Britain today must be considered only as a magistrate of the kingdom, while those who control other kingdoms in Christendom have full and free power'. I refer you for Scotland to Buchanan, for your own country France, where you seem to be a stranger, to Hotman's *Francogallia* and to Girard, the historian of France; concerning the rest, to others, of whom none as far as I know were Independents. From them you could have learned about royal right far different things from those you teach.

Since you cannot assert a tyranny for the kings of England by the rights of war, you now make trial of the right of parasites. Kings openly announce that they rule 'by the grace of God': what if they had announced they were gods? I believe they would easily have you as a priest; so the pontiff of Canterbury[17] publicly proclaimed that he was archbishop 'by the providence of God'. Do you because of your foolishness refuse the pope the right to be king in the church, so that you can set up a king who is more than a pope in the commonwealth?

[16] M quotes either from the transcription in William Camden, *Britannia* (London, 1607), p. 107, or John Sadler, *Rights of the Kingdom* (London, 1649), p. 69/sig. Ii3.

[17] I.e., William Laud (1573–1645) who became Archbishop of Canterbury in 1633.

But in the statutes of the kingdom he is called 'our lord the king'. You indeed have suddenly turned out wonderfully skilled in calling out the names[18] of our statutes, but you don't know that many are called lords who are not really so. You don't know how unfair it is to decide the right and truth of things from titles of honour, not to say of flattery. Make the same inference from the fact that it is called 'the king's parliament'; for it is also called the king's bridle,[19] and the king is not for that reason any more master of parliament than a horse is master of his own bridle. But 'why isn't it the king's parliament, since it is summoned by him?' I will tell you; because the senate also was summoned by a consul, but he was not for that reason master of that assembly either. And so a king summons parliament by virtue of his office and the duty which he has received from the people, so that he may consult those whom he summons about the difficult business of the realm,[20] not about his own. Or if any can be called his own, these were customarily always dealt with at the end; at the will of parliament too, not of himself. And the people whom it concerns to know this are in truth not ignorant that parliament, whether summoned or not, could have met by law twice in the course of a year in ancient times.[21] But 'the laws too are called the king's'. These are indeed the adornments pertaining to a king. But a king of England cannot make any law of himself; for he was not appointed to make laws but to guard those made by the people.

And you here admit that 'parliament meets to make laws'. Therefore it is called the law of the land and the law of the people. Hence King Athelstan in the preface of his laws, when he addresses all people, says: I have bestowed all things 'upon you in accordance with your own law';[22] and in the form of the oath by which the kings of England used to bind themselves before they were made kings, the people demand this formal promise from the king: 'Do you grant the just laws, which the people shall choose?'[23] The king replies, 'I do.'

[18] *nomenculator*: a name-caller, especially a slave who told his master the names of those met while canvassing.

[19] See p. 10.

[20] *de arduis regni negotiis consuleret*: a phrase from the parliamentary writ of summons.

[21] Cf. *E*, III, 399, where M. cites Sadler, *Rights*, p. 86/sig. M3v.

[22] For this phrase from the laws of King Athelstan (927–44), see William Lambarde's *Archaionomia*, appended to Abraham Wheloc's edition of Bede and the *Anglo-Saxon Chronicle* (Cambridge, 1644), p. 45.

[23] *Concedis justas leges quas vulgus elegerit?*: the tense of *elegerit* was hotly disputed in the pamphlet exchanges of 1642. The parliamentarians contended that it was future ('shall choose'), so binding the king to accept new statutes that might be chosen, the royalists

You also wander as far as the size of all England from the truth, when you say that 'the king, in the time when parliament is not in session, governs the whole state of the realm fully and clearly by royal right'. For he can decide nothing of great importance about war or peace, and not even in the administration of justice can he interfere with the decisions of the courts. And so judges swear that they will do nothing in giving judgements except according to law, even if the king himself by word or order or even by a letter sealed under his own ring, should command otherwise. Hence quite often under our law the king is called an 'infant' and said not to possess his rights and dignities except in the manner of a child or ward, *Spec. Just.* ch. 4, sect. 22.[24] Hence also that common saying amongst us: 'The king can do no wrong.'[25] This you interpret in this wicked fashion: 'It is not a wrong which a king does, because he is not punished for it.' Who would not see through the amazing impudence and dishonesty of the man, even by this single interpretation?

'It is', you say, 'the job of the head to command, not of the limbs; the king is the head of parliament.' Would you talk such nonsense, if your heart was wise? You are mistaken again (but is there any end to your mistakes?) in that you do not draw a distinction between the king's councillors and the houses of parliament; for a king must not even choose all his councillors, and none of the house of lords at all that were not approved by the rest; but as for choosing anyone for the house of commons, he never even took it upon himself to do so. Those to whom the people delegated this duty were chosen individually by their constituencies, by the votes of all. I speak of very well known things, and so I am briefer. But 'it is false', you say, 'that parliament was instituted by the people, as the worshippers of Saint Independence assert'. I see now why it is that you strive to overturn the papacy with so much violence: you carry another papacy in your belly, as they say: for what else ought you to be giving birth to, wife of your wife, he-wolf made pregnant by a she-wolf, but either a monster or some new papacy? Certainly as if you now were a genuine pope, you make male and female saints at your will. Kings too you absolve

that it was future perfect ('shall have chosen'), so merely committing him to abide by established laws. In *E*, M. says it 'requir'd him to give us such Laws as our selves shall choose', III, 519 (see also p. 414, and *Brief Notes*, VII, 484).

24 Horne, *Mirroir*, p. 271.

25 *rex non potest facere injuriam*: for this 'Law-Maxim' see *HB*, V, 391.

from all sin, and as if the pope, now your enemy, was laid low, you adorn yourself richly with the spoils. But the pope has not yet clearly fallen through your efforts, until the second and third, and perhaps fourth and fifth parts of that book of yours, *De primatu*, has appeared – that book which will kill many mortals from boredom before you have subdued the pope with it. Let it be enough meanwhile, I beg, for you to be able, at all events, to ascend to the anti-papacy; there is another female saint whom you have earnestly canonized among the rest, apart from that Independence who is jeered at by you, royal tyranny. So you will be chief priest of Saint Royal Tyranny; and so that you may be without none of the papal titles, you will be 'a slave also of slaves' – not of God, but of the court, since that curse upon Canaan[26] seems to have clung closely to your body.

'The people' you call 'a beast.' What meanwhile are you? For not that sacred council, nor that Saint Wolf can remove you, its master, from being one of the people or the mob; nor can it stop you from being that most loathsome beast which you are. Certainly the sacred books of the prophets customarily shadow forth the monarchy and domination of great kings under the name and guise of a huge beast.

'There is no mention', you say, 'of a parliament under kings before William.' I am not disposed to quarrel about a French word: the thing always existed:[27] and in Saxon times you grant that it used to be called 'a council of wise men'. And there are wise men among the common people just as in the ranks of the nobles. But 'in the Statute of Merton, in the twentieth year of Henry III,[28] mention is made of earls and barons only'. So names always deceive you, who have wasted your whole life on names. For we know well enough that Wardens of the Cinque Ports and city members of parliament, and sometimes merchants too in that age, were called by the name of barons; and there is absolutely no doubt that all members of parliament, however much commoners, were by that age, with much greater right, termed barons:[29] for the Statute of Marlbridge,[30] just like almost all the rest of the statutes, bears witness in plain words that also in the fifty-second year of the same king both the lords and commons were summoned. These commoners also, Edward III, in the preamble to the Statute of Staples,[31] which you very learnedly quote for me, called 'the great

[26] Gen. 9:25.
[27] Cf. *O*, III, 314–15.
[28] 1236.
[29] See p. 21.
[30] 1267.
[31] 1353.

men of the counties' – those indeed 'who had come from the separate cities to serve the whole county', who indeed made up the house of commons, and neither were nobles, nor could be. A book which is older than those statutes, called *Modus habendi Parlamenta*,[32] also records that a king may together with the commons alone hold a parliament and make laws, although the earls and bishops are not present; but the same is not possible for a king with earls and bishops, if the commons are not present. A reason is also added for this matter; because when the earls or bishops had not yet been established, kings together with the people still held parliaments and councils. Then earls came only on their own behalf, the commons each for their own constituency. Therefore the commons are understood to be present in the name of all the people; and in that name to be more powerful and more noble than the lords and in every way preferable.

But 'the power of judging' you say 'was never in the hands of the house of commons'. Nor was it ever in the hands of the king of England: remember however that in the beginning all power flowed from the people and still stems from them. As Marcus Tullius also shows most neatly in his speech *De lege Agraria*: 'As it is fitting that all powers, authorities and charges stem from the whole people, so most especially those which are set up for some profit and benefit to the people. In this case all the people choose one whom they think will most consult the interests of the people, and each individual by zeal and his own vote can pave a road for himself to obtain the post.'[33] You see the true origin of parliaments – one much older than those Saxon chronicles. While we may live in this light of truth and wisdom, you try in vain to spread around us the gloom of the dark ages. Let no-one think that this is said by me, as if I would wish to detract in any respect from the authority and sense of our ancestors. They certainly stood out more in the passing of good laws than either those ages, or their talent and learning seem to have promised. And although they rarely

[32] The *Modus Tenendi Parliamentum* was composed *c.* 1320 though it purported to describe procedures which predated the Norman Conquest: the authenticity of this claim about the antiquity of parliament was widely accepted in the seventeenth century. M. goes on to paraphrase part of clause XXIII, 'De Auxiliis Regis'/'Concerning Aids to the King' (*Parliamentary Texts of the Later Middle Ages*, ed. N. Pronay and J. Taylor (Oxford, 1980), pp. 77, 89–90), probably working from an intermediate source; e.g., William Hakewill's translation in *The Manner of Holding Parliaments in England* (1641), sig. D2v, or Sadler, *Rights*, p. 88/sig. L14v. But see p. 211.

[33] Cicero, *De lege Agraria*, II, 7, 17.

imposed laws that were not good, yet, being conscious of human ignorance and weakness, they decided that this should be handed down to posterity as the foundation of all laws, which our learned lawyers recognize too; that if any law or custom should conflict with the law of God or nature or, in short, reason, it should not be considered a valid law. Hence, even if you may find perhaps some edict or statute in our law by which tyrannical power is attributed to the king, since it is contrary to the will of God and nature and reason, understand that from the general and primary law of ours which I have advanced, it is rescinded amongst us and is invalid. But you will find no such royal right amongst us. For since it is agreed that the power of judgement was originally in the people themselves, and that the English never transferred it from themselves to a king by any *lex regia* (for a king of England is neither accustomed nor able to judge any man, except by laws already provided and established, *Fleta*, Bk 1, Ch. 17)[34] it follows that the same power is still situated whole and entire in the people. For you will not deny either that it was never handed over to the house of lords or (if it was) that it can be recovered from them by law.

But you say 'it is in the king's power to make a borough from a village and a city from that, so the king creates those who make up the lower house'. But, I say, towns and boroughs are more ancient than kings: even in the fields, the people are still the people.

Now we are greatly delighted by your Anglicisms; *County*[35] *Court*, *The Turn*, *Hundreda*: you have learned with amazing ease of learning to count your hundred Jacobuses in English!

> *Who procured* for Salmasius his 'Hundreda',
> and *taught* the magpie *to try out our words*?
> *His belly was his Master of Arts*, and one hundred
> Jacobuses the entrails of the exiled king's purse.
> *But if the hope of treacherous coin shall gleam*,
> the very one who recently threatened to scatter
> with one breath the primacy of the pope as antichrist
> will of his own accord *sing strains* to praise a cardinal.[36]

[34] *Fleta*, ed. John Selden (London, 1647), p. 16 (I, 17, 4).

[35] 1658: 1651Q and 1651F have 'Countie'. A 'Turn' (or 'Tourn') was the county sheriff's progress through the hundred-courts. M. mocks S. for giving the plural of 'Hundred' (a sub-division of a county) as 'Hundreda' rather than 'Hundreds'.

[36] The italicized phrases were taken from the model for M.'s epigram, the Prologue to Persius, *Satires*, 8–14.

Then you append a long dissertation about the earls and barons; so as to show that the king was the creator of all of them, which we readily concede, and for that reason they would generally serve kings; and for that reason we have rightly made provision that they should not be judges of a free people hereafter. 'The power of summoning parliament as often as he pleases and of dissolving it when he wishes', you assert, 'has been in the hands of the king time out of mind.' So whether we should trust in you, a mercenary, foreign jester who writes out the dictates of fugitives, or in the plain words of our laws, we will see below. 'But', you say, 'it is proven by another argument – and that an invincible one – that the kings of England have held power superior to that of parliament; the king's power is continuous and ordinary, and by itself administers the realm without parliament. The authority of parliament is extraordinary and only applies to certain matters and is not capable of deciding anything valid without the king.' Where should we say the great force of this argument lies hidden? In the words 'ordinary and continuous'? Yet many lesser magistrates have ordinary and continuous power, whom we call justices of the peace; do they therefore have supreme power? I have also said above that power has been handed over to the king by the people so that he might see, by the authority entrusted to him, that nothing was done contrary to the law, and to guard our laws, not to impose his own upon us. Consequently the power of the king is nothing except in the courts of the realm and through them; no, rather all the ordinary power is the people's who make judgements about all matters in juries of twelve men. And hence it is that when a defendant is asked in court, 'By whom will you be tried?', he always (by custom and law) replies, 'By God and the people' – not by God and the king, or the king's deputy. But the authority of parliament, which in deed and in truth is the supreme power of the people committed to that senate, if it must be called extraordinary, is called this only because of its eminence. Otherwise, as is well known, the actual estates of parliament are called orders, so are not extra-ordinary: and if not actually, as the saying is, yet virtually they hold continuous control and authority over all courts and ordinary powers; and this without the king.

Now I believe our barbarous utterances shock your refined ears; if I had the time, or it was worth the effort, I could set down so many barbarisms in this one book, that if you were punished with your deserts, certainly all schoolboys' rulers must be broken upon you, nor would so many gold pieces be given to you as once to that worst of poets, but far more blows over the ear. You say that 'it is an omen, more unnatural than the most monstrous of all opinions, that the fanatics should separate the person of the king from his power'. For my part I will not present the words of individuals. But, if by *person* you mean to say *the man*, Chrysostom, who was no fanatic, could have taught you that the man could, without absurdity, be separated from his power; he explains the apostle's command about higher powers by saying that by the power there the thing is meant, not the man. Why may not I say that a king who does anything contrary to the laws acts as a private citizen or tyrant, not as a king endowed with legal power? If you do not understand that in one man there can be several persons and that those are, in thought and meaning, separable from the man himself, you are clearly lacking in common sense and Latinity. But you say this so as to absolve kings from all sin, and so we may believe that you are clad in that primacy which you have snatched from the pope.

'The king', you say, 'is understood as being unable to sin, because no punishment follows upon his sin.' So whoever is not punished does not sin; it is not the theft but the punishment that makes the thief. Salmasius the grammarian does not commit solecisms, because he has withdrawn his hand from under the ruler. After the pope has been overthrown by you, let these indeed be the rules of your pontificate, or at least the indulgences, whether you prefer to be called the high priest of Saint Tyranny or Saint Slavery.

I pass over your abuse, heaped up at the end of your chapter, on 'the form of the English commonwealth and church'. For people like you, you most despicable man, usually curse most maliciously whatever is worthy of the most praise.

But so that I may not seem to have asserted anything rashly concerning the right of the king amongst us, or rather concerning the right of the people over the king, I will not regard it as a burden to bring forward from our records examples which, although they are few from many indeed, yet, they are such as will establish it clearly enough that the English recently judged their king according to the laws and institutes and also the custom of their ancestors. After the Romans departed from the island, the Britons for about forty years were *sui juris*, without kings; some of those whom they first created they put to death. Gildas criticizes the Britons for that on a very different charge from the one you make; certainly not because they had killed their kings, but because they had done so 'without judgement' or, to use his words, 'not in accordance with an examination into the truth'. Vortigern was because of his incestuous marriage with his daughter (on the testimony of Nennius,[37] the most ancient of our historians after Gildas) condemned 'by Saint Germain and all the council of the Britons', and the kingdom was handed over to his son Vortimer. These things happened not long after the death of Augustine. Hence your empty statement is easily disproved, when you asserted above that first of all a Pope, namely Zachary, taught that kings could be tried. About the year of our Lord 600, Morcantius, who then ruled in Cumbria, was for the murder of his uncle condemned to exile by Oudoceus, bishop of Llandaff, although he redeemed the sentence of exile by bestowing certain landed estates upon the church.[38]

Now let us come to the Saxons. Since their laws are extant, I shall omit their deeds. Remember that the Saxons were sprung from Germans, who gave their kings neither infinite nor free power and all used to take council together about more important issues. From them we may realize that parliament, if you except only the name, flourished even amongst the ancestors of the Saxons in supreme authority. And by them indeed it is everywhere named the council of wise men, from those very times down to those of Ethelbert, who, as Bede mentions, 'set up decrees of judgement according to the examples of the Romans with the council of wise men'.[39] So Edwin, king of the Northumbrians, and Ina, king of the West Saxons, published new laws 'after holding a council with their wise men and elders'.[40] Other laws Alfred promulgated likewise 'from a council of the most experienced; and they all decided', he said, 'that the observation of these be published'.[41] From these and many other passages of this kind, it is clearer than daylight that men chosen even from amongst

[37] Nennius was an eighth-century scholar and supposed author of the *Historia Britonum*, first published in 1691. M could have seen the two Nennius MSS at Cambridge or used an intermediate source like James Ussher, *De primordiis* (Dublin, 1639), p. 385. See *HB*, V, 7–8, 155, 166 (and, for an account of Vortigern's deposition not involving Germain, 150); *E*, III, 587–8. See Sadler, *Rights*, p. 56/sig. Gg4v.

[38] Cf. *E*, III, 588.

[39] Bede, *Historiae*, p. 120 (II, 5). For King Ethelbert (560–616), see *HB*, V, 196.

[40] For King Edwin of Northumbria (616–632) see Bede (1644), p. 141 (II, 13); for Ina (or Ine), West-Saxon king, 688–726, see Lambarde (1644), p. 1.

[41] For King Alfred (871–99) see Lambarde (1644), p. 22.

the people took part in the supreme councils; unless anyone judges that the nobles alone are wise.

There is also extant amongst us a very ancient book of laws, the title of which is *Speculum Justiciariorum*, in which it is related that the early Saxons, after the subjugation of Britain, when they were appointing kings, used to demand an oath from them that they would be subject to the laws and judgements like anyone else of the people, Ch. 1, sect. 2.[42] In the same place it says that it is right and fair that a king should have his peers in parliament to find out about the wrongs which a king or queen has done. During Alfred's reign it was ordained by the laws that every year parliament should be held twice in London or oftener if need be. When this law has fallen into disuse by the worst neglect of right, it was restored by two decrees under Edward III.[43] In another ancient manuscript also, which is titled *Modus Parlamenti*,[44] we read this: if the king dismisses parliament before all the matters are completed for which the council was summoned, he will be guilty of perjury, and he will be deemed to have broken that oath which he had given when about to become king. For how does he grant what he is sworn to – the just laws which the people shall choose – if he does not grant at the people's request their ability to choose them, either by summoning parliament less frequently, or by dismissing it more quickly than the people's business demands? And our lawyers have always regarded that oath by which the king of England binds himself as a most sacred law. And what remedy can be found for the greatest dangers to the commonwealth (which was the only end for summoning parliament), if that great and most august gathering may be dissolved at the pleasure of a king who is often quite stupid and wilful?

To be able to be absent from parliament is undoubtedly less than to dissolve parliament: but the king by our laws, as related in that book of the Manners, could not, nor ought not, be absent from parliament unless he is obviously ill; and not even then, unless his person has

[42] Horne, *Mirroir*, pp. 7–9.

[43] I.e., 4 Ed. III, c. 14 and 36 Ed. III, c. 10. Cf. *E*, III, 398 and Sadler, *Rights*, p. 183/sig. C4.

[44] *In alio etiam antiquo manuscripto, qui Modus Parlamenti inscribitur*: the reference to a MS and the changed title (the *Modus* was variously known) may be significant. For M.'s (later?) acquaintance with MSS of the *Modus* in the Cotton Library and belonging to his friend John Bradshaw, see M. to Emeric Bigot, 24 Mar. 1657, VII, 497–8. However, the material here from clause XXIV, 'De Departitione Parliamenti'/'Concerning the Departure of Parliament' (*Parliamentary Texts*, pp. 78, 90), was taken from Sadler, *Rights*, p. 31/sig. Dd4. Cf. *E*, III, 403.

been inspected by twelve peers of the realm, who could produce evidence for the king's ill health in parliament. Do slaves usually behave this way with a master? But on the other hand, the house of commons, without which parliament cannot be held, even when summoned by the king can be absent and, by withdrawing itself, can dispute with the king about the maladministration of the commonwealth: which the aforementioned book also testifies.[45]

But, and this is the chief point, among the laws of King Edward commonly called the Confessor, there is one excellent law which deals with the office of the king. If the king should fail in this office, 'the title of king shall not remain settled upon him'. In case this should not be sufficiently understood, it adds the case of Chilperic, king of the Franks, whose rule for that reason was abrogated by the people.[46] And that a bad king should be punished by the sentence of this law was indicated by that famous sword of St Edward, called Curtana, which the Earl Palatine used to carry in the procession at a king's coronation, 'in token' says our countryman Matthew Paris 'that he has the power by law to check even the king if he goes astray'.[47] And no-one virtually is punished by a sword except by losing his head. This law, along with the others of that good King Edward, William the Conqueror himself ratified in the fourth year of his reign: and in a very crowded council of the English near St Albans he confirmed it with a most solemn oath.[48] By doing so, he himself not only extinguished all right of conquest, if he held any over us, but also subjected himself to the judgement and sentence of this law. His son Henry also swore both to uphold all Edward's laws and to observe this particular one too, and upon those conditions only, while his elder brother, Robert, was still alive, he was chosen king.[49] All kings henceforth swore these same oaths before they received the trappings of the kingship. Hence that famous and ancient lawyer of ours, Bracton, says, Bk. 1, ch. 8: 'There is no king, one may be sure, where will is master, and not law'; and, Bk. 3, ch. 9: 'A king is a king so long as he rules well; and a tyrant, so long as he crushes with violent despotism

[45] A paraphrase of material from two clauses of the *Modus*; XIII, 'De Absentia Regis in Parliamento'/'Concerning the King's Absence in Parliament', and XXIII (*Parliamentary Texts*, pp. 72, 77, 85, 90). See Hakewill, *Manner*, sig. C2, D3.

[46] From 'De Regis officio' in *Leges Edovardi Regis*, Lambarde (1644), p. 142. For the contemporary significance of this, see the article by Greenberg cited in the Bibliography.

[47] See p. 21.

[48] See p. 10.

[49] For the confirmation by Henry I (1100–35), see Lambarde (1644), p. 175.

the people entrusted to him.' And in the same place: 'The king ought to exercise the power of right, as the deputy and servant of God; but the power to do wrong is the devil's not God's; when the king turns aside to do wrong, he is a servant of the devil.'[50] Practically the same words are used by another ancient lawyer, the author of that famous book which is entitled *Fleta*,[51] remembering in fact that law of Edward that was truly royal, and that primary rule in our law which has been mentioned by me above, by which nothing that is contrary to the laws of God and reason can be considered a law; as neither a tyrant can be considered a king, nor a servant of the devil as a servant of God. And so, since law is especially right reason, if a king and servant of God must be obeyed, by the very same reason and law a tyrant and a servant of the devil must be resisted.

And since debates arise more often about a name than a fact, the same authors relate that a king of England, even if he has not yet lost the name of king, both can and ought to be judged like anyone of the common people, Bracton Bk. 1, ch. 8; *Fleta* Bk. 1, ch. 17: 'No-one ought to be greater than the king in the deliverance of law; but he ought to be equal to the least in receiving judgement if he sins'; others read, 'if he seeks'.[52]

So since our king ought to be judged, whether under the title of tyrant or of king, it ought not to be difficult to say likewise who he has for lawful judges. It will not be amiss to consult the same authors about this, Bracton Bk. 2, ch. 16; *Fleta* Bk. 1, ch. 17: 'In ruling the people a king has his superiors, the law by which he became king, and his court, that is the earls and barons. *Comites* (earls) are so called, as they are the king's fellows; and he who has a fellow has a master. Therefore if the king would be without a bridle, that is without law, they ought to put a bridle on him.'[53] And we have shown above that the commons are included under the name of barons. Moreover the ancient books of our laws everywhere relate that the same men were

[50] Henry de Bracton, *De legibus et consuetudinibus Angliae* (1640), fo 5v (I, 8, 5); fo 107v (III, 9, 3).

[51] The first of the quotes from Bracton, III, 9, 3, is in *Fleta* (1647), at p. 16 (I, 17, 2); the second is at p. 17 (I, 17, 8).

[52] *si peccat*; alii legunt, *si petat*: M.'s only authority for this variant was Sadler, *Rights*, pp. 27–8/sig. Dd2 r-v: '*si Peccat*. For So, I need not feare, to read the words; (although some Copies read it *Petat* ...' Both Bracton 1569 and 1640 have 'si petat' at fo 5v (I, 8, 5); *Fleta* (1647) has 'si parcat' at p. 16 (I, 17, 2).

[53] Bracton (1640), fo 34 (II, 16, 3); *Fleta* (1647), p. 17 (I, 17, 9).

called peers of parliament also, and chiefly that book entitled the *Modus Parlamenti* says: 'There shall be chosen from all the peers of the realm twenty-five', of whom there will be 'five knights, five citizens', that is, representatives of cities, 'five burgesses: also two knights of the shire have a greater say in granting and gainsaying than the greatest earl of England,'[54] and deservedly indeed; for they vote on behalf of some whole county or constituency, the earls only for themselves. And who does not see that those earls 'by patent', as you call them, and 'by writ', since there are now no feudal lords, are the least suitable of all to judge the king by whom they were appointed? And since our law is, as it is in that ancient *Speculum*, that the king has peers who discover and judge in parliament 'if the king has done wrong to any of his people',[55] and if it is very well known that in our country anyone of the people in any of the lesser courts may bring a suit against the king for damages, how much more just and how much more necessary it is that if a king had done wrong to his whole people, he should have persons who cannot only bridle and check him but judge him and punish him too. For that commonwealth must be very badly and absurdly constituted in which a remedy is provided even for a private person in case of the most minor injuries done by the king, while no provision is made for the common good in the case of the greatest injuries, and none at all for the safety of all so that the king may not destroy them illegally when he could not legally injure even one man.

But since it has been shown that it is neither fitting nor advantageous for the earls to be the king's judges, it follows that that judgement belongs wholly and by the best right to the commons, who are both peers of the realm and barons, and are endowed with the power of all the people delegated to them. For since (as it is written in our law, which I have quoted above) the commons alone, together with

[54] *Eligentur* inquit *de omnibus regni paribus* 25, quorum erunt *quinque milites, quinque cives* id est urbium delegati, *quinque municipes: et duo milites pro comitatu majorem vocem habent in concedendo et contradicendo quam major comes Angliae*: this draws on two clauses of the *Modus*; XVII, 'De Casibus et Iudiciis Difficilibus'/'Concerning Difficult Cases and Decisions', and XXIII (*Parliamentary Texts*, pp. 75, 77, 87, 89). M.'s source was Sadler, *Rights*, p. 77/sig. Kk3, where the material is reversed: '*& duo Milites pro Comitatu majorem vocem habent in concedendo, & contradicendo, quam Major Comes Angliae, & c.* So, in doubtfull cases of Peace and *War, disputetur per Pares Parliamenti*: and if need bee, 25 shall bee chosen *de omnibus Paribus Regni*; which are so specified, 2 *Bishops*, 3 *Proctors*, 2 *Earls*, 3 *Barons*, 5 *Knights*, 5 *Citizens*, and 5 Burgesses.'

[55] Horne, *Mirroir*, pp. 7–9.

the king and without earls or bishops, constitute a parliament, because the king used to hold parliaments with the people alone even before the existence of earls or bishops, by the very same reason, the commons alone shall hold supreme power without the king and judge the king himself, because even before the creation of any king, they themselves had been accustomed in the name of the whole people to hold councils and parliaments, to judge, to pass laws and even to make kings – not so that they might be masters of the people, but so that they might manage the people's business. But if a king on the other hand should try to do wrong to them and crush them with slavery, by the very sentence of our law, the name of king does not remain settled upon him, he is no king; and if he be no king, why should we have far to seek his peers? For since he has already been judged a tyrant in actuality by all good men, there are none who are not peers and suitable enough to judge him worthy to be put to death in a court.

Since this is so, by bringing forward so many testimonies, so many laws, I think I have at last abundantly proved what I proposed: that, since it lies by very good right in the hands of the commons to judge kings, and since the commons have put the king to death because he had behaved very badly by the commonwealth and the church without any hope of cure, they acted rightly and regularly, in the public faith, with honour, and, finally, according to the laws of their native land. And I cannot here fail to congratulate myself upon our ancestors, who founded this commonwealth with no less good sense and freedom than did the Romans once or the most excellent of the Greeks. Nor could they, if they have any knowledge of our affairs, fail to congratulate themselves also about their posterity, who, when they had almost been reduced to slavery, so bravely and so prudently reclaimed a state, so wisely constituted and based upon so much liberty, from the uncontrollable despotism of the king.

CHAPTER IX

I think it is now clear enough that the king of England can be judged even by the laws of the English and that he has his lawful judges, which was the matter to be proven. How do you go on (for I shall not repeat my answers to your repetitions)? 'From the very matters now for which meetings are usually called', you say, 'it is all downhill to show that the king is above parliament.' Let it be as downhill a slope as you wish, you will instantly feel yourself being hurled headlong down it. 'Parliament', you say, 'is usually assembled upon affairs of great importance, in which the safety of the kingdom and people is concerned.' If the king summons parliament to attend to the people's business, not his own, and does not do even that except by the consent and at the judgement of those he summons, what else is he, I beg you, than a servant and agent of the people? Since, without the votes of those whom the people send, he cannot decide even the least thing either concerning others or even concerning himself. This also goes to prove that it is the king's duty to summon parliament whenever the people ask since it is the people's business, not the king's, that is dealt with in those assemblies, and that by the will of the people.

For although the king's assent was usually sought out of respect – and in matters of lesser importance concerning only the advantage of private persons he might not give it and might speak in accordance with that formula, 'The king will advise' – in matters which concern the common safety and liberty of all people, he could in absolutely no way say no, since that would be both against his coronation oath, by which he was held as if by the firmest law, and against the chief article of the Magna Carta, Ch. 29: 'We will not refuse, we will not delay right or justice to any man.' Will the king not refuse right or justice, and will he refuse the making of just laws? Not to any man, so not to all men? Not in any lesser court, so surely not in the highest court of all? Or shall any king assume so much for himself that he thinks he alone knows better than the whole people what is just and advantageous? Especially when 'he was made and chosen for this purpose, so he should do justice to all', Bracton Bk. 3, ch. 9;[1] that is, according to those laws 'which the people' shall choose. Hence that passage in our records, 7 H. 4., Rot. Parl. num. 59:[2] 'There is no royal prerogative which diminishes justice and equity in any respect.' And our ancestors have often compelled by force of arms kings who formerly refused to confirm acts of parliament, to wit the Magna Carta and others of this kind. Nor on that account do our lawyers state that those laws have less validity or are less lawful; since the king gave his assent under compulsion to those decrees to which he ought rightfully and voluntarily to have assented. While you strive to prove that kings of other nations too have been equally in the power of their sanhedrin or senate or council, you do not argue us into slavery, but them into liberty. In this you go on doing the same thing that you have done from the beginning, and what the stupidest of learned counsel quite often do, to argue unawares against themselves in a lawcase.

But we admit, you imagine, that 'the king, wherever he absents himself, is still deemed to be present in parliament by virtue of his power: so whatever business is dealt with there is understood as being dealt with by the king himself'. Then as if you had obtained some haul or even a small gain, won round by the memory of those gold pieces from Charles, you say 'we accept what they give us'. Accept then what you deserve – a great evil. For we do not grant what you hoped for: that, in consequence, 'that court possesses no other power than what is delegated by the king'. For if it is said that the king's power, whatever it is, cannot be absent from parliament, is it straight away said that it is supreme? Or does not rather the king's power appear to be transferred to parliament and as a lesser one to be comprised within the greater? Certainly if parliament can, without the will and consent of the king, revoke and rescind his acts and privileges granted to anyone, and circumscribe the king's own prerogatives as they think good, and moderate his annual income and the expenditure

[1] Bracton (1640), fo 107 (III, 9, 3).
[2] 1405–6. The reference is incorrect.

of the court, his own retinue and in short all the household business of the king; if they may remove even his intimate councillors and friends, or even snatch them from his bosom to punish them; if in short appeal is granted to any of the people by law concerning any matter from the king to parliament, but not likewise from parliament to the king – all of which both public records and the most learned of our lawyers bear witness both that it can happen and that it often has – I judge that there is no-one, at least if he is in his right mind, who would not admit that parliament is above the king. For even in an interregnum parliament flourishes, and – something which is very well attested in our histories – it has often, without any regard to hereditary descent, made king by free vote the man it thought fit.

So to sum up how the matter stands: parliament is the supreme council of the nation, set up by a completely free people and furnished with full power for this very purpose; to consult together over the most important matters. The king was created to take care that all the resolutions made by the advice and opinion of those estates should be fulfilled.

When parliament itself declared this publicly in its own recent edict[3] (for it did not refuse, in view of the justice of its actions, to render an account of its actions freely and of its own accord even to foreign nations), look at this man from a hovel, of no authority or credit or property, this native Burgundian slave, who accuses the supreme senate of England, when it is asserting its own and its country's right by law, of 'a detestable and horrible imposture'. Upon my word your country will be ashamed, scoundrel, of having borne a little man of such great impudence!

But perhaps you have some advice that you wish to give us for our good; go on, we are listening. 'What laws', you say, 'can parliament sanction in which not even the order of bishops agrees?' Did you then, madman, go to uproot bishops from the church, to put them into parliaments? O wicked man, who should be handed over to Satan, whom the church ought not to fail to excommunicate as a hypocrite and an atheist and no commonwealth receive as a common plague and stain to liberty. And moreover he strives to prove something (which is only to be proved from the gospel) from Aristotle and Halicarnassus,[4] and then from the papistical statutes of the most corrupt ages: that the

[3] *Parliamenti Angliae declaratio*, 22 Mar. 1649.
[4] Dionysius of Halicarnassus (*fl.* 30–8 BC), rhetorician and historian.

king of England is the head of the Church of England, so that he may as far as he can set over the holy church of God as fresh robbers and tyrants anew the bishops who have recently become his fellow-banqueters and intimates, who God himself drove out, and whose whole order, as being most destructive to christian religion, Salmasius has noisily contested in his previously published books ought to be exterminated root and branch. What apostate ever has fallen off in such a shameful and wicked desertion – I do not say from his own doctrine, which is unsettled, but from that of christianity, which he himself had asserted? 'If the bishops are removed from our midst, who under the king and by his judgement could have jurisdiction over the causes of the church', you ask, 'to whom will that jurisdiction devolve?' O villain, at last respect your own conscience! Remember while you may, unless I give you a warning that is already too late, remember that you will not go unpunished, that it is quite impossible to mock the holy Spirit of God thus. Pull yourself together at last and set some limit to your madness, lest the wrath of God, that has been set a-fire, should suddenly seize hold of you. For you wish to hand over Christ's flock and God's untouchable anointed, to be crushed and trampled again by those enemies and most savage tyrants from whom God's marvellous hand recently came forth and freed them. And you yourself instructed that they should be freed – I don't know whether for any advantage for them, or for your destruction and obduracy. But if bishops have no right to domination over the church, certainly kings have much less, whatever human statutes say. For those who have tasted the gospel with something more than their lips know that the government of the church is wholly divine and spiritual, not civil.

But when you say that 'in secular affairs the king of England has had supreme jurisdiction' – this our laws copiously declare to be false. Not the king but the authority of parliament either sets up or removes all the courts where judgements are made. Yet in them the least of the people might call the king to court; and quite often the judges used to pronounce against the king, and if the king tried to hinder this by prohibition or order or letter, the judges in accordance with their oath and the law did not obey him but rejected such orders and took no heed of them. The king could not throw anyone into chains or confiscate anyone's goods for public use; he could not punish anyone by death, unless he had first been summoned into some court where not the king but the usual judges gave sentence; and that often, as I have said above, against the king. Hence our Bracton, Bk. 3, ch. 9: 'The king's power is one to do justice, not to do wrong; and the king can do nothing else but only what he can do lawfully.'[5] Another thing is suggested to you by your advocates, who have recently gone into exile, based to be sure on certain statutes that are not ancient, made under Edward IV, Henry VII, and Edward VI. They did not see that whatever power those statutes grant to the king was all granted by parliament and begged as a favour so to speak, which that same authority can also revoke. Why have you so suffered your sagacity to be put upon that you believed you were proving the king's power to be absolute and supreme by the very argument which most proves that it depends upon acts of parliament? For our more venerable records also bear witness that our kings owe all their power not to heredity, nor to arms, nor to succession, but to the people. Such royal power we read was granted by the commons to Henry IV, such before him to Richard II, Rot. Parl. Hen. 4 num. 108;[6] just as any king usually grants prefectures to his governors and provinces by edict and letter of recommendation. Certainly, the house of commons ordered it expressly to be entered on public records that 'they had granted to King Richard' to enjoy 'the same good liberty as kings of England had before him'; and since that king abused it for the overthrow of the laws 'contrary to the faith of his oath', he was deprived of his kingdom by these same people. The same people also, as the same roll testifies, proclaim in parliament that having confidence in the discretion and moderation of Henry IV 'they wish and order that he have that same great royal liberty which his ancestors had'. But if the former had not been completely a matter of trust, as the latter was, certainly the houses of that parliament must have been foolish and vain to grant what was not theirs, and those kings too must have both injured themselves and their descendants in being willing to receive as a grant of others what was already their own; neither of which can be believed.

'A third of the royal power', you say, 'concerns the army. This part the kings of England have handled without peer and rival.' This is no truer than the rest that you have written on the word of deserters. For firstly that the judgement of peace and war was always in the hands of

[5] M. runs together two quotations from Bracton, fo 107–107v (III, 9. 3).
[6] 1399.

the great senate of the kingdom, our histories all throughout, and those of foreigners which have touched upon our affairs with any accuracy, bear witness. Also the laws of St Edward, on which our kings are bound to swear, make belief absolutely certain in the chapter *De Heretochiis*:[7] 'That there were certain powers set up throughout the provinces and all the counties of the realm, which were called Heretochs, in Latin *ductores exercitus*',[8] who were in charge of provincial troops, not only 'for the honour of the crown' but 'for the good of the realm.' And they were chosen 'by the common council, and by each of the counties in full popular assemblies, just as sheriffs too ought to be chosen'. Hence it is easily seen, that both the forces of the kingdom and the leaders of the forces were in ancient times and ought still to be in the power of the people not of the king, and that that most just law had no less strength in our kingdom than it once did in the Roman republic. About this it will not be beside the point to hear Marcus Tullius, *Philipp.* 10: 'All the legions, all the forces wherever they are belong to the Roman people. For not even the legions which abandoned Antony when he was consul are said to have belonged to Antony rather than the republic.'[9] And that law of St Edward, together with others of his laws, William, called the Conqueror, at the wish and command of the people, confirmed by oath; and also added this over and above, Ch. 56:[10] that 'all cities, boroughs, castles, be so guarded each night, as the sheriff and aldermen, and the rest of those put in charge by the common council shall think fit for the benefit of the realm'; and, in law 62,[11] 'for that reason castles, boroughs, cities were built for the protection of the nations and peoples of the realm, and therefore ought to be maintained with all liberty, integrity, and means'. What then? Shall fortresses and towns be guarded in peace time against thieves and evil-doers only by the common council of each locality, and not be guarded in greatest fear of war against enemies, be they foreign or internal, by the common council of the whole nation? Indeed unless this is granted, there will be neither 'liberty' nor 'integrity' nor 'means' in short in these places which need to be guarded: nor shall we gain any of those things, for which the law itself says that cities and fortresses are founded in the first place.

[7] Lambarde (1644), pp. 147–8. [8] *ductores exercitus*: leaders of the army.
[9] Cicero, *Philippics*, X, iv, 27.
[10] Lambarde (1644), p. 171; the confirmation is chapter 63, p. 173.
[11] M.'s material is from chapter 61 (not 62) in Lambarde (1644), p. 172.

Indeed our ancestors were accustomed to hand over anything to the king rather than their arms and the garrisons of towns, thinking that it was the same as if they personally went to surrender their liberty to the ferocity and lawlessness of kings. Since there are very copious examples of this in our histories, and already very well known, it would be superfluous to insert them in this place.

But 'the king owes protection to his subjects; how will he be able to protect them, unless he has arms and men in his power?' But, I say, he had all this for the advantage of the kingdom, as was said, not for the destruction of the citizens and ruin of the kingdom. Even in Henry III's time, a certain Leonard, a learned man, sensibly replied thus in an assembly of the bishops to Rustand, the pope's nuncio and the king's chancellor: 'All churches belong to my master the pope as we say all things belong to a prince: for protection, not for his enjoyment or by right of ownership', as they say; for defence, 'not for spoil.'[12] The same was also the opinion of the aforesaid law of St Edward; what else is this but power in trust, not an absolute one? Though a general in war has much the same sort of power – that is, delegated, not completely his own – he usually defends the people by whom he is chosen no more sluggishly whether at home or abroad. But in vain and surely in an unequal contest would parliaments have formerly contended with kings about the laws of St Edward and liberty, if they had thought that arms should be under the control of the king alone. For if the king had wanted to impose any unjust laws whatever, in vain would they have defended themselves against the sword by a 'Charter' however 'Great'.

'But what benefit will it be', you say, 'for parliament to have control of the army, since they cannot gather together even a farthing from the people to support them, without the king's consent.' Don't let that bother you! For firstly you make the false proposition that the estates in parliament 'cannot impose taxes on the people without the king's consent', when it is the people by whom these very members of parliament have been sent and whose cause they are upholding. Then it cannot escape you, who are so industrious an inquirer about other people's business, that the people of their own accord, by melting down their gold and silver vessels, spent a great amount of money on this war against the king.

[12] M. (*CB*, I, 440) notes this episode from Holinshed, *Chronicles*, III, 253.

Then you review the very large yearly revenues of our kings; you rattle on about nothing except 'five hundred and forty thousands'. You had heard greedily that 'out of the patrimony of the king very large grants' have customarily been made by those 'kings who have been conspicuous for praises of their generosity'. By this enticement, just like that notorious Balaam,[13] the traitors to their country brought you over to their side; so that you dared to curse the people of God and cry out against divine judgements. Fool, what benefit in the end was such boundless wealth to an unjust and violent king? What to you also? For I hear that nothing at all of what you had been devouring with mighty hope actually reached you except that one little money purse, covered with glass beads shaped like worms, and stuffed with one hundred gold pieces. Take, Balaam, that payment for your wickedness, which you so truly loved, and enjoy it. For you go on playing the fool.

'The setting up of the standard', that is, the 'banner, is the right of the king alone.' Why? Because

> Turnus raised the signal for war from the citadel of Laurentum.[14]

Do you really not know, grammarian, that this same duty is the office of any general at war? But 'Aristotle says,[15] it is necessary for a guard to stand by the king so he can protect the laws; so a king must have more military strength than all the people'. This man is used to twisting conclusions, as Ocnus does ropes in the underworld, which are of no use except to be eaten by asses.[16] For a guard given by the people is one thing, and power over all the armies is another. The latter, Aristotle, in the very passage which you have brought forward, declares does not belong to kings. A king must, he says, have as big a band of armed soldiers around him 'so he is stronger than any one man, or several men together, but in truth is still weaker than the people'; εἶναι δὲ τοσαύτην ἰσχὺν ὥστε ἑκάστου μὲν καὶ ἑνὸς καὶ συμπλειόνων κρείττω, τοῦ δὲ πλήθους ἥττω, *Pol.* Bk. 3, ch. 11.[17] Otherwise indeed, under pretence of protecting them, he could at once subject both people and laws to himself. And this is the

[13] Num. 22:5–34.

[14] Virgil, *Aeneid*, VIII, 1 (M. is quoting S. quoting Virgil).

[15] Aristotle, *Politics*, III, 15 (1286b).

[16] Ocnus was condemned in Hades to the futile task of making a straw rope which was eaten by an ass as fast as he made it. Cf. *DDD*, II, 346.

[17] Aristotle, *Politics*, III, 15 (1286b).

difference between a king and a tyrant; a king, by the consent and pleasure of the senate and people, has around him a sufficient guard against public enemies and seditious rebels: a tyrant, against the will of the senate and people, strives to get as big a guard as possible either of public enemies or of ruined citizens, against the very senate and people. And so parliament has thus granted to the king, as they did everything else, 'the raising of the standard'; not so that he might give signals dangerous to his own people, but to defend the people against those whom parliament had judged to be public enemies. If he had done otherwise, he should have been judged an enemy himself since, according to that very law of St Edward, or what is more sacred, the very law of nature, he lost the name of king. Hence in the aforesaid *Philippic*:[18] 'He who attacks the commonwealth with his sovereignty and army loses all right to that army and that sovereignty.' Nor was the king allowed to summon those 'feudal knights'[19] to a 'war' which the authority of parliament had not decreed, as is clear from many statutes. The same judgement was made about tolls and shipmoney,[20] which the king might not lawfully command from the citizens without an act of Parliament: and this was publicly resolved by the most learned of our lawyers about twelve years ago,[21] when the king's command was still very stable. So too long before then Fortescue, chancellor of Henry VI and a most eminent lawyer, said the king of England can neither change the laws nor impose taxes without the people's consent.[22]

But no-one can prove by any testimonies of the ancients that 'the government of the kingdom of England is purely monarchical'. 'The king', says Bracton, 'has jurisdiction over all.' That is, in the courts where in the king's name indeed, but according to our laws, justice is rendered. 'Everyone is beneath the king' – that means every

[18] Cicero, *Philippics*, X, v, 12.

[19] The last such feudal summons was in Aug. 1640.

[20] Although Parliament granted Tunnage and Poundage (customs duties) to Charles I for one year only (rather than for life as was customary) he continued to collect them from 1628. This practice was declared to have been illegal in the Tunnage and Poundage Act (June 1641). Ship Money (ostensibly naval requisitioning in the form of a rate) was levied from the maritime counties in 1634 and extended to the inland counties in 1635.

[21] In 1638 the judges actually found in favour of the king in Rex *v.* Hampden (the test case for Ship Money) by a majority of 7 to 5. Their judgement was overturned by the Act abolishing Ship Money (July 1641).

[22] Sir John Fortescue, *De laudibus legum Angliae* (1616), fo 26.

individual, and so Bracton himself explains in the passage I cited above.[23]

As to what remains, where you roll the same stone over and over again – in which you have the power, I believe, to tire out Sisyphus himself[24] – from what I have said above, it is abundantly answered. For the rest, if ever parliaments have conferred deference upon good kings with the fullest words just short of flattery and servility, this should not be understood as being conferred in the same way upon tyrants or to the detriment of the people; for liberty is not diminished by just deference. And as for what you cite out of Sir Edward Coke and others, that 'the kingship of England is an absolute power',[25] this is so if you consider any foreign king, or emperor; or, as Camden says, 'because it is not among the dependents of the empire'.[26] Furthermore each adds that this power exists not 'from the king' alone, but 'from the body politic'. Hence Fortescue says, *de laud. legum Angl.*, Ch. 9: 'The king of England' governs his people 'not by a pure royal power, but by a political; for the people are governed by those laws which' they make themselves.[27] This was known also to foreign writers; hence Philippe de Commynes, a very weighty author, in the fifth book of his *Commentaries* says: 'Amongst all the kingdoms of the earth, of which I have knowledge, there is none indeed in my opinion where public matters are handled with more restraint or where the king is allowed less power over the people than in England.'[28]

Finally you say 'the argument is ridiculous which they allege, that kingdoms existed before kings, as if you should say that light existed before the sun'. But we, my good fellow, do not say that kingdoms, but that people existed before kings. Meanwhile whom shall I call more ridiculous than you yourself, who deny that light existed before the sun, as if it were ridiculous. Thus while you wish to meddle in other people's business, you have unlearned the rudiments. You wonder lastly 'that those who have seen the king in a session of parliament sitting on his throne, under a gold and silken heaven,

[23] I.e., Bracton, I, 8, 5.

[24] Sisyphus was eternally condemned in Hades to rolling a rock to the top of a hill, from where it would always roll down.

[25] Quoted by S., *DR*, p. 248. See Coke, *Fifth Reports*, fo 8a (Caudrey's case).

[26] Quoted by S., *DR*, p. 249. See Camden, *Britannia* (1607), p. 118.

[27] Fortescue (1616), fo 25b.

[28] Philippe de Commynes, *Mémoires* (Paris, 1552), fo 94b (V, 18).

could have called into doubt whether majesty belonged to the king or the parliament'. You tell of unbelieving men indeed whom so lucid an argument petitioned from 'heaven', especially a 'gold and silken' one, has not moved. This golden heaven you, a stoic, have so devoutly and singly contemplated that it seems you have quite forgotten the heavens of Moses and Aristotle: since in the former's you have denied that 'light existed before the sun', and in the latter's you have taught above that there are three temperate zones. How many zones you have observed in that gold and silken heaven of the king I do not know, but this I do know: you have removed one zone, well tempered with one hundred gold stars, from that heavenly contemplation of yours.

CHAPTER X

This whole controversy about right, whether of kings in general, or of the king of England in particular, has become more difficult because of the obstinate struggles of factions than through the actual nature of the business. So I hope that for those who prefer the pursuit of truth before faction, I have from the law of God, and the right of nations, and finally from the institutes of my country brought forward abundant proofs that might leave it beyond doubt that a king of England can be judged and also punished by death. As for the rest – whose minds either superstition has seized, or premature admiration of the king's splendour has so dulled the edge of their wits that they can see nothing glorious or splendid in true virtue and liberty – whether we battle with reason and arguments or with examples, we strive in vain.

Truly you, Salmasius, as with all the rest, seem to do this too to the limit of absurdity, as you, who cannot stop heaping all kinds of insults upon all Independents, assert that the very king whom you are defending was the most independent of all: for 'he did not owe his kingdom to his people, but to his family'. Then the man whom you forcefully grieved at the beginning of your book 'was forced to plead for his life', you now complain 'perished unheard'. But in truth, if you like to inspect the whole pleading of his cause, which is most faithfully published in French,[1] perhaps you will be otherwise persuaded. Although Charles was certainly granted for some days on end the fullest opportunity of speaking, he did not indeed make any use of it

[1] *Histoire entière & veritable du Procez de Charles Stuart*, 20 Jan. 1650.

to clear the crimes that he was charged with, but only to reject wholly that jurisdiction and his judges. And it is no wrong for any defendant who is either silent or always makes irrelevant replies, if he is clearly guilty, to be condemned even unheard.

If you say that Charles 'died a death clearly answering to his life' I agree; if you say that he ended his life piously, holily, and 'fearlessly', know that his grandmother, Mary, an infamous woman, died on the scaffold with an equal appearance of piety, holiness and constancy. And in case you attribute too much to that presence of mind which is often very great in any common wrong doer at his death, often desperation or a hardened heart puts on a certain show and, so to speak, mask of courage, and often stupidity puts on that of tranquillity: the worst men wish to seem good, undaunted, innocent and sometimes holy no less in their death than in life; and at the very moment of capital punishment for their crimes, they are accustomed to make a last parade of their hypocrisy and deceptions, as spendidly as they are able; and, as is the habit of the most silly poets or actors, to strive most conceitedly for applause even at their exit.

Now you say 'you have reached that part of the investigation in which the question must be discussed of who were the chief authors of the condemnation of the king', although inquiry should rather be made about you – how you, a foreigner, and a French vagabond, have reached the point of holding an enquiry into our affairs, so foreign to you. At what price were you bought? Truly that is well enough known. But who, finally, instructed you in your earnest enquiries about our affairs? Of course those deserters and enemies to their country who got hold of a most vainglorious man in you, and by bribery easily brought you to speak ill of us. Then you were given some little treatise about the state of our affairs either written by some mad, half-papist chaplain or some servile courtier; the job was given to you of turning it into Latin. Hence these made up stories of yours which, if you please, we will investigate a little.

'Not a hundred-thousandth part of the people agreed to this condemnation.' So what about the rest of them, who allowed so great a crime to happen without their consent? Were they blocks of wood, or maimed trunks of men, or truly such spiritless creatures as those in Virgil's scene?

> Interwoven Britons hold up purple hangings[2]

[2] Virgil, *Georgics*, III, 25.

For you seem to me not to mean true Britons at all, but some Picts or even men painted by the needle.[3] And since it is unbelievable that a warlike nation should be sent beneath the yoke by so few, and those the lowest of their common people – which in your story is the first thing that happens – that appears to be quite false.

'The ecclesiastical order had been ejected by the senate itself.' And so your madness is the more unhappy, for you do not yet realize you are mad, when you complain that those people *were* ejected by parliament who you yourself write in a very lengthy book *ought* to be ejected from the church. 'A second order of the senate which consisted of the nobles, dukes, earls and viscounts was cast down from its rank.' And deservedly, for since they were not returned by any constituency, they sat for themselves only, and had no right over the people, but yet used generally to oppose their right and liberty, by some custom of their own. They had been appointed by the king, and were his companions, and servants, and so to speak shadows. Once he was removed, they had themselves to be reduced to the level of the people from whom they arose. 'One part – and that the worst – of parliament ought not to have claimed for itself the power of judging kings.' But the house of commons, as I told you above, was not only the most important part of parliament, even under kings, but by itself it formed a parliament in all respects absolute and lawful, even without the lords, much less the clergy. But 'not even the whole of this actual part was admitted to vote about the king's death'. That part certainly was not admitted which had openly defected in spirit and in counsel to one whom it had judged a king in word but an enemy in deed. The English estates of parliament along with those representatives who had been sent likewise from the parliament of Scotland, had written on 13 January 1645[4] in reply to his request for a deceitful truce and discussions to be held with them in London, that they could not allow him into the city until he gave satisfaction to the commonwealth for the civil war which had been raised by his doing in three kingdoms and for the deaths of so many of his subjects carried out by his order, and had made provision for a stable and true peace upon the terms which the parliaments of both kingdoms had offered

[3] *pictos nescio quos, vel etiam acu pictos*: involves a pun on *pictus* as both painted, tattooed or decorated, and Pict.

[4] *idibus Januarii* 1645: M's date is Old Style. The text to be forwarded to the king was agreed on by the Committee of Both Kingdoms and the Scottish commissioners and approved by the Commons on 13 Jan. 1646. Cf. *E*, III, 596.

him so often and would offer again. He himself on the other hand had either rejected with deaf replies or had evaded with ambiguous ones their very just demands which had now been most humbly presented to him seven times. The houses at last, after the patience of so many years, feared that the cheating king would ruin by all his delays while in prison that commonwealth which he had not had the power to subdue in battle, and, by plucking the very pleasant fruit of our disagreements, be restored and, even though a public enemy, actually celebrate a triumph produced by himself over his conquerors. So they decreed that hereafter they would not take any account of the king; that they would send him no further requests or receive any from him.[5] Yet after these resolutions, there were found – out of the actual number of the estates – men who, from hatred of that most invincible army, whose very great deeds they envied, and which after its great services they desired to dismiss in disgrace, obeyed the will of some seditious ministers to whom they were miserably subject. They gained an opportune time for themselves, when many of those whom they knew utterly disagreed with them were absent in the provinces, where they had been sent by the house itself to settle the riots of the Presbyterians which were already spreading, and with a strange levity – not to say treachery – they decreed that an inveterate public enemy, king in name only, with practically no satisfaction received from him or precaution taken, should be brought back to the city, and restored to the highest dignity and power, just as if he had deserved honourably of the commonwealth.[6] So they set the king before their religion, liberty, even lastly that covenant which had been so often boasted about by them. What did those men do meanwhile who were sound and saw such destructive counsels in motion? Ought they to have failed their country and not provided for their own safety because the infection of that disease had penetrated into their own house?

But who excluded those who were diseased? 'The English army' you say; that is, not one of foreigners but of most brave and loyal citizens, most of whose officers were the very members who those excluded patriots had judged should be excluded from their own country and sent far off into Ireland![7] The Scots meanwhile, with a

[5] The Vote of No Addresses, 3 and 15 Jan. 1648.

[6] The Commons yielded to pressure from the City on 24 May 1648 by voting to resume negotiations with the king. On 5 July the Lords backed a petition for the king to return to London 'in honour, freedom and safety' for the treaty.

[7] Refers to the policy promoted in the spring of 1647 by Denzil Holles (later one of the

now doubtful good faith, were occupying with large forces four counties of England nearest to their borders; they were holding the strongest towns of these regions with garrisons; they were keeping the king himself in custody: they were also supporting factions and riots of their people – more than threatening to parliament itself – everywhere both in the city and the country. These riots shortly after broke out, not only into civil war, but Scottish war as well.

And if it has always been most praiseworthy for private citizens also to come to the aid of the commonwealth by advice or arms, there is certainly no reason that the army can be blamed, which obeyed its orders when it was summoned to the city by the authority of parliament, and easily crushed the rioting of the royalist faction which often threatened the house itself. And matters had been brought to such a crisis point that either we must needs be crushed by them or they by us. On their side stood most of the pedlars and workmen of London, and all the most factious of the ministers; on our side an army known for its great loyalty, restraint and courage. When it was possible by means of them to keep the liberty and safety of the commonwealth, do you think all this should have been betrayed by cowardice and stupidity?

The leaders of the royalist party, when subjugated, had unwillingly laid down their arms indeed, but not their hostility. Intent on all opportunities of renewing the war, they had withdrawn to the city. Although these men were their greatest enemies, the Presbyterians, when they saw they were not allowed both civil and ecclesiastical domination over everyone, had begun to associate with them in secret counsels which were most unworthy of both their previous words and deeds. They advanced to such a point in bitterness that they preferred to deliver themselves over to be the property of the king again, than admit their own brothers to that part of liberty which they too had acquired with their own blood; and preferred to try as a master again a tyrant who was drenched in the blood of so many citizens, burning with anger and with a vengeance he had already conceived against the survivors, rather than to endure as their peers, with equal rights, their brothers and friends. Only those called Independents knew how to be true to themselves to the end and to use their victory. They did not want a man who, when king, had made himself an enemy, to turn

eleven impeached members) for disbanding the New Model Army and deploying a force in Ireland.

himself from an enemy into a king again – wisely, in my opinion. They were not undesirous of peace for this reason, but sensibly feared either fresh war or eternal slavery wrapped up in the name of peace.

And so that you can slander our army more copiously, you begin a confused and meagre account of our affairs, in which although I find much false and frivolous, and much delivered by you as faults which should be considered praiseworthy, yet I judge that it achieves nothing to set another narrative from the opposite point of view against this one. For this is a contest in reasonings not narrations and both sides will credit the former but not the latter. And indeed matters are of such a nature that they cannot be spoken of according to their worth except in a just history. And so I think it better, as Sallust said of Carthage,[8] to be silent about such important matters rather than to say too little. Nor shall I sin so as to interweave in this book amongst your reproaches the praises not only of illustrious men but chiefly of Almighty God which ought most often to be repeated with regard to this amazing chain of events. So I will, as is my custom, pick out only those things which seem to hold an appearance of argument.

As you say, 'the English and the Scots in a solemn covenant promised to preserve the majesty of the king' – omitting the terms upon which they promised it: namely, if it might be done certainly, with the safety of their religion and their liberty. To both of these that king was so wicked and treacherous up to his last breath that, if he lived, it was easily apparent that their religion would be endangered and their liberty would perish.

But you return now to those authors of the king's execution. 'If the matter itself be rightly judged according to its weight and importance, the conclusion of the unspeakable deed must be imputed to the Independents, so that the Presbyterians could claim for themselves the glory of its beginning and progress.' Hear, Presbyterians, how does it now help, how does it affect the estimation of your innocence and loyalty that you seemed so much to shrink from punishing the king? According to the most wordy advocate of the king, your accuser, you 'went more than half way'; you, 'to the fourth act and beyond, were observed stammering in this drama of vaulting from one horse to

[8] Sallust, *Bellum Jugurthinum*, XIX, 2.

another'.[9] [But meanwhile, O man of far-fetched eloquence, why do you so easily imitate those whom you so laboriously accuse – 'observed' so often in this defence of the king 'stammering' yourself while 'vaulting from one horse to another'?][10]

You Presbyterians 'ought deservedly to be marked with the crime of killing the king, as you paved the way for his death'; you 'and no others struck that wicked axe upon his neck'. Woe to you first of all, if ever Charles's stock recover the kingdom of England hereafter. You, believe me, will have to pay for this. But fulfil your vows to God: love your brothers who liberated you, who so far have kept that calamity and certain destruction from you, though against your wills. You are accused likewise because 'some years before by various petitions you endeavoured to lessen the rights of the king, because you inserted and published expressions abusive of the king in those very papers which you presented to the king in the name of parliament'; to wit 'in that declaration of the lords and commons of 26 May 1642.[11] You openly confessed what you thought of the king's authority in some mad proposals that breathed treason. Hotham, by reason of such an order received from parliament shut the gates of the town of Hull against the coming of the king';[12] you 'desired to find out by this first trial of rebellion what the king would bear'. What could be said more fitted than this to reconcile the hearts of the English to each other and alienate them completely from the king? Since from this they can understand that if a king returns, they will be punished not only for the king's death, but also for petitions once made by them, and the acts of a full parliament about liturgy and abolishing bishops,[13] about

[9] S.'s mixed metaphors resist translation, but the basic charge of vacillation and changing loyalties on the part of the Presbyterians is clear enough.

[10] 1658.

[11] I.e., *A remonstrance of the Lords and Commons assembled in Parliament, or, the reply of both Houses, to . . . His Majesties answer to . . . A remonstrance, or the declaration of the Lords and Commons . . . in answer to a declaration under His Majesties name, concerning the business of Hull* (London, 1642).

[12] On 5 March 1642 the two Houses passed the Militia Ordinance and placed Sir John Hotham in charge of the strategic garrison at Hull. He refused to admit the king on 23 April. See *E*, III, 423–32, 451.

[13] *frequentissimi Parlamenti acta de liturgia et episcopis abolendis*: the offices of archbishops and bishops were left intact by the Bishops' Exclusion Act (Feb. 1642) and were not actually abolished until the *ordinance* of Oct. 1646, though the ordinance itself shared in the widespread assumption that they had been. Cf. *E*, III, 401. For ordinances dealing with the Book of Common Prayer, see *E*, III, 503–8.

the triennial parliament[14] and whatever was ratified by the greatest consent and applause of the people, as being the seditious and 'mad proposals of the Presbyterians'.

But this most fickle of men suddenly changes his mind, and what just now, 'when he was judging the matter very correctly', seemed to him to be due to the Presbyterians alone, now it seems to him, 'turning over the' same 'matter from on high', to be wholly due to the Independents. Just now he was asserting that the Presbyterians 'proceeded against the king with open force of arms' and that by them he was 'conquered in war, captured and thrown into prison'; now he writes that all 'this doctrine of rebellion' belongs to the Independents. O the trustworthiness and constancy of the man! What need is there now to compare another narrative with yours, which has so shamefully boiled itself away into nothing?

But if anyone doubts whether you are a good or a bad man, let him read your following lines: 'it is time', you say, 'to unfold whence and at what time the sect hostile to kings burst forth: truly these fine Puritans began to come forth from the darkness of hell in the reign of Elizabeth, and thence to throw the church into confusion first, or rather the commonwealth itself; for they are no less plagues to the commonwealth than to the church'. Now your very utterance pronounces you truly Balaam; for where you were desirous of vomiting out all the poison of your bitterness, there unknowingly and unwillingly you have spoken a blessing. For this is very well known throughout the whole of England, that if any people were eager to follow a purer way of divine worship after the example of either French or German churches, whichever they judged was more reformed, almost all of which our bishops had corrupted by their ceremonies and superstitions, if any in short stood out among the rest in piety towards God, or in integrity of life, they were named Puritans by the supporters of the bishops. These are the men whose doctrine you shout out is unfriendly to kings; and not these alone, for you say 'the majority of protestants, who have not sworn by the other points of their teaching, still seem to have approved of this one thing which opposes the tyranny of a king'. So while you most harshly speak ill of the Independents, you praise them in that you derive their origins from the purest family of christians; and a doctrine which you

[14] The Triennial Act (Feb. 1641) stipulated that, in the absence of any writ of summons, Parliament should meet every three years for fifty days. See *E*, III, 398–401.

everywhere assert is peculiar to the Independents, you now confess that the 'majority of protestants have approved'. You have advanced up to that point of audacity, impiety and apostasy that even the bishops, whom you recently instructed ought to be torn up by the roots from the church and exterminated as plagues and antichrists, you now affirm 'ought to have been protected by the king', so that he might not indeed 'detract at all from his coronation oath'. There is nothing further now in crime and infamy to which you can advance, but one sole remaining step – to forswear as soon as possible the protestant religion, which you pollute. And as for your saying that we 'tolerate all sects and heresies', don't accuse us of that, so long as the church still tolerates your impiety, your emptiness, lies and hired trickery and finally, your apostasy, in that you dare to say that the most holy of christians and even the majority of protestants, your opponents, 'came forth from the darkness of hell'.

And why should I not omit then your deceits, upon which you expend a great part of the rest of the chapter, and those monstrous tenets which you invent for the Independents, to heap ill-will upon them? For they have absolutely no bearing upon this case about the king and are generally such as to deserve everyone's laughter or scorn rather than refutation.

CHAPTER XI

You seem to me to approach this eleventh chapter, Salmasius, though without shame yet with some consciousness of your worthlessness. For when you proposed that you would inquire in this place 'by what authority' the sentence was pronounced on the king, you add something which nobody was expecting of you, that 'it is in vain that such inquiry is made': indeed 'the nature of the men who did it has left hardly any room for this question'. So since your discovery of your impoliteness and impudence in taking up this cause matches your consciousness now of your loquacity, you will therefore get a shorter answer from me. To your question now 'by what authority' the house of commons either judged the king itself, or delegated the judgement to others, I reply by the highest. How they hold the highest authority, you will learn from those things which were said by me above when I was disproving your diligent foolishness. And if you believed yourself at least able to say at any time what is sufficient, you would not be in the habit of most hatefully repeating so often the same sing-song. The house of commons could delegate their judicial power to others in the same way indeed in which you say the king, who also himself received all his power from the people, could delegate his to others. Hence in that 'solemn covenant' which you have brought against us, both the highest estates of England and Scotland solemnly declare and promise to exact from traitors the punishment with 'which the supreme judiciary power of each nation, or those who have power delegated from it', had judged they ought to be punished.[1] Now you hear the

[1] Article IV of the Solemn League and Covenant. Cf. *E*, III, 594.

parliament of each nation testifying that they can delegate to others their judicial authority which they themselves call 'supreme'; so empty and frivolous is the controversy you raise about the delegation of this power.

But you say 'with these judges who were chosen from the lower house were joined also judges taken from the ranks of the military; but it was never the job of soldiers to judge a citizen'. I will blunt your argument in very few words, for remember that we are not now talking of a citizen but of a public enemy: if a commander in the field, with his military officers, should wish to try such a man before a court-martial when he had been taken prisoner in war (and could be summarily executed, if it was so decided) will he be thought to have done anything beyond the rights or custom of war? And a man who is an enemy to the commonwealth and has been taken prisoner in war cannot even be considered a citizen, much less a king, in that commonwealth. This is the purport of that most sacred law of King Edward which denies that a bad king either can be a king or ought to be called by the name of king.

But against your statement that it was not a 'whole' house of commons but one 'maimed and mutilated' that tried the case of the king's life, set this: the number of those who thought that the king should be punished was far greater than those who ought by law to transact any business in parliament, even in the absence of the rest. Since they were absent by their own fault and failure (for inward desertion to the common enemy was the worst kind of absence), they could not delay those who had remained faithful from preserving that commonwealth which, when it was swaying and almost reduced to slavery and annihilation, the whole people had first entrusted to their loyalty, prudence and courage. And they indeed performed the deed energetically. They threw themselves against the lawlessness, frenzy and treachery of an exasperated king; they placed everyone's liberty and safety before their own; they outdid all parliaments before this, all their ancestors in good sense, magnanimity and constancy. Yet a large part of the people, although it had promised all loyalty, exertion and help, deserted them ungratefully in the midst of the course. This part wished for slavery and peace with idleness and luxury under any terms; but the other part were demanding liberty, and peace only if it was stable and honourable. What was the parliament to do here? Was it to defend the latter, the sound part, faithful both to it and the country, or was it to follow the former, the deserter of both? I know what you will say it ought to have done; for you are not Eurylochus, but Elpenor,[2] that is a miserable animal of Circe, a filthy pig, accustomed to the most shameful slavery even under a woman. Hence you have no taste of virtue and the liberty which is born of it. You want all men to be slaves, because you feel nothing in your breast that is noble or free. You speak and breathe nothing that is not ignoble and slavish.

You add further the scruple that 'the man about whom we decided was also king of Scotland', as if for that reason he might do anything in England without being punished. Finally, so you can at least end this chapter, which is dislocated and dry above all the rest, with some witty saying, you say 'there are two little words, consisting of the same (and the same number of) elements, differing only in the position of the letters but differing immensely in their meaning, *Vis* and *Ius*'.[3] Of course it is no great wonder that you, a man of three letters,[4] could carve out such an artful little quibble about three letters. Much more wonderful is what you assert throughout all your book: that two things, 'differing' so much from each other in all other ways, are one and the same thing in kings. For what act of might was ever committed by kings which you have not affirmed to be the right of kings?

These are the points which in nine very long pages I could notice as worthy of an answer; the rest are matters which either have been repeated again and again and I have more than once refuted, or have no influence on the discussion of this case. And so if I am briefer than is customary, it will be imputed not against my diligence, which I do not suffer to languish in this great boredom, but against your loquacity so empty and vacant of matter and reason.

[2] See Ovid, *Metamorphoses*, XIV, 252–88. Cf. *E*, III, 488.
[3] *Vis, et Jus*: might and right.
[4] See Plautus, *Aulularia*, II, 1, 35, where *fur* (thief) is 'a man of three letters'.

CHAPTER XII

I would wish for my part, Salmasius, so I shall not seem to anyone to be unfair or bitter against King Charles who has fulfilled his fate and punishment, that you had passed over in silence this whole passage about 'his crimes', which would have been more advisable both for you and your party. But now, since it has pleased you more to speak about them too overconfidently and wordily, I will make you perceive indeed that nothing more thoughtless could have been done by you than to save up till last the worst area of your cause, namely his crimes, to be torn open again and inquired into in greater detail. When I have shown these to have been real and most terrible, they will at the very end leave in the minds of your readers both a memory of him which is displeasing and hateful to all good men, and a very great hatred of you, his defender.

You say 'the accusation against him can be divided into two parts: one deals with blame attached to his way of life; the other with the crimes which he might have committed as king'. It will be easy for me to be silent about his life, which slipped away amid banquets and games and troops of women. For what is there about luxury worth relating? Or what would these things have mattered to us if he had been only a private citizen? After he chose to be king, he could not live for himself, just as he could not even sin for himself alone. For firstly he harmed his subjects most violently by his example. In the second place, all the time he spent upon his desires and sports – which was very great – he withdrew from the commonwealth which he had undertaken to govern. Finally he squandered upon domestic luxury immense wealth, countless riches which were not his own but the public's. And so it was at home that he first began to be a bad king.

But 'let us pass over' rather to those crimes 'which he is charged with having committed in misruling'. Here you grieve that he was judged 'a tyrant, a traitor and a murderer'. That this was not done to his wrong will be proven. But first let us define a tyrant, not according to the opinion of the mob, but according to the judgement of Aristotle and all learned men.

A tyrant is one who regards only his own advantage, not that of the people. So Aristotle in the tenth book of the *Ethics*[1] and elsewhere; so very many others. As to whether Charles regarded his own advantage or the people's, these few examples out of many, which I will only touch upon, will act as testimony.

When his patrimony and the royal revenues were not sufficient for the expenses of the court, he laid very heavy taxes upon the people. When these were used up, he devised new ones; not to increase or adorn or defend the commonwealth but to convey into and heap up for himself in one house, or squander in one house, the wealth of more than one nation. When he had scraped together an unbelievable amount of money illegally in this way, he tried either to abolish parliament completely, which he knew was the one thing that could act as a bridle on him, or, by summoning it no oftener than suited his purposes, to render it accountable to himself alone. After dragging this bridle from himself, he himself cast another bridle upon the people. He had German cavalry and Irish infantry stationed through the cities and towns, as if they were garrisons, when there was no war. Does he seem too little like a tyrant still to you? In this also, as in many other things, which I have shown above on an occasion granted me by you (although you consider it improper for Charles to be compared to that very cruel Nero), he very much resembled Nero: for he too had very often threatened to remove the senate from the commonwealth.

Meanwhile he was unduly hard upon the consciences of religious men, and compelled all to the practice of certain ceremonies and superstitious forms of worship which he had brought back into the church from the heart of popery. Those who declined he punished with exile or imprisonment. He made war on the Scots twice for this reason.[2] Thus far he may seem to have deserved the name of tyrant at least 'once over'.

[1] Aristotle, *Ethics*, 1160b.
[2] The Bishops' Wars of 1639 and 1640.

Now I will explain why the name of traitor was added to the indictment. When he had affirmed to this parliament again and again by promises, edicts and solemn oaths (which he broke) that he was making no endeavours against the commonwealth, at that very time he was either holding levies of papists in Ireland, or by sending ambassadors secretly to the king of Denmark,[3] was seeking weapons, horses and help expressly against parliament, or he was seducing an army now of Englishmen, now of Scots by bribery. To the former he promised the ransacking of the city of London, to the latter the annexation of the four northern counties beneath the rule of the Scots if they were willing to lend their efforts to him to remove parliament by any means. Since this did not succeed, he gave to a certain Dillon,[4] a traitor, secret instructions for the Irish, whom he ordered to assault all the English settlers of that island in a sudden attack. These more or less are the proofs of his betrayals, which have not been gathered from empty rumours, but discovered from his very own letters,[5] signed and sealed by his very own hand.

I think finally that no-one will deny that he was a murderer, when the Irish, on receipt of his orders, took up arms and killed, together with the application of particular torments, five hundred thousand English who at the height of peace feared nothing of the kind; and when he also stirred up so great a civil war himself in the other two realms. For I add that in the talks on the Isle of Wight, the king openly took upon himself both the blame and the charge of this war and freed parliament of it all in his very well-known confession.[6] You have now in brief why King Charles was judged a tyrant, a traitor and a murderer.

But you ask 'why was he not' judged thus either in that 'solemn covenant' or afterwards when he was surrendered, either 'by the Presbyterians' or by 'the Independents', but rather 'was received as it befitted a king to be received, with all respect?' By this argument alone any intelligent man can be convinced that it was only at long last and after they had borne all, and tried all and steadfastly suffered all, that the estates determined to cast off the king. You alone maliciously seize upon this too much as a grudge, when it will bear witness among

[3] Christian IV, king of Denmark-Norway, 1588–1648. See *E*, III, 449, 538.
[4] Thomas, Viscount Dillon. See *E*, III, 475–6.
[5] The king's papers were seized after his defeat at Naseby (June 1645) and published with a commentary as *The Kings Cabinet Opened.* See *E*, III, 537–43.
[6] See p. 31.

all good men of their extreme patience, restraint and perhaps too lengthy tolerance of the king's pride.

But 'in the month of August which preceded his execution, the house of commons, which already then ruled alone and was answerable to the Independents, wrote a letter to the Scots,[7] in which it testified that it never intended to change the form of government which up till this time had prevailed in England under the king, the house of lords, and of commons'. See now how the deposing of the king is not attributed to the doctrine of the Independents. These men, who do not usually conceal their doctrine, profess, even when they had control of affairs, that 'they never intended to change the form of the kingdom'. But if something later came into their mind that they did not intend at first, why might they not follow that course which seemed above all to be more right and for the good of the commonwealth? Especially when Charles could not in any way be either begged or moved to consent to their most just demands, which they had presented always in identical form from the beginning. He persisted in those same most perverse opinions about religion and his own rights which he preserved from the beginning and which were so disastrous for us: changed not at all from that Charles who had brought so many evils upon us all both in peace and in war. If he assented to anything, he would indicate by signs which were hardly obscure that he did it unwillingly and as soon as it was in his power he would consider it of no validity. His son would openly declare the same thing (at the time when he took away with him part of the fleet), in a written publication. The same thing the king did too by means of a letter to certain of his supporters in the city.

Meanwhile he had secretly cemented a peace with the Irish, the most savage enemies of the English, on disgraceful terms, despite the protestations of parliament, but whenever he invited the English to uselessly repeated peace discussions, the whole time he was cooking up war against them with all his efforts. At this point where should they, to whom the commonwealth had been committed, turn? Should they deliver into the hands of our bitterest enemy the safety of us all

[7] The Houses agreed on a declaration 'touching not altering the fundamental Government of the Kingdom by King, Lords, and Commons' on 6 May 1648; see *Journals of the House of Commons*, v, 552, and *Journals of the House of Lords*, x, 247. For the text referred to by S., see *A Great and Bloody Fight at Scarborough-Castle ... Together, with the Parliaments Message and Propositions, to their Brethren of Scotland, concerning the Kings Majesty* (14 Aug. 1648), p. 6.

which had been entrusted to them, or should they leave us to another seven years of almost internecine war (not to prophesy anything worse) to bear again and suffer to the end? God inspired them with a better thought – to prefer, as a result of that very Covenant, the commonwealth, religion and liberty to their previous thoughts (for they had not yet come to resolutions) of not deposing the king. All this they saw – later indeed than they ought but still at the last – could not stand while the king stood. Certainly parliament ought always to be impartial and free to consult the commonwealth's interests as well as is possible according to the occasion; nor should they be so devoted to their previous opinions that they should feel scruples later on about voting more wisely for themselves or the commonwealth when God has given them the understanding and the opportunity to do so.

But 'the Scots do not think the same and, what is more, when writing to Charles the son, they call his father a most sacred king and the deed by which he was killed most accursed'. Take care not to speak further of the Scots, whom you do not know. We know the time when they called the same king 'most accursed', a murderer and a traitor, and the deed by which he might be killed as a tyrant 'most sacred'.

Now you criticize the indictment we drew up against the king as being not properly drafted, and you ask 'why it was necessary to add to that count of tyrant the titles of traitor and murderer, since the name tyrant includes all evils'. Then you actually instruct us grammatically and lexicographically what a tyrant is. Off with your trivia, grammarian, which the one definition of Aristotle which has just been cited will blow away without any trouble; and it will instruct you, instructor, that the name tyrant, since you don't care to understand anything but names, can stand short of traitor and murderer.

But 'the laws of England do not say that the king incurs a charge of treason if he has fostered sedition against himself or his people'. Nor do they declare, I say, that parliament is guilty of *lèse-majesté*, if it removes a bad king, or has ever been so, though it has often removed one previously. But they do clearly bear witness that a king can injure and diminish his own majesty, or even lose it outright. For the expression in that law of St Edward, 'to lose the name of a king', is none other than to be deprived of the office and dignity of a king, as happened to Chilperic, king of France, whose example the law itself places in the same passage for the sake of illustrating the matter. But there is no lawyer amongst us who can deny that high treason can be committed against the kingdom just as much as against the king. I appeal to Glanville himself, whom you produce. 'If anyone commits any act to kill the king, or create rebellion in the kingdom, it is a charge of treason.'[8] So that design by which certain papists were preparing to scatter to the breezes the houses of parliament, along with the estates themselves, in one explosion of gunpowder was judged to be 'high treason', not only against the king but against the parliament and the realm, by James himself and both houses of parliament.[9] What further need is there in so clear a matter to mention, as I easily could, our statutes? Since it is clearly absurd and contrary to reason itself that treason can be committed against the king, but cannot against a people, on account of whom, thanks to whom, by whose good grace, so to speak, a king is what he is. In vain then do you babble about so many of our statutes, in vain do you vex and distress yourself with old books of English laws; in the ratifying or repealing of these the authority of parliament has always prevailed, and it is their concern alone to explain what is treason and what *lesè majesté*. And I have already shown repeatedly that this majesty has never so far passed from the people to the king that it is not to be seen to be much more lofty and majestic in parliament.

But who can bear to hear you, a French good-for-nothing quack, expounding our rights? But you, English deserters, all you bishops, doctors, lawyers who proclaim that all literature and learning has fled from England with you, did no-one of your number know how to defend the king's cause and his own with enough energy and Latin and set it out for the judgement of foreign nations, so that that hare-brained purse-snatcher of a Frenchman must needs be summoned for hire to your side to undertake the defence of an impoverished king, crowded about as he was by the speechlessness of so many doctors and priests? All of you will burn, believe me, with great infamy for this amongst foreign nations too; and all men will consider that in any case you deservedly failed in a cause which you had not the power to uphold even in words, much less in arms or courage.

[8] Glanville, *Tractatus de legibus & consuetudinibus regni Anglia* (1604), fo 113b (XIV, 1). The quotation is also given by S., *DR*, p. 317, and Sadler, *Rights*, p. 23–4/sig. Cc4r-v.

[9] Cf. M., *In Quintum Novembris*, 161–2. M.'s youthful fascination with the Gunpowder Plot of 5 Nov. 1605 is further reflected in a group of epigrams, *In Proditionem Bombardicam*.

But I return to you, good man, so skilled in speaking, if you for your part have returned to yourself; for I catch you snoring so near the end and sleepily yawning some irrelevant thing about voluntary 'death'; then you at once deny that 'it can befall a king in possession of his right mind to tear apart his people with seditions, hand over his own armies to be defeated by the enemy, and to raise factions against himself'. Since all of these things have been done both by many other kings and by Charles himself, you cannot doubt, especially being a Stoic, that like all wicked men, so all tyrants too are quite mad. Hear Horace:

> He who is driven blindly on by wicked stupidity and any ignorance of truth, Chrysippus' portico and followers assert is mad. This principle includes peoples and great kings, except for the wise man.[10]

So if you wish to remove from king Charles the charge of any mad act, you will have to remove the wickedness from him before the madness.

But you say 'the king could not commit treason against those who were his own vassals and subjects'. Firstly, since we are as free as any nation of men, we will suffer no barbarous custom to impose upon us. Next, imagine that we were the 'vassals' of the king; not even so did we consider it necessary to endure a tyrant as our master. All such subjection, as our own laws state, is limited to what is 'honourable and beneficial', Leg. Hen. I, 1, ch. 55.[11] All our lawyers relate that this pledge is 'mutual', so long as the master shows 'his liege protection', as they say. But if on the contrary he should be too savage or do him some terrible wrong, 'all tie of homage is dissolved and utterly extinguished'. These are the very words of Bracton and Fleta.[12] Hence there are times when law itself arms the vassal against the master, and hands him over to be killed by the vassal in single combat, if it so happens. If a whole state or nation may not do the same to a tyrant, the condition of freemen will be worse than that of slaves.

Now you strive to excuse Charles's murders partly with murders done by other kings and partly with their just deeds. About Irish

[10] Horace, *Satires*, II, 3, 43–6.

[11] From the 'Leges Henrici Regis', Lambarde (1644), p. 194 ('De privilegio Domini super hominem suum'). But see Sadler, *Rights*, p. 20/sig. cc2v.

[12] M. is presumably referring to Bracton, II, 35, 12 (1640, fos 80v–81v), and *Fleta*, III, 16, 23–35 (1647, pp. 207–9). However, the exact form of words he uses can be found in Sadler, *Rights*, p. 18/sig. cclv.

butchery 'you refer the reader to that well known work of the king, *The King's Image*': and I refer you to *The Image Breaker*.[13] You do not wish the 'capture of La Rochelle', the betrayal of the inhabitants, 'the aid that was boasted of rather than given' to be imputed to Charles.[14] I have nothing to say about whether it is deservedly imputed. He committed sins enough and more at home to trouble to follow up foreign affairs: meanwhile you condemn under the same charge of rebellion all the protestant churches that have at any time defended themselves in arms against kings who were enemies to their religion. Let them themselves consider how important it is for the preservation of church discipline and their own integrity not to neglect this insult offered by their own nursling to them. We have taken it bitterly that we English too were betrayed in that expedition. For a man who long intended to turn the kingdom of England into a tyranny did not judge that he could accomplish his ideas unless the strength and flower of his citizens' army was previously blotted out.

Another crime of the king was that certain words were erased by his order from the oath that is customarily given when kings accede to the throne, before he had sworn it. O unworthy and execrable action! If he who did it is impious, what shall I say of him who defends it? For by immortal God, what treachery, or what violation of right could be greater? What ought to have been more sacred to him, next to the holy sacraments themselves, than that oath? Who, I ask, is more wicked – he who sins against the law, or he who takes pains to make the law itself sin along with him, or finally removes the law altogether so he may not seem to sin? Come now: this oath which he ought most conscientiously to have taken, your king broke. But so he might not yet seem to have broken it openly, he corrupted it by trickery, in some most shameful adulteration. And so he might not be said to have perjured himself, he turned the very oath into perjury. What else could be expected but that he would reign most unjustly, most deceitfully and most unfortunately, when he began his rule with so detestable a wrong, and dared to adulterate that principal law which he thought would be his only impediment to perverting all the laws? But that 'oath', for so you defend him, 'cannot bind kings any more than the laws do; and they assert that they are willing to be bound by laws

[13] For M.'s own thoughts on these titles, see *E*, III, 343.
[14] The disastrous expedition to La Rochelle, led by Buckingham, was in 1627.

and live according to them, when they are yet in reality unbound by them'. Whoever could be so sacrilegious and so sinful in speech as to assert that a most religious sacrament, given while touching the gospels, can be broken with no reason as if it were in itself a mere trifle? But Charles himself has disproved you, criminal and monster; as he, since he thought that sacrament was not in itself a trifle, for that reason preferred either to escape its obligation secretly, or cheat it by some deception rather than openly break it; and he preferred to be a corrupter and falsifier of this oath rather than a perjurer openly.

But truly 'the king swears to his people, as the people do in turn to the king; but the people swear allegiance to the king, not the king to the people'. Truly an elegant fabrication of man! Does not a man who under oath promises and pledges that he will fulfil something faithfully, bind his faith to those who demand the oath from him? Every king indeed swears 'faith, service and obedience to the people' in the fulfilment of that which he promises. At this point you come back to William the Conqueror, who himself was compelled more than once to swear to fulfil not what was pleasing to him, but all that the people and the great men demanded of him.

But if many kings do not 'receive the crown' with solemn ritual and accordingly do not swear and still rule, the same reply can be made about the people, of whom a large part have never sworn allegiance. If a king will be unbound for that reason, so will the people be also. But the part of the people which swore, swore not only to the king but to the kingdom and laws, by which the king was created, and indeed to the king only so far as he should observe the laws 'which the common people', that is, the community or the house of commons, 'shall choose'. For he would be rather stupid who wished to turn the language of our laws always into purer Latin. This clause, 'which the common people shall choose', Charles, before he received the crown, caused to be deleted from the form of the royal oath.[15] But you say 'without the king's assent the people would choose no laws', and under this point you quote two statutes: one, Year 37 Hen. 6. c. 15, the other, 13 Edward 4. c. 8. But so far are either of the two from appearing anywhere in the book of statutes that in the years cited by you, neither of those kings promulgated any statute at all. Now you

[15] Although it was alleged that this clause (originally sworn by Edward II in 1308) had first been substituted at Charles's coronation, this may have happened earlier.

have been tricked, go and complain of the bad faith of those deserters for dictating to you unheard of statutes; while other people wonder at your impudence as well as your emptiness for being unashamed to want to seem thoroughly well-versed in books which you have so clearly proven that you have never inspected nor even seen.

But as for that clause in the oath which you dare to call 'fictitious', you bold-faced buffoon, you say 'the king's defenders say that it may happen' that it might be extant in some ancient copies 'but that it fell into disuse because it did not have suitable meaning'. But it is on this very account that our ancestors put that clause in this oath sworn by the king, so that it should always have a meaning not suitable for tyranny. And if it had fallen into disuse, which however is quite false, who would deny that it should be recalled by a much better law? In vain, if I listen to you: since that custom 'in kings of swearing, which has been received today is merely ceremonial'. But the king, when it was necessary for the bishops to be abolished, pleaded that he might not because of that oath: so that most sacred sacrament, according to whether it is serviceable to the king or not, will be something solid and stable, or only empty and 'ceremonial'.

Again and again, Englishmen, take notice of what I beseech you, and think over to yourselves what kind of king you will have, if he should return. For it would never have come into the mind of this wicked, foreign grammarian to wish, or to be able, to write about the right of the king of England, except that that exiled son of Charles, dyed in his father's teaching, along with those most profligate instructors of his, had with all eagerness supplied what they wanted to be written about this subject. These men dictated to him that 'the whole of parliament could be charged with treason against the king' even for this reason alone: 'that without the king's assent, it declared all to be traitors who have taken up arms against the parliament of England; parliament of course being the king's vassal'. But the king's oath is 'merely ceremonial', so why not the 'vassal's' too? In this way no respect for the laws, nor any loyalty to oath, or scruple of conscience will have any power to restrain either the lust of an unbridled king, or the vengeance of an angry one from the lives and fortunes of you all, since he has been so instructed from childhood that he thinks all laws, religion and finally his own good faith ought to be his vassals and servants to his pleasure. How much more preferable and worthy of yourselves, if you want wealth, liberty, peace and power, not to hesitate to seek all these by your virtue, hard work, prudence and fortitude, rather than to hope for them in vain under the domination of a king? Certainly those who do not think that these can be acquired without a king and master, it cannot be said how meanly, how dishonourably – I do not say how unworthily – they make up their mind about themselves: for what else are they doing but confessing that they are idle, feeble, lacking in intelligence and good sense, born to slavery with body and soul? And all slavery indeed is shameful to a freeborn man. But for you, after recovering your freedom, by God's championship and your own fighting, after so many brave deeds and so memorable an example made of a very powerful king, to desire to return again to slavery, even against your destiny, will be not only most disgraceful but also impious and wicked; and your crime will be equal to the crime of those who, seized by a longing for their former slavery in Egypt,[16] at last were divinely destroyed by many and various disasters, and paid the penalty to God their liberator for so servile a heart.

What say you meanwhile, O advocate of slavery? 'The king', you say, 'could grant pardon for treason and other crimes, which is sufficiently convincing that he was unbound by laws.' For treason indeed, not such as had been committed against the kingdom but such as had been committed against himself, a king could like anyone else grant pardon: he could also perhaps pardon certain other wrongdoers, although not always. For that reason shall he who has some right to save a wrongdoer sometimes likewise have forthwith as an immediate consequence any right to destroy all good men? When summoned into court, and that an inferior one, a king like anyone of the people indeed, is not bound to answer except through his attorney. Shall he therefore, when summoned into parliament by everyone, not come? Shall he not answer in person?

You say that we 'try to defend our action by the example of the Dutch', and hence, fearing for your pay of course, by which the Dutch support such a plague and a pest as you, so you do not seem by slandering the English to have also slandered the Dutch who support you, you wish to demonstrate how 'unlike is what the latter and what the former have done'. I shall omit this comparison of yours, although certain parts of it are absolutely false, and others smell of flattery, in

[16] Cf. *Readie & Easie Way*, VII, 463.

case you should not perhaps make a satisfactory offering for your salary. For the English deny that they need to defend their acts by the example of any foreigners at all. They have their native laws which they have followed, which are the best in this respect in all the world. They have people to imitate, their ancestors, very brave men who never gave way to the unrestrained powers of kings. Many of them they killed as punishment for behaving themselves in an intolerable fashion. They were born in freedom, they are self-sufficient, they can make for themselves the laws they want. One law before all others they cherish, a most ancient law made by nature herself which judges all laws, all civil right and power not by the lust of kings but by the safety of good citizens above all.

Now I see nothing left but rubbish and rubble of earlier chapters; and since you have heaped together a big enough pile of these indeed at the end, I don't know what else you wanted for yourself except to forestall the collapse of this structure of yours. At long last, after your immeasurable loquacity, you shut off your streams 'calling God to witness that you undertook to defend this cause, not only because you were asked, but because your conscience advised you that you could defend none better'. Merely because you were asked, do you meddle with our affairs which are quite foreign to you, without us asking you? Would you slander with the most unworthy and insulting words, and defame by the publication of an infamous book, the highest magistrates of the English people, doing what is their duty within their own jurisdiction in accordance with their authority and the power entrusted to them, without being provoked by any wrong yourself (for they didn't even know you were born)? But by whom were you asked? Was it by your wife, I believe, who exercises a royal right over you, as they say, and who like the notorious Fulvia in the obscene epigram[17] from which you recently (p. 320) stitched together patchworks, says to you whenever she pleases 'either' write 'or let us fight'. Hence you preferred to write rather than have the signal sounded for war. Or perhaps you were asked by the younger Charles and that most desperate crowd of wandering courtiers, like a second Balaam summoned by a second King Balak, to deign by ill-speaking to set upright the cause of a king that was lying in ruins and lost by ill fighting? So indeed it could have been, except that there was a certain difference,

[17] Martial, *Epigrams*, XI, 20.

of this kind: for he was a clever man sitting upon a talkative little ass when he came to curse; you are a very talkative ass, sat on by a woman, and, covered over by the healed heads of the bishops whom you had wounded, seem to present a miniature emblem of that beast in Revelation.[18]

But they say that you were sorry for this book, shortly after you had written it. It is very well; and so to bear witness to your repentance to everyone, you should do nothing before making out of yourself merely one long letter in place of so long a book. For such was the repentance of that famous Judas Iscariot, whom you resemble. Young Charles knew it too, and for that reason he sent you as a gift a purse, that mark of the traitor Judas, because he had heard first, and afterwards knew, that you were an apostate and the devil: that Judas betrayed Christ, and you Christ's church; you had taught that bishops were antichrists, but you have deserted to them; you have undertaken the cause of people whom you had condemned to hell; Christ freed all men, you have tried to reduce them all to slavery. Do not doubt, after you have been so impious towards God, towards the church, towards all of mankind, that the same end awaits you too. Led by despair rather than penitence, and thoroughly tired of yourself, at last you will hang from the unhappy tree, just like that equal of yours did once upon a time, and burst in the middle. And that faithless and treacherous conscience, persecutor of good and holy men, you will send ahead to the place of torment that is at some time destined to receive you.

So far I seem now to have completed with God's good aid the task which I had set out in the beginning – to defend the excellent deeds of my fellow countrymen against the mad and most spiteful rage of this raving sophist both at home and abroad, and to assert the common right of the people against the unjust domination of kings, not indeed out of hatred of kings, but of tyrants. And I have not knowingly passed over without reply any argument or example or testimony brought by my opponent which seemed indeed to have any solidity at all to it or any power of proof. Perhaps I have gone closer to the opposite kind of fault in that, by rather too often replying also to his follies and quite hackneyed subtleties as if they were arguments, I may seem to have given them an importance which they did not deserve.

One thing remains, perhaps the most important – which is that you

[18] Rev. 13:1.

too, my countrymen, yourselves refute this opponent of yours; and I see no other way of doing this than by striving forever to surpass the evil words of all men by your own best deeds. Your vows and burning prayers God kindly granted when you fled to him for refuge, crushed by more than one kind of slavery. He has most gloriously freed you first of all nations from what are truly the two greatest evils in the life of men, and the most destructive to virtue; tyranny and superstition; he has cast upon you such greatness of spirit that you, first of mortals, did not hesitate to judge a king, when he was conquered by your weapons and taken prisoner, with a famous sentence and punish him once he was condemned. After so shining a deed, you will have to think and do nothing mean and narrow, nothing that is not great and lofty. To attain this glory there is this one path to walk upon; if, as you have vanquished enemies in war, so you will show that you also, unarmed and in the midst of peace, can most bravely of all mortals conquer ambition, greed, wealth and the corruptions of prosperity, which subdue the other nations of men; and if you show in preserving freedom as much justice, temperance and moderation as you showed courage in driving off slavery. By these arguments and testimonies only can you convince people that you are not those whom this man pursues with the reproaches of 'traitors, robbers, cut-throats, parricides, fanatics'; that you have not butchered a king because you were spurred on by ambition or a desire to take possession of the rights of others, or by sedition or any wicked lusts, not by madness or fury, but that you punished a tyrant because you were burning with love of freedom, religion, justice, honour and finally love of your native land.

But if – which, good God, may you not allow – you have otherwise in mind, if you will be brave in war but dishonourable in peace, when you have had the evident power of God working so propitiously for you and so grievously for your enemies, and by the example so remarkable and memorable placed before your eyes you have not learned to fear God and worship justice, as far as I'm concerned, I will concede indeed and confess, for I will not be able to deny, that all those very wicked things, which now slanderers and liars either say or think about you, are true: and in a short time you will find God far more angry than either your enemies have found him hostile, or you have found him kind and favourable, beyond all the other races that are on the earth today.

[While it is now some years since I published this hastily, as reason of state then demanded, I kept thinking that if ever I should take it in hand again at leisure, as sometimes happens, I might afterwards polish or perhaps remove or add something. This I now judge that I have accomplished, though more briefly than I used to think would be the case. The memorial, as I see, is such as it is, and will not easily die. If anyone will ever be found who has defended civil freedom more freely than in this, yet surely there will hardly be found anyone who has defended it in a greater and more glorious case. If, then, the doing of an exemplary deed so elevated and famous is believed to have been as successfully accomplished as not without divine prompting to have been attempted, let this surely be a reason that it may seem to have been celebrated and defended by the same aid and impulse as is also evident in these praises. I would much prefer this to be thought by all than that any other success, whether of talent, or judgement or diligence, be given me. Only this: as with that famous Roman consul who, when retiring from his magistracy, swore in a public meeting that the commonwealth and that city was safe because of his exertion alone;[19] so I, as I now put the finishing touches to this work, would dare to say, calling God and men to witness, that in this book I have shown and brought to the surface from the greatest authors of wisdom, both divine and human, matters in which I trust both the English people has been satisfactorily defended in this cause (to the everlasting fame of its posterity), and many mortals (except such as would prefer themselves to be slaves) who have been before deceived by foul ignorance of their right and the false show of religion have been satisfactorily freed. The oath of that Roman consul indeed, such and so great as it was, the whole Roman people at that meeting swore and approved with one voice and one consent: this persuasion of mine, I have long realized, all the best, not only of my countrymen but also of foreigners, approve with the loud voices of nations everywhere.

I thankfully enjoy this fruit of my labours, the highest which I have set myself in this life and, at the same time, think most particularly how I can best testify not only to my country, to which I have paid the most I had, but also to men of whatever nation, and above all to the

[19] See Cicero, *Epistulae ad Familiares*, V, 2, 7; *Pro Sulla*, XI, 34; *In Pisonem*, 3, 6–7; *De Re Publica*, I, 4, 7.

christian cause, that I am pursuing yet greater objects than these if I can, and I will be able to succeed if God grants it; and for their sake I am at their service meanwhile, and reflecting.][20]

THE END.

[20] 1658.

Biographical notes

ANTONY: MARCUS ANTONIUS (*c.* 82–30 BC), soldier and triumvir; Shakespeare's 'Mark Antony'. On Julius Caesar's staff in Gaul and, despite an earlier quarrel, joint consul with him in 44. At first conciliatory towards the conspirators against Caesar, he was appointed a triumvir with Lepidus and Octavian in 43, and then defeated Brutus and Cassius at Philippi (42). Served in Asia Minor, though an expedition against the Parthians (36) ended disastrously. His liaison with Cleopatra alienated his brother-in-law Octavian who in 32 secured his dismissal by the senate. Defeated at Actium in 31, he committed suicide the following year.

BEZA, THEODORE, or THEODORE DE BEZE (1519–1605), French theologian, translator, and successor of CALVIN at Geneva. Studied law at Orleans (1535–9), and was professor of Greek at Lausanne before being appointed rector of the new academy at Geneva (1559). His Greek editions and Latin translations of the New Testament were of fundamental importance. Published *The Right of Magistrates*, one of the major Calvinist works on resistance, in French in 1574 and in Latin in 1576. M. knew of it from THOU (*CB*, I, 500–01), though he also attributed the *Vindiciae contra tyrannos* (actually by Philipp du Plessis Mornay or, possibly, Hubert Languet) to Beza (*DS*, IV, 659).

BRACTON, HENRY DE (d. 1268). From 1245 until his death, Bracton (or Bratton, or Bretton) appeared as a justice of assize in the southwestern counties, and was also a judge in the king's central court (what was to become the king's bench) until he retired or was dismissed in 1257. His *De legibus et consuetudinubus Angliae* – a kind of *summa* which frequently cites the Roman law – was the crowning achievement of English medieval jurisprudence: first printed by Tottel in 1569.

BUCER, MARTIN (1491–1551), German theologian and reformer. Converted to protestantism in 1521, and became leader of the reformation in Strasburg from 1527. A conciliatory figure, who mediated between the various protestant factions, he nevertheless failed to secure a compromise between LUTHER and ZWINGLI at the Colloquy of Marburg (1529). Following the protestants' defeat at Mühlberg in 1547, he left for England where he became Regius Professor of Divinity at Cambridge (1549) and wrote his *De Regno Christi* to further the reformation under Edward VI (1547–53). The second of M.'s divorce pamphlets, *The Judgement of Martin Bucer*, consists largely of translated excerpts from this.

BUCHANAN, GEORGE (1506–82), Scottish humanist. Although Buchanan's reputation was primarily that of a great Latin poet and dramatist – as Montaigne, whom he taught at Bordeaux, Sir Philip Sidney, and M. (see *DS*, IV, 592) all agree – his education was emphatically scholastic. At fourteen he was being taught in Paris by the theologian John Mair, whom he followed to the university of St Andrews (1524–6). His Calvinism meant he could only return to Scotland again after the deposition in 1559 of the Regent, Mary of Guise, and the reformation effected by KNOX and others. He began to develop his political ideas in response to the problem posed by Mary, Queen of Scots – a catholic monarch of a reformed kingdom – and her deposition in 1567, finally publishing *De Iure Regni apud Scotos* in 1579 and *Rerum Scoticarum Historia* in 1582.

BUCKINGHAM: *see* VILLIERS, GEORGE

CALVIN, JEAN (1509–64), French theologian and leader of the reformation at Geneva. Calvin studied theology (Paris), law (Orleans and Bourges), and Greek (Paris again), experiencing a conversion between 1528 and 1533. In 1536 he began the task of thoroughgoing reformation in Geneva. His success in this struggle, together with the influence of his great *Institutes of the Christian Religion* (first published in 1536 but constantly revised and enlarged until 1559), established the model of presbyterian discipline. M. does not quote Calvin's equivocal remarks on resistance in the *Institutes*, but draws on the more forthright *Readings on the Prophet Daniel* (1561).

CARTWRIGHT THOMAS (*c.* 1535–1603), presbyterian controversialist. Became Lady Margaret Professor of Divinity at Cambridge in 1569 but was ejected by John Whitgift the following year for his 'seditious' talk of reform. From 1573 to 1586 he was in exile at Geneva and elsewhere. The influence of Burghley and Leicester secured his return but could not prevent constant investigation by the Ecclesiastical Commission.

CHARLES I (1600–49), King of Great Britain and Ireland. Born in Scotland, the second son of King James VI and I of Scotland and England and Queen Anne of Denmark. Spent his formative years in the shadow of his elder brother, Prince Henry (d. 1612) before coming under the influence of BUCKINGHAM. Married Henrietta Maria, daughter of Henry IV of France, shortly before his succession in 1625. Difficulties with his first three parliaments (1625, 1626, and 1628–9), particularly over foreign policy, were compounded by military fiascos at Cadiz (1625) and the Isle de Rhé off La Rochelle (1627). The dissolution of parliament in Mar. 1629 began a period of eleven years'

Personal Rule marked by a rapprochement with Spain in foreign policy, the promotion of Archbishop Laud's preferences in the church, and the use of often antiquated fiscal devices to increase revenue. The policy collapsed with the Scots' armed resistance – in the so-called Bishops' Wars – to the imposition of a Laudian ecclesiastical programme: this necessitated summoning first the Short and then the Long Parliament in 1640. Although Charles was forced to accept a series of bills which amounted to a constitutional revolution, civil war broke out in 1642, ending in his surrender to the Scots in May 1646. From then until 1649 (a period including the second Civil War in 1648), he sought to play off various groups against each other to secure his reinstatement on acceptable terms. The Army intervened in Dec. 1648, and the Rump (effectively the Commons acting without the cooperation of the Lords) appointed a High Court, the jurisdiction of which Charles refused to recognize. He was found guilty of high treason and 'other high crimes', and executed on 30 Jan. 1649.

CHRYSOSTOM, SAINT JOHN (340–407), eminent father of the church, renowned for eloquence (his surname means 'golden-mouthed'). Came to prominence as deacon, presbyter and preacher at Antioch (381–98) before succeeding to the episcopate at Constantinople (398–404) from where he was driven into exile by the emperor Arcadius and his wife Eudoxia. M. admired him as an expositor since he rejected the allegorical method of interpreting scripture in favour of grammatical techniques.

COCHLAEUS, or JOHANNES DOBENECK (1479–1552), catholic theologian and controversialist. From 1529–39, he served as secretary to Duke George of Saxony, one of the most committed opponents of LUTHER.

COOK, JOHN (d. 1660), regicide. Trained as a lawyer at Gray's Inn (probably admitted 1594) and travelled extensively on the continent, living for several months with the Diodati household at Geneva (which M. also visited). Appointed solicitor-general, 8 Jan. 1649, to act as prosecutor at the king's trial in the absence through illness of the attorney-general, William Steele. Campaigned with Ireton in Ireland, where he wrote *Monarchy No Creature of Gods Making* (1652). Tried and executed Oct. 1660.

DU HAILLAN: *see* GIRARD, BERNARD DE

FENNER, DUDLEY (1558?–1587), puritan divine. Educated at Peterhouse, Cambridge, he later assisted CARTWRIGHT at Antwerp. Imprisoned on his return to England, he retired to the reformed church at Middleburgh.

FLETA. The name of the legal treatise rather than a person. Derived largely from Bracton, and written *c.* 1290 as a manual with the practising lawyer in mind, its author was traditionally supposed to have been one of the corrupt judges incarcerated by Edward I in the Fleet prison.

FORTESCUE, SIR JOHN (1394?–1476?), legal writer. Became chief justice of the king's bench in 1442 and may also have served as Henry VI's lord chancellor. Strongly pro-Lancastrian, he nevertheless recognized Edward IV in 1471 and was pardoned and admitted to the council.

GIRARD, BERNARD DE, seigneur du Haillan (*c.* 1535–1610). After enjoying the patronage of the Duke of Anjou, he was appointed as Historiographer by Charles IX of France (1560–74), and confirmed as such by his successor Henry III (1574–89). He published the *Histoire générale des Rois de France* in 1576, though he was no less well-known for his other constitutionalist work, *De l'état et succès des affaires de France* (1570).

GLANVILLE, RANULF DE (d. 1190). Became chief justiciar of England (1180) and was active in Henry II's service in France and England. Although reputed the author of the *Tractatus de legibus & consuetudinibus regni Anglia* (commonly known as 'Glanville'), this may merely have been written during his justiciarship.

GOODMAN, CHRISTOPHER (1520?–1603), puritan divine. Became Lady Margaret Professor of Divinity at Oxford in the reign of Edward VI but left England for Strasburg in 1554 to escape the Catholic reaction following the accession of Mary Tudor (1553–58). There was, however, a schism among the exiled reformers (the 'troubles' at Frankfurt) and Goodman withdrew with WHITTINGHAM and others to Geneva where he was chosen (with KNOX) as pastor. In 1558, he assisted Whittingham in the preparation of the Geneva Bible (1560) and published *How Superior Powers oght to be obeyd of their subjects.*

GROTIUS, HUGO (1583–1645), Dutch jurist, statesman, poet, theologian and historian. Studied at Leyden (1594–7) and at the law faculty of Orleans (1597–9) before being appointed Historiographer of the States of Holland in 1599. From 1612 he was involved in an Erasmian project to effect a reunion of the christian churches, seeking support on a visit to England in 1613. Hopes for this scheme – together with his career in Dutch politics – ended abruptly when he was tried for treason in 1619 in the aftermath of the Calvinists' triumph over the Arminians at the Synod of Dort. While imprisoned at Lowenstein, he began *De Veritate Religionis Christianae* (first published in Dutch in 1622) and his *De Iure Belli ac Pacis* (published in 1625), the two works for which he was most famed in his lifetime. In exile, he received an irregular pension from Louis XIII before being appointed (1634) as Swedish ambassador in France. He died at Rostock in 1645, returning from Stockholm where he had been discharged. M. was especially interested in his tragedy *Adamus Exul* (1601) and his *Annotations of the Old and New Testament* (1641–50).

HAMMOND, HENRY (1605–60), anglican divine. Educated at Oxford where he was a member of the so-called Great Tew circle which met at Lord Falkland's country house. Became one of the royal chaplains in 1645 and later attended CHARLES I at Hampton Court and Carisbrooke Castle. A prolific scholar, he quarrelled only reluctantly with SALMASIUS.

HOTMAN, FRANÇOIS (1524–90), French lawyer, historian and polemicist. Studied law at Orleans then, in 1547, became CALVIN's amanuensis at Geneva. He later taught law at the universities of Strasburg, Valence and Bourges, from where he fled to Geneva in 1572 to escape the massacre of the Huguenots. There he revised a draft of *Francogallia* (apparently seen by BEZA at the time) and published it in 1573 (final version in 1586). This was an account of the ancient French constitution in which he sought to effect a synthesis between existing constitutionalist and Calvinist strains of political thought, by identifying the powers of the Three Estates (emphasized by the former) with that of elected 'ephoral' authorities (stressed by the latter).

JUNIUS-TREMELLIUS. Composite name of the most widely-used protestant Latin Bible which was the work of two Heidelberg professors, Immanuel Tremellius (1510–80) and his son-in-law, Franciscus Junius, or Du Jon (1545–1602). It comprised Tremellius' translation of the Old Testament; Junius' translation of the Apocrypha from the Greek; and BEZA's translation of the New Testament from the Greek (together with Tremellius' translation of those parts of it found in Syriac). M. uses (though he also departs from) this text in the *Defence*: he criticized the translation in *T*, II, 615.

JUSTINIAN: FLAVIUS PETRUS SABBATIUS JUSTINIANUS (483–565), Byzantine emperor (from 527). His great achievement was the codification of Roman law which was begun in 528 by a commission of ten which published the first Code (*Codex Vetus*) in 529. In 530, under the chairmanship of Tribonian, work was begun on the Digest (*Digesta* or *Pandectae*), which came into force simultaneously with the Institutes (*Institutiones*) in Dec. 533, followed by the revised *Codex* a year later. Justinian's own laws were unofficially collected as the Novels (*Novellae* or, sometimes, *Authentics*). For M.'s mounting hostility to Justinian because of his revocation of earlier legislation on divorce by THEODOSIUS II, see *T*, II, 701.

KNOX, JOHN (1505–72), Scottish reformer. An early promoter of the protestant cause in Scotland, he fell victim to the catholic resurgence in 1547 when the French captured St Andrews and he was condemned to the galleys. Driven from his exile in England (1549–53) on the accession of Mary Tudor, Knox spent six years at Geneva before returning to Scotland in 1559 where he played a leading role in expelling the French and establishing the presbyterian kirk.

LUTHER, MARTIN (1483?–1546), theologian and leader of the German reformation. Luther joined the Augustinian order instead of pursuing a career in the law, but was afflicted by spiritual doubts and depression until, *c.* 1513, he arrived at a belief – henceforth central to his theology – in justification by faith alone. He provoked a doctrinal dispute in 1517 with his famous ninety-five theses at Wittenberg, and defended himself against the authorities at Augsburg (1518), Leipzig (1519) and the Diet of Worms (1520), after which he was proclaimed an outlaw of the Empire. A dependence on secular rulers for protection meant he initially preached a doctrine of passive obedience, and denounced social and religious radicals. However in 1530, at Torgau, Luther with other leading theologians formally accepted the lawfulness of resistance.

MARTYR, PETER: *see* VERMIGLI, PIETRO MARTIRE

PARAEUS, DAVID (1548–1622), German theologian. Paraeus was a professor of theology at Heidelberg whose *Commentary upon Romans* (1609), in which he, like M., refused to allow any material differences between foreign and domestic tyrants, was burned at Oxford and Cambridge. M. first quotes from Paraeus' commentary on Revelation in *Church-Government* (I, 815), and cites him constantly in the divorce tracts.

SADLER, JOHN (1614–74), lawyer. Acquired an expertise in Hebrew and other oriental languages at Emmanuel College, Cambridge before studying law at Lincoln's Inn. Despite initial reservations about the legality of the Purge, he was intruded as Master of Magdalene College, Cambridge in 1650; served on the Hale Commission for law reform in 1652; became a member of the Council of State in 1653; served as an MP in 1653 and 1659; and was one of the Commissioners for the Great Seal in 1659. He was probably on friendly terms with M. (who cites *Rights of the Kingdom* in Chapter V of *E* and often draws on it for material in the later chapters of the *Defence*) by Aug. 1648.

SALMASIUS, or CLAUDE DE SAUMAISE (1588–1653), French classicist. Displayed a remarkable facility with languages at an early age: having been taught Latin and Greek by his father, he went on to Hebrew, Arabic, and Coptic by himself. Studied philosophy at Paris (1604) and law at Heidelberg (1606). He married Anne Mercier in 1622 (?), by report a domineering woman, and accepted a position at Leyden in 1631, though declining the title of professor. His reputation rested on a formidable list of editions of classical texts, though he also wrote on religious and ethical topics, notably his *De Usuris* (1638). After publishing the *Defensio Regia*, he accepted an invitation to Stockholm in 1650. Although it was rumoured that M.'s reply broke him and led to his dismissal from the court of Queen Christina, he had been ill earlier and in fact overstayed his leave of absence from Leyden. An incomplete reply to M.'s *Defence* was published posthumously in 1660.

SCHICKARD, WILHELM (1592–1635), German orientalist and mathematician. He was successively professor of languages (1619) and of mathematics (1631) at the university of Tübingen. M.'s extensive use of *Jus Regium* (first noted by J. B. Carpzov in the second edition (Leipzig, 1674), pp. 149, 164) casts doubt on some of the claims made about the depth of his rabbinical learning. For a balanced account see Golda Werman, 'Milton's Use of Rabbinic Material', in *Milton Studies*, XXI, (Pittsburgh, 1985), pp. 35–47.

SELDEN, JOHN (1584–1654), lawyer, historian, orientalist and parliamentarian. After leaving Oxford, Selden established himself at the Inner Temple, publishing a series of books on the history of the law culminating in the controversial *History of Tythes* (1617). He entered parliament in 1623: active in the attack on BUCKINGHAM and in other controversies, he was imprisoned shortly before the 1629 dissolution. Although he made his peace with the government, partly by publishing *Mare Clausum* (a reply to GROTIUS' *Mare Liberum*) in 1635, he sided with parliament in the Civil War. M. (see I, 452; II, 350, 513; IV, 624–5; VI, 378; VII, 299) greatly admired his *De Iure Naturali et Gentium juxta Disciplinam Ebraeorum* (1640) and *Uxor Ebraica* (1646).

SEYSSEL, CLAUDE DE (*c.* 1450–1520), French lawyer and historian. Seyssel served in the Parlement of Paris and as a member of Louis XII's Grand Council. He published *La Grand Monarchie de France* in 1519, though M. used the Latin translation by SLEIDAN, first published in 1545.

SLEIDAN, or JOHANN PHILIPPSON (1506–56), German historian. Studied ancient languages at Liége and Cologne, and law and jurisprudence at Paris and Orleans. Acted as an interpreter for the French king, Francis I, at the Diet of Hagenau; was pensioned for a time by Edward VI of England; and was an envoy (1551–2) from Strasburg (where he had become a professor of history in 1542) to the Council of Trent. Philip of Hesse made him the historian of the Schmalkaldic League, a task he completed in 1554.

THEODOSIUS II (401–50), eastern emperor. Succeeded his father Arcadius while still a child in 408. Published the *Codex Theodosianus* in 438: accepted by Valentinian III (western emperor, 423–55), it came into force for the empire as a whole in 439. For M.'s approval of these emperors see *T*, II, 700 and *E*, III, 590; for M.'s fascination with Valentinian, see *CB*, I, 375, 400, 430.

THOU, JACQUES-AUGUSTE DE (1553–1617), French historian. Devoted most of his life to writing the *History of His Own Time* (final version published in 1620). One of the most frequently cited authors in M.'s *CB*.

THUANUS: *see* THOU, JACQUES-AUGUSTE DE

VERMIGLI, PIETRO MARTIRE (1500–62), Italian-born reformer also known as PETER MARTYR. Rose to prominence in the Augustinian order at Spoleto and Naples before his unorthodox views led to a ban on preaching. Invited by BUCER to Strasburg in 1542, where he became professor of theology, then moved to England in 1547, where he became Regius Professor of Divinity at Oxford (1548) and helped promote the Edwardian reformation. Imprisoned on the accession of Mary Tudor, he eventually left England for Zurich. M. was familiar with his extensive commentaries on the scriptures.

VILLIERS, GEORGE, first duke of Buckingham (1592–1628). Rose to prominence as the favourite of James VI and I, dominating the court by 1618. The parliament of 1621–2 attacked Buckingham (created Marquess, 1618, and Duke, 1623) obliquely, by impeaching the monopolists Mompesson and Mitchell. Criticism of Buckingham, especially his foreign policy, continued in CHARLES I's first parliament (June–Aug. 1625), and culminated in impeachment proceedings in the second (Feb.–June 1626) leading to its dissolution. Despite reversing his pro-French policy (which left Britain at war with both France and Spain), the failure of the La Rochelle expedition ensured that attacks continued in the third parliament (prorogued June 1628). Buckingham was assassinated in Aug. 1628 by John Felton, a veteran of Cadiz and the Isle de Rhé.

WHITTINGHAM, WILLIAM (1524–97), English reformer and translator. Interrupted his studies at Oxford to travel in France and Germany where he adopted extreme protestant views. Went into exile in 1554 at Strasburg, then followed KNOX to Geneva after dissension among the exiles. When other exiles returned to England on the death of Mary Tudor he stayed behind to see through the completion of the Geneva Bible. M.'s allegorical treatment of error and custom in the 1644 edition of *DDD* (II, 223) may be indebted to Whittingham's preface to GOODMAN's *Superior Powers.*

ZWINGLI, HULDREICH (1484–1531), Swiss reformer. Educated at Vienna and Basle, he began to develop the outlines of a reformed theology before being appointed preacher at Zurich in 1518 and coming across the work of LUTHER. Differences between them, particularly over the Eucharist (which Zwingli regarded as strictly symbolic) were never resolved despite attempts at mediation by BUCER. He led the reformation at Zurich in the 1520s: while Berne and Basle followed suit other cantons resisted, and he was killed at the battle of Kappel in the struggle which resulted.

Index of scriptural citations

Index of subjects

Index of subjects

Index of subjects

Index of subjects

Index of subjects

Index of subjects

Index of proper names

Index of proper names

Index of proper names

Index of proper names

Index of proper names

Index of proper names

Index of proper names

Index of proper names

Index of proper names

WITHDRAWN FROM STOCK

Index of proper names

CAMBRIDGE TEXTS IN THE HISTORY OF POLITICAL THOUGHT

Titles published in the series thus far

Aristotle *The Politics* (edited by Stephen Everson)

Bakunin *Statism and Anarchy* (edited by Marshall Shatz)

Bentham *A Fragment on Government* (introduction by Ross Harrison)

Bossuet *Politics drawn from the Very Words of Holy Scripture* (edited by Patrick Riley)

Cicero *On Duties* (edited by M. T. Griffin and E. M. Atkins)

Constant *Political Writings* (edited by Biancamaria Fontana)

Filmer *Patriarcha and other writings* (edited by Johann P. Sommerville)

Hobbes *Leviathan* (edited by Richard Tuck)

Hooker *Of the Laws of Ecclesiastical Polity* (edited by A. S. McGrade)

John of Salisbury *Policraticus* (edited by Cary Nederman)

Kant *Political writings* (edited by H. S. Reiss and H. B. Nisbet)

Leibniz *Political Writings* (edited by Patrick Riley)

Locke *Two Treatises of Government* (edited by Peter Laslett)

Luther and Calvin on Secular Authority (edited by Harro Höpfl)

Machiavelli *The Prince* (edited by Quentin Skinner and Russell Price)

J. S. Mill *On Liberty* with *The Subjection of Women* and *Chapters on Socialism* (edited by Stefan Collini)

Milton *Political Writings* (edited by Martin Dzelzainis)

Montesquieu *The Spirit of the Laws* (edited by Anne M. Cohler, Basia Carolyn Miller and Harold Samuel Stone)

More *Utopia* (edited by George M. Logan and Robert M. Adams)

Paine *Political Writings* (edited by Bruce Kuklick)